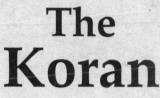

The
Koran
TRANSLATION

Translated by
S.V. Mir Ahmed Ali

Edited by
Yasin T. al-Jibouri

Published by
Tahrike Tarsile Qur'an, Inc.
80-08 51st Avenue
Elmhurst, New York 11373

Published by
Tahrike Tarsile Qur'an, Inc.
80-08 51st Avenue
Elmhurst, New York 11373
E-mail: read@koranusa.org
http://www.koranusa.org

First U.S. Edition 2004

Library of Congress Catalog Number: LC82-80220

British Library Cataloguing in Publication Data

ISBN: 0-940368-36-6

Front Cover: Courtesy of NASA

www.spaceimages.com

In the Name of Allah, the most Gracious, the most Merciful

PREFACE

The Holy Qur'an is often described as Islam's living miracle. A "miracle" is the inability or incapability to imitate an extra-ordinary feat. One who is capable of effecting something which nobody else can effect is the doer of a miracle. None other than the Almighty is capable of doing so. He, and only He, is the One Who decrees, Who manifests His might over others, including, of course, the natural phenomena and the cosmos at large. A miracle is something that challenges what is already established, proving what is out of the ordinary, violating the rules of normalcy.

Consider the miracle of the *isra'* (the night journey from Mecca to Jerusalem) and *mi'raj* (ascension to the heavens). It is one of the most glorious of all miracles, one whereby Muhammed (s.a.w.w.) became the only human being ever to be raised so high. How could the Messenger of God travel, all alone and during part of the evening, the lengthy distance from Mecca to Jerusalem without any means of transportation? How could he, moreover, traverse the domain of the heavens and physically go through all these barriers and distances, leaving the earth without a plane, a spaceship, or a rocket? Actually, even the spaceships launched nowadays to relatively limited distances, compared to the distance the Messenger of God (s.a.w.w.) had reached when he went through the seven heavenly strata, are liable to develop malfunctions. How could this Messenger (s.a.w.w.), then, describe in minute details all what he had seen in the seven heavens in one single night, his observations, and the places he had reached? Is there any human being who can refute his description or contest his documented statements? Even his contemporary opponents could not disprove his statements.

The Holy Qur'an remains the eternal miracle of our prophet Muhammed (s.a.w.w.), one whereby he challenged the jinns and mankind to produce a book like it, or a chapter, or even ten fabricated "verses." This happened when just about everyone was a genius in mastering the language. Yet none was able to face this challenge; so, the Arabs resorted to once fighting the prophet and once offering him position and wealth.

The Holy Qur'an is a miracle in the true sense of the word:

> *And they say: Why are no Signs (miracles) sent down upon him from His Lord? Say: The Signs (miracles) are With God alone, and I am only a plain warner. Is it not enough for them that We have revealed to you the Book which is recited to them? Most surely there is mercy in this and a reminder for people who believe.*
> (Qur'an, 29:50-51)

The Holy Qur'an was the evident miracle which sufficed all mankind as proof testifying to the truth of the message brought by Muhammed (s.a.w.w.). Every syllable in it is a miracle by itself: "Say: If men and jinns should join (forces) together in order to bring the like of this Qur'an, they will never be able to bring the like thereof, even if some of them were to aid the others. And certainly We have explained for men in this Qur'an every kind of similitude, but most men do not consent to aught but denying" (Qur'an, 17:88-89).

No human being can ever be acquainted with all the knowledge embedded in the Holy Qur'an, for it is the speech of the Almighty, the Praised and the Glorified One, Who has said, "Say: If the sea were ink for the words of my Lord, the sea would surely be consumed before the words of my Lord are exhausted even if We were to bring the like of it to add thereto" (Qur'an, 18:109).

There are miracles in the Holy Qur'an which are continuous, perpetual, eternal, ever present, impressing one generation after another: each generation will by itself discover the miracles of this Book and may come to know that the miracles of the Holy Qur'an never end, nor will its wonders. All the miracles which violated the laws of nature and whereby God strengthened His messengers and prophets, who were sent by Him to mankind before Muhammed (s.a.w.w.), had taken place within the sphere of the earth, and they are now history and tales told. But the Almighty revealed to this messenger, Muhammed (s.a.w.w.), the most enduring of all miracles, one that will always shine through each and every age and time, thus granting him the very uppermost kingdom of the heavens. Other heavenly books have been distorted, altered, tampered with, yet nobody can ever attribute the same to the Holy Qur'an. This by itself is, indeed, a miracle, a divine proof of Providence's watchful and caring eyes.

God Almighty has said in the Holy Qur'an, "We will soon show them Our Signs in the universe and in their own selves till it becomes quite clear to them that it is the truth" (Qur'an, 41:53). The Qur'an's challenge, and the fact that it tears down the veil separating us from the future, is another difficult front which the enemies of God have to face. Its knowledge of the future may be divided into two time categories: 1) the present and the near future, which is not distant from the time when the Holy Qur'an was revealed, and 2) the distant future. Let us deal with these categories in a little more detail.

The Holy Qur'an states the following:

In the Name of God, the most Gracious, the most Merciful. Aleef, Lam, Meem. The Romans have been vanquished, in a near land, and they, after being

*vanquished, shall be the vanquishers, within a few
years. God's is the command before and after, and on
that day the believers shall rejoice, with the help of
God; He helps whomsoever He pleases, and He is the
Mighty, the Merciful.*
(Qur'an, 30:1-5)

Let us now review history in reference to the verses
cited above.

Young Muhammed (s.a.w.w.) was in Syria twice: 1) in
about 582 A.D., when he was twelve years old, in the
company of his uncle Abu Talib, and 2) in 595 A.D.,
thirteen years later, as a businessman trading on behalf
of Khadija daughter of Khuwaylid who shortly thereafter became his wife. While he was there, one of his observations was the historical fact that a feud was brewing
between the then mightiest "superpowers" on earth, the
Persian and the Roman empires, each vying for hege-
mony over Arabia's fertile crescent. Indeed, such an ob-
servation was quite accurate, for after only a few years, a
war broke out between them that ended with the Romans losing it, as the Holy Qur'an tells us in the verses
cited above of Chapter 30 (The Romans). This Chapter
was revealed in 7 A.H./615-16 A.D., only a few months
after the fall of Jerusalem to the Persians. Only four years
prior to that date, the Persians had scored a sweeping
victory over the Christians, spreading their control over
Aleppo, Antioch, and even Damascus. Muhammed
(s.a.w.w.) was concerned about either of these two empires extending its control over the land inhabited by
his then fiercely independent Pagan people. The loss of
Jerusalem, birthplace of Christ, Jesus son of Mary (peace
be upon them both), was a heavy blow to the prestige of
Christianity. This war was between the Byzantine (Eastern Roman) emperor Heraclius (575 - 641 A.D.) and the
Persian king Khusrau (Khosrow) Parwiz (Parviz) or
Chosroes II (d. 628 A.D.). It was one of many wars in
which those mighty nations were embroiled and which
continued for many centuries. The hands of Divine

Providence were already busy paving the path for Islam: the collision between both empires paved the way for the ultimate destruction of the last Persian empire, the Sassanian (or Sassanid), and in Islam setting root in that important part of the world. Moreover, Muhammed (s.a.w.w.)'s offspring came to marry ladies who were born and raised at Persian as well as Roman palaces. Imam Husain (p.b.u.h.), younger son of Imam Ali ibn Abu Talib (p.b.u.h.), Muhammed (s.a.w.w.))'s grandson, married the daughter of the last Persian emperor Jazdagird (Yazdegerd) III son of Shahryar and grandson of this same Khusrau II. Jazdagerd ruled Persia from 632-651 A.D. and lost the Battle of Qadisiyya to the Muslim forces in 636 A.D., thus ending the rule of the Sassanians. Having been defeated, he fled for Media in northwestern Iran, homeland of Persian Mede tribesmen, and from there to Merv, an ancient Central Asian city near modern day Mary in Turkmenistan (until very recently one of the republics of the Soviet Union), where he was killed by a miller. The slain emperor left two daughters who, during their flight attempt, following the murder of their father, were caught and sold as slaves. One of them, Shah-Zenan, ended up marrying Imam Husain (p.b.u.h.), whereas her sister married the renown scholar and acclaimed *muhaddith* (traditionist) Muhammed son of caliph Abu Bakr. Shah-Zenan was awarded a royal treatment and was given a new name in her Persian mother tongue: Shahr Banu, which means Ahead of the ladies of the city."

Now let us ask the following: "Could prophet Muhammed (s.a.w.w.) predict the result of a war that would be waged between two giant nations of that time after a few years? Can the leader predict the outcome of a war and guarantee the victory of one army over another? Let us suppose that the Romans had lost the war after a few years, and that the Persians were the victors; what would the fate of the Holy Qur' an then be?" In the latter case, the Holy Qur'an would have committed a grievous error if the Romans had been defeated; so, how could the Messenger of God, Muhammed (s.a.w.w.), put all the creed of Islam and the credibility of the Holy Qur'an in jeopardy just like that, making statements like these and asserting that the Romans would defeat the Persians? But he is not the one who is doing so; it is the Almighty Who knows what is, what was, and what will be.

Now let us discuss the challenge the Holy Qur'an posed during the lifetime of the Prophet (s.a.w.w.).

The nature of this type of challenge is that it confronted the unbelievers, including an uncle (one of ten) of Muhammed (s.a.w.w.), namely Abu Lahab, God condemn him, who disbelieved and ferociously fought the Islamic call. The Almighty, because of that, revealed the following verses condemning Abu Lahab:

> *In the Name of God, the most Gracious, the most Merciful.*
> *Perdition overtake both the hands of Abu Lahab, and he will perish. His wealth and what he earns will not avail him. He shall soon burn in a fire that flames, and so will his wife, the bearer of (fire) fuel; upon her neck (there shall be) a halter of a strongly twisted rope.*
> (Qur'an, 111:1-5)

When these verses were revealed, Abu Lahab was still alive, and he never retreated from his disbelief; so, what stopped him from retreating and claiming to embrace the faith just to disprove his nephew=s truthfulness? What could the consequences of a mistake like this have been? But these verses are not statements made by Prophet Muhammed (s.a.w.w.); rather, they express the speech of Muhammed's Lord, the speech which suffers no alteration. The Qur'an's facts can never be changed simply because this greatest of all Books challenges all times till the Day of Judgment.

There is another fiery challenge which puts an end to any confusion, forcing the unbelievers to recognize the fact that there is no doubt in this speech, the speech of God, the One and Only God, and that it is capable of facing the unknown regarding the past, the present, and the future. This additional challenge is embedded in the verses saying,

> *You will most certainly ride in a stratum (of sphere)*
> *over a stratum.*
> (Qur'an, 84:19)

This statement was made about one thousand and four hundred and fifty years ago when there were no planes, rockets, spacecraft, nor attempts to probe the earth's outer sphere, and when means of transportation were confined to riding the backs of animals. God, Glory and Praise are His, has included in His miracle called the Holy Qur'an many cosmic mysteries in order to give it the chance for a continuous output till the time of the Hour, and so that each generation may derive such an output from it "... till it becomes clear to them that it is the truth," that is, till they realize that the Holy Qur'an is the truth revealed by God. Thus can we indicate that cosmic wonders are in harmony with the verses of the Holy Qur'an. The verse saying, "We will soon show them Our Signs [or miracles, *ayat*]" means that God Almighty will reveal to us the wonders and mysteries of the universe; these can be demonstrated to both believers and non-believers alike "till it becomes clear to them that it is the truth."

Surat al-Inshiqaq states the following: "By the moon when it grows full, you will most certainly ride one stratum (of sphere) after stratum. But what is the matter with them that they do not believe, and when the Qur'an is recited to them, they do not prostrate? Nay! Those who disbelieve belie the truth. And God knows best what they hide; so announce to them a painful punishment, except those who believe and do good deeds; for them there is a reward that shall never be cut off" (Qur'an, 84:18-25).

The Almighty promised the humans that they would "ride one stratum (of sphere) after stratum," that is, that they would be able to traverse the universe and move from one spheric orbit to another. This is quoted from the *tafsir* (exegesis) of Ibn Abbas in his book *Al Miqyas li Ibn Abbas*... By the way, Ibn Abbas was one of Prophet Muhammed's cousins: he was Abdullah ibn [son of] Abbas ibn Abd al-Muttalib, of Banu Hashim, of Quraish. Referred to as the Islamic nation's scribe, he was a highly respected *sahabi* whose *ahadith* are classified by al-Bukhari and Muslim as "*sahih*," accurate, authentic. He was born in Mecca, and he kept the Messenger of God company and narrated his traditions. In his later years, he became blind, so he retired to a'if where he died in 68 A.H./687 A.D. In both al-Bukhari's and Muslim's *Sahih* books, there are 1,160 *ahadith* transmitted through Ibn Abbas alone. Qur'an, 84:18-25 clearly refer to space exploration; so, where did Prophet Muhammed (s.a.w.w.) obtain this knowledge from?! Airplanes had not yet been invented. Now they have become a reality, and they are traversing the air layers, moving humans from one layer to another, while spaceships are now moving them from one sphere, orbit, stratum, or pathway, to another.

Let us bring another Qur'anic challenge, a miracle in the breach of the veils separating us from the future. This challenge speaks to the pedants who profess knowledge, who know a little and are ignorant of a lot and yet who think that they know it all. In it, the Holy Qur'an proves to them that they do not know anything except what God has taught them to know, for He is the One Who knows everything, and that the Holy Qur'an is His speech which falsehood cannot approach at all. In Surat al Dukhkhan we read,

In the Name of God, the most Gracious, the most Merciful.
Ha, Meem. I swear by the Book that makes (the truth) manifest. Surely we revealed it (Qur'an) on a blessed night; surely We are ever warning; therein every wise

affair is made distinct. (It is) a command from Us; surely We are the senders (of messengers), (as) a mercy from your Lord; He is the Hearing, the Knowing, the Lord of the heavens and the earth and what is between them, if you believe. There is no god but He; He gives life and causes death, your Lord and the Lord of your fathers of yore. Nay! They are in doubt; they sport. Keep waiting, therefore, for the day when the sky brings an evident smoke that shall overtake men; this is a painful punishment. Lord! Remove from us the punishment; surely we are believers. How shall they be reminded, and there came to them a Messenger making (the truth) clear, but they turned their backs on him and said: One taught (by others), a madman? Surely We will remove the punishment a little (but) you will surely return (to evil). On the day when We seize (them) with a most violent seizing, surely We will then inflict retribution.

(Qur'an, 44:1-16)

God Almighty is saying here that the Holy Qur'an is the speech of the Creator, God, Glory to Him and all Praise, which He revealed to His Messenger Muhammed (s.a.w.w.) in a blessed night in order to warn all people, and so that He may determine in it every decree of what will come to pass. To the skeptics who doubted the truth in the Message revealed to Muhammed (s.a.w.w.) does the Lord of Dignity and Honor, the Praised One, say, through His servant and Messenger, Muhammed (s.a.w.w.), "Keep waiting, therefore, for the day when the sky brings an evident smoke that shall overtake men" (Qur'an, 44:10-11). The Prophet, in a tradition dealing with the signs denoting the approach of the Day of Judgment, is quoted as saying, "The first of such signs is the smoke [referred to in these verses]." He was asked what smoke it would be. He said, "It will cover the east of the earth and the west; it will remain for forty days and nights. It will affect the believer just as a cold [catarrh] affects him. As to the unbeliever, he will feel as though he is intoxicated; it [smoke] will come out of his nostrils, ears and rear ends." Imam Ja`fer al-Sadiq (p.b.u.h.) is quoted as saying, "There will be smoke that will overwhelm both ends (east and west or north and south) of the earth, causing the death of two thirds of the world population." This smoke can now be said as caused by the explosion of nuclear and hydrogen bombs and by the poison gases they release. "Evident" in this verse means it can be easily seen and identified. It will cover all people and fill the earth. It will be, as the verse describes it, "a painful punishment." How it will punish people is explained above by the *hadith* of the Prophet (s.a.w.w.), that is, it will come out of the nostrils, ears and rear ends of the unbelievers, and they [the two thirds of the world population] will all perish.

Just as it defies the past and the future, the Holy Qur'an defies the present as well, putting people on the spot, giving them the choice to either submit and recognize the Power of God Almighty and the admission that His speech, which He revealed to His servant and Messenger Muhammed (s.a.w.w.), is the truth from God, or to remain in their stubbornness, disbelief, and renunciation of the truth and thus continue straying; the truth is veiled from their visions and hearts.

Is there another example which we can bring about the Holy Qur'an defying the present? Yes, there is. Here the Holy Qur'an challenges us with regard to the creation of humans. God Almighty says in the Holy Qur'an, "So let man consider what he is created of. He is created of water pouring forth, coming from between the back and the ribs. Most surely He is able to return him (to life)" (Qur'an, 86:5-8), and He also says, "We certainly created man of an extract of clay, then We made him a small seed in a firm resting-place, then We made the seed a clot, then We made the clot a lump of flesh, then We made in the lump of flesh bones, then We clothed the bones with flesh, then We caused it to grow into another creation; so, blessed be God, the best of creators" (Qur'an,

23:12-15). Is there any description of our creation more eloquent than this? Is there anyone who can alter this sequence in our creation? If all human beings are unable to come into this world in any way other than the one stated in these verses, then it is the speech of the Almighty, the Creator of everything and everyone, the Lord of the Worlds. So Praise be to God and Exalted is He above what they describe.

Let us now quote these verses: "Every soul shall taste of death" (Qur'an, 3:185), "Wherever you may be, death will overtake you, though you may be in lofty towers" (Qur'an, 4:78). This by itself is a challenge God Almighty includes in the Holy Qur'an, He Who decreed death to His creation, for who among the humans can run away from death? Are these verses the speech of humans? Does this challenge end at any period of time?

The majority of Muslim scholars are of the view that the Holy Qur'an, in its entirety, in the rules and regulations it contains, and in its order and organization, wisdom, eloquence and clarity, and because of the legislation it contains, the news of the unseen, and due to other considerations, is, indeed, a miracle the like of which mankind is unable to produce. There are many proofs in and aspects of the miraculous nature of the Holy Qur'an embedded in the Book itself. One such miraculous aspect is its logic and eloquence; it tells about the unseen, its legislative miracle, its scientific miracles in their various forms such as the medical, cosmic, geographical, physical, numerical, and many other aspects.

Among the miraculous aspects of the Holy Qur'an is the fact that no other book, religious or secular, has ever received as much attention as the Holy Qur'an. Since its revelation, Muslims learned its verses and chapters by heart, taking time and effort to explain them and record what the Messenger of God (s.a.w.w.) has commented in their regard and what other scholars of exegesis have. As time passed by, a new class of scholars of exegesis was created, and books were written by commentators. There are now books dealing with verses with a fixed meaning, and with verses bearing similar meanings. There are studies dealing with the causes of revelation and classifications dividing the Qur'anic chapters into either Mecci or Medeni, and studies dealing with the arts of its recitation, and books in the methods of its reading, and others in its miraculous aspect. Books have been authored dealing with the grammar of the language of the Holy Qur'an, others with its imagery, and yet others computing its verses and dividing its chapters and *hizb*s, the half and the quarter of the latter, in addition to books classifying which verses abrogate others and which are abrogated. There are linguistic studies confined to the study of the Holy Qur'an, to its eloquence, organization, clarity of argument and the meanings of words and diction, the tribal accents in its recitation, the virtues of its chapters, the rewards of reciting it, and the etiquette of such recitation. The attention paid to the Holy Qur'an reached the degree that its words and letters were computed and the ratio between these words and letters, verses, and chapters, was determined. In Medina, there is a manuscript that dates back to the first Hijri century and quotes a group of scholars explaining how they were computing the letters of the Holy Qur'an using barley grains and recording their statistics in a small dissertation placed among old containers preserved till the present time. The dissertation contains the total number of the verses and letters, and the total number of characters in the Holy Qur'an, in addition to other data.

A review of the past fourteen centuries or more during which Islam was fought with various norms of wars in which different nations on earth participated, wars wherein every possible weapon was used with the exception of accepting the challenge, proves that all those opponents proved their inability to face the challenge of the Holy Qur'an. The perfect definition of the Holy Qur'an can be found only in the Holy Qur'an itself, and nobody can attain such knowledge except those whose breasts God Almighty has expanded for such a task, enabling them to comprehend and absorb such knowledge.

It is for the seekers of such knowledge, for the open-minded non-Muslim reader as well as the Muslim reader who wishes to be closer to his Maker, that we publish this edition of the English translation of the Holy Qur'an, hoping and praying that it will be blessed by the Almighty and appreciated by you.

Yasin T. al-Jibouri
Falls Church, Virginia, U.S.A.
Jumada I 1420/August 1999

CONTENTS

The Exordium
(al-Fatiha)

In the name of God, the Beneficent, the Merciful.

2.   (All) praise is due (only) to God, Lord of the worlds.

3.   The Beneficent, the Merciful.

4.   The Master of the Day of Judgment.

5.   You (alone) do we worship, and from You (only) do we seek help.

6.   Guide us (O Lord) on the Right Path.

7.   The path of those upon whom You have bestowed Your bounties, not (the path) of those inflicted with Your wrath, nor (of those) who strayed.

The Cow
(al-Baqarah)

In the name of God, the Beneficent, the Merciful.

1. Alif, Lam, Mim.

2. This is the Book; there is no doubt therein, a guidance for the pious,

3. Who believe in the unseen, establish (regular) prayers, and spend (in the way of their Lord) of what We have provided them,

4. Who believe in that which has been revealed to you (O, Our Messenger Muhammad) and that which has been revealed (to other messengers) before you, and are sure of the hereafter.

5. These are on the right guidance of their Lord, and these are the successful ones.

6. As for those who disbelieve, indeed it is the same for them whether you warn them or not; they will never believe.

7. God has sealed their hearts and hearing; upon their sight is a covering, and for them is a great chastisement.

8. Of people are some who say: "We believe in God and in the Last Day," (while in fact) they are not believers at all.

9. They intend to deceive God and those who believe, while they deceive only their own selves, but they do not perceive it.

10. In their heart is a disease, and God increases their disease; for them is a painful chastisement because of the lies they were telling.

11. When it is said to them: "Do not make mischief in the world," they say: "Verily, we are only doers of good."

12. Beware! Verily, they are the mischief-mongers, but they do not perceive it.

13. When it is said to them: "Believe as other people have believed," they say: "Shall we believe as the fools believed?" Beware! Verily, they are the fools, but they do not know.

14. When they meet with those who believe, they say: "We believe," but when they go apart to their devils, they

say: "Surely we are with you. Verily, we are only jesting."

15. God taunts them and allows them to continue bewildered in their rebellion.

16. These are they who trade error for guidance, hence their transaction does not profit them, nor are they guided aright.

17. Their similitude is like one who kindles a fire and, when it lights all around him, God takes away their light and leaves them in darkness; they do not see.

18. (They are) deaf, dumb and blind; hence they will never return (to the Right Path).

19. Or like a rainstorm from heavens fraught with darkness, thunder and lightning; they put their fingers in their ears against the thunderclaps for fear of death, and verily God surrounds the disbelievers.

20. The lightning well-nigh snatches away their sight from them. As long as it flashes for them, they walk therein, but when it is dark for them, they halt. Had God willed, He could have taken their hearing and sight away. Verily, God has power over all things.

21. O mankind! Worship only your Lord Who created you and those before you so that you may guard (yourselves against evil),

22. Who made the earth a resting place for you and the sky a structure, and caused water to descend from the heavens and thereby produced fruits for your sustenance; therefore, do not set up equals to God while you already know.

23. If you are in doubt about what We have revealed to Our servant (Muhammad), then produce a surah like it, and call your witnesses other than God if you are truthful.

24. But if you do not, and you shall never do it, then guard yourselves against the Fire whose fuel shall be people and stones, prepared for the disbelievers.

25. Give the glad tidings to those who believe and do good deeds that for them shall be gardens through which rivers flow. Whenever they are provided with fruits as sustenance therefrom, they shall say: "This is what we were provided with before!" and they shall be provided with the like of it, and for them shall be purified spouses; they shall dwell therein forever.

26. Verily God is not ashamed to set forth the similitude of a gnat, or anything more or less than it. Those who believe know that it is the truth from their Lord, but those who disbelieve say: "What does God mean by this parable?" He leads many astray thereby, and guides aright many others, but He leads astray thereby only the transgressors-

27. Who violate the covenant of God after it has been agreed upon, and sever that which God commands to be joined, and make mischief in the world; these are the losers.

28. How can you disbelieve in God while you were lifeless (in your mother's womb) and he brought you to life? He causes you to die and again He will restore you to life, then unto Him alone will you be returned.

29. He it is Who created for you all that is in the earth and directed (His command) to the heavens and fashioned them into seven heavens; He is the Knower of all things.

30. Behold! Your Lord said to the angels: "Verily, I am going to appoint a vicegerent on earth." They said: "Will You appoint therein one who will cause mischief and shed blood, while we celebrate Your praise and hallow You alone?" The Lord said to the angels: "Verily, I know what you do not."

31. And He taught Adam the nature of all things, then He placed them before the angels and said: "Inform Me of the names of these if you are truthful."

32. They said: "Glory be to You! We have no knowledge save what You have taught us. Verily, You alone are the all-Knowing, the Wise."

33. He said: "O Adam! Inform them of their names," and when he had informed them of their names, (the Lord) said: "Did not I say to you that verily I know the secrets of the heavens and the earth, and that I know what you declare and conceal?"

34. When We said to the angels: "Prostrate before Adam," they all prostrated save Iblis; he refused and was puffed up with pride and thus turned into a disbeliever.

35. We said: "O Adam! Dwell, you and your mate, in the Garden and eat therefrom freely as you please, but do not approach this tree lest you should become transgressors!"

36. But Satan made them slip and drove them out of the

state in which they had been. We said: "Get you down! Each of you is an enemy of the other, and there shall be an abode for you on earth and a provision for a fixed period of time."

37. Adam learned (certain) words from his Lord, and God turned to him (mercifully), for verily He is the oft-Turning (in mercy), the Most Merciful.

38. - "Get you down therefrom all together, and when guidance comes from Me to you, no fear shall come to those who follow My guidance, nor shall they grieve."

39. But those who disbelieve and falsify Our signs shall be the fellows of the Fire; they shall abide therein forever.

40. O children of Israel! Remember My bounty which I bestowed upon you, and fulfill your covenant with Me (so that) I fulfill My covenant with you; and fear only Me.

41. And believe in what I have revealed testifying to that which is with you (of the scriptures); do not be the first to disbelieve therein; do not barter My signs for a mean price, and take shelter in Me alone.

42. Do not mix the truth with falsehood, and do not hide the truth when you know it.

43. Establish prayers and pay zakat, and bow down (praying) with those who bow down.

44. Do you enjoin righteousness upon people while forgetting it yourselves, even while you read the scripture? Do you not understand?

45. Seek help (from God) through patience and prayer; it is indeed a hard task, save upon the humble,

46. Who think that they will surely meet their Lord, and that surely to Him they will return.

47. O children of Israel! Remember My bounty which I bestowed upon you, and that I gave you preference over other nations of the world.

48. Guard yourselves against the Day when no soul makes up for anything another soul lacks, nor shall intercession be accepted from it, nor shall any ransom be taken, nor shall they ever be helped.

49. And (remember) when We delivered you from Pharaoh's people who afflicted you with grievous torment by slaying your sons and letting your women live, and in that there was a great trial from your Lord.

50. And (remember) when We split the sea for you and rescued you, drowning Pharaoh's people even as you were looking on.

51. And when We appointed forty nights for Moses, then you took the calf (for your god) after he had left you, and thus you transgressed.

52. Yet after that We forgave you so that you might be grateful.

53. We bestowed the Scripture and the Criterion (of good and evil) upon Moses that you might be guided.

54. And (remember) when Moses said to his people: "O my people! Verily you have wronged your own selves by taking the calf (for god), so turn (penitent) to your Creator and slay yourselves (the wrong-doers among you); that will be better for you with your Maker." Thus did He turn to you (mercifully, and pardoned you). Verily, He is the Oft-turning (in mercy), the Most Merciful.

55. And (remember) when you said: "O Moses! We will never believe in you until we see God manifestly," so the thunderbolt seized you while you looked on.

56. Then We raised you after your death, perchance you might be thankful.

57. We caused clouds to shadow you; We sent down to you the manna and quails, (saying): "Eat of the good things wherewith We have provided you." They did not wrong Us. They were unjust to their own selves.

58. Remember when We said: "Enter this city, and eat as you please of the plenty therein, and enter the gates prostrating (in obeisance) and (praying): `Pardon us,' We shall forgive your sins, and increase Our favours to the doers of good unto others."

59. But those who were unjust changed the word into other than that which they had been told, so We sent down upon those who were unjust a torment from heavens for what they were perverting.

60. And (remember) when Moses sought water for his people, We said: "Strike the rock with your staff!" Then twelve springs gushed out therefrom; each group knew its (respective) drinking place. "Eat and drink of God's provision, and do not commit evil in the world or behave mis-

chievously!"

61. And (remember) when you said: "O Moses! We can never endure only one kind of food, so pray to your Lord on our behalf that He may (help) produce for us of what the earth grows: its herbs, cucumbers, garlic, lentils, and onions!" He said: "Do you seek to exchange the better for the worse? Go down to settle in some town, and there you shall have what you ask for." Humiliation and wretchedness were stamped upon them, and they drew to themselves the Wrath of God. This is so because they were rejecting the signs of God and slaying the Prophets unjustly; it is so because they disobeyed and were transgressing.

62. Verily those who believe (in Islam), and those who are Jews, and the Christians, and the Sabians: for those who believe in God and the Last Day and do good deeds shall be a reward with their Lord, and there shall be no fear on them, nor shall they grieve.

63. And (remember) when We made a covenant with you and raised Mount Tur above you, (saying): "Hold fast onto that which We have bestowed upon you with strength (of determination), and remember that which is therein so that you may guard yourselves against evil."

64. (Yet) thereafter you turned back. Had it not been for the grace and mercy of God on you, you would surely have been among the losers.

65. And, indeed, you know of those amongst you who transgressed on the Sabbath, so We said to them: "Be apes, despised and rejected."

66. So We made it a lesson for those of their own times and for those who came thereafter, and an exhortation for those who guard themselves against evil.

67. And (remember) when Moses said to his people: "Verily, God commands you to sacrifice a cow," they said: "Do you ridicule us?" He said: "I seek the protection of God against being ignorant."

68. They said: "Pray for us to your Lord to make it plain to us what cow it is." He said: "Indeed, He says `Verily, she is a heifer, neither too old nor too young, but of mid-age betwixt that (and this); act therefore as you are commanded."

69. They said: "Pray on our behalf to your Lord that He

may make clear to us of what colour she is." He said: "Indeed, He says that she is a yellow cow; her colour is brightly yellow, delighting the beholders."

70. They said: "Pray to your Lord on our behalf to make it further clear to us what cow she is. Lo! Cows are all alike to us, and if God wills, we shall surely be guided aright."

71. (Moses) said: "Indeed, He says that she is a cow not yet used to till the soil nor irrigate the tilth; sound and without blemish." They said: "Now you have brought the truth." So they sacrificed her, though they almost did not.

72. And (remember) when you slew a man and then disputed about it; God was to bring forth (into the light) what you hid.

73. (Wherefore) We said: "Strike him with a part of it." Thus God brings the dead to life and shows you His signs, so that you may understand.

74. (Yet) afterwards, your hearts became hardened as stones or harder still; for there are some stones from which streams gush forth, and others which split asunder and water comes out therefrom, and there are some that fall down for fear of God; and God is not heedless of what you do.

75. Do you then hope that they will believe in you, while a party of them used to hear the word of God and then knowingly alter it after understanding it, and they knew (what they were doing)?

76. When they meet those who believe, they say: "We believe," and when they are alone with one another, they say: "Do you talk to them of what God has revealed against you (in the Torah) that they may argue with you about it before your Lord?" Do you not then understand?

77. Do they not know that God knows what they conceal and what they proclaim?

78. Among them are unlettered folks who do not know the scripture except from hearsay, and they do nothing but conjecture.

79. Then woe unto those who write the book with their own hands and then say: "This is from God" so that they may sell it for a petty price; thus woe unto them for what they earn thereby.

80. They say: "The Fire shall never touch us but for a

number of days." Say: "Have you taken a promise from God, for He never breaks His Promise?! Or do you say about God what you do not know?"

81. Those who earn evil and are surrounded by their sins are the fellows of the Fire, therein they shall abide forever.

82. As for those who believe in God and uphold righteousness, they are the inmates of the Garden; therein they shall forever abide.

83. (Remember) when We made a Covenant with the children of Israel (saying): "You shall worship only God, and you shall do good deeds to parents and kindred, orphans and the needy; speak kindly to all men, and establish the prayer and pay zakat." Then you turned back, save a few of you, and still you backslide.

84. And (remember) when We made a Covenant with you: "Do not shed your blood, nor turn yourselves out of your dwellings." Then you solemnly accepted this, while you yourselves were witnesses thereto.

85. Yet after this you cause your own slaughter, and banish a party of you from their own homes, backing each other against them through sinning and transgression. If they would come to you as captives you would ransom them, while their very banishment was unlawful to you. Do you then believe in a part of the Book and reject the other? Then what shall be the return for those who do so save disgrace in the life of this world, and on the Day of Judgment they shall be returned to the most grievous punishment, and God is not heedless of what you do?

86. These are they who have bought the life of this world in exchange for the life hereafter; so their punishment shall not be lightened, nor shall they be helped.

87. We bestowed the scripture upon Moses, and We caused him to be succeeded by messengers. We gave Jesus, the son of Mary, clear evidence, and aided him with the Holy Spirit. Is it that whenever a messenger comes to you with that which you did not desire, you swell with pride? Some (messengers) you called impostors, and some you slew.

88. They say: "Our hearts are covered." Nay! God has

cursed them for their blasphemy; little is it that they believe.

89. When a Book is brought to them from God confirming what is with them, although before it they had been praying for victory over those who disbelieved, and when there comes to them that which they recognize, they (still) disbelieve.; God's curse is on the disbelievers.

90. Vile is it (the price) for which they have sold their souls that they deny the revelation from God, feeling offended and envious that God, out of His Grace, sends it to whomsoever of His servants He pleases. They have incurred wrath upon wrath, and for the disbelievers there is a most disgracing punishment (in store).

91. When it is said to them: "Believe in what God has revealed," they say: "We believe in what was revealed to us." They disbelieve in what is besides it even though it is the truth confirming what is with them. Say: "Why, then, did you slay the Prophets of God aforetime if you indeed believe?"

92. Verily Moses came to you with clear evidence, yet in his absence you took the calf for your god and behaved unjustly.

93. And (remember) when We made a Covenant with you and raised Mount Tur above you (saying): "Hold fast by that which We have given you and hearken (to Our Word)," they said: "We have hearkened and disobeyed." They were made to imbibe (deep love of) the calf into their hearts for their wrong belief. Say: "Vile is that to which your belief bids you, if you are believers at all."

94. Say: "If the ultimate abode with God in the hereafter is exclusively for you, not for others of mankind, then you must desire death if you are truthful."

95. But they will never desire it because of what their hands have committed before. Verily, God well knows the unjust.

96. You will surely find them the greediest of mankind for life. Also among the idolaters: each is covetous to live even a thousand years, and yet his living a long life will in no way remove him further from the wrath; verily God sees what they do.

97. Say: "Whoever is an enemy to Gabriel-for, verily, it is he who has brought it (Qur'an) to your heart by God's command, confirming what has already been revealed before, and a guidance and glad tidings to the believers-

98. "Whoever is an enemy to God and His angels, and His messenger, and Gabriel and Michael, then verily God is an enemy to the disbelievers."

99. Verily We sent down to you clear signs, but none disbelieved in them except the perverse.

100. Is it not true that every time they make a covenant, a party of them would cast it aside? Nay, most of them do not believe.

101. When a messenger from God comes to them confirming what was already with them, some of those to whom the scripture was given cast the Book of God behind their backs, as if they did not know it.

102. They followed what the devils recited (falsely) against Solomon's kingdom; not that Solomon disbelieved, but it was the devils that disbelieved; they taught sorcery to men and what had been revealed to the two angels, Harut and Marut, in Babylon. Neither of them taught anyone without saying: "We are only a trial; so, do not commit blasphemy." They learned from them means to sow discord between husband and wife; but they could harm none thereby except by God's permission. They learned what harmed them and did not benefit them, and indeed they knew that whoever traded in that (art) would have no share in the happiness of the hereafter. Vile was the price for which they sold their own selves, had they only known it.

103. Had they believed in God and guarded themselves against evil, their reward from God would have surely been better, had they only known it.

104. O you who believe! Do not say (to the Prophet) "Ra'ina," (i.e. words of ambiguous import), but say "Unzurna," and hearken; there is a grievous punishment for the disbelievers.

105. Neither do those who disbelieve from among the people of the Book, nor do the idolaters, like that anything good should be sent to you from your Lord. But God chooses for His mercy whomsoever He pleases; God is of Mighty

Grace.

106. Whatever We abrogate of a sign or cause to be forgotten, We bring (in its place) one better than it or its peer. Do you not know that God has power over all things?

107. Do you not know that to God belongs the kingdom of heavens and earth, and that there is none for you, besides God, to protect or to help?

108. Do you like to question your Messenger (Muhammad) as Moses was questioned aforetime? He who exchanges faith for infidelity has verily strayed from the right path.

109. Many among the people of the Book wish to turn you back to infidelity after you had believed, out of selfish envy on their part, (even) after the truth has been manifested to them; but forgive and overlook till God brings about His command. Verily God has power over all things.

110. Establish prayer and give zakat, and whatever of good you send forth for your souls, you shall find its reward with God; verily God sees what you do.

111. They say: "None shall enter Paradise unless he is a Jew or a Christian." These are their vain wishes; say (O Our Prophet Muhammad): "Bring your proof if you are truthful."

112. Yea! Whosoever submits himself entirely to God and is a doer of good, his reward shall be with his Lord, and on such shall be no fear, nor shall they grieve.

113. The Jews say: "The Christians rest on naught." The Christians say: "The Jews rest on naught." Yet both read the Book! (Even) those who do not know say likewise. God will judge between them on the Day of Judgment in what they differ.

114. Who is more unjust than he who bars entry to the mosques of God so that His name may not be remembered therein, and strives to ruin them? Is it not fit for such men to enter them but in awe? For them is disgrace in this world and a great punishment in the hereafter.

115. To God the East and the West belong; therefore, wherever you turn, there is the Face of God. Verily God is all-Pervading, all-Knowing.

116. They say: "God has taken a son." Glory be to Him!

Nay! To Him belongs all that is in the heavens and the earth;
Him alone does everything obey (in supplication),

117. Originator of the heavens and the earth. When He
decrees an affair, He only says "Be," and it is.

118. Those (pagans) who do not know say: "Why does
not God speak to us?" or "Why does a sign not come to us?"
Thus did those before them speak. Their hearts are alike.
We have indeed made the signs clear for people who have
certainty.

119. Verily We have sent you with the truth, a bearer of
glad tidings and a warner, and you shall not be questioned
about the companions of the blazing Fire.

120. The Jews will never be pleased with you, nor will
the Christians, until you follow their creed. Say (O Our
Prophet Muhammad): "Verily the guidance from God is the
true guidance." Verily if you follow their whims after (all)
the knowledge which has come to you, none will help you
nor protect you from God.

121. Those to whom We have given the Book read it as
it should be read; it is they who believe therein. And those
who disbelieve in it are the losers.

122. O Children of Israel! Remember the bounties which
I bestowed upon you, and that I have given you preference
over the people of the world.

123. Guard yourselves against the Day when no soul
shall make up for anything another soul lacks, nor shall any
compensation be accepted from it, nor intercession profit it,
nor shall they be helped.

124. And (remember) when Abraham was tried by his
Lord with certain commandments which he fulfilled. He
said: "Verily I shall make you an imam over mankind."
(Abraham) said: "And of my offspring?" He said: "My covenant will not include the unjust."

125. And (remember) when We made the House a resort for mankind and a sanctuary (saying): "Take the station
of Abraham as a place of prayer." And We covenanted with
Abraham and Ishmael (saying): "Purify My House for those
who circumambulate it, for those who abide in it to pay
devotion (in prayer), for those who bow down (in prayer),
and for those who prostrate."

126. And (remember) when Abraham said: "Lord! Make this city a place of security, and provide the dwellers therein with fruits to those among them who believe in God and the Last Day." He said: "I will grant whoever disbelieves an enjoyment for a short while, but I will soon drive him to the doom of Fire, and what an evil destination it is."

127. And (remember) when Abraham raised the foundations of the House with Ishmael, (praying): "Lord! Accept (this service) from us. Verily You, and You alone, are the all-Hearing and the all-Knowing.

128. "Lord! Make us (both) Muslims (submitting only) to You, and of our progeny a Muslim people submitting only to You. Show us the ways of our devotion, and turn to us (mercifully), for verily You, and You alone, are the oft-Returning (in mercy), the Most Merciful.

129. "Lord! Raise up amongst them a messenger from among themselves who shall recite to them Your revelations and teach them the book and wisdom and purify them for You; You alone are the Mighty, the Wise."

130. Who turns away from the creed of Abraham other than one who debases himself with folly? Indeed we Have chosen him (Abraham) in this world, and verily in the hereafter he is among the righteous.

131. And (remember) when his Lord said to him: "Surrender yourself to me," he said: "I have surrendered myself to the Lord of the worlds."

132. Abraham bequeathed it to his sons, and so did Jacob, saying: "O my sons! Verily God has chosen the religion (Islam) for you; therefore, you must not die except as Muslims."

133. Were you witnesses when death approached Jacob? He said to his sons: "What will you worship after me?" They said: "We will worship your God and the God of your fathers, Abraham and Ishmael and Isaac, One God, God alone, and only to Him do we submit."

134. This is a group that has passed away; for them is the reward which they have earned, and you shall not be questioned about what they were doing.

135. They say: "Be (either) Jews or Christians so that you may be rightly guided." Say (O Our Prophet

Muhammad): "Nay! Only the creed of Abraham, the one firm in faith; and he was not of those who associate others with God."

136. Say: "We believe in God, and that which has been revealed to us, and that which was revealed to Abraham, Ishmael, Isaac, Jacob, and the tribes, and which was bestowed upon Moses and Jesus, and in that which was bestowed upon the Prophets from their Lord. We make no distinction between one and another of them, and to Him alone have we submitted ourselves."

137. So if they believe as you believe in Him, they are indeed rightly guided; but if they turn away, it is they who are schismatics; then God will be sufficient (as a defense) for you against them; He is the all-Hearing, the all-Knowing.

138. (This is the manner of) God's colouring, and who is better than God at colouring; and we worship Him alone?

139. Say: "Do you dispute with us about God, whereas He is our Lord and yours? Our deeds are ours, and your deeds are yours; to Him alone are we exclusively loyal."

140. Or do you say that Abraham, Ishmael, Isaac, Jacob and the Tribes were Jews or Christians? Say: "Do you know better, or does God? Who is more unjust than those who conceal the testimony they have from God?" God is not heedless of what you do.

141. That is a group that has passed away. What they have earned is theirs, and what you have earned is yours, and you will not be questioned about what they were doing.

142. The fools among men will say: "What has turned them from their qibla which they used to face?" Say (O Our Prophet Muhammad): "To God belongs the East and the West; He guides whomsoever He pleases to the Right Path."

143. Thus have We made you a middle people, that you may be witnesses over mankind and the Prophet a witness over you. We did not fix the qibla towards which you faced except to distinguish him who follows the Prophet, from him who turns upon his heels. This was surely a hard thing for any except those whom God has guided. God would not render your faith in Him futile; verily God is Affectionate and Merciful to mankind.

144. Verily We see the turning of your face in the heavens, so We shall turn you (in prayer) towards a qibla with which you shall be pleased. Turn then your face towards the Sacred Mosque, and wherever you may be, turn your faces towards it (in prayer). Verily those who have been given the Book know it is the truth from their Lord; and God is not heedless of what they do.

145. If you were to bring all kinds of signs to those who have been given the Scripture, even then they would not take the direction of your qibla, and you cannot take the direction of their qibla, nor will some of them take the direction of the "other" qibla. If you were to follow their inclinations after the knowledge that has come to you, then you would surely be of the unjust ones.

146. Those to whom We have given the Book know him (the Prophet) even as they know their own sons, and verily some of them conceal the truth though they know it.

147. It is the truth from your Lord; so do not be of those who doubt.

148. Everyone has a direction to which He turns. Hasten then to outdo each other in everything good. Wherever you may be, God will bring you all unto Him, for verily God has power over all things.

149. And from wherever you go forth, turn your face (in prayer) towards the Sacred Mosque. Verily that is the truth from your Lord, and God is not heedless of what you do.

150. So from wherever you have gone forth, turn your face towards the Sacred Mosque, and wherever you are, turn your faces thither, so that men may have no argument against you (O Muhammad), save those that are unjust. So do not fear them; rather, fear Me! And that I may perfect my bounties on you, and that you may be guided aright.

151. We have sent you a Prophet from amongst your own selves who recites to you Our signs, purifies you, teaches you the Book and the wisdom, and teaches you that which you did not know,

152. Therefore, (if you) remember Me, I will remember you (too); be thankful to Me, and do not be ungrateful.

153. O you who believe! Seek help with patience and

prayer. God is with those who are patient.

154. Do not say of those who are slain in the path of God that they are dead. Nay, (they are) living, but you do not perceive it.

155. Surely We shall test you with some fear, hunger, loss of wealth, lives and fruits; but give glad tidings to the patient ones,

156. Who, when a misfortune befalls them, say: "Verily we are God's, and unto Him we shall return."

157. Those are they on whom are blessings from their Lord and mercy, and they are the ones that are (rightly) guided.

158. As-Safa and al-Marwah are among the signs of God. Whoever therefore makes a pilgrimage to the House or performs umrah, there shall be no blame on him to go round them both, and whoever of his own accord does anything good in deed, verily God is Appreciative, all-Knowing.

159. Those who conceal what We have sent of (Our) manifest evidence and guidance, after what We have so clearly shown mankind in the Book, are those whom God curses, and all those who curse (such ones) curse them too,

160. Except those who turn (repentant), amend (themselves), and make the truth manifest; they are the ones to whom I turn (mercifully), and I am the oft-Returning (in mercy), the all-Merciful.

161. Those who disbelieve and die disbelievers, on them shall be the curse of God, the angels, and mankind all together.

162. Abiding in it, the torment shall not be lightened from them, nor shall they have a respite.

163. Your God is only one God! There is no god but He! He is the Beneficent, the Merciful;

164. In the creation of the heavens and the earth, in the alternation of the night and the day, in the ships that sail in the sea with what profits mankind, in the water which God sends down from the skies and enlivens therewith the earth after its death and scatters therein of (every kind of) animal, and in the changing of the winds and the clouds controlled for service between the heavens and the earth, there are signs for the guidance of those who understand.

165. Yet among men are some who take to themselves equals (to God) besides God, and love them as they love God; but the Believers are stauncher in their love for God. If only those who are unjust could see (what they will realize) when they behold the torment, that indeed to God belongs all power, and God is severe in punishing;

166. When those who were followed renounce them that followed them, and they see the torment and the ties between them are rent asunder;

167. Those who followed shall say: "If only there were for us a return, then we would renounce them even as they have renounced us." Thus will God show them their deeds (which shall be the cause) of intense regret for them, and they shall not come out of the Fire.

168. O men! Eat of what is lawful and good in the earth, and do not follow the footsteps of Satan, for he is an open enemy to you.

169. He commands you to what is evil and shameful, and that you should say against God that which you do not know.

170. When it is said to them: "Follow what God has sent down," they say: "Nay! We follow that which we found our fathers doing." Even if their fathers had no sense at all, and were not rightly guided?

171. The parable of those that disbelieve is like one who shouts at someone who can only hear a cry; (they are) deaf, dumb, blind and thus do not understand.

172. O you who believe! Eat of the good things with which We have provided you, and thank God if it is Him that you worship.

173. He has prohibited only that which dies of itself, the blood and flesh of the pig, and whatever has had a name other than the name of God been invoked upon it. But whoever is forced to it without the desire for it rather than to transgress (the limits), then it is no sin on him; God is Forgiving, Merciful.

174. Those that conceal what God has sent down and trade it for a petty price eat nothing but fire inside their bellies; God will not speak to them on the Day of Resurrection, nor will He purify them, and for them there shall be a

grievous torment.

175. These are they who have bartered error for right guidance, and torment for forgiveness. O how (bold) they are to endure the Fire!

176. This is (their doom) because God has revealed the Book with the truth. Verily, those who dispute about the Book are in a schism (far away from the Truth).

177. Righteousness is not (a matter of whether) you turn your faces towards the East or the West; rather, righteous is one who believes in God and the Last Day, in the angels, the Book, and the Prophet, and gives his wealth out of love for Him to (his) kindred, the orphans, the needy, the wayfarer, the one who asks, and for those in slavery, and (who) establishes prayer and pays zakat, fulfills the promise when one is made, patient in distress and affliction and in time of war, these are they who are truly righteous, and these are they who are the pious.

178. O you who believe! Equality is prescribed for you in the matter of murder: the freeman for the freeman, the slave for the slave, the woman for the woman; but if any remission is made (to anyone) by his (aggrieved) brother, then the recognized course must be adopted and payment made to him in a handsome manner. This is an ease and a mercy from your Lord, and whosoever transgresses the limit after this, for him there shall be a painful chastisement.

179. For you there is (security of) life in (the law of) equality, O men of understanding, so that you may guard yourselves (against evil).

180. It is prescribed for you that when death approaches any of you, if he leaves behind any goods, that he make a bequest for his kinsmen in goodness, a duty incumbent upon the pious.

181. Whosoever alters the bequest after he has heard it, the guilt shall be on those who alter it. Verily, God is Hearing and Knowing.

182. But he who fears from a testator anything unjust or sinful and establishes agreement between them, (there shall be) no sin on him; God is Forgiving and Merciful.

183. O you who believe! Fasting has been ordained to you as it was ordained to those before you so that you guard

yourselves (against evil).

184. It is for a fixed number of days, but whoso among you is sick or on a journey, then (he shall fast) the same number of other days. Those who find it a hardship which they cannot bear may effect a redemption by feeding a poor man, and (even so) whoso of his own accord performs a good deed, it is better for him, and if you fast, it is better for you if you know.

185. The month of Ramadan (is the month) in which the Qur'an was sent down (as) a guidance for mankind, a clear evidence of guidance, the criterion of right and wrong; so whosoever of you witnesses the month, he shall fast therein, and whosoever is ill or on a journey (he shall fast) the same number of other days. God desires ease for you, and He does not desire hardship for you, should you complete the (prescribed) number (of days), and that you may glorify God for guiding you, and that you may be thankful (to Him).

186. When My servants ask you about Me, then (say to them that) verily I am nigh; I answer the prayer of the supplicant when he beseeches Me. So let them hearken to Me and believe in Me, so that they may be led aright.

187. It is made lawful to you on the nights of the fast to cohabit with your wives; they are an apparel for you and you are an apparel for them. God knows that you were cheating yourselves, so He has turned (in mercy) towards you and forgiven you. Therefore, cohabit with them and seek what God has prescribed for you, and eat and drink until the white streak (of dawn) becomes manifest to you from the black streak (of night), thereafter complete the fast until night. And do not cohabit with them while you are at mosques. These are the limits prescribed by God, therefore, do not approach them. Thus does God make His signs clear to mankind so that they may guard themselves (against evil).

188. Do not swallow up your property among yourselves by wrongful means, nor seek gaining access thereby to the authorities that you may knowingly swallow up a portion of the property of man wrongfully.

189. They ask you (Our Messenger Muhammad) concerning the new (phases of the) moon; tell them that they

are indications of (the phases of) time fixed for men and for the pilgrimage. It is not righteousness that you should enter your houses from behind, but righteous is the one who guards himself (against evil). So Enter the houses through their doors and take shelter in God so that you may be successful.

190. And fight in the cause of God (against) those who fight you, but do not be aggressive; (for) God does not love the aggressors.

191. And slay them wherever you find them and drive them away from wherever they drove you away, for mischief is more grievous than slaughter. But do not fight them near the (Inviolable) Sacred Mosque until they fight you therein, but if they fight you, slay them, (for) such is the recompense of the disbelievers;

192. But if they desist, then verily God is Forgiving, Merciful.

193. And fight them until there is no more mischief, and the religion is only God's; but if they desist, then there should be no hostility save against the aggressors.

194. A sacred month (in reprisal) for a sacred month, and reprisal (is lawful) in all things sacred; whoever then inflicts aggression on you, inflict a similar aggression on him as was inflicted by him on you, and fear God, and know that God is (always) with the pious ones.

195. Expend in the path of God, and do not cast yourselves into perdition with your own hands. Do good deeds, for God loves the beneficent ones.

196. Complete the hajj and umrah seeking to please God; but if you are prevented, then send whatever offering is easily available (to you), and do not shave your heads until your offering reaches its place; but whosoever among you is sick and has had an ailment in his head, then let him effect a compensation by fasting, or (by) charity or sacrifice. But when you are secure (from the hindrance), then whoever gratifies (his desires) from the umrah till the hajj, let him offer whatsoever offering is easily available; but he who is not able to find (any offering) should fast for three days during the pilgrimage, and seven days when you return; this is ten complete days; this is for him whose people do

not dwell near the Sacred Mosque. Fear God and know that God is severe in requiting evil.

197. The hajj is in the well-known months. So, whosoever undertakes the pilgrimage therein, let there be no sexual intercourse, nor bad language, nor wrangling during the pilgrimage, and whatever of good you do, God knows it. So, make provision (for your journey), and the best provision is piety, and fear me, O you people of understanding.

198. There shall be no sin on your part that you seek bounty from your Lord. And when you march from 'Arafat, remember God near the Holy Monument, al-Mash'ar, and remember Him as He has guided you, although you were surely, before this, among those who strayed.

199. Then march on whence other people march on, and seek the pardon of God; God is Forgiving, Merciful.

200. And when you have performed your rites, remember God as you remember your fathers, rather with a more intense remembrance, for among men are those who say: "O Lord! Grant us in this world," and for them there shall be no share in the Hereafter,

201. Among them are some who say: "Lord! Grant us good in this world and good in the Hereafter, and save us from the torment of the Fire."

202. These shall have a portion of what they have earned; God is quick in reckoning.

203. And remember God on the prescribed days, and whosoever hastens off in two days, it will be no sin on him, and whoso tarries (there), on him there will be no sin, nor for him who is pious; so take shelter in God and know that to Him you shall all be gathered.

204. Among men there are those whose talk about the life of this world marvels you, and he takes God to witness to what is in his heart, yet he is the most violent of adversaries.

205. And when he turns his back (to you), he strives on earth that he may cause mischief therein and destroy the arable land and the livestock, while God does not love mischief.

206. And when it is said to him: "Fear God," pride drives him on to sin; so, Hell will suffice him, and it is an evil

abode indeed.

207. Among men is he that trades his life for the pleasure of God, and verily, God is affectionate to His (faithful) servants.

208. O you who believe! Enter into submission (to God) and do not follow the footsteps of Satan, for he is an obvious enemy to you.

209. But if you slip after that which has come to you of the clear signs, then know that God is Mighty, Wise.

210. They await aught but that (the wrath of) God should come to them under canopies of bright cloud, and the angels (of wrath should come upon them) and the (whole) matter decreed away, and to God all matters shall return.

211. Ask the Children of Israel how many clear signs We have given them, and whosoever changes the bounty of God after it has come to him, then, God is severe in requiting (evil).

212. The life of this world has been made alluring to those who disbelieve, and they scoff at those who believe, but those who guard themselves against evil will have the upper hand on the Day of Judgment, and God provides sustenance to whomsoever He pleases without measure.

213. Mankind was but one nation, then God sent prophets as bearers of glad tidings and warners, and He sent with them the truth to judge thereby between men when they differ, and none differed therein but those very people to whom it was given even after clear signs had come to them, through revolt among themselves, whereupon God guided those who believed, by His Will, to the truth about which people differed, and God guides whomsoever He wills to the Right Path.

214. Or do you think that you will enter the Garden while there has not yet come upon you like that which came upon those who passed away before you? Distress and affliction came upon them; they were shaken so (much so) that ultimately the Messenger and those who believed with him said: "When will the help of God come"? Verily God's help is nigh.

215. They ask you (O our Messenger Muhammad) what they should spend. Say that whatever of good you spend, let

it be for your parents and near of kin, the orphans, the needy, and the wayfarer, and whatever good you do, verily God knows it.

216. Fighting (in the cause of God) is ordained upon you, and it is hateful to you, and perchance you hate a thing whereas it is good for you, and perchance you love a thing whereas it is bad for you, and God knows while you do not.

217. They ask you (O our Messenger Muhammad) concerning the sacred month, if there is fighting therein. Say that fighting therein is a grave (sin), and to hinder people from the way of God, and to deny Him, to prevent access to the Holy Mosque, and to drive its people therefrom, is graver still with God, and mischief is more grievous than carnage. They will not cease fighting you until they turn you from your faith, if they can, and whoever of you reneges, he dies an infidel; such are they whose deeds shall be in vain in this world as well as the hereafter, and they are the inmates of the Fire, therein shall they abide forever.

218. Those who believed and those who migrated and strove in the way of God are they who hope for the Mercy of God, and God is Forgiving, Merciful.

219. They ask you (O our Messenger Muhammad) concerning wine and drawing lots. Say that in both there is great sin, and also (some) benefit for man, but their sin is greater than their benefit. They ask you what they should spend. Say: "Anything which can be spared." Thus does God make the signs clear for you so that you may ponder.

220. Concerning this world and the next, they ask about orphans. Say that to set (their affairs) right is best for them. But if you become co-partners with them, then they are your brethren, and God distinguishes the corrupt from the well-doer. Had God willed, He could surely have made it hard for you. Indeed, God is Mighty, Wise.

221. Do not marry women who associate others with God until they believe; a believing slave-girl is definitely better than a free idolatress even though she may allure you. And do not give (your women) in marriage to men who associate others with God until they believe; a believing slave is better than a (free) idolater even though he may allure you. They beckon to the Fire, and God beckons to the

Garden and a forgiveness by His leave, and makes His signs clear for men so that they may be mindful.

222. They ask you concerning menstruation. Say: "It is an upset; therefore, keep away from women during menstruation and do not be intimate with them until they are cleansed, then when they are cleansed, approach them as God has ordained you." God loves those who turn to Him constantly and loves those who clean themselves.

223. Your women are a tilth for you, so, enter your tillage as you please. And provide in advance for yourselves (for the life hereafter) and take shelter in God, and know that you will meet Him. Bear (these) glad tidings to the faithful.

224. Do not make (the name of) God a hindrance in your oaths against doing good deeds, being pious, and bringing about peace among men; verily God is Hearing, Knowing.

225. God will not call you to account for thoughtless oaths, but He will call you to account for what your hearts have earned, and God is Forgiving, Forbearing.

226. For those who swear to abstain from their wives, a waiting for four months is ordained, and if then they go back (on their oath), then God is Forgiving, Merciful.

227. If they resolve on divorce, then God is Hearing, Knowing.

228. Divorced women shall wait until after three periods (of menstruation), and it shall not be lawful for them to conceal what God has created in their wombs, if they believe in God and the Last Day. Their husbands shall have the greater right to take them back during the period if they desire reconciliation, and for the women shall be similar rights (over men) in fairness, but for men on women is a degree above, and God is Mighty, Wise.

229. Divorce (shall be lawful) only twice then (you should) either keep her in fairness or send her away with kindness, and it shall not be lawful for you to take away anything from which you have given them, unless both fear that they shall not keep the limits of God. If you fear that they shall not maintain the limits of God, there shall be no sin on either of them about what she gives up to get herself

freed (from wedlock). These are the limits ordained by God; do not exceed them. Those that exceed the limits ordained by God are the ones that are unjust.

230. So if he divorces her (for a third time), she shall not then be lawful to him until she weds another husband, and if he (also) divorces her, then there shall be no sin on either of them if they return to each other should they think that they shall keep themselves within the limits ordained by God (which) He makes clear for people who know.

231. When you have divorced women and they reach their prescribed period, then retain them in fairness or set them free with fairness, and do not retain them to hurt them that you may transgress. Whosoever does so is indeed unjust to his own self. And do not take the commandments of God as a joke, and remember the bounty of God upon you and that He has sent you the Book and Wisdom, admonishing you thereby, and take shelter in God and know that God knows all things.

232. Having divorced your women, and they have completed their term, you must not prevent them from marrying their husbands when they agree among themselves in fairness; by this is admonished whosoever among you who believes in God and the Last Day. This is more beneficial and is purer for you. Indeed, God knows and you do not.

233. Mothers shall suckle their children two entire years, should (the father) desire to complete the term of suckling, and on the father shall be their sustenance and their clothing in fairness. No soul is burdened save to (the extent of) its ability, neither shall a mother be made to suffer on account of her child, nor a father because of his child, and on the heir (of the father) devolves a similar responsibility. If both parents decide on weaning, by mutual consent and consultation, there shall be no blame on them; but if you decide to engage a wet nurse for your children, there shall be no blame on you, provided you pay what you promise in fairness. Fear God and know that God sees what you do.

234. Some of you die leaving widows; the latter shall wait four months and ten days, and when they have completed their prescribed term, there shall be no blame on you if they dispose of themselves justly and reasonably. God is

fully aware of whatever you do.

235. But there shall be no blame on you in (an indirect) proposal of marriage (before the completion of the waiting term) that you make to women or keep concealed within yourselves; God knows that you will mention them, but make no promise in secret to them except if you speak in fairness, and do not resolve on wedlock until the prescribed term is completed, and know that God knows what is in your hearts; therefore, be mindful of Him, and know that God is Forgiving, Forbearing.

236. There is no blame on you if you divorce women as long as you have not touched them nor settled any dowry for them, but provide for them-the wealthy according to their means and the poor according to their means-a provision with fairness; (this is) an obligation on the doers of good.

237. If you divorce them before you have touched them and have already settled a dowry for them, then you shall give them half of what you have settled unless they remit it, or is remitted by that who holds the marriage agreement, and that you yourselves voluntarily remit is more in accordance with righteousness. Do not forget generosity among yourselves; God beholds whatever you do.

238. Be strict in observance of the prayer and (in particular) the midday prayer, and stand up in devotion to God.

239. If you fear (a foe) then (pray as you may) on foot or riding, but when you are safe, remember God, pray as He has taught you what you did not know.

240. Those of you who die leaving widows shall bequeath their wives a year's maintenance without causing them to leave their homes; but if they leave their homes of their own accord, there shall be no blame on you in what they may do for themselves in fairness, and God is Mighty, Wise.

241. For the divorced women, too, there shall be a provision in fairness, an obligation on those who are God-fearing.

242. Thus does God make His signs clear to you so that you may understand.

243. Did you not see those who went forth leaving their

homes, in thousands, fearing death, then God said to them: "Die," and after that He restored them to life? Verily God is gracious to people but most people are not thankful.

244. Fight in the path of God, and know that God is Hearer and Knower of all things.

245. Who is he that will lend God a fair loan, so that He will multiply it to him manifold? It is God that holds and extends, and to Him you shall be returned.

246. Have you not seen the chiefs of the children of Israel, after Moses, when they spoke to their Prophet (saying): "Appoint for us a king, that we may fight in the path of God"? He said: "Is it not possible that if fighting is ordained upon you, you will not fight?" They said: "What ails us that we should not fight in the path of God when we have indeed been driven out from our homes and children?" But when fighting was ordained to them, they turned back, save a few; God well knows the unjust.

247. Their Prophet said to them: "Verily, God has raised up Saul for you (to be) king (over you)." They said: "How can the kingdom be his, over us, when we have more right to it than he, and he is not endowed with abundant wealth?" He said: "Verily, God has favoured him over you and has increased him abundantly in knowledge and physique. And God grants His (divine) authority to whomsoever He pleases, and God is Omniscient, all-Knowing."

248. Then their Prophet said to them: "Verily, the sign of his authority shall be that the Ark of Covenant shall come to you with an assurance of tranquility from your Lord, and the relics of what the family of Moses and the family of Aaron left behind, borne by angels. Verily, therein shall be a sign for you, if you are indeed believers."

249. When Saul set forth with his armies, he said: "Verily God will test your patience at a stream; whosoever drinks from it is not of me, and whosoever does not taste of it is of me, save he who drinks a draught with the hollow of his hand." But they drank of it save a few, and when he and those who believed with him had crossed it, they said: "We have no strength this day against Goliath and his hosts." But those who thought (rightly) that they would meet God said: "How often by God's permission has a small army van-

quished a big one, and God is with those who persevere?"

250. When they set forth against Goliath and his hosts, they said: "O Lord! Shower on us (Your blessings of) endurance, set our feet firm, and help us against the disbelieving people."

251. Whereupon they routed them by God's permission, and David slew Goliath, and God granted him the kingdom and wisdom and taught him as He pleased. Were it not for God's repelling some men with others, the earth would have been filled with mischief, but God is gracious to all the worlds.

252. These are the signs of God; We rehearse them to you (O our Messenger Muhammad), and in truth, you are one of (Our) messengers.

253. We have exalted some of these messengers above others; of them are some to whom God has spoken, and some He has raised in degrees, and We bestowed upon Jesus son of Mary clear proofs and aided him with the Holy Spirit. Had God willed, those who came after them would not have fought among themselves after clear proofs had come to them, but they differed, and of them there were some who believed and some who disbelieved. Had God so willed, they would not have fought among themselves, but God does whatever He pleases.

254. O you who believe! Spend out of what We have provided you with before a Day comes wherein there shall be no bargaining, nor friendship, nor intercession, and those who disbelieve are the unjust ones.

255. God! There is no God but He, the ever-Living, the self-Subsistent. Slumber does not seize Him, nor does sleep; to Him belongs whatsoever is in the heavens and whatsoever is in the earth. Who is he that can intercede with Him except with His permission? He knows what is before them and what is behind them, while they cannot comprehend any of His Knowledge save that which He pleases. His Throne extends over the heavens and the earth, and the preservation of them both does not tire Him, and He is the Most High, the Most Great.

256. There is no compulsion in religion; indeed truth has been made manifestly distinct from error; therefore, he

who disbelieves in the taghut (evil) and believes in God has indeed laid hold onto the strongest handle which will not break, and God is Hearing, Knowing.

257. God is the Guardian of those who believe. He takes them out of the darkness into the light. The taghuts (evil ones) are the guardians of those who disbelieve; they take them out of light into darkness; they are the companions of the Fire, they shall abide therein forever.

258. Did you not see him who disputed with Abraham about his Lord because God had granted him (temporal) authority? Abraham said: "My Lord gives life and causes death," he said: "I (also) give life and cause death." Then Abraham said: "Verily, God causes the sun to rise from the east, so, you cause it to rise from the west," whereupon he who disbelieved was confounded. God does not guide the unjust people.

259. Or (did you not see) the like of he (Uzair) who passed by a town and it had fallen into complete ruin? He exclaimed: "How can God (ever) bring it to life (again) after its death?" Whereupon God caused him to die a hundred years and thereafter brought him back to life. He (God) asked him: "How long did you tarry thus?" He said: "Perhaps I have tarried a day or a portion thereof." He said: "Nay! You have tarried a hundred years. So behold your food and your drink, they do not (in the least) indicate the passing of any time, changing (its original state), and look at your donkey-and indeed We will make you a sign (of Our might) to mankind-and look (further) at the bones, how We assemble them together and thereafter (how We) clothe them with flesh." When it became clear to him, he said: "(Now) I know that God has power over all things."

260. Behold! Abraham said: "Lord! Let me see how You bring the dead to life." He said: "Do you not believe it?" He said: "Yea, but (I ask You) only that my heart may rest convinced." He said: "Take four birds and tame them to come to you, and (cut them into portions, then) place a portion of them on each mountain, then call them-they will come to you rushing. And know then that God is Mighty, Wise."

261. The similitude of those who spend their wealth in the path of God is like a grain of corn that grows seven ears,

in each ear a hundred grains grow. Verily God gives manifold increase to whomsoever He pleases, and God is Omniscient, Knowing.

262. For those who spend their wealth in the path of God, and afterwards do not follow it with obligation or injury is a reward with their Lord; neither shall they have any fear, nor shall they grieve.

263. A kind word and a pardon is better than charity followed by injury, and God is self-Sufficient, Forbearing.

264. O you who believe! Do not render your charities worthless by your obligation and injury, like one who spends his wealth just to be noticed by men, while disbelieving in God and the last day. His comparison is with a smooth hard rock on which there is a little soil; when rain heavily falls upon it, it leaves it a bare stone. They shall not be able to gain anything of what they have earned, and God does not guide the disbelieving people.

265. The similitude of those who spend their wealth seeking God's pleasure and strengthening their souls is like a garden on a hill. When rain heavily falls upon it, it yields its fruit twofold, and if heavy rain does not fall upon it, then a gentle shower suffices. And God beholds all that you do.

266. Would any of you like that there should be a garden for him of palms and vines, with streams flowing underneath, and all kinds of fruits for him therein, being stricken with old age, his offspring being weak, then a whirlwind strikes his garden with fire, setting it ablaze? Thus does God make His signs clear to you that you may reflect.

267. O you who believe! Give in charity only out of the good things which you have earned, and of that which We have produced for you from the earth, and do not aim at the bad things to spend thereof (in charity) while you yourselves would not accept it but look at it with disdain, and know that God is self-Sufficient, praise-Worthy.

268. Satan threatens you with poverty and enjoins sordidness on you, whereas God promises you pardon from Him and a grace; God is Omniscient, all-Knowing.

269. He grants wisdom to whomsoever He pleases, and he who has been granted wisdom is granted abundant good; none shall mind it save those endowed with wisdom.

270. Whatever charity you spend, or whatever vow you make, verily God knows it, but for the unjust there shall be no helpers.

271. If you disclose charity, it is good for you, and if you hide it and give it to the poor, it will be better still for your souls; it will remove some of your sins from you, and God is aware of all what you do.

272. It is not incumbent on you (O our Messenger Muhammad) to guide them, but God guides aright whomsoever He pleases. Whatever good you spend charitably shall be for your own selves. Do not give except seeking the pleasure of God, and whatever you spend of good shall be rendered back to you in full, and you shall not be wronged.

273. (Charity is) for those poor that are besieged in the path of God and thereby prevented from moving about in the land. The ignorant one thinks they are rich on account of their restraint (from seeking assistance). You may recognize them by their countenance-they do not beg of men importunately, and whatever of good things you give in charity, God fully knows it.

274. For those who spend their wealth by night and day, secretly and openly, a reward shall be with their Lord; fear shall not be on them, nor shall they grieve.

275. Those who swallow usury will not stand (at the Resurrection) except like the one whom Satan has confounded with his touch; this is so because they say that trade is only like usury, whereas God has decreed trade lawful and usury unlawful; wherefore whosoever desists shall have what has gone before, and his affairs rest with God. Those who return (to it even after the admonition) are the inmates of the Fire; they shall abide therein forever.

276. God blots out (the gains of) usury and causes charities to grow, and God does not love any ingrate sinner.

277. Verily those who believe, act righteously, establish prayer, and pay zakat shall have their reward with their Lord; they shall neither have any fear, nor shall they grieve.

278. O you who believe! Take shelter in God and forego what remains (due to you from usury) if you are indeed believers.

279. And if you do not do it, then be apprised of war

from God and His Messenger, and if you repent, then you shall have your capital. Do not treat others unjustly, and you will not be dealt with unjustly.

280. If any debtor is in straitened circumstances, then let there be a respite until his ease. If you forego, it is better for you, had you only known.

281. Fear the Day wherein you shall return to God; what each had earned shall be measured back in full, and they shall not be wronged.

282. O you who believe! When you contract each other a loan for a fixed term, write it down, and let a scribe write it down justly for you, and the scribe should not refuse to write as God has taught him; so let him write, and let him who owes dictate, and he should take shelter in God his Lord against diminishing anything of it. But if he who owes is witless or infirm, or if he is not able to dictate himself, then let his guardian dictate justly, then call to witness two testifiers from among your men; if you cannot find two men (to testify), then a man and two women of those whose testimony you approve of, so that if one of the two (women) forgets, the second may remind her; the witnesses should not refuse when summoned (to evidence). Do not disdain writing the transaction down, be it small or big, with its fixed term. This is the most equitable (procedure) with God, the most sure evidence, and the nearest to certainty that you may not fall into any kind of doubt thereafter except when it is a ready (hand to hand) transaction of trade in which you give and take among yourselves, then there is no blame on you if you do not write it, and have a witness when you thus transact. No scribe or witness should cause or suffer harm, and if you do so, then you will be transgressing. Take shelter in God; God admonishes you, and God knows all things.

283. If you are on a journey and do not find a scribe, take a pledge with possession; but if one of you trusts the other, let the trusted one fulfill his trust and take shelter in God his Lord. Do not conceal evidence; whosoever conceals it, then surely his heart is sinful, and God knows all that you do.

284. To God belongs whatsoever is in the heavens and the earth, and whether you manifest what is in your minds

or conceal it, God will call you to account for it; then He will forgive whomsoever He pleases and punish whomsoever He pleases, and God has power over all things.

285. The Prophet believes in what has been revealed to him from his Lord, and so do the believers; all believe in God, and in His angels, books, and messengers. (They say): "We make no difference between any one of His Messengers," and they say: "We have heard and obeyed (and we implore) Your forgiveness, O Lord, and to You is our return."

286. God does not impose on any soul except according to its (individual) ability; in its favour shall be what it has acquired (of good), and against it (shall be the evil) it has wrought. Lord! Do not hold us responsible if we forget or make a mistake. Lord! Do not lay on us a burden as You laid on those before us. Lord! Do not lay on us that which we have no strength (to bear); pardon us, and forgive us, and have mercy on us. You are our Lord, so help us against the unbelieving people."

The Family Of Imran
(aale-Imran)

In The Name of God, the Beneficent, the Merciful.

1. Alif, Lam, Mim.

2. God! There is no god but He, the ever-Living, the self-Subsistent.

3. He has revealed to you the Book in truth confirming what was before it, and He revealed the Torah and the Evangel aforetime, a guidance for people, and He revealed the Criterion (al-Furqan).

4. Verily for those who disbelieve in the signs of God is a severe punishment; God is Mighty, Master of Retribution.

5. Indeed, there is nothing hidden from God in the earth, or in the heavens.

6. He it is Who fashions you in the wombs of your mothers as He pleases; there is no god but He, the Almighty, the all-Wise.

7. He it is Who has revealed to you (O Our Prophet

Muhammad) the Book, some verses of which are decisive: these are the bases of the Book, while others have several possible meanings. Those in whose hearts there is perversity go after that which is unclear therein seeking thereby to mislead and to interpret (to suit their selfish motives), while none knows its interpretation except God and those firmly rooted in knowledge. They say: "We believe in it; all is from our Lord." But none heeds (this) save those endowed with wisdom.

8. (They pray:) "O Lord! Do not suffer our hearts to go astray after You have rightly guided us, and grant us mercy from You, for verily You, and You alone, are the Bestower.

9. "Lord! Verily You are the Gatherer of mankind on the Day about which there is no doubt." Verily, God does not fail in His Promise.

10. Neither the wealth nor the offspring of those who disbelieve shall ever avail them aught against (the Wrath of) God, and they are the fuel of the Fire.

11. Like wont of the people of Pharaoh and those before them. They falsified Our signs, so God seized them for their sins, and verily God is severe in requiting evil.

12. Say to those who disbelieve: "You shall be vanquished and gathered together to Hell, what a wretched resting place it is!"

13. Indeed there was a sign for you in the two hosts that met together in the encounter: one host fighting in the path of God and the other disbelieving in Him; they saw them twice their number with their own vision. Verily, God strengthens with His support whomsoever He pleases, in this indeed there is a lesson for those who have (sound) vision.

14. The craving for women and sons, the hoarding of treasures of gold, silver, well-bred horses, cattle and farm-land, is all made attractive to men. This is but the provision of life in this world, and with God is the best returning place.

15. Say: "Shall I tell you of what is better than all these for the righteous? Gardens, with their Lord, beneath which rivers flow, to abide therein with pure spouses, and God's pleasure; God is well-Aware of His servants-

16. Who pray saying: "Lord! Indeed we believe, so forgive us our sins and save us from the torment of the Fire."

17. The patient, the truthful, the devout, those who spend in the way of God, and those who seek forgiveness before dawn.

18. God bears witness that there is no god but He, and so do the angels and those who possess knowledge; standing firmly for justice; there is no god but He, the Almighty, the all-Wise.

19. Verily the religion according to God is Islam, nor did the people of the Book differ therefrom except after knowledge had come to them, out of envy among themselves. Whosoever disbelieves in the signs of God, then, verily God is quick in reckoning.

20. But if they dispute with you (O Our Prophet Muhammad) say: "I have submitted myself wholly to God and so does everyone who follows me." Tell those who have been given the Book and the unlettered (ones): "Have you too submitted?" If they submit, then indeed they are rightly guided; if they turn away, your duty then is only to convey the message to them, and God is mindful of His servants.

21. Announce a grievous penalty to those who deny the signs of God, kill the prophets without a just cause, and are not equitable in their dealing with other people.

22. They are the ones whose deeds shall bear no fruits in the life of this world nor in the life hereafter, and there shall be none to help (them).

23. Have you not seen those (Jews) who have been given a portion of the Book? When they are summoned to the Book of God-so that it may judge between them-a faction of them turns back, and they are the ones who withdraw.

24. This is so because they say: "The Fire shall not touch us except for days." What they have invented deceives them in the matter of their religion.

25. How then (will it be) when We gather them together for the Day about which there is no doubt, when every soul shall be paid in full that which it has earned, and they shall not be wronged?

26. Say: "O God, Master of the Kingdom, You grant au-

thority to whomsoever You like, and You take authority away from whomsoever You please! You exalt whomsoever You like and abase whomsoever You wish; in Your hands is all good; verily You are mighty over all things.

27. "You cause the night to pass into the day, and You cause the day to pass into the night; You bring forth the living out of the dead, and the dead out of the living, and You give sustenance to whomsoever You like without measure."

28. Let not the believers take the disbelievers for their friends in preference to the believers. Whoso shall do this then nothing of God is his, except when you have to guard yourselves against them in apprehension, but God cautions you of Himself, for to God is the end of your (life's) journey.

29. Say: "Whether you conceal what is in your hearts or manifest it, God knows it; He knows all that is in the heavens and in the earth, and God has power over all things."

30. (Remember) the Day when every soul finds present whatever it has wrought of good and whatever it has wrought of evil, it will wish that the interval between it and itself were wide. But God cautions you of Himself, and God is affectionate to His faithful servants.

31. Say (O Our Prophet Muhammad): "If you love God, then follow me, God will love you and forgive you your sins, and God is Forgiving, Merciful."

32. Say (O Our Prophet Muhammad): "Obey God and the Messenger." But if they turn back, then verily God does not love the disbelievers.

33. Indeed, God favoured Adam and Noah and the descendants of Abraham and the descendants of Imran above all nations,

34. Offspring, one from another, and God is Hearing, Knowing.

35. The wife of Imran said: "Lord! Verily I have vowed to You that which is in my womb (dedicated) to You (exclusively for Your service), freed (from all worldly responsibilities); therefore accept it from me, You are the all-Hearing, the all-Knowing."

36. And when she delivered her, she said: "Lord! I have delivered a female," and God knew best what she deliv-

ered, "and the male is not like the female, and I have named her Mary and commend her to Your Protection, and also her offspring, from Satan the outcast, the accursed."

37. So her Lord accepted her with a gracious acceptance, and made her grow up in grace, and entrusted her to the charge of Zachariah. Whenever Zachariah entered to see her in the sanctuary, he found her with sustenance. He said: "O Mary! From where does this come to you?" Said she: "It is from God. Verily God provides whomsoever He pleases without measure."

38. There Zachariah prayed to his Lord: "Lord! Grant me good from Your bounty; verily You hear the prayer."

39. Then the angels called unto him while he stood praying in the sanctuary: "Verily God gives you glad tidings of (a son) Yahya (John), honourable and chaste, and a Prophet from among the virtuous ones."

40. He said: "My Lord! How can there be a son born to me, since old age has indeed affected me and my wife is barren?" He (angel) said: "Even so, God does whatsoever He pleases."

41. He said: "Lord! Appoint a sign for me." He said: "The sign for you shall be that you shall not speak to men for three days except by signs, and remember your Lord much, and glorify Him in the evening and at day-break."

42. And when the angels said: "O Mary! Verily, God has chosen you and purified you and favoured you over all the women of the world.

43. "O Mary! Be devout to your Lord and prostrate yourself and bow down (in prayer) with those who bow down."

44. This is of the news of the unperceivable which We reveal to you (O Our Prophet Muhammad), for you were not with them when they cast their lots with their pens as to which of them should have the charge of Mary, nor were you with them when they disputed among themselves.

45. Behold! The angels said: "O Mary! Verily, God gives you glad tidings of a Word from Him whose name shall be the Messiah, Jesus son of Mary, illustrious in this world and in the Hereafter, and one of those close to God.

46. "And he shall speak to men (both when) in childhood and when mature, and (he shall be) of the righteous

ones."

47. She said: "My Lord! How can I have a son when no man has touched me?" He said: "Even so does God create whatsoever He pleases; when He decrees a thing, He only says to it `Be,' and it is.

48. "And He will teach him the Book and the Wisdom, the Torah and the Evangel,

49. "And (appoint him) a messenger to the children of Israel (to declare): `Lo! I have come to you with a sign from your Lord. I will make for you out of clay a figure of a bird, and I will breathe into it, and it shall become a flying bird by God's permission, and I shall heal the blind and the leper and will raise the dead to life by God's permission; and I will declare to you what you eat and what you store up in your houses. Verily, in this will be a sign for you if you are (indeed) believers.

50. "`And (I come) confirming that which is before me of the Torah, and to allow you some of that which has been forbidden to you. And I come to you with a sign from your Lord, so take shelter in God, and obey me,

51. "`Verily God is my Lord and yours; therefore, worship (only) Him. This is the Right Path.'"

52. When Jesus perceived disbelief on their part, he said: "Who will be my helpers towards God?" The disciples said: "We will be your helpers towards God! We believe in God and bear witness that we are Muslims."

53. And they prayed to God, saying: "Lord! We believe in what You have revealed and we follow the Messenger (Jesus), so include us among those who bear witness (to him)."

54. They (the Jews) planned, and God too planned, and surely God is the best of planners.

55. Behold! God said: "O Jesus! I shall take you away and raise you to Me; (so) purify yourself of those who disbelieve and I shall make those who follow you triumphant upon those who disbelieve till the Day of Resurrection, when your return shall be unto Me, and I shall judge between you in what you differ."

56. As for those who disbelieve, I will chastise them with a severe chastisement in this world and the hereafter,

and there shall be no helpers for them.

57. As to those who believe and do good deeds, He will pay them their recompense in full, and God does not love the unjust.

58. This We recite to you of the signs and the Wise Reminder.

59. Verily, the similitude of Jesus with God is like (that of) Adam: He created him of dust then He said to him "Be," and he was.

60. It is the truth from your Lord; therefore, do not entertain any doubt.

61. And to him who disputes with you therein after knowledge has come to you, say (O Our Prophet Muhammad): "Come, let us summon our sons, and (you summon) your sons, and our women and your women, and ourselves your own selves, then let us invoke and lay the curse of God upon the liars!"

62. Verily, this is the true narrative; there is no god but God, and verily, God is Almighty, all-Wise.

63. But if they turn back, then, indeed God knows the mischief-makers.

64. Say (O Our Prophet Muhammad): "O People of the Book! Come to a word common between us and you: that we worship none but God and shall not associate any with Him, and that we shall not take any others for lords other than God." If they turn back, then say: "Bear witness that we are Muslims."

65. O People of the Book! Why do you dispute about Abraham when the Torah and the Evangel were not revealed till after his time? Do you not then understand (even that much)?

66. Lo! You are those who disputed about that of which you had knowledge, but why do you dispute about that of which you do not have any knowledge? And God knows, while you do not.

67. Abraham was neither a Jew nor a Christian, but upright in faith, a Muslim, and he was not polytheist.

68. The nearest of men to Abraham are surely those who followed him, and this Prophet (Muhammad), and those who believe; God is the Guardian of the faithful.

69. A group among the People of the Book fervently desires to mislead you, but they mislead only their own selves, though they do not sense it.

70. O People of the Book! Why do you disbelieve in the signs of God while you yourselves witness them?

71. O People of the Book, why do you hide the truth when you know it?

72. A group among the People of the Book said: "Believe in what has been revealed to the believers at daybreak, and deny it at its close, perchance (by this device) they may return (to disbelief).

73. "And do not believe in any but those who follow your religion." Say: Verily, the true guidance is the guidance from God. Are you envious that any others should also have been given similarly to what has been given to you? Or do you fear that they would dispute with you (even) in the presence of your Lord? Say: "Grace is in the hands of God, He grants it to whomsoever He pleases, and God is Omniscient, Knowing.

74. "He singles out for His Mercy whomsoever He pleases, and God is the Lord of bounties unbounded."

75. Among the People of the Book is he who, if you entrust him with (even) a heap of gold, will return it to you, and among them are such who, if you entrust him with even a dinar, he will not restore it to you unless you keep standing over him, demanding. This is so because they say: "It is not incumbent on us to keep our word to the ignorant." Thus they utter a lie against God while knowing it.

76. Yea, whoso keeps his promise and guards himself (against evil), verily God loves those who guard themselves (against evil).

77. Indeed, for those who barter their covenant with God and their oaths for a petty price there is no share in the Hereafter, and God will not speak to them nor look towards them on the Day of Resurrection, nor will He purify them, and for them shall be a grievous punishment.

78. Indeed among them are those who twist their tongues with the Book that you may reckon it to be of the Book, but it is not of the Book, and they say: "It is from God," and it is not from God; they tell a lie against God while they well

know it.

79. It is not for a man that God should give him the Book, judgment, and messengership, and yet he should say to people: "Be my worshippers, rather than God's," but he would say: "Be godly, for you are used to teaching the Book, and used to reading it yourselves."

80. Nor would he enjoin you to take the angels and the messengers for lords; would he enjoin you to disbelief after becoming Muslims?

81. Behold! God took the pledge of the prophets (saying): "I bestow upon you of the Book and wisdom; when a Prophet comes to you confirming that which is with you, you shall believe in him and you shall support him." He said: "Do you thus agree to take this Covenant as binding upon you?" They said: "We agree." He said: "Then bear witness for I am a witness with you."

82. Therefore, whoever turns away after this are surely transgressors.

83. Do they seek other than the religion of God, when to Him submits whosoever is in the heavens and in the earth, willingly or unwillingly, and to Him they shall be returned?

84. Say: "We believe in God, and in what has been revealed to us, and in what has been revealed to Abraham, Ishmael, Isaac, Jacob, and the Tribes, and in what was bestowed upon Moses, Jesus, and the prophets from their Lord; we make no distinction among them, and we have surrendered to Him."

85. Whosoever seeks any religion other than Islam, it shall never be accepted from him, and in the hereafter he shall be among the losers.

86. How shall God guide a people who disbelieved after (a time of) their belief, and after they had borne witness that the Messenger (Muhammad) was true, and after clear evidence had come to them? God does not guide the unjust people.

87. Their recompense is that the curse of God, the angels, and all mankind shall rest upon them.

88. Therein they shall abide; their torment shall not be lightened, nor shall they be respited,

89. Except those who after this repent and amend, for

indeed God is Forgiving, Merciful.

90. Verily, those who disbelieve after their belief, then increase in their infidelity, never shall their repentance be accepted, and these are they who have gone astray.

91. Verily, those who disbelieve and die disbelievers, never shall even the world full of gold be accepted from any of them should they offer it as ransom. A painful torment awaits them, and they will find no helpers.

92. You shall never attain righteousness until you give away (in the way of God) of what you love, and of whatsoever you give, verily God knows it.

93. All food was allowed to the children of Israel except what Israel (Jacob) had himself forbidden before the Torah had been revealed. Say: "Bring then the Torah here and read it, if you are truthful."

94. Those who fabricate a lie about God, after this, are indeed the unjust.

95. Say: "God has spoken the truth, so follow the creed of Abraham the upright in faith, and he was not a polytheist."

96. Verily, the First House (of worship) made for mankind is the blessed one at Bakka, a guidance for the world.

97. In it are clear signs, the standing place of Abraham, and whoever enters it is secure, and purely for God is the pilgrimage to the House incumbent upon people, for those who can afford to journey thereto. Whoever disbelieves, then verily God is self-Sufficient, Independent of the worlds.

98. Say (O Our Prophet Muhammad): "O People of the Book! Why do you disbelieve in the signs of God, while God is a witness over what you do?"

99. Say: "O People of the Book! Why do you hinder him who believes from the path of God, and seek to make it (seem) crooked, when you are its witnesses? And God is not heedless of what you do."

100. O you who believe! If you obey a (certain) group among those who have been given the Book, they will turn you infidels after your believing.

101. How can you disbelieve when the signs of God are recited unto you, and His Messenger (Muhammad) is among you? And whoever holds fast to God is guided to the Right

Path.

102. O you who believe! Fear God as you should, and see that you do not die but as Muslims.

103. And hold fast to the Rope of God all together, and do not be divided among yourselves, and remember the bounty of God bestowed upon you when you were enemies (of each other); He united your hearts together with (mutual) love, and thus through His favour did you become brethren, and while you were on the brink of the pit of the Fire, He delivered you therefrom. Thus does God clearly make His signs manifest for you so that you may be guided.

104. And that there should be among you a group that calls (mankind) to virtue and enjoins what is good and forbids evil, and these are they who shall be successful.

105. And do not be like those who became divided and disagreed after clear evidences came to them, and for these shall be a great torment.

106. On the Day when some faces will be bright and some blackened; as for those whose faces are turned black, (it will be said: "Did you disbelieve after believing? Taste, then, the chastisement in which you disbelieved."

107. And as for those whose faces shall be bright, they shall be in the mercy of God; they shall abide therein forever.

108. These are the signs of God; We recite them to you in truth, and God does not intend injustice to mankind.

109. To God belongs whatsoever is in the heavens and in the earth, and to God alone shall all matters return.

110. You are the best group that has been brought forth for mankind; you enjoin goodness and forbid evil, and you believe in God. Had the People of the Book believed (similarly), it would have surely been better for them; of them (only some) are believers and most of them are perverse.

111. They shall never harm you except slightly, and if they fight you, they shall turn their backs to you, then they shall not be helped.

112. Abasement is made to cleave to them wherever they are found, except under a covenant with God and a covenant with men, and they have incurred the wrath of God. (Besides,) humiliation is stamped upon them; this is so

because they used to disbelieve in the signs of God, and they slew the prophets unjustly; this is so because they disobeyed and used to transgress.

113. They are not all alike. Among the People of the Book is a group so upright in faith that they recite the signs of God all night long, and prostrate themselves in adoration.

114. They believe in God and the Last Day, enjoin goodness and forbid evil, and hasten to do good deeds; these are among the righteous.

115. Whatever good they do, none of it shall be rejected, and God well knows those who are righteous.

116. As for those who disbelieve, their possessions and offspring shall never avail them anything against God; they shall be the inmates of the Fire, therein they shall forever abide.

117. The similitude of what they spend in this life is like a freezing wind which smites the farmland of a people who have wronged themselves and destroys it. God did not do injustice to them; it was they who were doing injustice to their own selves.

118. O you who believe! Do not be intimate with anyone other than those who are your fellow-believers. Others will not fail to corrupt you. They desire what distresses you the most. Their spite has already shown itself out of their mouths, but what is concealed in their hearts is greatest still. Indeed, We have made the signs clear to you, if you would understand.

119. Lo! You love them, but they do not love you, though you believe in the entire Book. When they meet you, they say: "We believe," but when they are apart, they bite their fingers in rage against you. Say (O Our Prophet Muhammad): "Die in your rage!" Verily God well knows whatever is in people's hearts.

120. If any good touches you, it grieves them, and if ill afflicts you, they rejoice thereat. But if you are patient and guard yourselves (against evil), their guile shall not harm you, for verily God encompasses whatever they do.

121. (Remember) when you set from your family at early dawn so that you would prepare the encampment for

the believers to prepare for the battle (of Uhud), and God hears and knows.

122. Two of your groups had contemplated flinching, and God was the Guardian of both, in God (alone) should the believers trust.

123. Indeed God has succored you also at (the battle of) Badr when you were contemptibly weak; so take shelter in God so that you may be thankful.

124. And (also) when you said to the believers: "Does it not suffice you that your Lord should help you with three thousand angels sent (from heaven)?"

125. Yea! If you are steadfast and take shelter in God, and they (the enemy) come upon you in this sudden manner, your Lord will help you with five thousand (such) angels splendidly equipped.

126. God did not effect this but as good tidings for you, and that your hearts might thereby rest assured. There is no succor but from God, the Almighty, the all-Wise.

127. That He might cut off a part of those who do not believe, or cast them down to make them return disappointed.

128. Nothing of the authority is for you at all, whether He turns to them (mercifully) or chastises them, for verily they are transgressors.

129. And to God belongs whatever is in the heavens and in the earth. He forgives whomsoever He pleases and punishes whomsoever He pleases; God is Forgiving, Merciful.

130. O you who believe! Do not devour usury, doubling it over, and take refuge in God that you may be successful.

131. And fear the Fire that is prepared for the disbelievers.

132. And obey God and the Messenger (Muhammad), that you may receive mercy.

133. And hasten to forgiveness from your Lord, and to Paradise, vast as the heavens and the earth, prepared for the pious,

134. Who spend (in God's way) in both prosperity and strain, and who restrain their anger and forgive the faults of

men; God loves those who do good (to others).

135. They are those who, when they commit a shameful deed or wrong their own selves, remember God and implore pardon for their sins; and who forgives sins other than God? And they are not obstinate in knowingly persisting to do wrong.

136. As for these, their reward is pardon from their Lord and gardens beneath which rivers flow, to abide therein forever, and excellent is the reward of those who act (righteously).

137. Indeed, there have already been examples before you, so travel throughout the world and see what the end of those who reject (the Prophets of God) has been.

138. This is a clear statement for mankind, a guidance and admonition for the pious.

139. Do not lose heart, and do not grieve, for you shall gain the upper hand if only you truly believe.

140. If a wound has afflicted you, a similar wound has also afflicted the disbelieving people. We bring about these days (of varying fortunes) among men by turns, so that God may ascertain those who have sincerely believed, and that He may take witnesses from among you, and God does not love the unjust.

141. So that God may purge those who believe and destroy the infidels.

142. Do you imagine (O Muslims!) that you will (all) enter paradise when God does not yet ascertain those of you who have striven hard among you, nor test the steadfast?

143. And you did indeed desire death before you met it, so indeed you have now seen it, even while you look on.

144. Muhammad is only a Messenger; messengers have already passed away before him; therefore, if he dies or is slain, will you turn upon your heels? He who turns upon his heels will not harm God the slightest, and soon will God reward the grateful ones.

145. It is not for any soul to die except by God's permission, (according to) the Book that fixes its term. He who desires his reward in this life, We give him thereof. And he who desires his reward in the Hereafter, We give him thereof. And soon shall We reward the grateful ones.

146. How many a prophet fought, and myriads of godly men with him, while they did not lose heart at what befell them in the way of God, nor did they weaken, nor did they demean themselves? God loves the steadfast ones.

147. And their saying was nothing but a prayer: "Lord! Forgive us our sins and excesses in our affairs, and set our feet firm and help us against the disbelieving people."

148. God gave them a reward in this world and an excellent reward in the Hereafter, and God loves those who do good (to others).

149. O you who believe! If you obey the disbelievers, they will make you turn on your heels, thus will you turn back losers.

150. Nay! God is your guardian, and He is the best to help.

151. We will cast terror into the hearts of the disbelievers for associating with God that for which He never revealed any authority, and their abode shall be the Fire; how bad is the abode of the unjust!

152. Indeed God fulfilled His Promise to you when you routed them by His permission, till you flinched and disputed the (Prophet's) command and disobeyed after He had shown you that which you loved. Some of you desire this world, and some the Hereafter. Then He made you turn away from them, so that He might test you. He has forgiven you now, and God is the Lord of Grace for the believers.

153 (Remember) when you ran away climbing the high ground without even looking back at anyone, and the Messenger behind you calling you back. So He inflicted upon you anguish after anguish, so that you might learn not to grieve at what eluded you, nor at what befell you, and God is fully aware of what you do.

154. Then, after the anguish, God sent tranquility upon you, (in the form of) slumber; it overcame a group of you, while the other group, who cared only for their own lives, were thinking about God quite unjustly thoughts of ignorance. They were saying: "Is there anything for us of authority?" Say (O Our Prophet Muhammad): "Verily, the authority rests wholly with God." They hid in their hearts what they would not reveal to you; they were saying: "Had we

had any authority, we would not have been slain at this place." Say: "Even if you had remained in your homes, those who were decreed to be slain would have gone forth to the places where they (now) lie, so that God might test what was in your hearts and that He might purge what was in your hearts, for God knows what you hide."

155. Verily those of you who turned back on the day of Uhud when the hosts met, (it was) only Satan who made them slip because of some of their (sinful) deeds, but indeed God has pardoned them, for God is Forgiving, Forbearing.

156. O you who believe! Do not be like the disbelievers who said of their brethren upon travelling throughout the world or engaged in fighting (in the way of God): "Had they been with us, they would not have died and would not have been slain," so that God may make this an intense regret in their hearts; and it is God Who gives life and causes death; and God beholds what you do.

157. If you are slain in the way of God, or you die, then pardon from God and mercy is better than all that they amass.

158. If you die or are slain, verily to God alone you shall be gathered.

159. Thus it is God's mercy that you are lenient to them; had you been severe and hard-hearted, they would surely have dispersed away from around you. So forgive them and seek pardon for them, and take their counsel in affairs, but when you are resolved, put your trust in God, for God loves those who put their trust in Him.

160. If God supports you, none shall overcome you; but if He forsakes you, who is there that could help you after that? On God then should the believers rely.

161. It is not for any prophet to defraud. He who defrauds shall bring his deception with him on the Day of Resurrection; then every soul shall be paid what it has earned, and they shall not be dealt with unjustly.

162. Is then he who abides by the pleasure of God like him who has brought on himself the wrath from God, and whose abode shall be Hell? What an evil destination it is!

163. They are of diverse ranks with God, and God beholds what they do.

164. Indeed God conferred His favour upon the believers when He raised a Messenger (Muhammad) from among themselves to recite to them His signs, and to purify them, and to teach them the Book (Qur'an) and wisdom, though before this they were in manifest error.

165. When a misfortune befell you (at Uhud), while you had already inflicted twice as much (on the disbelievers at Badr), you said: "Whence is this?" Say (O Our Prophet Muhammad): "This is from your own selves; verily, God has power over all things."

166. And what befell you on the day when the two hosts met was by God's permission, and that He might test the believers.

167. And that He might know the hypocrites; and it was said to them: "Come! Fight in the way of God! Or (at least) repel the foe." They said: "Had we known there would be a fight, we would have followed you." Nearer were they then to infidelity than to faith. They speak with their mouths what was not in their hearts, and God knows best what they conceal.

168. (These are those) who said to their brethren while they themselves remained at home: "Had they obeyed us, they would not have been slain." Say (O Our Prophet Muhammad): "Ward off death from yourselves if you are truthful."

169. And do not think of those who are slain in the way of God as dead. They are alive with their Lord, being sustained,

170. Rejoicing in what God of His Grace has granted them, and rejoicing for those who have not yet joined them that no fear shall come to them, nor shall they grieve.

171. They rejoice in the grace from God and His bounty, and truly God does not suffer the reward of the believers to be lost.

172. (As for) those who responded to the call of God and the Messenger (Muhammad, even) after wounds had been inflicted upon them, such of those who do good (to others) and guard (themselves) against evil, shall have a great reward.

173. Those to whom people said: "Verily people have

mustered many strong against you, therefore fear them," it only increased their faith, and they said: "God is (quite) sufficient for us and a most excellent Protector."

174. They returned, therefore, with favour from God and His Grace, without any evil touching them, and they sought the pleasure of God; and God is the Lord of Mighty Grace.

175. It is only Satan that frightens his friends. Do not fear them, but fear Me, if you are true believers.

176. Do not let those who hastily vie in their infidelity grieve you; verily, they shall never harm God one whit. God intends that He shall not assign any share for them in the life hereafter, and there is a painful chastisement (in store) for them.

177. Verily, those who trade infidelity for faith shall never harm God one whit; there is a painful chastisement (in store) for them.

178. Do not let those who disbelieve think that Our giving them respite is good for them; We only give respite to them so that they may increase their sins, and there is a disgraceful chastisement for them.

179. It is not for God to leave the believers in the state in which you are, but only until He has distinguished the wicked from the good, and it is not for God to acquaint you with the unperceivable; God chooses His messengers as He pleases; believe then in God and His messengers; and if you believe and fear God, for you then there is a great reward.

180. Let not those who are niggardly in giving what God has granted them of His Grace reckon that it is good for them. Nay! It is bad for them; that which they have been niggardly of shall soon be a collar around their necks on the Day of Resurrection. (Only) God's is the heritage of the heavens and the earth, and verily God is aware of what you do.

181. God has indeed heard the statement of those who say: "God is poor and we are rich." Certainly, We shall record what they say, and their unjust slaying of the prophets, and We shall say: "Taste the torment of burning.

182. "This is for what your own hands have sent forth before you, and because God is not (in the least) unjust to the servants."

183. To those who say: "Verily, God has covenanted with us that we should not believe in any messenger until he presents to us an offering which is devoured by a fire (from heaven)," say (O Our Prophet Muhammad): "Indeed messengers came to you before me with miracles and with that which you said; why then did you slay them, if you speak the truth?"

184. And if they accuse you of lying, then verily other messengers before you, who came with clear proofs (miracles) and scriptures and the enlightening book, were also accused of speaking falsehood.

185. Every person tastes death, and verily you shall be paid your recompenses in full on the Day of Resurrection. Whosoever is removed from the Fire and admitted into Paradise has indeed achieved his goal, and the life in this world is only a provision of vanity.

186. Certainly you shall be tried in your possessions and in your own selves, and certainly you shall bear much annoyance from those who were given the book before you, and from those who associate other gods with God, and if you are patient and guard yourselves (against evil), then verily that is a matter of (very great) resolve.

187. Behold! God took a pledge from those who were given the book: "You shall surely make it known to mankind, and you shall not hide it," then they cast it behind their backs and attained therewith a small price. How bad (then is what) they obtained!

188. Do not think that those who rejoice for what they have brought about, and love to be praised for what they have not done,- think not that they will escape the chastisement; indeed there is a grievous torment (in store) for them.

189. And to God (alone) belongs the kingdom of the heavens and the earth; and God has power over all things.

190. Verily, in the creation of the heavens and the earth and the alternation of the night and the day are signs for men who possess wisdom.

191. Those who remember God standing and sitting and reclining on their sides, and think seriously about the creation of the heavens and the earth, (saying): "Lord! You have not created all this in vain! Glory be to You! Save us

then from the torment of the Fire.

192. "Lord! Whomsoever You cause to enter the Fire, surely You have disgraced him; the unjust have none to help.

193. "Lord! We have indeed heard the voice of a Caller (Messenger) calling us to faith saying: `Believe in your Lord!' and we believed. Lord! Forgive us then our sins and remove away from us our evil deeds, and cause us to die with the virtuous ones.

194. "Lord! Grant us what You promised us through Your messengers, and do not disgrace us on the Day of Resurrection. Verily, You do not break Your promise."

195. So their Lord responded to them: "I will not suffer the work of any of you that works to be lost, be they males or females, each one of you is from the other; therefore, those who migrated and were turned out of their homes and suffered in My way and who fought and were slain, I will most certainly blot out their sins from them, and I will most certainly admit them into gardens beneath which rivers flow, a reward from God! And with God alone is the Excellent Reward."

196. Do not let the ups and downs (in prosperity) of those in the cities deceive you.

197. It is a brief comfort; thereafter their abode is Hell, and what a bad resting place it is!

198. As to those who fear (the wrath of) their Lord, for them are the gardens beneath which rivers flow; they shall abide therein forever. Such is their reception with God, and whatever is with God is the best for the righteous.

199. Among the People of the Book are those who believe in God, and in what has been revealed to you and in what has been revealed to them, humbling themselves before God; they do not sell the signs of God for a mean price. For these there is a recompense with their Lord. Indeed, God is quick in reckoning.

200. O you who believe! Be patient and vie with (each other) in endurance and be ever-garrisoned, and fear (the wrath of) God, so that you may be successful.

Women
(an-Nisa)

In the name of God, the Beneficent, the Merciful.

1. O men! Reverence your Lord Who created you from a single person and created from him his mate, and spread from these two a multitude of men and women, and be heedful before God in Whose Name you importune one another, and be mindful of kinship; indeed God is Vigilant over you.

2. Give orphans what is theirs and do not substitute your worthless things for their good ones, and do not devour their substance along with your own, for verily it is a great sin.

3. If you fear that you cannot act justly among orphans, then marry women who seem good to you, two or three or four, and if you fear that you shall not deal justly (with many), then (marry) only one, or whom your right hands have acquired; that is more proper for you else you should err.

4. Give women their dowry freely (without any) restraint; but if they of their own accord are pleased to give up to you anything thereof, then (you may) spend it with pleasure (and it shall be) wholesome (to you).

5. Do not give away your property which God has made for you (a means for) sustenance to the weak-minded, but maintain them therewith, and clothe them, and speak to them with words of kindness and counsel.

6. Test the orphans until they reach the age of marriage; then if you find in them mental maturity, release their property to them, and do not consume it wastefully or hastily (fearing) lest they should attain full age; whoever's guardian is rich, let him abstain (altogether), and whoever is poor, let him take (for himself) within reason. When you transfer to them their property, have (the transaction) witnessed in their presence, and God suffices as a Reckoner.

7. For men there shall be a share in what their parents and kindred leave, and for women shall be a share in what their parents and kindred leave, be it small or big, a decreed share.

8. When those of kin, the orphans, and the needy, are present at the division, provide them also with (something) from it, and speak to them kindly.

9. Let those who fear (regarding the orphans) lest they might leave behind them weakling offspring, worrying on their account, be heedful of God, and let them utter appropriate comfort.

10. Verily, those who eat away the properties of the orphans unjustly swallow only fire into their bellies, and they shall enter the blazing Fire.

11. God enjoins you this regarding your children: The male shall have a share equal to that of two females, and if they are females, (two or) more than two, they shall have two thirds of that which (the deceased) has left. But if she is the only daughter, she shall have the half, and the father and the mother of the deceased shall each have a sixth part of what he has left if he has a child, but if he has no child and his parents are his heirs, then his mother shall have the third, and if he has brothers, his mother shall have the sixth, after paying the bequest he may have bequeathed and his debt. Your father or your children, you do not know which of them is the most advantageous to you. These injunctions are ordained by God; surely God is Knowing, Wise.

12. Yours shall be half of what your wives leave if they have no children, but if they have a child, for you shall be a quarter of what they leave after paying any bequest they may have bequeathed or any debt, and for them shall be a quarter of what you leave if you have no child; if you have a child, for them (shall be) the eighth of what you leave, after the payment of any bequest you may have bequeathed or any debt; if a man or woman leaves (his or her property) to be inherited by distant relatives, and he or she has a brother or a sister, each of these two shall have the sixth, but if there are more, they shall share the third after the payment of any bequest he may have bequeathed or any debt, without loss to anyone. This is an Ordinance from God; God is Knowing, Forbearing.

13. These are the limits set by God; whosoever obeys God and His Messenger (Muhammad), He will admit him into gardens beneath which rivers flow to abide therein

forever; this is the supreme achievement.

14. Whosoever disobeys God and His Prophet (Muhammad) and oversteps His limits, He shall admit him into the Fire to abide therein forever, and for him shall be a shameful torment.

15. As to those who are guilty of lewdness from among your women, bring four witnesses against them from among yourselves, and if they bear witness, confine them to their houses till death takes them away or God makes some way for them.

16. If any two among you commit it (lewdness), punish them both; then if they (both) repent and amend, turn away from them; indeed, God is oft-Returning (to Mercy), all-Merciful.

17. Verily, repentance before God is only for those who do evil in ignorance and then turn (to God) thereafter; these it is to whom God will turn (mercifully), and God is all-Knowing, Wise.

18. Repentance is not for those who (continue to) do evil until, when death comes to one of them, he says: "Now surely I repent," nor for those who die unbelievers; these are they for whom We have prepared a grievous torment.

19. O you who believe! It is not lawful for you to take women as inheritance against their will; do not make life difficult for them in order that you may take a part of what you have given them, unless they are guilty of manifest lewdness; deal kindly with them, and if you dislike them, it may be that you dislike a thing while God has placed in it abundant good.

20. If you intend to take one wife in place of another, and have given one of them a heap of gold, then do not take anything from it; would you take it by slandering and with manifest wrong-doing?

21. How could you take it when one of you has cohabited with the other, and they have taken from you a firm covenant?

22. Do not marry women whom your fathers had married, except what has already passed, for it is shameful and abominable and an evil way.

23. Forbidden to you are your mothers, daughters, sis-

ters, paternal aunts and maternal aunts, the daughters of your brothers and the daughters of your sister, your foster-mothers and your foster-sisters, the mothers of your wives, and your stepdaughters in your guardianship (born) of your wives to whom you have had cohabitation-but if you have not cohabited with them, it shall not be a sin on you (to marry them)-and the wives of your sons who are of your own loins, and that you combine two sisters (at one and the same time in wedlock), except what has already passed; God is Forgiving, Merciful.

24. All protected (married) women (are forbidden unto you) save those whom your right hands possess. (This is) God's written guidance to you. Other women are lawful for you, provided that you seek them with (dowries from) your own property, taking them honourably, not in debauchery. Those whom you marry for a fixed period of time (i.e. in mut'a), give them their dowries, and there is no blame on you concerning whatever you mutually agree after what is appointed. Verily, God is all-Knowing, Wise.

25. Whoever of you does not have enough means to marry believing women, then (let him marry) from among those whom your right hands possess (slaves or captives) from among your believing maidens; God has full knowledge of your faith. You are one from the other, so marry them, with the permission of their masters, and give them their dowries justly, being chaste, not committing lewdness, nor receiving lovers (secretly), and after they are protected (in wedlock), if they are proved guilty of lewdness, then on them shall be half the punishment (prescribed) for free women. This is permission for him among you who fears his falling into evil; and that you show self-restraint is better for you, and God is Forgiving, Merciful.

26. God desires to explain to you (His ordinances), and to guide you in the ways of those (gone) before you, and to turn (merciful) to you; God is all-Knowing, all-Wise.

27. God wishes to turn mercifully unto you, but those who follow their own lust only desire that you should deviate a great deviation.

28. God desires to lighten your burden, and man has been created weak.

29. O you who believe! Do not devour each other's property among yourselves unlawfully save that it be trading by mutual consent, and do not kill yourselves, God is Merciful to you.

30. If any do so, in rancor and injustice, then soon shall We cast them into the Fire; such is easy for God.

31. If you avoid the great sins which you are forbidden, We will remit from you your misdeeds, and We will admit you into Paradise, an honourable place it is indeed.

32. Do not covet that whereby God has raised some of you above others; for men shall have the benefit of what they earn, and women shall have the benefit of what they earn, and ask God of His Grace; surely God knows all things.

33. To everyone We have appointed heirs of what their parents and near relatives have left behind, and regarding those with whom your right hands have made a covenant, give them their share; God is ever Witness over all things.

34. Men have authority over women on account of that with which God has caused one of them to excel over the other, and for what they spend of their sustenance; therefore, righteous women are obedient, guarding the unperceivable just as God has guarded. As for those whose disloyalty you fear, admonish them, then keep away from them in bed, then beat them (lightly), and if they obey you, do not seek a way against them; God is ever-High, ever-Great.

35. If you fear a breach between the couple, then send one arbitrator chosen from his family, and one from hers; if they both desire a compromise, God will effect harmony between the couple; God is all-Knowing, all-Aware.

36. Worship God and do not associate anything with Him, and do good deeds to your parents, kinsfolk, orphans, the needy, the close neighbour and the neighbour who is a stranger, to a companion by your side and to the wayfarer, and to that whom your right hands possess; surely God does not love the proud, the boastful.

37. Those who are niggardly and bid people to niggardliness, hiding away what God has given them of His bounty, We have prepared for the disbelievers an ignominious torment.

38. Those who spend their property (in charity) only to be noticed by people, disbelieving in God and the Last Day: he whose companion is Satan, what an evil companion he is!

39. What harm would it have done them had they believed in God and the Last Day and spent benevolently of what God had provided them with? Verily God is fully aware of them.

40. Verily, God does not do injustice even the weight of an atom, and if there be any good deed, He multiplies it and gives on His part a great reward.

41. How will it be then when We bring forth a witness from every nation and bring you (Muhammad) as a witness over those (witnesses)?

42. On that Day, those who disbelieve and disobey the Prophet shall wish that the earth had been levelled with them. But they shall hide no word from God.

43. O you who believe! Do not approach prayer when intoxicated until you know well what you say, nor junub (needing ghusul), unless you are travelling, until you bathe. If you are sick, or on a journey, or if one of you comes from the privy, or you have touched women and you do not find water, then take pure earth and wipe (with it a part of your face and hands); God is Pardoning, Forgiving.

44. Have you not seen how those to whom a portion of the scripture is given traffic in error, and wish that you too should stray from the (straight) path?

45. But God best knows your enemies, and God suffices as a Protector and Helper.

46. Among the Jews are those who displace words from their proper places and say: "We hear and we disobey," and "Hear what is not heard," and "Raina," with a twist of their tongues, slandering the faith. Had they said: "We hear and we obey," and "Do hear," and "Do look at us," it would have been better for them and more proper, but God has cursed them for their disbelief; (only) few of them will believe.

47. O you to whom the Scripture has been given! Believe in what We have revealed confirming what is (already) with you, before We alter faces and turn them on their backs,

or We curse them as We cursed the people of the Sabbath, and the Command of God is ever executed.

48. Verily God does not forgive that anything is associated with Him, but He forgives what is besides that to whomsoever He pleases, and whoever associates anything with God has indeed committed a great sin.

49. Have you not seen those who consider themselves pure? Nay, it is God who purifies whomsoever He pleases, and they shall not be wronged in the least.

50. Behold how they invent lies about God, and that (itself) is sufficiently a manifest sin.

51. Have you not observed those to whom a portion of the Scripture has been given? They believe in jubt and taghut (Satan) and they say about the disbelievers: "These are better guided in the path than those who believe (in God)"?

52. Those are they whom God has cursed; you shall never find any helper for whomsoever God curses.

53. Or do they have a share in the Kingdom? Yet they would not give people even the speck in the date-stone.

54. Or do they envy the people for what God has given them of His grace? Indeed We bestowed upon Abraham's children the Book and the Wisdom, and We bestowed upon them a great authority.

55. So among them is he who believes in him (Muhammad), and among them is he who turns his face away from him; Hell suffices as a blazing fire.

56. Verily, We shall soon cast those who disbelieve in Our signs into the Fire. As often as their skins are burnt away, We will change them for other skins, so that they may taste the torment; indeed God is Mighty, Wise.

57. As for those who believe and do good deeds, We will admit them into gardens beneath which rivers flow; therein they shall abide forever; therein they shall have pure spouses, and We shall admit them into dense shades.

58. Verily God commands you to return what was entrusted to you to their owners, and when you judge between men, to judge with justice; how excellent is that to which God exhorts you; indeed, God is the Hearer and the Seer.

59. O you who believe! Obey God and obey the Messen-

ger and those vested with authority from among you. Then if you dispute about anything, refer it to God and the Messenger, if you believe in God and in the Last Day. This is the best and the fairest way of ending (the dispute).

60. Have you not observed those who think they believe in what has been revealed to you and what has been revealed before you? They intend to resort to the judgment of taghut (Satan) though they were commanded to abjure him, and Satan intends to mislead them far astray.

61. When it is said to them: "Come, (let us refer) to what God has revealed (the Holy Qur'an) and to the Prophet (Muhammad)," you see the hypocrites turn away from you with utter aversion.

62. But how, then, when some misfortune befalls them on account of what their own hands have sent before, they come to you swearing: "By God, we only desired (to promote) good and concord"?

63. These are the ones about whose hearts God knows what is concealed therein; therefore, turn aside from them and admonish them, and speak to them words which will get through to them concerning their own selves.

64. We did not send any messenger but to be obeyed by God's permission. Since they were being unjust to their own selves, had they only come to you and sought forgiveness of God, and the Messenger (also) had asked pardon for them, surely they would have found God oft-Returning (to Mercy), most Merciful.

65. But no, by your Lord! They will not be true believers until they have set you up as their judge in all their disputes, and then they do not find any vexation (at all) in their hearts against what you decide, and submit themselves with a total submission.

66. Had We prescribed for them to sacrifice their lives or to go forth from their dwellings, they would not have done it, except a few of them. Had they done what they had been exhorted to do, it would certainly have been better for them and more effective for strengthening their faith,

67. Then We would certainly have given them, on Our part, a great recompense,

68. And We would certainly have guided them on the

straight path.

69. Whoever obeys God and the Prophet (Muhammad) shall be with those upon whom God has bestowed favours among the Prophets, the truthful, the witnesses, and the righteous companions.

70. This is a Grace from God, and suffices God that He knows all things.

71. O you who believe! Take your precautions, then sally forth in detachments or all together (in a body).

72. Among you is he who would surely tarry behind. If a misfortune befalls you, he says: "God had been gracious to me, that I was not present with them,"

73. But if grace comes to you from God, he will certainly say, as if there had not been (any ties of) affection between you and him, "Oh! Would that I had been with them! I would then have obtained a great achievement."

74. Let those then fight in the way of God who barter the life of this world for the hereafter, and to him who fights in the way of God, whether he be slain or victorious, We shall grant him a great recompense.

75. What has happened to you that you do not fight in the way of God for the weak among men, women and children who (in helplessness) say: "Our Lord! Take us out of this town whose inhabitants are tyrants, and appoint for us from You a guardian, and appoint for us from You a helper"?

76. Those who believe fight in the way of God, and those who disbelieve fight in the way of Satan. Fight therefore against the friends of Satan; indeed, Satan's plotting is weak.

77. Have you not seen those to whom it was said: "Withhold your hand (from war) and establish prayer and pay zakat," but when fighting was prescribed for them, lo, a party of them feared men with what should be the fear of God, or even with a greater fear? They said: "Lord! Why have You ordained fighting upon us? Wherefore did You not grant us respite to a near end?" Say (O Our Prophet Muhammad): "The provision of this world is insignificant, and the hereafter is better for him who guards (himself against evil), and you shall not be wronged (even to the extent of) the membrane covering of a date stone."

78. Wherever you are, death will claim you, even if you

are in lofty towers. If good befalls them they say: "This is from God," but if evil befalls them they say: "This is from you." Say, (O Our Prophet Muhammad): "All is from God." But what has happened to these people that they make practically no effort to understand anything they are told?

79. Whatever good happens to you (O man) is from God, and whatever evil befalls you is from your own selves. We have sent you (O Our Prophet Muhammad), to mankind as Our Messenger, and God is sufficient a Witness (thereto).

80. Whosoever obeys the Messenger, he indeed obeys God, and whosoever turns away, We have not sent you to watch over them.

81. They claim obedience, but when they go out from your presence, a party of them broods by night over doing other than what you enjoin. And God writes down what they brood by night, so, turn aside from them and trust in God, and God is sufficient as a Protector.

82. Do they not think carefully about the Qur'an? Had it been from any other than God, they would surely have found much discrepancy therein.

83. When there comes to them news of (public) safety or of alarm, they spread it abroad; had they referred it to the Messenger and to those in authority among them, those among them who can extract it would know (what to do about) it, and had it not been for the grace of God upon you and His mercy, you would surely have followed the devil, except a few.

84. Fight, then, in God's way; it is not imposed (on any) except in relation to yourself. And urge the faithful; God may restrain the fury of those who disbelieve, and God is the strongest in might, the severest in punishment.

85. Whoever intercedes with a good intercession shall have a share therefrom, and whoever intercedes with a bad intercession shall bear its burden; God keeps control over all things.

86. When you are greeted with a greeting, answer it with a better one or reciprocate it; verily, God takes account of all things.

87. God! There is no god but He! He will certainly gather you all together on the Day of Resurrection; there is no

doubt in it. Who can be more true in word than God?

88. What has happened to you (that) you should be divided into two parties about the hypocrites? God has caused them to return for what they have earned; do you intend to guide those whom God has left to stray? For those whom God has left to stray you shall never find a way.

89. They long that you should disbelieve as they, so that you may be all alike; so do not take friends from among them until they migrate in God's way; but if they turn back, seize them and slay them wherever you find them, and do not take any of them as friends or helpers-

90. Except those who reach a people between whom and you there is a peace treaty, or those who come to you with their hearts restraining them from fighting you or their own people. Had God pleased, He would have given them power over you, so certainly they would have fought you; therefore, if they withdraw from you and do not fight you, and offer you peace, then God has made no way for you to fight them.

91. Soon will you find others who desire security from you and from their own people; every time they are returned to mischief, they plunge into it headlong; therefore, if they do not withdraw from you, nor seek peace, nor restrain their hands, then seize them and slay them wherever you find them, and it is these against whom We have given you a clear authority.

92. A believer is not to kill a believer except by mistake, and whosoever a believer kills by mistake should set free a believing slave, and blood-money should be paid to his people unless they remit it as a charity. But if his tribe is hostile to you and he is a believer, the freeing of a believing slave suffices, and if he is from a tribe between whom and you there is a treaty, the blood-money should be paid to his people along with the freeing of a believing slave; but he who does not find (the means) to do this should fast for two consecutive months as a penance from God, and God is all-Knowing, Wise.

93. Whosoever kills a believer intentionally, his recompense shall be Hell; he shall abide therein, and God's wrath shall be on him and so shall His curse, and a great torment

is set up for him.

94. O you who believe! When you march forth to fight in the way of God, be careful to distinguish (the enemy), and do not say to anyone who extends a greeting of peace to you: "You are not a believer," (just because) you covet the perishable goods of this life, whereas with God there are abundant gains. Like this you were yourselves before, but God conferred His grace on you; therefore, carefully distinguish; God is all-Aware of what you do.

95. Those of the believers who stay behind without suffering any injury, and those who strive in the way of God with their wealth and their lives are not equal; God has given a higher degree to those who strive with their wealth and lives over those who stay behind. To each, God has promised good, but He has favoured those who strive and fight above those who sit (at home) by a great recompense-

96. Of high degrees from Him, pardon and mercy; God is oft-Forgiving, Merciful.

97. Verily, those whom the angels take away (at death), wronging their own selves, they (the angels) shall say to the sinning souls: "In what state were you?" They shall say: "We were oppressed in the land." They will say: "Was not the land of God vast enough for you to migrate therein?" So these (are those) whose refuge shall be Hell, and what an evil destination!

98. Except the (really) weakened ones among men, and the women and children who have no power or means to escape from the unbelievers, nor can they find the (right) way.

99. So God may pardon them, and God is Clement oft-Forgiving.

100. Whosoever migrates in the way of God will find in the world many places of refuge and vastness, and whosoever goes forth from his house migrating to God and His Prophet (Muhammad), and then death claims him, his recompense has surely become incumbent upon God; God is oft-Forgiving, Merciful.

101. When you travel throughout the world, there shall be no blame on you if you shorten the prayers, if you fear that those who disbelieve will cause you distress; the infi-

dels are open enemies to you.

102. When you (O Our Prophet Muhammad) are among them (during a battle) and you establish (congregational) prayer with them, let a party of them stand up with you, and let them take their arms; when they have concluded their prostrations, let them take their position at your rear, and let the other party which has not prayed yet come forward to pray with you, but let them take their precautions and their arms. Those who disbelieve desire that you should neglect your arms and your baggage, so that they may turn upon you all at once. But there shall be no blame on you if you should be inconvenienced by rain, or should become ill, to put your arms away, but take your precaution; indeed God has prepared a disgraceful torment for the infidels.

103. When you have finished the prayer, remember God standing, sitting, and reclining. When you are secure (from danger), continue to perform the prayer; indeed, prayer is (imposed) upon the believers as a timed ordinance.

104. Do not slacken in pursuit of the enemy; if you suffer pain, surely they too suffer as you suffer, but you hope from God what they do not hope, and God is all-Knowing and Wise.

105. Verily, We have revealed to you the Book (Qur'an) with the truth that you may judge between people by what God shows you, and do not plead for the treacherous.

106. And pray for the pardon of God (for your followers); indeed, God is oft-Forgiving, Merciful.

107. And do not plead on behalf of those who deceive their own selves; God does not love anyone who is treacherous, sinful.

108. They hide from people but they cannot hide from God, and He is with them when they hold nightly discourses with which He is not pleased, and God encompasses all that they do.

109. Behold! You pleaded for them in the life of the world, but who shall plead with God for them on the Day of Resurrection, or who shall be their defender?

110. Whoever does evil, or wrongs his own self, and thereafter seeks pardon of God, shall find God oft-Forgiving, Merciful.

111. Whoever commits a sin, he commits it against his own self, and God is all-Knowing, Wise.

112. Whoever commits a fault or a sin and accuses an innocent, he indeed burdens (himself) with calumny and a manifest sin.

113. Had God's grace not been upon you nor His mercy, a party among them would certainly have resolved to lead you astray, but they shall only lead their own selves astray, and they shall not harm you in the least. God has revealed the Book to you and granted you wisdom, and taught you what you did not know, and great is God's grace upon you.

114. There is nothing good in most of their whisperings except (in his) who bids charity or goodness or peace among people, and whoever does this seeking the pleasure of God, We shall give him a great recompense.

115. Whoever opposes the Prophet (Muhammad) after guidance has been made manifest to him, following a way other than that of the believers, We will turn him to that which he has (himself) turned, and will cast him into Hell, and what an evil destination it is!

116. Verily God does not forgive that (anything) be associated with Him, but He forgives anything besides this to whomsoever He pleases, and whoso associates any with God has indeed strayed far, far away (from the right path).

117. They do not invoke anything besides Him but idols, and they invoke only Satan, the persistent rebel,

118. Whom God has cursed, and he (Satan) said: "Most certainly I will take an allotted share of Your servants,

119. "Surely I will lead them astray and stir vain desires in them, and will certainly bid them slit the ears of cattle, and I will certainly command them to change the creation of God." Whoever takes Satan as a guardian besides God truly suffers a manifest loss.

120. He (Satan) gives them false promises and stirs vain desires in them, but Satan promises nothing but (sheer) deception.

121. The abode of these shall be Hell, and they shall not find any escape from it.

122. But We shall admit those who believe and do righteous deeds into gardens beneath which rivers flow; they

shall forever abide therein; it is a promise of God. (It is) true indeed, and who can be more true in utterance than God?

123. (It shall) not be according to your desires nor the desires of the people of the Book; (but) whoever does evil shall be recompensed for it, and he will not find any guardian or helper.

124. Whosoever does deeds of righteousness, whether male or female, and is a believer, then these shall enter the Garden, and they shall not be wronged even the membrane covering of a date-stone.

125. Who is better in creed than he who resigns himself entirely to God, and is righteous, following the creed of Abraham, the upright one? And God took Abraham for a friend.

126. To God belongs whatever is in the heavens and the earth, and God encompasses all things.

127. They ask you for a decision about women; say, (O Our Prophet Muhammad): "God makes His decision known to you about them, and that which is recited to you in the Book concerning orphan girls whom you do not give what is assigned to them while you desire to wed them, and also (concerning) the weak among the children, that you stand firm for the orphans with justice; and whatever of good you do, verily God knows it."

128. If a woman fears ill-treatment or desertion from her husband, it shall be no fault on the twain if they effect reconciliation between them amicably, for reconciliation is good, and avarice is made to be present in (people's) minds, and if you do good deeds and guard yourselves (against evil), then verily God is all-Aware of what you do.

129. You will never be able to do justice between your wives, even though you may be intent (on it), so do not turn away (from a woman) altogether, so as to leave her (as if it were) hanging (in the air), and if you effect a reconciliation and guard yourselves (against evil), verily, then God is oft-Forgiving, Merciful.

130. And if they separate, God will render each free from want out of His abundance; and God is omni-Scient, Wise.

131. To God belongs whatever in the heavens and the

earth, and indeed We enjoined on those who were given the Book before you, and on you too, that you should take refuge in God, and if you disbelieve, then verily to God belongs whatever in the heavens and the earth; God is self-Sufficient.

132. To God belongs whatever in the heavens and the earth, and God is sufficient as Protector.

133. If He pleases, He can destroy you, O people, and bring others (instead), and for this God has the power.

134. Whoever desires the reward of this world, with God is the reward of this world and the hereafter, and God is all-Hearing and all-Seeing.

135. O you who believe! Stand firmly with justice, witnesses for God's sake, though it be against your own selves or your parents or your kindred, be he rich or poor, for God is closer (than you) to them both; therefore, do not follow your inclinations lest you should deviate (from the truth), and if you swerve (from the truth) or turn aside, then verily God is all-Aware of what you do.

136. O you who believe! Believe in God, His Messenger, and the Book which He has revealed to His Prophet (Muhammad), and the Book which He revealed before (him). Whoever denies God and His angels and Books, His Messengers and the Last Day, he has indeed strayed off, far away (from the right path).

137. Verily those who believed and thereafter disbelieved, then again believed, and yet again disbelieved, and thereafter increased in their disbelief; it is not for God to pardon them, nor will He guide them to the right way.

138. Announce to the hypocrites that there shall be a painful torment for them.

139. Do those who take the disbelievers for friends rather than the believers seek honour from them? Then indeed all honour belongs to God.

140. Indeed, He has revealed to you in the Book that when you hear the signs of God being defied and ridiculed, then do not sit with them until they enter into some other discourse; otherwise, you will become like them; verily, God will gather the hypocrites and the infidels in Hell all together.

141. Those keep watching you, if there is a victory from God for you, they say: "Were we not with you?" And if the infidels have a share (in the victory), they say: "Did we not acquire mastery over you and protect you from the believers?" Therefore God shall judge between you on the Day of Resurrection, and God will not make a way for the infidels (to triumph) over the believers.

142. Verily the hypocrites strive to deceive God, but He is deceiving them, and when they stand up for prayer, they stand up sluggishly (without earnestness)-they do it only to be observed by people, and they remember God only a little.

143. Wavering between that (and this), neither towards these (believers) nor those (infidels), and whoever God leaves to stray, you shall never find a way for him.

144. O you who believe! Do not take the disbelievers for friends rather than the believers; do you desire to furnish God with a manifest proof against your own selves?

145. Verily, the hypocrites shall be in the lowest stage of the Fire, and you shall never find any helper for them,

146. Except those who repent, amend, hold fast to God, and purify their religion wholly for God. These then shall be with the (true) believers, and God will grant the believers a great reward.

147. What can God gain should He torment you while you are grateful, and if you believe? God recognizes (all good) and is all-Knowing.

148. God does not love the open utterance of evil in speech except by one who has been wronged; God is the Hearer, the Knower.

149. If you do good openly or conceal it, or pardon an evil, then verily God is pardoning, omni-Potent.

150. Verily those who deny God and His Messengers, and desire to differentiate between God and His Messengers and say: "We believe in some and we deny some," intend to take between this and that a middle course;

151. These are truly the infidels, and we have prepared a disgraceful torment for the infidels.

152. Those who believe in God and His Messengers and do not differentiate between any one of them and another,

are those whom He will grant their recompense; God is oft-Forgiving, Merciful.

153. The people of the Book ask you (O Our Prophet Muhammad) to bring them a book from heaven; indeed they demanded of Moses a greater thing than that, for they said: "Show us God manifestly," whereupon lightning struck them for their wickedness. Then they took a calf (as a god) even after clear signs had come to them, but (even then) We pardoned them for this, and We bestowed upon Moses a clear authority.

154. We lifted Mount Tur (Sinai) over them at (the taking of) their covenant, and We said to them: "Enter the door prostrating," and We said to them: "Do not exceed (Our limits) on the Sabbath," and We took a firm covenant from them.

155. So, for the breaking of their covenant and denial of the signs of God, and their slaying the prophets unjustly, and their saying: "Our hearts are covered," God set a seal upon them for their disbelief, so they believe but a little.

156. And for their disbelief, and for their utterance of a grievous calumny against Mary;

157. And for their saying: "Verily we have slain the Messiah, Jesus son of Mary, the messenger of God." But they did not slay him, nor did they crucify him; it only seemed so to them, and indeed those who differ concerning this are only in doubt about it; they do not have any true knowledge about it except pursuance of a conjecture, and they certainly did not slay him.

158. Nay! God took him up unto Himself, and God is Mighty, Wise!

159. There shall not be anyone of the people of the Book but he must certainly believe in him before his death, and on the Day of Resurrection, he (Jesus) will be a witness against them.

160. For the iniquity of the Jews, We forbade them those good things which had been made lawful for them before, and for their obstructing many people from the path of God,

161. And for taking usury, though they were forbidden it, and their wrongful devouring of people's property, and We have prepared a painful torment for the disbelievers

from among them.

162. But those who are well grounded in knowledge among them, and those who believe in what has been revealed to you and what has been revealed (to Our messengers) before you, and those who keep up prayers, and those who pay zakat, and the believers in God and the Last Day., these it is whom We shall give a great recompense.

163. Verily, We have revealed to you (O Our Prophet Muhammad) as We revealed to Noah and the messengers after him, and We revealed to Abraham, Ishmael, Isaac, Jacob, Jesus, Job, Aaron, and the Tribes, and Solomon, and We bestowed the Psalms (Zabur) upon David.

164. And messengers We have already mentioned to you before, and messengers We have not mentioned to you, and God spoke to Moses directly in words.

165. We sent messengers to convey glad tidings and to warn, so that no argument may remain for people against God, after the coming of the messengers, and God is Mighty, Wise.

166. God Himself bears witness that whatever He has revealed to you (O Our Prophet Muhammad) He sent with His Knowledge; and the angels, too, bear witness, and God is sufficient as Witness.

167. Verily those who disbelieve and obstruct people from God's way have indeed strayed off far away (from the Right Path).

168. It is not for God to pardon those who disbelieve and act unjustly, nor will He guide them to the way,

169. Except the way to Hell, to abide therein forever. And this is quite easy for God.

170. O mankind! Verily the Messenger (Muhammad) has come to you with the Truth from your Lord; believe, then, in him; that is best for you, and if you disbelieve, then to God belongs whatever in the heavens and the earth, and God is all-Knowing, all-Wise.

171. O people of the Book! Do not exceed the limits in your religion, and do not say anything about God except the truth; verily, the Messiah Jesus son of Mary is only a messenger of God and His Word which He conveyed to Mary and a Spirit proceeding from Him; believe therefore

in God and His messengers and do not say that there are three gods; to desist is best for you; verily, there is only One God! Far it is from His Glory that He should have a son; to Him belongs whatever in the heavens and the earth; God is sufficient as Protector.

172. The Messiah never disdains to be a slave of God, nor do the angels who are near unto Him, and whosoever disdains serving Him out of pride, He will gather them to Him all together.

173. As for those who believe and do good, He will pay them their full recompense, and will increase them of His grace. As for those who disdain and are proud, He will chastise them with a painful torment. They shall not find for themselves any guardian or helper besides God.

174. O mankind! Indeed an undeniable proof from your Lord has come to you, and We have revealed to you a manifest Light.

175. As for those who believe in God and hold fast to Him, soon will He admit them to mercy from Him and a grace, and will guide them to Himself on the Straight Path.

176. They ask you for a decree of the Law, say, (O Our Prophet Muhammad), "God gives you a decision about distant kindred. If a man dies and he has no offspring, and he has a sister, for her shall be half of what he leaves, and he shall be her heir, if she has no son, and if there are two sisters, then they shall both have two thirds of what he leaves, and if there are brethren, men and women, then the male shall have the like of the shares of two females. God makes it clear for you lest you should err, and God knows all things."

The Table Spread
(al-Ma'ida)

In the name of God, the Beneficent, the Merciful.

1. O you who believe! Fulfill your contracts. The grass-eating quadrupeds are made lawful for your food, except those which are recited to you, not allowing the game while you are under (the prescribed) pilgrimage restrictions; verily God commands whatever He intends.

2. O you who believe! Do not violate the sanctity of the monuments of God, nor the sacred month, nor the offering, nor the symbolic garlands (wearings), nor those resorting to the Sacred House, seeking the Grace of their Lord and His Pleasure. When you are free from the prescribed restrictions of the pilgrimage, then you may hunt, and do not let the malice of those who hindered you from the sacred Mosque incite you to exceed the limits. Help one another in righteousness and piety, and do not help one another in sin and aggression; take shelter in God, for verily God is severe in punishment.

3. Forbidden to you are: dead meat, blood, the flesh of swine, what has been slaughtered in the name of any other than God, the strangled, the beaten to death, the dead by a headlong fall, the gorged to death by a horn, and that which the wild beasts ate, except what you yourselves lawfully slaughter. Also forbidden to you is whatever was sacrificed on altar stones (to idols), and that which you divide by consulting arrows; all these are abominations. This day, those who disbelieve have despaired of your (reverting from your) religion, so do not fear them but fear Me. This day have I perfected your religion for you, completed My favour upon you, and chosen Islam as your religion; but whosoever is helplessly forced by hunger, not inclining to sin, then verily God is oft-Forgiving, Merciful.

4. They ask you (O Our Prophet Muhammad) what food is made lawful for them; say: "The good things have all been made lawful for you: whatever you have taught the hunting beasts to catch: train the dogs which you have taught even as God has taught you, then eat of what they catch for you, and mention the name of God on the prey (when you set the beast on it), and fear God; verily, God is swift in reckoning."

5. This day have been made lawful for you all good things, and the food of the people of the Book has been made lawful to you, and your food is lawful for them, and the chaste ones from those who have been given the Book before you are lawful (wives) for you when you have given them their dower with chaste intention of lawful wedlock, nor fornicating, nor secretly taking them for paramours;

whoever denies Faith, indeed, all his deeds become vain, and in the Hereafter he shall be of the losers.

6. O you who believe! When you get ready for prayers, wash your faces and hands along with the elbows, and wipe a part of your heads and feet to the ankles, and if you are polluted, then cleanse yourselves, and if you are sick or on a journey, or if one of you comes from the privy, or you have had contact with women, and you do not find water, then betake to pure earth and wipe a part of your faces and hands with it; God does not intend to lay a hardship on you, but to purify you instead so that He may complete His favour on you, you may be grateful.

7. And remember the bounties of God on you, and the Covenant He has bound with you when you said: "We have heard (Your Commandment) and we have obeyed it sincerely," and fear God, verily God knows whatever is hidden in your hearts.

8. O you who believe! Be always upright for God, bearing witness to justice, and do not let the hatred of a people incite you not to act equitably; act equitably, that is nearer to piety; fear God, verily God is fully aware of all what you do.

9. God has promised those who believe and do good deeds that there is for them pardon and a great reward.

10. As for those who disbelieve and belie Our signs, they are the fellows of the Fire.

11. O you who believe! Remember God's bounties on you when some people were determined to stretch forth their hands against you, but He withheld their hands from you; so, fear God, and upon God alone let the faithful rely.

12. Certainly God took a Covenant from the children of Israel, and We raised up from among them twelve chieftains, and God said: "Verily, I am with you; if you keep up prayer and pay zakat, and believe in My messengers and support them and lend God a goodly loan, I will certainly wipe out your sins from you; and I will certainly permit you into gardens beneath which rivers flow; but whosoever disbelieves after this, from among you, he shall certainly have missed the Right Path.

13. But for the breaking of their Covenant, We cursed

them and made their hearts hard; they shift the words (of the Scripture) from their proper places, and have forgotten a part of what they were admonished with; nor will you cease to be informed of deceit from among them, except from a few of them; so forgive them and overlook; verily God loves the beneficent.

14. Of those also who say: "Verily, we are Nazarenes," We took their Covenant, too, but they have forgotten a portion of what they were admonished with; therefore, We stirred up among them enmity and hatred till the Day of Resurrection, and soon will God inform them of what they were doing.

15. O people of the Book! Indeed Our Prophet (Muhammad) has come to you revealing to you much of what you have been concealing of the Book, and yet overlooking even more; indeed, Light and a manifesting Book (Qur'an) have come to you from God,

16. Whereby God guides that who follows His Pleasure into the ways of peace, and takes them out of darkness into the Light by His Will, guiding them to the Straight Path.

17. Certainly, they are blasphemous those who say: "God is the Messiah son of Mary;" say: "Who could hold anything against God if He intends to destroy the Messiah son of Mary, his mother, and all that is on earth altogether? For to God belongs the dominion of the heavens and the earth, and what is between both; He creates what He wills, and God has power over all things."

18. The Jews and the Christians say: "We are the sons of God and His beloved ones;" say: "Why then does He punish you for your sins? Nay, you are but human like others He has created; He pardons whomsoever He pleases and punishes whomsoever He pleases, and to God belongs the dominion of the heavens and the earth and whatever is between them, and to Him is the ultimate return of all."

19. O people of the Book! Indeed, Our Prophet (Muhammad) has come to you, explaining to you after the break in (the series of) Our Prophets, lest you say that no bearer of glad tidings nor a warner came to you; but now a bearer of glad tidings and a Warner (Our Prophet Muhammad) has come to you, and God has power over all

things.

20. Behold! Moses said to his people: "O my people! Remember the bounties of God upon you when He raised prophets among you, and made you kings and gave you what He has not given anyone else in the world.

21. "O my people! Enter the holy land which God has assigned for you, and do not turn your backs, for then you will turn losers."

22. They said: "O Moses! Verily, there are in it people of might, and verily we will never enter it until they get out of it, and if they get out, we will certainly enter then."

23. Then two men of those who feared God, and upon both of whom God had bestowed His favour, said: "Enter upon them suddenly by the gate, for once you have entered it, you shall verily be victorious, and upon God you should rely, if you are true believers."

24. They said: "O Moses! Verily, we shall never enter it at all while they remain therein; go, therefore, you and your God, and fight; verily we shall stay here waiting."

25. He said: "Lord! I have no authority except over myself and my brother, so cause a separation between us and the rebellious people."

26. God said: "The land shall be forbidden to them for forty years; they shall wander perplexedly in the world; therefore, do not grieve over the rebellious people."

27. Recite unto them the story of the two sons of Adam with truth. They both offered an offering, but it was accepted from one of them and rejected from the other. (One of them) said (to the other): "I shall certainly slay you." (The other) said: "Verily, God accepts (an offering) only from those who guard themselves against evil.

28. "Should you stretch your hands towards me to slay me, I will not stretch mine to slay you. Verily, I fear God, Lord of the worlds.

29. "Verily, I intend that you bear my sin and also your own, so you will be among the companions of the Fire, the recompense of the unjust."

30. So his passion led him to slay his brother; he slew him and thus became one of the losers.

31. Then God sent a crow digging the earth to show him

how he should cover the unsightly corpse of his brother; (seeing this) he said: "Woe unto me! Am I unable to be like this crow to cover the unsightly corpse of my brother?" And so did he repent.

32. On that account, We ordained to the children of Israel that he who slays anyone for any reason other than (a punishment for) murder or mischief in the land, it shall be as though he slays all mankind, and he who saves it shall be as though he saves all mankind, and certainly messengers came to them with clear evidences, yet many of them, even after all that, committed excesses in the land.

33. The recompense of those who wage war against God and His Messenger and strive in the land spreading mischief is only that they be slain or crucified, or that their hands and feet be cut off from opposite sides, or that they be banished from the land. For them shall be a disgrace in this world, and in the hereafter a great torment awaits them,

34. Except those who repent before you gain power over them; know that God is oft-Pardoning, Merciful.

35. O you who believe! Fear God and seek an approach to Him, and strive hard in His way so that you may prosper.

36. Had those who disbelieve had what is in the earth altogether and the like of it with which to ransom them from the torment of the Day of Resurrection, it shall not be accepted from them, and for them there shall be a painful torment.

37. They would desire to get out of the Fire but they shall not be able to do so, and for them shall be a lasting torment.

38. As for male or female thieves, cut off their hands, a punishment for what they earn, an exemplary punishment by God, and God is Mighty, Wise.

39. Whoever turns to God repentant after his iniquity and reforms himself, verily God turns to him (mercifully); indeed, God is oft-Pardoning, Merciful.

40. Do you not know that to God belongs the dominion of the heavens and the earth? He punishes whomsoever He pleases and pardons whomsoever He pleases, and God has power over all things.

41. O Prophet (Muhammad)! Do not let those who has-

ten in infidelity grieve you. Be it among those who say: "We believe" while their hearts do not believe. Or be it among the Jews who listen to lies; they listen to other people who have not come to you; they distort the words from their original places (in the law), saying: "If you are given this (by Muhammad), take it, and if you are not given, beware!" As for that whom God desires to try, you can never prevail with God in anything. They are the ones whose hearts God does not wish to purify; theirs is a disgrace in this world, and a greater punishment in the Hereafter.

42. They listen to lies and devour illicit gain; therefore, if they come to you (O Our Prophet Muhammad), you are (at liberty) to judge between them or turn aside from them, and if you turn aside from them, then they shall never harm you in any way; but if you judge, then judge between them with equity; verily God loves those who deal equitably.

43. But how shall they make you their judge, while the Torah is with them wherein is the clear judgment of God, and yet they turn away even after that? These, in fact, are not believers.

44. Verily, We revealed the Torah; therein was guidance and light; with it Our messengers who submitted judged between the Jews and the divines (rabbis) and scholars (doctors of divinity) in accordance with what they were entrusted of the Book of God, and they were witnesses thereof; therefore, do not fear people but fear Me, and do not barter away My signs for a miserable price; those who do not judge by what God has revealed are indeed infidels.

45. We prescribed for them therein that a life for a life, an eye for an eye, a nose for a nose, an ear for an ear, a tooth for a tooth, and a reprisal for wounds; but whoever remits it (in charity), it shall be an expiation of his sins, and whoever does not judge according to what God has revealed is indeed among the unjust ones.

46. We sent Jesus son of Mary in their footsteps, confirming the law (Torah) which was before him, and We bestowed the Evangel upon him, wherein there is guidance and light, confirming what was before it of the Torah, a guidance and admonition for those who are God-fearing.

47. Let the people of the Evangel judge according to what

God has revealed in it; whoever does not judge by what God has sent down are the transgressors.

48. We have revealed to you (O Our Prophet Muhammad) the Book (Qur'an) with truth, confirming what is before it of the book and a guardian thereof; therefore, judge between them by what God has revealed, and do not follow their (vain) desires, diverging from what has come to you of the truth. For each of you We appointed a law and a way: Had God desired, He would have made all of you a single community, but He wished (instead) to try you in what He has given you; therefore, compete excelling one another in goodness; to God alone is the return of all of you; it is then that He shall declare to you that wherein you differed.

49. (God commands) that you should judge between them by what God has revealed, and do not follow their vain desires; be cautious of them lest they should beguile you from any part of what God has sent you, and if they turn back, know then that God desires to afflict them for some of their sins, and verily many are transgressors.

50. Is it the judgment of the times of pagan ignorance that they desire? Who else can be better than God to judge for a people of assured faith?

51. O you who believe! Do not take the Jews nor the Christians for friends and protectors; they are friends of one another, and whoever among you takes them for friends is verily one of them; indeed, God does not guide the unjust people.

52. So you see those in whose hearts there is a disease hastening towards them, saying: "We fear lest a reverse (of fortune) befalls us." But it may be that God brings about a victory (for you), or something from Himself, then they will regret what they hid in their hearts.

53. Then those who believe will say: "Are these the ones who swore by God with the most forcible of their oaths that they certainly were with you?" In vain shall all their good deeds go, and they shall be losers.

54. O you who believe! Whoever among you turns back from his religion, God will soon bring forward a people whom He loves and they love Him, humble before the be-

lievers, mighty against infidels, striving hard in God's way, and they do not fear the censure of those who censure. This is the Grace of God, He bestows it upon whomsoever He pleases, and God is ample-Giving, all-Knowing.

55. Verily, your guardian is (none but) God and His Prophet (Muhammad), and those who believe, establishing prayer and paying charity even while bowing down (in prayer).

56. Whoever takes God, His Messenger (Muhammad), and those who believe as his guardians, verily he has joined the fellowship of God; they are the ones that shall always triumph.

57. O you who believe! Do not take (for guardians) those who hold your religion in mockery and ridicule from among those who have been given the Book before you and the infidels; fear God, if you are believers (in Him).

58. When you proclaim the call to prayer, they make it a mockery and a sport; this is so because they are people who lack understanding.

59. Say (O Our Prophet Muhammad): "O people of the Book! Do you find fault with us for aught except that we believe in God and in what has been revealed to us and what had been revealed before, while most of you are transgressors?"

60. Say (O Our Prophet Muhammad): "Shall I inform you of worse than this in retribution from God? (It is he) whom God has cursed and brought His Wrath upon his own self, some of whom He transformed into apes and swine, and he who worshipped Taghut (tyranny); they are worse in rank and far more astray from the Right Path."

61. When they come to you, (O Our Prophet Muhammad), they say: "We believe," while indeed they come with infidelity (in their hearts), and indeed they have left with it, and God knows best what they have been concealing in their hearts.

62. You see many of them vying in sin and exceeding the limits, and their eating of what is foul; certainly evil is what they have been doing.

63. Why do not the learned men and the doctors of law prohibit them from uttering what is sinful, and their eating

of what is forbidden? Evil indeed is what they do.

64. The Jews say: "The hand of God is tied up." Be their hands tied up, and be they cursed for what they say; nay, His hands are wide outstretched; He expends as He pleases. What has been revealed to you from your Lord will certainly increase many of them in transgression and infidelity, and We have caused enmity and hatred among them to last till the Day of Resurrection; every time they kindle a fire for war, God extinguishes it, and they strive to spread mischief on earth, and God does not love mischief-makers.

65. Had the people of the Book believed and guarded themselves against evil, We would certainly have blotted out their sins and admitted them into gardens of bliss.

66. Had they (the Jews and Christians) upheld the Torah and the Evangel, and that which was revealed to them from their Lord (Qur'an), they would certainly have had the sustenance of good things from above them and beneath their feet; of them are those who are moderate, but most of them are evil-doers!

67. (O Our Prophet Muhammad) Deliver what has been revealed to you from your Lord, and if you do not do so, then (it will be as though) you never delivered His Message at all, and surely God will protect you from (mischievous) people; verily, God does not guide the infidel people.

68. Say (O Our Prophet Muhammad): "O people of the Book! You have no ground to stand until you stand fast by the Law and Evangel and what has been revealed to you from your Lord," and surely that which has been revealed to you (O Muhammad) will increase many of them in transgression and infidelity; therefore, do not grieve for the infidel people.

69. Surely those who believe, and those who are Jews, the Sabians, and the Christians, whoever believes in God and the Last Day and does good deeds, no fear shall be upon them nor shall they grieve.

70. Certainly We took a Covenant from the children of Israel and We sent them messengers. Whenever a messenger comes to them with what they did not like, some they called liars and others they slew.

71. They thought that there would be no affliction, so

they became blinded and deafened; then God turned mercifully to them, yet again many of them became blinded and deafened, and God well sees what they do.

72. Certainly infidels are those who say: "Surely God is the Messiah son of Mary," whereas the Messiah himself had said: "O children of Israel! Worship only God, my Lord and yours; surely whoever associates any with God, then God forbids him from the Garden, and his abode shall be the Fire, and there shall be no helper for the unjust at all."

73. Surely disbelievers are those who say: "Certainly God is the third of a triad," and there is no god but only the One God; if they do not desist from saying so, a grievous torment shall befall those who disbelieve.

74. Will they not then turn to God and ask His pardon? And God is oft-Pardoning, Merciful.

75. The Messiah son of Mary is but a messenger; indeed prophets before him have passed away, and his mother was a truthful lady; they used to eat food; behold how We make Our signs clear for them, yet behold how they are turned away from the Right Path!

76. Say to them: "Do you worship besides God that which does not possess for you any harm, nor profits you aught, while God is all-Hearing, all-Knowing?"

77. Say: "O people of the Book! Do not exceed the bounds of your religion, following the vain desires of people who had gone astray aforetime, leading many others astray, and deviating from the Right Path."

78. Cursed were those among the children of Israel who did not believe by David and Jesus son of Mary, for they disobeyed, and persisted in their excesses.

79. They used not to forbid each other the hateful things which they wrought; indeed, how evil was that which they were doing!

80. You will see many of them befriending those who disbelieve; surely evil is that which their souls have sent before; God's Wrath is upon them, and they shall forever abide in torment.

81. Had they believed in God and the Messenger, and in what was revealed to him, they would not have taken them for friends, but most of them are evil-doers.

82. You will certainly find the most violent of people in enmity towards the believers to be the Jews and those who are polytheists, and you will certainly find the nearest in friendship to the believers to be those who say: "We are Christians." This is so because there are among them priests and monks, and they are not elated with arrogance.

83. When they hear what has been revealed to Our Messenger, you will see their eyes overflowing with tears on account of what they recognize of the truth; they say: "Lord! We believe, so include us among the witnesses (to the truth).

84. "And what reasons have we not to believe in God and in the truth that has come to us while we earnestly wish that our Lord should admit us (to heaven) with the righteous ones?"

85. God therefore rewarded them for what they had said with gardens beneath which rivers flow to abide therein forever; and this is the recompense of the doers of good.

86. As for those who disbelieve and belie Our signs, these shall be the inmates of the flaming Fire.

87. O you who believe! Do not deprive yourselves of the good things God has made lawful for you, and do not transgress the limits; verily, God does not love the transgressors.

88. Eat of what God has given you (for food) that which is lawful and good, and fear God in Whom you believe.

89. God does not call you to account for what is vain of your oaths, but He calls you to account for making deliberate oaths; so its expiation is the feeding of ten poor men out of the average food whereby you feed your families, or their clothing, or the freeing of a slave; but whosoever does not find means (to do any), then let him fast for three days; this is the expiation of your oaths when you swear; keep then your oaths; thus does God clarify His signs for you that you may be grateful.

90. O you who believe! Intoxicants and games of chance and (the dedication of) stones (idols) and divination by arrows are only an abomination of Satan's handiwork, so keep away from it so that you may be successful.

91. Satan only desires to cause enmity and hatred in your midst through intoxicants and gambling and to keep you

away from remembering God and from prayers; will you then abstain?

92. Obey God, and obey the Messenger, and be on your guard; but if you turn back, know then that Our Prophet (Muhammad) is bound only to deliver a clear announcement (on Our behalf).

93. On those who believe and do good there is no blame for what they ate (before the time) when they guarded themselves, believed and did good deeds; still more they guard themselves and believe even more strongly, still (further more) they guard themselves and do (greater) deeds, and God loves the doers of good.

94. O you who believe! God will surely try you with something about the game which your hands can reach and your lances, that God may distinguish those who fear Him in the unseen, and whoever exceeds (the limits) thereafter, for him shall be a painful chastisement.

95. O you who believe! Kill no game while in the pilgrim garb, and whoever among you kills it intentionally, the compensation of it is the like of what he killed from cattle, as decided by two just men among you, an offering to be brought to the Ka'ba, or the expiation (of it) is the feeding of the poor or the equivalent thereof in fasting, that he may taste the penalty of his deed; God has pardoned what is gone by, and whoever returns to it then God will exact penalty from Him, and God is Mighty, Lord of Retribution.

96. The game of the sea is allowed to you and eating thereof provision for you and for the travellers, and the game of the land is forbidden to you as long as you are in the pilgrim garb; fear God to Whom you shall be gathered.

97. God has made the Ka'ba, the Sacred House, a sanctuary for mankind, and the sacred month and the offerings and the (animals with the) garlands, so that you may know that God knows whatever in the heavens and in the earth, and that verily God knows all things.

98. Know that God is severe in punishing, and that God is oft-Forgiving, Merciful.

99. Nothing incumbent upon the Messenger but the delivering of the Message, and God knows what you reveal and conceal.

100. Say (O Our Prophet Muhammad): "The bad and the good are not equal though the abundance of the bad may enchant you; so then fear God, O men of understanding, that you may be successful."

101. O you who believe! Do not ask about things which if revealed to you will only trouble you, and if you inquire about them while the Qur'an is being revealed, they shall be declared to you; God pardons as to these matters; for God is oft-Forgiving, Forbearing.

102. Surely people before you asked such questions and then became disbelievers therein.

103. God has not ordained (the making of) a slit-ear she-camel, or to let loose a she-camel for free pasture, or idol sacrifices for twin-births in animals, or the freeing (from work) of stud-camels. Blasphemers are those who invent a lie against God, but most of them lack wisdom.

104. When it is said to them: "Come to what God has revealed and to the Messenger," they say: "Suffices us what we found our fathers doing." Even if their fathers knew nothing and were not rightly guided?

105. O you who believe! On you rests the burden of guarding yourselves; he who strays cannot hurt you when you follow the right guidance; to God is the return of all of you; He shall declare to you what you used to do.

106. O you who believe! When death approaches any of you, take witnesses, when making a bequest, two just persons from among you, or two others from those other than you, if you are travelling in the land and death afflicts you; detain the two (witnesses) after the prayer; then if you doubt (them), they shall both swear by God saying: "We will not take for it a price though he be a kinsman, and we will not hide the testimony of God; certainly then we would be among the sinners."

107. Then if it becomes known that they have both been guilty of a sin (of perjury), then two others shall stand in their place from among those who have a claim against them, two nearest of kin, so they both should swear by God that: "Certainly our testimony is truer than the testimony of those two, and we have not exceeded the limits, (for if we did) then most surely we should be of the unjust."

108. Thus, it is more proper that they testify in a proper manner or fear that their oaths be taken after theirs; fear God and listen, and God does not guide the transgressing people.

109. Beware! On the Day of Judgment, God will assemble all the messengers and then ask: "What response were you given (to your guidance, from your people)?" They shall reply: "We have no knowledge; verily You are the all-Knowing of the unseen."

110. God shall ask: "O Jesus son of Mary! Remember My favour on you and your mother; when I strengthened you with the Holy Spirit, that you spoke to the people in the cradle, and when grown up, and I taught you the Book, the wisdom, the Torah, and the Evangel, and when you made of clay a figure like that of a bird by My leave, then you breathed into it, it became a bird by My leave, and you healed the blind (since birth) and the lepers by My leave, and you brought life back to the dead by My leave, and I withheld the children of Israel from harming you when you came to them with clear signs (miracles), but those who disbelieved among them said: "This is nothing but clear sorcery."

111. And when I revealed to the disciples, "Believe in Me and My messenger (Jesus)," they said: "We believe, and bear witness that we are Muslims (submitting to God)."

112. Behold! The disciples said: "O Jesus son of Mary! Is your Lord able to send us a table furnished with food from heaven?" Jesus said: "Fear God, if you truly believe in Him!"

113. They said: "We desire to eat from it, and that our hearts be satisfied, and that we may know that you have indeed spoken the truth to us, and that we may be witnesses thereto."

114. Jesus son of Mary said: "O God! Our Lord! Send down to us from heaven a table set with food that it may be for us a recurring happiness, to the first of us and to the last, and a sign from You, and provide us with our sustenance, and You are the best of Sustainers."

115. God said: "Verily, I will send it down to you, but whoever disbelieves thereafter among you, surely I will chastise him with a chastisement the like of which I will not

chastise anyone else in the world."

116. God shall ask: "O Jesus son of Mary! Did you tell the people: to take you and your mother as two gods besides God?" and he will reply: "Glory be to You! It was not for me to say that which I had no right to say; had I said it, You would have indeed known it; You know whatever is in my conscience, whereas I do not know what is in Yours; verily You are the great Knower of the unseen.

117. "I did not say to them aught except what You commanded me, that is, `Worship God, my Lord and yours', and I was a witness over them as long as I was among them. When You took me up, You were the Watcher over them, and You are the Witness over all things.

118. "Should You chastise them, verily they are Your servants; should You forgive them, verily You are Almighty, Wise."

119. God shall then say: "This is the Day when truthfulness avails the truthful; for them shall be gardens beneath which rivers flow to abide therein forever; God is well pleased with them and they with Him; this is the great achievement."

120. God's is the kingdom of the heavens and the earth and whatever therein, and He alone has power over all things.

The Cattle
(al-An'am)

In the name of God, the Beneficent, the Merciful.

1. All praise belongs to God Who created the heavens and the earth, and caused the darkness and the light; yet those who disbelieve hold (others) as equals with their Lord.

2. He it is Who created you of clay, then decreed the term (of your life); and a determined term is with Him, yet you doubt thereof.

3. He is God in the heavens and the earth! He knows your secrets and your disclosures! And He knows what you earn (for yourselves by your deeds).

4. Whenever any sign of their Lord reached them, they turned away from it.

5. They indeed rejected the truth when it came to them;

therefore, very soon the tidings will come to them of what they mocked at.

6. Do they not see how many a generation before them, whom We had established in the earth (to the extent to) which We have not yet established you, We have destroyed? We sent the clouds to shower upon them abundantly, and We made the rivers flow beneath (their dwellings), yet We destroyed them for their sins and raised after them another generation.

7. Had We revealed to you a book written on paper, and had they touched it with their hands, surely those who disbelieved would have said: "This is naught but obvious sorcery."

8. They say: "Why has no angel been sent down with Him?" Had We sent an angel down, the matter would have certainly been decided (once and for all) and they would not have been respited.

9. Had We made him an angel, We would have certainly made him a man, and We would certainly have confused them in what they already are confused about.

10. Certainly many messengers were mocked before you, but that which they mocked encompassed the scoffers among them.

11. Say (O Our Prophet Muhammad): "Travel throughout the world, then see what the end of those who reject (Our messengers) has been."

12. Say: "To whom belongs what is in the heavens and the earth?" Say: "To God; He has prescribed mercy on Himself; most certainly He will gather you on the Day of Resurrection, there is no doubt about it; as for those who have ruined their souls, they will never believe."

13. To Him belongs whatever dwells in the night and the day, and He is the all-Hearing, the all-Knowing.

14. Say: "Shall I take a guardian besides God, Originator of the heavens and the earth? While He feeds others and is not Himself fed?" Say: "I am commanded to be the first to submit to God, not to be one of the polytheists."

15. Say (O Our Prophet Muhammad): "Verily I dread, should I disobey my Lord, the chastisement of a great day.

16. "From whomsoever it is averted on that day, indeed

He had mercy on him, and this will be the manifest triumph.

17. "If God touches you with affliction, none can remove it but He, and if He touches you with good, then He has power over all things.

18. "He is the Supreme Lord above His servants, and He is the all-Wise, the all-Aware."

19. Say: "What is the weightiest in testimony?" Say: "God is witness between me and you, and this Qur'an has been revealed to me that I may thereby warn you, and whomsoever it reaches. Do you really bear witness that there are other gods with God?" Say: "I bear no such witness!" Say: "Verily, He is the One God, and verily I am away from that which you associate with Him."

20. Those to whom We have given the Book know this as they know their own sons; yet those who have lost their souls will never believe.

21. Who is more unjust than that who forges a lie against God, or belies His signs? Verily, the unjust will never succeed.

22. On the day of Judgment, We shall gather them all together, then We shall say to those who associated others (with God): "Where are your associate-gods about whom you used to conjecture?"

23. Their excuse would be nothing but their cry: "By God, our Lord! We were not polytheists!"

24. Behold how they lie against their own selves, and that which they forged has passed away from them.

25. Of them are those who hearken to you, and We have cast veils over their hearts lest they should understand it, and a heaviness into their ears. Even if they see every sign, they will not believe in it; when they come to you, they only dispute with you; those who disbelieve say: "This is naught but the legends of the ancient."

26. They prohibit others from it, and they themselves keep far away from it; they only destroy their own souls, but they do not perceive it.

27. Could you but see when they are made to confront the Fire, how they shall say: "Would that we were sent back, we would not reject the signs of our Lord, and we would be of the believers."

28. Nay, it has been manifested to them what they had concealed before; had they been sent back, they would certainly have returned to what they were forbidden, and most certainly they are liars.

29. They say: "There is nothing beyond this life of ours in this world, and we are not to be raised again."

30. Could you but see when they are made to stand before their Lord how He will say: "Is this not the truth?" They will say: "Yes, indeed, by our Lord!" He will say: "Taste then the chastisement for what you disbelieved."

31. They are indeed losers those who disbelieved in the meeting of their God, until the hour (or Resurrection) suddenly approaches, they will say: "O our grief for our neglecting it!" And they shall bear their burdens on their backs; indeed, it is evil that which they will bear.

32. The life of this world is naught but play and vain sport, and certainly the abode of the hereafter is the best for those who guard (themselves against evil); do you not then understand?

33. Indeed, We know that what they say certainly grieves, but verily it is not you that they reject; it is the sign of God which the wrong doers deny.

34. Most certainly Our messengers before you were rejected, but they were patient on being rejected, and were persecuted until Our help came to them; none can alter the words of God, and most certainly the tidings about the messengers have come to you (from Us).

35. If their turning away is hard upon your mind, then even if you are able to seek an opening into the earth, or a ladder (to ascend) to the heavens, so that you bring them a sign, it will still be in vain. Yet if only God desired, He would certainly have gathered them all on the right guidance; so, do not be of the ignorant.

36. Verily, only those who listen (to the Word of God) will accept; as for the dead, God will raise them, then to Him will they all return.

37. They say: "Why is not a sign sent down to him from his Lord?" Say: "Verily, God is able to reveal a sign," but most of them do not know.

38. There is no animal that walks upon the earth, nor a

bird that flies with its two wings, except that they are communities like you; We have not neglected anything in the Book (Qur'an), then to their Lord shall they all be gathered in the end.

39. Those who rejected Our signs are deaf and dumb, in utter darkness; God allows whomsoever He pleases to stray, and He guides to the Straight Path whomsoever He wills.

40. Say: "Do you think that if the chastisement of God comes to you, or if the Hour (of resurrection) approaches you, you will call for help anyone other than God? Then say it if you are truthful."

41. Nay, you will call upon Him, and He shall remove that for which you earnestly pray Him if He pleases, and you would forget (the false gods) you set up (with Him).

42. We sent (messengers) to nations before you; then We caught them in distress and adversity so that they might humble themselves.

43. Yet why did they not humble themselves when Our punishment came to them? Their hearts were hardened, and the devil made that which they were doing alluring to them.

44. When they forgot the warning they had received, We opened for them the gates of all things (of enjoyment) until, when they rejoiced in what they were given, We caught them suddenly, and lo, they were in utter despair.

45. So the roots of the people who were unjust were cut off, and all Praise is due to God, Lord of the worlds.

46. Say: "Do you think that if God takes away your hearing and your sight, and seals your hearts, who is the god other than He that can bring it back to you?" See how We explain the signs, yet they turn aside.

47. Say (O Our Prophet Muhammad): "Do you think, if the chastisement of God comes to you suddenly or openly, will anyone be destroyed except the unjust?"

48. We do not send messengers except as heralds with glad tidings and as warners; then whoever believes and acts aright shall have no fear, nor shall they grieve.

49. As for those who reject Our signs, Our chastisement shall afflict them for what they used to transgress.

50. Say (O Muhammad): "I do not tell you that the treasures of God are with me, nor that I know the unseen, nor do

I say to you that I am an angel; I only follow what is revealed to me." Say: "Are the blind and the seeing alike? Do you not then reflect?"

51. Convey this warning to those in whose hearts rests the fear that they shall be brought before their Lord, besides Whom they have neither protector, nor intercessor, that they may fear God.

52. Do not drive away those who call upon their Lord, in the morning and the evening, seeking His countenance. It is neither on you to answer for anything on their account, nor is it on them to answer for anything on yours so that you drive them away and thus be of the unjust.

53. Thus did We try some of them through others so that they say: "Are these they upon whom God has conferred His Favours from among us?" Does not God know best who the grateful ones are?

54. When those who believe in Our signs come to you, say: "Peace be on you; your Lord has inscribed (the rule of) mercy upon Himself, so if any among you commit evil in ignorance, then he turns repentant after that and amends, verily He is the oft-Forgiving, Most Merciful."

55. Thus did We explain the signs in detail so that the way of the sinners may become manifest.

56. Say (O Our Prophet Muhammad): "I am forbidden to worship those whom you call upon besides God." Say: "I do not follow your inclinations, for then indeed I would have gone astray, and I will not then be of those who are guided (aright)."

57. Say: "Verily, I have manifest proof from my Lord, yet you rejected it; I do not have with me that (chastisement) which you hasten for; the judgment belongs to none but God Who declares the truth and He is the best to decide."

58. Say: "Had what you hasten been with me, the matter between me and you would have been decided, and God knows best the unjust."

59. With Him are the keys (of the treasures) of the unseen-none but He knows what is in the land and the sea; not even a leaf falls but He knows it, nor a grain in the darkness of the earth, nor anything wet or dry but (it is) in a clear Book.

60. He it is Who takes your souls by night (in sleep), and He knows what you acquire in the day, then He raises you up therein that a prefixed term of life be fulfilled; then to Him is your ultimate return, then He will declare to you what you were doing.

61. He is the all-Dominant above His servants, and He sends guardians over you. When death comes to one of you, Our messengers (angels) take him away, and they never fail (in their duty).

62. Then they shall be returned to God, their Master, the only Real One. Beware! His alone is the judgment, and He is the swiftest to reckon.

63. Say: "Who delivers you from the dread of the darkness of the land and the sea, when you pray Him openly, humbling yourselves, and secretly, saying: "If He delivers us from this, certainly we shall be of the grateful ones"?

64. Say: "God delivers you from them, and from every distress, yet again you associate others with Him."

65. Say: "He has power that He may send on you a chastisement from above you or from under your feet, or He would involve you in confusion, in party dissensions, and make some of you taste the vengeance of others;" behold how We repeatedly explain the signs so they may understand.

66. And your people rejected it, though it is the very truth. Say (O Our Prophet Muhammad): "I am not a guard over you."

67. For every message there is a prefixed term, and soon shall you know it.

68. When you see those engaged in vain talk about Our signs, get away from them until they enter into (some) other discourse, and if the devil causes you to forget this, then do not keep company after recollecting the unjust people.

69. No responsibility of the reckoning of their deeds shall fall upon the righteous, but they only remind them, perchance they may guard themselves against evil.

70. Leave those who have taken their religion for a play and a vain sport, and those whom the temporal life of this world has beguiled, and admonish them by it (Qur'an) lest a soul should be fettered with what it has earned. There

shall be no protector nor intercessor besides God, and if it seeks to give every compensation, it shall not be accepted from it. These are they who are fettered with what they earned. For them shall be a drink of boiling water and a painful chastisement for their disbelief.

71. Say (O Our Prophet Muhammad): "Shall we call on any besides God that neither profits us nor harms us, and shall we turn back on our heels after God has guided us, like that who is infatuated by the devils, perplexed in the earth, even though he has companions who call him to guidance saying: `Come to us'?" Say: "Verily the guidance of God is the true guidance, and we are commanded that we should submit ourselves to the Lord of the world.

72. "And that you establish prayers and fear Him; He it is to Whom you shall be gathered.

73. "He it is Who created the heavens and the earth true proportions, The day He says: `Be', behold, and it is! His word is the truth; His is the authority on the Day when the trumpet is blown; Knower of the unperceivable and the perceivable worlds; the all-Wise, the all-Aware."

74. Abraham said to his father Azar: "Do you take idols for gods? Verily I see you and your people in obvious error!"

75. Thus did We show Abraham (the laws of) the Kingdom of the heavens and the earth, and that he may be of those who have certitude.

76. Thereafter, overshadowed by the night, he saw a star and said: "This is my Lord." When it set, he said: "I do not love the setting ones."

77. Then when he saw the moon rising in splendour, he said: "This is my Lord, this is the greatest;" then when it, too, set, he said: "O my people! I am clear of what you associate with God."

78. When he saw the sun rising in splendour, he said: "This is my Lord; this is the greatest," but when it too set, he said: "O my people! I am indeed free from the partners you ascribe to God.

79. "Verily I have turned my face wholly to Him Who originated the heavens and the earth, being upright, and I am not of the polytheists."

80. When his people disputed with him, he said: "Do you dispute with me about God while indeed He has guided me? I fear none of what you associate with Him save any that My Lord wills; my Lord comprehends everything in His knowledge, will you not then be mindful?

81. "How should I fear that which you have associated with Him while you do not fear since you have associated with God that for which no authority has been sent down on you? Then which of the two parties has greater right to security, if only you know?

82. "Security is for those who believe and do not mix their faith with iniquity, and they are the ones who are rightly guided."

83. This is Our argument which We gave to Abraham rebutting his people; We exalt whoever We please; verily your Lord is Wise, all-Knowing.

84. We bestowed upon him Isaac and Jacob; each We guided, and Noah did We guide before, and among his progeny are David and Solomon, Job and Joseph, Moses and Aaron; thus do We reward those who do good deeds.

85. And Zakariya and John and Jesus and Elias: all in the ranks of the righteous.

86. And Ishmael and Elisha and Jonas and Lot: each We exalted over the worlds,

87. (To them and to) their fathers, descendants and brethren, and We chose them (for Our Message), and We guided them to the Straight Way.

88. This is God's guidance; He guides with it whomsoever of His servants He pleases, and if they were to associate others with Him, what they were doing would avail them naught.

89. These are they upon whom We bestowed the Book, authority and prophethood; so, if these people disbelieve in it, indeed We have already entrusted it to a people who shall not disbelieve therein.

90. These are they whom God has guided; therefore, follow their guidance. Say (O Our Prophet Muhammad): "I do not ask for any recompense from you for it (prophethood); it is but a reminder to the world."

91. They do not esteem God with the estimation due to

Him when they say: "God sends down nothing to man!" Say: "Who then revealed the Book which Moses brought as a light and a guidance for mankind? You transcribe it into (separate) sheets whereof you publish a part and conceal much? And you were taught what you did not know, neither you nor your fathers." Say: "(It is none but) God!" Then leave them sporting in their vain discourses.

92. We have sent this blessed Book (Qur'an) confirming that which preceded it, so that you may warn (the people of) the mother-city (Mecca) and those around it. Those who believe in the Hereafter believe in it, and they are (constantly) guarding their prayers.

93. Who is more unjust than he who forges a lie against God or says: "I have received a revelation," while nothing has been revealed to him, or he who says: "I can reveal like what God has revealed"? And if you could see when the unjust are in the agonies of death, and the angels stretch forth their hands saying: "Surrender your souls; today you shall be recompensed with a disgraceful chastisement for what you unjustly spoke against God, scornfully rejecting His signs."

94. Indeed you will come to us (bare and) alone as we created you at first, leaving behind your backs that which We bestowed on you, and We do not see your intercessors with you, those whom you asserted were in your affairs the associates (of God), and indeed the ties between you are now severed, and what you falsely asserted has departed from you.

95. Verily God is the splitter of grain (seed) and date stone (to sprout); He brings out the living from the dead and the dead from the living; that is God! How then are you turned away deluded?

96. He cleaves the dawn-break, and He has made the night for rest and the sun and moon for reckoning (time); this is the measuring of the Almighty, the all-Knowing Lord.

97. He it is who made the stars for you that you may be rightly guided in the land and the sea; indeed, We have made the signs plain for people who understand.

98. He it is who has produced you from a single soul, then there is (for you) a receptacle and a depository; We

have made the signs plain for people who understand.

99. He it is who sends down water from heaven, then we bring forth with it buds of all plants; from it green (foliage) from which We produce grain piled up in ears; and of the palm trees, of the sheaths of it come forth clusters (of dates) within reach, and gardens of grapes and olives and pomegranates, alike and not alike; see the fruit of it when it yields the fruit and the ripening of it; verily, in this are signs for people who believe.

100. Yet they make the jinns, His creation, equals with God, and they falsely and without knowledge attribute to Him sons and daughters! Praise and glory be to Him above what they attribute!

101. (He is the) Originator of the heavens and the earth; how could He have a son while He has no consort? He created all things, and He knows all things.

102. (Behold!) that is God, your Lord; there is no god but He, Creator of all things; therefore, worship Him; He is indeed the Guardian over all things.

103. Vision cannot perceive Him, while He perceives all vision; He is the Subtle, the all-Aware.

104. Indeed clear proofs have come to you from your Lord; whosoever therefore sees it, it is for his own self, and whosoever (willfully chooses to be) blind, then it is against his own self; I am not a keeper over you.

105. Thus do We explain the signs, so that they may say: "You have been taught" and that We may make it clear to people who know.

106. Follow what has been revealed to you from your Lord; there is no god but He, and turn away from the polytheists.

107. Had God so pleased, they would not have associated (others with Him), and We have not made you a keeper over them, nor are you their guardian.

108. Do not abuse those whom they invoke besides God lest they should abuse God in transgression without knowledge; thus have We made to every people their deeds fair-seeming to them, then to their Lord is their return, so He will inform them of what they did.

109. They swear by God with the strongest of their oaths

that if a sign came to them, they would most certainly believe in it; say (O Our Prophet Muhammad): "Verily signs are with God, but what should make you know that when it comes they will not believe?"

110. We will turn their hearts and visions aside even as they did not believe in it the first time, and We will leave them in their contumacy blindly wandering on.

111. Even if We send the angels down to them, and the dead speak to them, and (even if) We had gathered all things before them, they would not believe unless God so pleases, but most of them deliberately choose to ignore.

112. Thus did We appoint an enemy for every messenger. The devils, from mankind and the jinn, inspire each other (with) tinsel discourses to deceive (them); had your Lord pleased, they would not have done it; therefore, leave them and what they forge alone,

113. Thus the hearts of those who do not believe in the life hereafter may incline towards it, so that they may be well-pleased therewith, and that they may earn what they may.

114. Should I seek other than God for a judge, while He has revealed to you the Book (Qur'an) fully explained? And those to whom We have given the Book know that it has been sent down from your Lord with truth; so, do not be of those who doubt.

115. Perfect is the Word of your Lord in truth and justice; there is none that can change His words; He is the all-Hearing, the all-Knowing.

116. If you obey most of those on earth, they will lead you astray from God's Way; they only follow conjecture; they only falsely guess.

117. Verily, your Lord knows best who strays from His Way, and He knows best those who follow the right guidance.

118. Eat, therefore, (the meat) over which the Name of God has been mentioned, if you believe in His signs.

119. What has happened to you that you do not eat of that (meat) over which the Name of God has been mentioned, while He has indeed made plain to you what He has forbidden to you, except what you were compelled to? Many

would lead people astray by their vain desires without knowledge; verily, your Lord knows best the transgressors.

120. And give up open and secret sins; verily those who earn sin will be recompensed with what they earned.

121. Do not eat of that over which God's Name was not mentioned; verily it is transgression, and verily the evil ones inspire their friends that they should contend with you, and if you obey them, verily you will (all) be polytheists.

122. Is he who was dead, then We raised him to life and made for him a light whereby he walks among people, like unto him that whose similitude is one who is in utter darkness, whence he cannot come forth? Thus has been made fair-seeming for the disbelievers what they did.

123. Thus did We make in every town leaders to be its guilty ones, that they may plot therein, and they do not plot but against their own selves, but they do not perceive it.

124. When a sign comes to them, they say: "We will never believe until we are given the like of what was given to the messengers of God." God knows best where to place His Message. Soon shall humiliation from God befall those who are guilty, and a severe chastisement for what they cunningly plot.

125. Whomsoever God chooses to guide aright, He expands his breast for Islam, and whomsoever He intends to leave straying, He makes his breast strait and narrow as though he is climbing into the very skies. Thus does God lay ignominious chastisement on those who disbelieve.

126. This is the path of your Lord, a straight one; indeed, We have made the signs clear for people who take heed.

127. For them shall be the abode of peace with their Lord, and He is their Guardian because of what they used to do.

128. On the Day when He gathers them all together (and says). "O assembly of jinn! You increased your strength (by seducing a great number of) men;" and their friends from among men will say: "O Lord! Some of us profited by others and we have reached our term which You appointed for us." He shall say: "The Fire is your abode, be you the

dwellers therein save what pleases God; verily your Lord is Wise, all-Knowing."

129. Thus do We make some of the iniquitous befriend others because of what they earned.

130. "O assembly of jinn and men! Did not prophets come to you from among you, relating to you My signs, and warning you of the meeting of your day (of requital)?" They shall say: "We testify against ourselves." This world's life deceived them, and they shall bear witness against their own selves that they were disbelievers.

131. This is so because your Lord does not destroy any town unjustly while their occupants were negligent.

132. And for all are degrees in accordance with what they do, and your Lord is not heedless of their deeds.

133. Your Lord is self-Sufficient, Lord of Mercy; if He pleases, He may take you away and make whomsoever He pleases successors after you, just as He raised you from the posterity of other people.

134. Verily, what you are promised will certainly come to pass, and you cannot make (God) helpless against it.

135. Say (O Our Prophet Muhammad): "O my people! Act according to your ability; verily I too act, then you will soon know for whom of us will be the (best) end in the hereafter; verily, the unjust shall not succeed."

136. They assign to God from what He has created of tilth and cattle, and say: "This is for God," according to their assertion, "and this is for our associates." Then what is for their associates does not reach God, and what is for God reaches their associates! How evil is their judgment!

137. Thus, their associates have made fair-seeming to most of the polytheists the slaying of their own children that they might cause them to perish, and have confounded to them their religion. Had God desired, they would not have done so; therefore, leave them and what they forge alone.

138. They say: "These cattle and tilth are a taboo (consecrated); none shall eat them save as we please." This is according to their own assertion, and (there are) cattle whose yoke or burden is forbidden, and cattle over which they do not mention the Name of God (when slaughtered), forging

a lie against Him; soon He will requite them for what they forge.

139.   They say: "What is in the wombs of these cattle is exclusively for our males and is forbidden to our wives, and if it is still-born, then all of them are partners therein. Soon will He recompense them for falsely attributing it to God; verily, He is Wise, all-Knowing.

140.   Indeed, those who slay their children foolishly without knowledge and prohibit what God has given them, forging falsehood against God; indeed, they have gone astray and they are not guided aright.

141.   He it is Who produces gardens (of vine) trellised and untrellised, and date palms and tilth of various kinds of food produce and olives and pomegranates, similar (in kind) and different (in variety); eat of its fruit when it yields fruit and give His share, on the day of reaping, and do not act extravagantly; verily, He does not love the extravagant ones.

142.   And of cattle are some bearers of burden and some (low fit only) for spreading; eat of what God provides you with, and do not follow the footsteps of Satan; verily he is your declared enemy.

143.   Take eight in pairs, two of sheep, and two of goats. Say: "Has He forbidden the two males or the two females or what is contained in the wombs of the two females? Inform me with knowledge, if you are truthful."

144.   And two camels and two oxen, and say: "Has He forbidden the two males or the two females or that which the wombs of the two females contain? Or were you witnesses when God enjoined this?" Who then is more unjust than he who forges a lie against God to lead people astray without knowledge? Verily, God does not guide those who are unjust.

145.   Say: "I do not find in what has been revealed to me anything forbidden to an eater to eat except what dies by itself, or blood poured forth, or flesh of swine, for verily that is unclean, a transgression, to invoke the name of any other than God's; but even so, if one is forced (to eat it), not lusting, nor willfully transgressing the limits, then verily your Lord is oft-Forgiving, Merciful."

146.   To those who were Jews We forbade every animal

having undivided hoofs, and oxen and sheep We forbade to them the fat of both, save what is upon their backs or entrails or what is mixed with bones; this We recompensed them for their rebellion, and verily We are Truthful.

147. If they reject you (O Our Prophet Muhammad), then say: "Though your Lord is full of mercy, all-Embracing, yet His Wrath shall not be returned from the guilty people."

148. Those who are polytheists will say: "Had God wished, we would not have associated (aught with Him), nor our fathers, nor would we have forbidden anything." Thus, those before them rejected until they tasted Our Wrath. Say: "Do you have any (certain) knowledge? Then produce it to us; you follow naught but conjecture, and you utter naught but guessing."

149. Say: "Then God's alone is the decisive argument. Had God wished, He would surely have guided you all aright."

150. Say: "Bring your witnesses who testify that God has forbidden this." Then (even) if they bear witness, do not bear witness with them, and do not follow the inclinations of those who reject Our signs nor those who do not believe in the Hereafter, making others equal with their Lord.

151. Say (O Our Prophet Muhammad): "Come! I will recite to you what your Lord has forbidden to you, so that you do not associate with Him anything, and that you be good to your parents and do not slay your children for fear of poverty;" We provide for you and for them, and do not draw close to shameful deeds, those that are apparent and those that are concealed, and do not kill the soul which God has forbidden save to effect justice; this He enjoined you with, so that you may understand.

152. Do not approach the property of an orphan save that it be in the best manner till he attains his maturity; give full measure and full weight in justice; We do not task a soul except according to its ability. And when you speak, be just, though it be against a kinsman, and fulfill God's Covenant; this He enjoins you with, so that you may be mindful.

153. And (know) verily that My Path is straight; so, follow it, and do not follow other ways for they will scatter you away from His Path; thus does He enjoin you so that

you may guard (yourselves against evil).

154. Besides, We gave Moses the Book completing (Our Favours) on those who do good deeds and explaining all things in detail, and guidance and mercy, so that you may receive mercy.

155. This (Qur'an) is a Book: We have sent it down, blessed, so follow it, and guard (yourselves against evil) so that you may receive mercy.

156. Lest the (polytheists) should say: "The book (from God) was revealed to two parties (Christians and Jews) before us, and verily we were unaware of what they read."

157. Or lest you should say: "If only a book had been sent to us, we should have been better guided than them." So indeed has now come to you a manifest Proof from your Lord, guidance and mercy; who then is more unjust than he who rejects the signs of God and turns away from them? Soon shall We recompense those who turn away from Our signs with an evil chastisement for their turning away.

158. They wait only (to see) that the angels come to them or your Lord (Himself) comes, or that some signs of your Lord come to them; on the Day when some of the signs of your Lord come, the faith of a soul which did not believe, nor earn good through its faith, shall not avail it. Say (O Our Prophet Muhammad): "Wait! Verily, we, too, are waiting."

159. Verily those who divided their religion and became parties, you have no concern with any of them; their affair is only with God, then will He inform them of what they did.

160. Whosoever comes with a good deed, for him shall be ten like it; and whosoever commits an evil deed, he shall be only recompensed with the like of it, and they shall not be dealt with unjustly.

161. Say (O Our Prophet Muhammad): "Verily my Lord has guided me to the Straight Path, the established religion, the faith of Abraham, the upright one, and he was not a polytheist."

162. Say: "Verily, my prayer and sacrifice, my life and death, (are all only) for God, Lord of the worlds.

163. "No associate (is there) for Him, and thus I am commanded; I am the first of the Muslims (those who sub-

mit to God)."

164. Say: "Shall I seek other than God for a Lord while He is the Lord of all things, and no soul earns (any evil deed) but against itself, and no bearer of a burden shall bear the burden of another; then to your Lord is your return, so He will inform you of what you used to differ (therein)."

165. He it is Who has made you as (His) Vicegerent on earth and raised some of you above others in ranks, that He may try you in what He bestowed upon you; verily, your Lord is quick in the requital of evil, yet verily He is the oft-Forgiving, the Merciful.

The Heights
(al-A'raaf)

In the name of God, the Beneficent, the Merciful.

1. Alif, Lam, Mim, Sad.

2. A Book (Qur'an) has been revealed unto you; so, there should be no oppression in your heart about it, so that you may warn thereby, and so that it may be a reminder to those who believe.

3. (O people) Follow what has been revealed to you from your Lord, and do not take anyone other than Him for guardian; (yet) little do you mind.

4. How many a town have We destroyed? Our Wrath approached them by night, or while they reposed at noontime.

5. So their cry when Our wrath approached them was none but: "Verily, we were unjust."

6. We shall certainly question those to whom (Our Messengers) were sent, and certainly We shall also question the ones We send (as messengers).

7. Then We shall certainly relate to them with knowledge, for We were never absent.

8. The measuring (of deeds) will then be quite fair; so, whosoever's weight (of good deeds) is heavy shall be the successful one.

9. The souls of those whose measure is light will suffer for being unjust towards Our signs.

10. Indeed, We have facilitated for you to live on earth

and provided you with means of livelihood therein; little do you appreciate.

11. We created you, gave you your form, then said to the angels: "Prostrate to Adam," so they all did except Iblis; he refrained from joining those who prostrated.

12. He (God) said: "What prevented you from prostrating since I commanded you?" He (Iblis) said: "I am better than him; You created me of fire while creating him (Adam) of clay."

13. He (God) said: "Then get down, for it is unfit for those who behave arrogantly therein. Get out of it; indeed, you shall be among the despised."

14. He (Iblis) said: "Grant me a respite till the Day when they are resurrected."

15. He (God) said: "Verily, you shall be granted a respite."

16. He (Iblis) said: "Just as You have deprived me of it, I will surely wait for them even on Your Straight Path.

17. "Then I will surely approach them from front and from behind, from their right side and from their left, and You shall find most of them ungrateful."

18. He (God) said: "Get out of it despised and driven away! I shall fill Hell with you and whosoever of them that follows you.

19. "O Adam! Dwell, you and your wife, in the garden; eat, both of you, from wherever you desire, but do not draw near this tree, for then you both will be unjust (to your own selves)."

20. Then Satan whispered evil suggestions to the two so that he might reveal to them that which was kept hidden from them of their shame. He said: "Your Lord has not forbidden you from drawing near this tree except so that you both might not become angels, or lest you both should become immortal."

21. He swore to them both saying: "Verily, I am a sincere advisor to you."

22. Then he instigated both of them through deceit, so when they tasted of the tree, their shame became manifest to their eyes, and they both began covering themselves with leaves of the garden, and their Lord called out to them say-

ing: "Didn't I forbid you both from nearing this tree and (moreover) told you that Satan is the avowed enemy of both of you?"

23. They said: "O Lord! We have been unjust to our-selves, and if You do not forgive us and be merciful unto us, then we will certainly be of the losers."

24. He said: "Get down, some of you being enemies of one another; and for you there is in the earth an abode and a provision for a fixed time."

25. He said: "Therein you shall live, and therein you shall die, and from it you shall be brought out."

26. O children of Adam! Indeed, We have sent upon you a raiment to cover your shame and as adornment, and the raiment of piety is the best; this is one of the signs of God so that you may be mindful.

27. O children of Adam! Do not let Satan involve you into affliction as he got your parents out of the garden, strip-ping off their raiment, that he might expose to them their shame; he watches you, and so does his tribe, from whence you do not see them; indeed, We have made the devils guard-ians of those who do not believe.

28. When they act lewdness they say: "We found our fathers (acting) upon it, and God has enjoined it upon us." Say (O Our Messenger Muhammad): "Verily, God does not enjoin lewdness; do you say against God what you do not even know?"

29. Say: "My Lord has enjoined justice and set your faces upright when prostrating. Call upon Him sincerely, turn-ing to Him exclusively in religion, even as He brought you forth in the beginning, so to Him shall you also return."

30. He has guided a party among you aright, while the other party entitled themselves to error; indeed they have taken the devils for their guardians other than God, think-ing that they are the ones who are rightly guided.

31. O children of Adam! Be adorned at the time of pros-tration; eat and drink and do not commit excesses; indeed He does not love those who are excessive.

32. Say (O Our Messenger Muhammad): "Who has pro-hibited the adornment of God which He has brought forth for His servants, and the good things of the provisions?"

Say: "These are, in the life of this world, for those who believe, and exclusively theirs on the Day of Judgement." Thus
do We explain the signs in detail for people who understand.

33. Say: "Verily my Lord prohibited only shameful
deeds, those apparent and those concealed, and sin and
rebellion without right, and that you associate with God
that for which He has sent no authority, and that you say
against God what you do not know."

34. For every people is a term, so, when their (appointed) term comes, they shall not remain behind it (even)
an hour, nor can they go before.

35. O children of Adam! When Messengers come to you
from among you relating to you My signs, then whosoever
guards himself against evil and amends (himself), no fear
shall then come upon them nor shall they ever grieve.

36. Those who reject Our signs and arrogantly turn away
from them are the inmates of the Fire, and they shall (forever) abide therein.

37. Who is then more unjust than one who forges a lie
against God or rejects His signs? Those are they who shall
receive their share (as decreed) in the Book until Our Messengers come to them, causing them to die, then ask them:
"Where is that which you called upon besides God?" They
would say: "They have deserted us," and they shall bear
witness against themselves that they had been infidels.

38. He will say: "Enter among the people who indeed
have passed away before you, of jinn and men, into the Fire.
Every time some (new people) enter it, they shall curse their
brethren, until they have all come together into it, the latter
shall say about the former: "O Lord! These are they who led
us astray; therefore, give them double (our) chastisement of
the Fire." He will say: "For Everyone (of you) double, but
you do not know."

39. The former of them will say to their latter: "So (now)
there is no advantage for you over us; therefore taste the
chastisement for what you earned."

40. Verily those who reject Our signs and arrogantly
turn away therefrom, the gates of heaven shall not open for
them, nor shall they enter the garden until the camel passes

through the needle eye; thus do We recompense the guilty.

41. For them shall be the bed of Fire, and from above them its covering. Thus do We recompense the unjust.

42. Those who believe and do good deeds, We do not task any soul but to its ability. They are the dwellers of the garden (of bliss). They shall (forever) abide therein.

43. We will remove whatever rancor in their hearts. Rivers shall flow beneath their abodes, and they will say: "All praise is due only to God Who guided us to this, and We would not have been guided had God not guided us; indeed, the Prophets of our Lord came with the truth." And it shall be said aloud to them: "Behold! This is the garden of which you are made heirs, a reward for what you did."

44. The inmates of the garden will call out to the inmates of the Fire saying: "Indeed we have found what our Lord promised us to be true; have you too found what your Lord promised you to be true?" They will say: "Yes, indeed." Then a caller will call out between them saying that the curse of God be upon the unjust,

45. Those who hinder (people) from God's Path and seek to make it (look) crooked, and they disbelieve in the Hereafter.

46. And between the two shall be a veil, and on the heights shall be men who know all by their marks, and they shall call out to the inmates of the garden: "Peace be upon you." They shall not have yet entered it, though they do hope so.

47. When they turn their eyes towards the inmates of the Fire, they shall say: "Lord! Cause us not to be with the unjust people."

48. Men will call the occupants of the heights whom they can recognize by their marks. They will say: "Of no avail had been your amassing and that in which you used to act proudly.

49. "Are these they on whom you swear that God will not bestow His mercy? To them God now says: `Enter into the garden! No fear shall be on you, nor shall you ever grieve.'"

50. The inmates of the Fire shall call to the inmates of the garden saying: "Pour upon us of the water, or of what God

has provided you with." They shall say: "Verily God has forbidden both to the infidels,

51. "Those who make their religion a pastime and a play, and whom the life of the world had deceived." So today We neglect them as they neglected meeting this day of theirs, and as they denied Our signs.

52. Indeed We have brought them a Book which We have explained with knowledge, a guidance and a mercy for people who believe.

53. Do they wait for anything but the final fulfillment? On the day when the final fulfillment comes, those who neglected it before will say: "Indeed, the messengers of our Lord came with the truth; are there for us (now) any intercessors that they may intercede for us? Or could we be sent back so that we might act other than we did before?" Indeed they have lost their souls, and what they forged has abandoned them.

54. Verily your Lord is God Who created the heavens and the earth in six days, then established Himself upon the Throne. He throws the veil of night over the day, which pursues it incessantly, and the sun and the moon and the stars He made subservient to His Command. Be it known that His is the creation and the command; blessed is God, Lord of the worlds.

55. Call on your Lord, humbly and secretly; God does not love the transgressors.

56. Do not make mischief in the earth after its reformation, and call on Him fearing (His Wrath) and hoping (for His Mercy); indeed the mercy of God is well-nigh to those who do good.

57. He it is Who sends forth the (heralding) winds bearing good tidings before His Mercy; until they bring up laden clouds. We drive it to a land which is dead, then We send down water upon it, then We bring forth therewith fruits of all kinds; likewise, We shall bring forth the dead that you may be mindful.

58. And the good land, its vegetation springs forth (abundantly) by the Will of its Lord, and that which is bad, (herbage) does not come forth from it except scantily; thus do We display Our signs to people who give thanks.

59. Indeed We sent Noah to his people, so he said: "O my people! Worship God alone; you have no god other than Him; indeed I fear for you the chastisement of a dreadful day."

60. The chiefs of his people said: "Verily we see you in obvious error."

61. He said: "O my People! No error is in me, but I am a messenger from the Lord of the worlds;

62. "I deliver to you the message from my Lord and advise you, and I know from God what you do not know.

63. "Or do you wonder that an admonition has come to you from your Lord through a man from among you, that he might warn you and that you might guard (yourselves against evil), and that mercy might be shown to you?"

64. But they rejected him, so We delivered him and those with him in the ark, and We drowned those who rejected Our signs; indeed they were a blind people.

65. And to (the people of) Ad We sent their brothers Hud. He said: "O my people! Serve God alone; you have no god other than Him. Will you not then guard (yourselves against evil)?"

66. The chiefs of those who disbelieved among his people said: "Verily we see you in folly, and indeed we think you are a liar."

67. He said: "O my people! There is no folly in me, but I am a messenger of the Lord of the worlds;

68. "I deliver to you the message of my Lord and I am a trusted advisor to you.

69. "Do you wonder that an admonition has come to you from your Lord through a man from among you that he might warn you? Remember how He made you successors of Noah's people, and increased you in stature, so remember the bounties of God that you may be successful."

70. They said: "Do you come to us just so that we may serve God alone and give up what our fathers used to serve? Then bring down to us that which you threaten us with, if you are truthful."

71. He said: "The punishment and the Wrath have indeed fallen upon you from your Lord. Do you dispute with me about the names which you and your fathers have named

(as idols), for which no authority has been sent from God? Wait then, and indeed I too am with you waiting."

72. So We delivered him and those with him by mercy from Us, and We cut away the roots of those who rejected Our signs, and they were not believers.

73. And to the people of Thamud We sent their brother Salih. He said: "O my people! Worship God alone. You have no god other than Him; indeed a clear proof from your Lord has come to you. This is God's she-camel which is a sign for you; so, leave it to pasture (freely) in God's earth and do not touch her with any harm else you should be seized with a painful chastisement.

74. "And remember when He made you successors of the people of Ad, and settled you on earth; you build mansions on its plain, hewing the mountains into dwellings; so remember the bounties of God, and do not seek evil in the world, making mischief."

75. The chiefs of those who were puffed up with pride among his people said to those believers among them who were reckoned weak: "Do you know that Salih is sent by his Lord?!" They said: "Verily, we in what he had been sent with are disbelievers."

76. Those who were puffed up with pride said: "Verily, we are disbelievers in that which you believe."

77. They hamstrung the she-camel and rebelled against the command of their Lord and said: "O Salih! Bring us what you threatened us with, if you are a messenger at all."

78. Then the earthquake seized them (without a warning); so they became stiffened in their dwellings.

79. Then he turned away from them and said: "O my people! Indeed I delivered to you the message of my Lord, and admonished you, but you do not love those who admonish."

80. We sent Lot; he said: "Do you commit lewdness which none in the world committed before you?!

81. "Verily you approach men in lust instead of women; nay, you are people who transgress."

82. There was no answer from his people except their saying: "Turn them out of your town; indeed they are a people who seek to purify (themselves)."

83. So We delivered him and his family, except his wife: she was among those who remained behind.

84. And We pelted them with a shower (of stones); behold the end of the criminals.

85. And to the people of Midian We sent their brother Shu'ayb. He said: "O my people! Worship God alone; you have no god other than Him; indeed, a clear proof has come to you from your Lord; so, give full measure and weight, and do not diminish to men their things, and make no mischief in the earth after its reform. This is better for you if you believe.

86. "Do not sit in every path threatening and hindering those who believe in God from treading His Path, seeking to make it (look) crooked. And remember when you were few and He multiplied you. Behold what the end of mischief-makers had been.

87. "If one party among you has believed in what you have been sent with, and another that has not, then wait with patience until God judges between us; He is the best of judges."

88. The chiefs of those who were puffed up with pride among his people said: "We will certainly turn you out, O Shu'ayb, together with those who believed in you, from our town, or you return to our faith." He said: "Even if we detest it?!

89. "Indeed we shall have forged a lie against God if we return to your faith after God had rescued us from it; it does not befit us that we return to it save if God our Lord wills; our Lord's knowledge encompasses everything, and on God alone do we rely. Lord! Decide between us and our people with truth; You are the best of those who judge."

90. The chiefs of those who disbelieved from among his people said: "(Beware!) If you follow Shu'ayb, you shall certainly be losers."

91. Then an earthquake seized them, and they became motionless (corpses) in their own dwellings.

92. Those who rejected Shu'ayb became as if they had never dwelt therein. Those who called Shu'ayb a liar were the ones who lost.

93. So he turned away from them and said: "O my people!

Indeed I delivered to you the message of my Lord and admonished you; how then shall I be sorry for a disbelieving people?"

94. We sent no prophet to a town but We seized its people with distress and adversity so that they might humble themselves.

95 Then We changed their suffering into prosperity, until they multiplied, and they said: "Indeed, adversity and happiness touched our fathers, too." We seized them suddenly while they were not aware.

96. Had the people of the towns believed and feared God, We would have opened up for them blessings from the heavens and the earth, but they rejected (the prophets); so, We seized them for what they earned.

97. Do people of the towns then feel secure from Our torment coming to them by night while they are asleep?

98. Or do people of the towns feel secure against Our torment approaching them in the morning while they are sporting?

99. Do they then feel secure against God's plan?! None feels secure from God's plan except people who are (doomed to be) losers.

100. Is it not (a lesson) admonishing those who inherit the earth after its former people that if We please We would afflict them for their sins, and set a seal on their hearts that they would not hearken?

101. We relate to you some of the events of these towns, and indeed their messengers came to them with clear evidences (miracles), but they would not believe in what they considered before as lies. Thus does God set a seal on the hearts of the infidels.

102. We did not find in most of them any (adherence to the) Covenant, and We found most of them to be transgressors.

103. Then We raised after them Moses with Our signs to Pharaoh and his chiefs, but they were mischievous about it. Behold then what the end of the mischief-makers was.

104. Moses said: "O Pharaoh! Verily I am a messenger from the Lord of the worlds.

105. "It is incumbent upon me to say nothing about God

save the truth; indeed I have come to you with clear signs
from your Lord; so, send with me the children of Israel."

106. He said: "If you have come with a sign, bring it, if
you are truthful at all."

107. So he (Moses) threw down his rod, and lo! It was a
serpent clearly seen.

108. Then he drew forth his hand and lo! It was (shining) white to all beholders.

109. The chiefs of Pharaoh's people said: "This is indeed
a most learned sorcerer.

110. "He intends to turn you out of your land; what is it
then that you counsel?"

111. They said: "Put him off, and his brother, too, and
send into the cities collectors,

112. "That they may bring you every learned sorcerer."

113. The sorcerers came to Pharaoh and said: "Will there
be a reward for us if we triumph?"

114. He said: "Yea! You shall surely be nearest to me."

115. They said: "O Moses! Will you cast (your rod) first,
or shall we be the first (to cast)?"

116. He (Moses) said: "You cast (first)." So when they
cast, they bewitched people's eyes and terrified them, producing a great magic.

117. We revealed to Moses: "Cast your rod!" Then lo! It
swallowed all that they had falsely demonstrated.

118. So was the truth established, rendering all that they
were doing vain.

119. So (Pharaoh and his magicians) were defeated manifestly, returning humiliated.

120. So did the sorcerers prostrate themselves in adoration.

121. They said: "We believe in the Lord of the worlds,

122. "The Lord of Moses and Aaron."

123. Pharaoh said: "Do you believe in Him before I give
you permission? Verily this is a plot you have plotted in the
city so that you may turn its people out of it, but you shall
soon know (the consequences).

124. "I will surely cut off your hands and feet from opposite sides, then I will crucify you altogether."

125. They said: "Verily to our Lord we return.

126. "You only wreak vengeance on us because we believed in the signs of our Lord when they came to us. O Lord! Pour out upon us patience and cause us to die submitting (to You)."

127. The chiefs of Pharaoh's people said: "Do you suffer Moses and his people make mischief in the earth and desert you and your gods?" He said: "Soon we will slay their sons and leave their women suffer as they live; verily we have a firm hold over them."

128. Moses said to his people: "Seek help from God and be patient; indeed the earth is God's; He grants it as a heritage to whomsoever He pleases from among His servants." The end is (only) for those who guard themselves against evil.

129. They said: "We have been persecuted before you came to us, and since you came to us, too." He (Moses) said: "Your Lord may destroy your enemy and make you inheritors in the world so that He may see how you act (therein)."

130. Indeed We seized Pharaoh's people with droughts and diminution of fruits that they might be admonished.

131. But when any good reached them, they said: "This is due to us," and when any evil smote them, they ascribed it to ill-luck due to Moses and those with him. Be it known that their ill-luck is only with God; but most of them do not know.

132. They said: "Whatever you bring us of a sign to enchant us, we will not believe in you."

133. So We sent upon them widespread calamities, the locust and the lice, the frogs and the blood-clear signs, yet they still behaved arrogantly, and so they became a guilty people.

134. Whenever torment fell upon, they said: "O Moses! Pray to your Lord as He covenanted with you, if He removes the torment from us, we will surely believe in you, and we will surely send the children of Israel with you."

135. But whenever We removed the torment from them, till a fixed term which they had to reach, lo, they broke their promise.

136. So We inflicted retribution upon them, and We drowned them in the sea because they rejected Our signs

and were heedless thereto.

137. We made the people who were deemed weak inheritors of the eastern parts of the earth as well as the western which We have blessed (with fertility), and the good Word of your Lord was fulfilled regarding the children of Israel for what they suffered, and We destroyed what Pharaoh and his people had wrought, and whatever shade they made.

138. We let the children of Israel safely cross the sea, then they came upon a people devoted to worshipping idols of their own making. They said: "O Moses! Make us a god as these folks have gods of their own." He said: "Verily you are a people behaving ignorantly.

139. "As regarding these people, surely what they are doing shall be destroyed, and what they have wrought is vain."

140. He said: "Shall I seek for you a god other than (the true) God, while He has exalted you over the world?"

141. And (remember) when We rescued you from the people of Pharaoh who afflicted you with grievous torment, slaying your sons and leaving your women live, and in this was a great trial for you from your Lord.

142. We appointed for Moses thirty nights and completed it with ten more; thus was the term of his Lord completed, forty nights, and Moses said to his brother Aaron: "Take my place among my people; act rightly and do not follow the path of mischief-makers."

143. When Moses came at Our appointment and his Lord spoke to him, he said: "Lord! Manifest Yourself to me so that I may look towards You." He said: "You shall never see Me, but look towards the mountain: if it remains firm in its place, then you will see Me." When his Lord manifested His Glory unto the mountain, He made it crumble, and Moses fell down stunned, and when he recovered his senses, he said: "Glory be to You! I turn to you (repentant); I am the first to believe (in You)."

144. He said: "O Moses! Verily I have favoured you above the people with My Messages and with My words; take then what I give you and do not be among the ungrateful."

145. We ordained for him in the Tablets laws of every kind and the explanation of everything, saying: "Uphold these with firmness and bid your people uphold fast to what is best for them thereof; soon will I show you the abode of the wicked.

146. "Soon will I allow those who are unjustifiably proud in the world to turn away from My signs, while (even) if they see a sign, they will not believe therein, and (even) if they see the Right Path, they will not adopt it as a way, and if they see the path of error, they will adopt it for a way; this is so because they rejected Our signs and were heedless thereto."

147. Those who reject Our signs and the meeting of the Hereafter, vain shall be their deeds; shall they be recompensed save for what they have wrought?

148. The people of Moses made of their ornaments a calf, a mere body that seemed to low; could they not see that it neither spoke to them nor guided them in any way? They adopted it (for worship) and they were unjust.

149. When they repented and saw that they had gone astray, they said: "If Our Lord is not merciful unto us, and does not forgive us, surely we shall be losers."

150. When Moses returned to his people, wrathful and grieved, he said: "It is evil that which you have neglected after me; did you make haste about the matter of your Lord?" And he threw the Tablets down and seized his brother by the head, dragging him. He (Aaron) said: "O son of my mother! Verily the people reckoned me weak and almost slew me; so, do not make my enemies rejoice, and do not count me among the unjust."

151. He (Moses) said: "Lord! Forgive me and my brother; admit us into Your mercy; You are the most merciful of those who have mercy."

152. Verily those who adopted the calf (for a god), a wrath from the Lord shall soon reach them, and an indignation in the life of this world; thus do We recompense the forgerers of lies,

153. Those who do evil deeds, then they repent thereafter, and truly believe, indeed your Lord after that is certainly oft-Forgiving, Merciful.

154. When the anger of Moses dissipated, he took up the Tablets, in the writings therein was guidance and mercy for those who fear for the sake of their Lord.

155. Moses chose of his people seventy men for Our appointment, then when a shock seized them, he prayed: "Lord! Had You pleased, You could have destroyed them and me too before; would You destroy us for what the fools among us have done? It is naught but Your trial; You cause whomsoever You will to stray, and You guide whomsoever You please; You are our Guardian; so, forgive us and bestow Your mercy upon us; You are the best to forgive.

156. "Ordain for us in this life good and in the life hereafter; indeed we turn to You." He said: "I inflict My chastisement upon whomsoever I will, and My mercy encompasses all things; therefore, I will soon ordain it for those who are pious and who pay regular charity, and those who believe in Our signs.

157. "Those who follow the unlettered messenger-prophet, whose name they find written in the Torah and the Evangel; he enjoins them to whatever is good and forbids everything evil; he makes lawful to them all things that are good, and he prohibits them from bad ones, and he removed from them their burdens and yokes which were upon them; so, those who believe in him, honour, and support him, and follow the Light sent down with him, are the ones who are truly successful."

158. Say (O Our Messenger Muhammad): "O people! Verily I am the Prophet of God to all of you, of Him to Whom the kingdom of heavens and earth belongs. No god is there but He. He grants life and causes death; so, believe in God and His unlettered Messenger, the Prophet who believes in God and His Words; therefore, follow him so that you may be rightly guided."

159. Among the people of Moses there is a party that guides with the truth and thereby effects justice.

160. We divided them into twelve tribes (or) nations, and We inspired to Moses when his people asked him for water: "Strike with your rod." Twelve springs gushed forth: each tribe knew its drinking place, and We caused the clouds to shade them, and We sent down to them manna and quails,

saying: "Eat of the good things with which We have provided you." And they (still rebelled, though) did not harm Us but harmed their own selves, and were doing injustice (to their own souls).

161. It was said to them: "Dwell in this town and eat thereof as you please and say: `Put down from us our burden (of sins),' and enter the gates making obeisance, We will then forgive your faults. We will soon bestow more unto those who do good deeds to others."

162. But those who did injustice among them changed a word other than that which was spoken to them, so We sent upon them a pestilence from heavens, for they had been doing injustice.

163. Ask them about the town which was by the sea; when they exceeded (the limits) in the Sabbath, their fish came to them on the day of their Sabbath, appearing on the surface of the water, and on the day they did not observe the Sabbath, they did not come to them. Thus did We try them for they were transgressing.

164. And when a party of them said: "Why do you admonish a people whom God would destroy, or whom He would chastise with a severe torment?" they said: "To be free from blame before your Lord, perchance they may fear God."

165. So when they did forget what they were warned with, We delivered those who forbade evil and seized those who were unjust with a dreadful chastisement because they were transgressing.

166. So when they proudly defied what they had been forbidden, We said to them: "Be apes scouted (away from human society)."

167. Behold! Your Lord declared that He would surely send against them until the Day of Resurrection those who would afflict them with a grievous torment; verily your Lord is certainly quick to requite, and indeed He is the oft-Forgiving, Merciful.

168. We scattered them throughout the world into (various) peoples; some of them are righteous, and some are otherwise, and We tried them with good and with evil, so that they might return (to the Right Path).

169. Then (an evil) posterity succeeded after them who inherited the Book, choosing the vanities of this low life saying: "Everything will be forgiven us." And if similar vanities came to them, they would seize them, too. Was not a Covenant of the Book taken from them that they read what is therein? But the abode of the Hereafter is the best for those who guard (themselves against evil). Do you not then understand?

170. Those who hold fast to the Book and establish prayer, indeed We do not waste the recompense of those who amend.

171. When We shook the Mountain over them as if it were a covering, and they thought that it was going to fall down upon them, We said: "Uphold firmly to what We give you and be mindful of what is therein, perchance you may fear God."

172. When your Lord brought from the children of Adam, from their loins, their descendants, and made them bear witness upon their own selves, saying: "Am I not your Lord?" They replied: "Yes, indeed! We do bear witness." (This We did) lest you should say on the Day of Judgment: "Verily we were unaware of this."

173. Or lest you should say: "Verily, only our fathers before us associated (with God), and we are their descendants after them; will You then destroy us for what the vain doers did?"

174. Thus do We explain the signs in detail so that you might return (unto Us).

175. Relate to them the news of that unto whom We bestowed Our signs but he withdrew therefrom, so Satan followed him, and he became one of those who went astray.

176. Had We willed, We would certainly have exalted him thereby, but he clung to the earth and followed his vain inclinations; so his similitude is like the parable of a dog: if you attack him, he lolls out his tongue, and if you leave him alone, he still lolls out his tongue; such is the similitude of the people who reject Our signs; so, relate to them the tales so that they may reflect.

177. How evil is the similitude of the people who reject Our signs and are unjust to their own selves.

178. Whomsoever God guides, he it is that is rightly guided, and whomsoever He suffers to stray, it is they that (are doomed to) lose.

179. Indeed We have created for hell many jinn and men; they have hearts but they do not understand thereby, and they have eyes but they do not see thereby. They have ears but they do not hear thereby; they are like cattle; nay, even more astray. These are they who are heedless.

180. To God alone belong all the most Beautiful Names; so call unto Him thereby, and leave alone those who are profane while using His names; soon shall they be recompensed for what they were doing.

181. Of those whom We created are a people who guide others with the truth and themselves are justly adhering thereto.

182. We shall gradually draw those who reject Our signs to ruin from whence they do not know.

183. And I grant them a respite. Verily My scheme is unfailingly strong.

184. They do not reflect that their companion (Muhammad) is not seized with madness; he is only a discerning warner.

185. Or do they not look into the kingdoms of the heavens and the earth and whatever things (God) created, and may be that their term has drawn nigh; then in what other words after this would they believe?

186. Whomsoever God suffers to stray, there is no guide for him, and He leaves them alone in their transgression blindly wandering.

187. They ask you about the Hour (of resurrection) when its fixed time will be. Say: "The knowledge of it is only with my Lord. None shall manifest it at its time but He. Heavy shall its burden be in the heavens and the earth; it will not come to you but suddenly." They ask you as if you were solicitous about it. Say: "Its knowledge is only with God," but most people do not know.

188. Say: "I neither own for myself any benefit, nor harm, except what God wills, and had I known the unseen, indeed I would have had much of good, and evil would not have touched me, and I am only a warner and a bearer of

glad tidings for those who believe."

189. It is He Who created you from a single self and from it He created its mate to dwell resting thereto; when he covers her, she bears a light burden and carries it; when it grows more heavy, they both pray to their Lord: "If You grant us a good child, we shall certainly be grateful."

190. But when He grants them a good child, they even ascribe partners with Him in what He has given them; most exalted is God above what they associate with Him.

191. Do they associate (with Him) that which does not create anything, while they are themselves the created ones?

192. They cannot help them, nor can they help their own selves.

193. If you invite them to guidance, they will not follow you; it is the same if you invite them or hold your peace.

194. Verily, those whom you call upon besides God are subservient (to God) like your own selves. So call on them, then let them answer if you are truthful.

195. Have they feet with which they walk? Or hands with which they hold? Or eyes with which they see? Or ears with which they hear? Say (O Our Messenger Muhammad): "Call all your associates and then scheme against me and give me no respite;

196. "Verily my Protector (against your schemes) is God Who revealed the Book (Qur'an) and He guards the virtuous ones.

197. "Those whom you call upon besides Him are not able to help you, nor can they help their own selves."

198. If you invite them to guidance, they would not listen, and you see them looking towards you while they do not see.

199. Adopt moderation and enjoin virtue and turn away from the ignorant ones.

200. If an enticement from Satan assails you, seek refuge with God; indeed He is all-Hearing, all-Knowing.

201. Verily those who guard (themselves against evil), when afflicted by an evil thought from Satan, become mindful (of God) then lo! They see (aright).

202. Their brethren drag them deeper into error, so they

do not halt their efforts.

203. When you do not bring them a sign, they say: "Why don't you forge it?" Say: "Verily I only follow what is revealed to me from my Lord; these are clear proofs from your Lord, a guidance and mercy for people who believe."

204. When the Qur'an is recited, listen to it and be attentive, perchance you may receive mercy.

205. And remember your Lord within your self in humility and awe, not in a loud voice, in the morning and the in the eve, and do not be of the negligent ones.

206. Verily those who are with your Lord are not too proud to worship Him; they glorify Him and (while doing so) they prostrate.

The Spoils of War
(al-Anfaal)

In the name of God, the Beneficent, the Merciful.

1. They ask you about the Anfal (accessions); say (O Our Messenger Muhammad): "The Anfal are for God and the Prophet; so, fear God and set aright matters between yourselves, and obey God and His Prophet if you are believers."

2. Indeed those are believers whose hearts are thrilled when God is mentioned, and when His Signs are recited unto them, their faith is strengthened, and on God alone do they rely.

3. They establish prayer and spend of what God has provided them with.

4. They, and they alone, are the believers in truth; for them are (exalted) gardens with their Lord, forgiveness, and a graceful sustenance.

5. Even as your Lord caused you to go out of your house with the truth, though a party of the believers were certainly averse;

6. They dispute with you about the truth even after being made manifest (to them), as if they were (helplessly) being driven to death while they saw it.

7. When God promised you one of the two (enemy) parties, that it should be yours, you wished that the one

unarmed should be yours, yet God intended to establish the truth with His words, and to cut off the roots of the infidels,

8. That He may establish the truth of what was true, and falsehood bring to naught, though the guilty ones disliked it.

9. You implored help from your Lord, so He answered you: "Verily, I will aid you with a thousand angels, rank behind rank."

10. God did not cause but as good tidings (to you), so that your hearts might thereby be convinced; and no help is there save from God; verily God is ever-Triumphant, Wise.

11. He caused upon you a slumber as a security from Him, and He sent down water from heavens that He might purify you therewith, and remove from you the uncleanliness of Satan, and that He might fortify your hearts, and plant your feet firmly with it.

12. When your Lord revealed to the angels saying: "Verily, I am with you; give firmness then to those who believe. Soon I will cast terror into the hearts of those who disbelieve, therefore strike off their necks; and smite their fingertips.

13. "This is so because they opposed God and His Prophet (Muhammad), and whosoever opposes God and His Prophet is verily to be punished by God severely."

14. Taste it, then, and beware that for the infidels is the torment of the Fire.

15. O you who believe! When you meet those who disbelieve on the battlefield, do not turn your backs to them.

16. Whoever turns his back to them on that day, except if he turns aside (maneuvering) for the fighting, or in joining (another) contingent, he deserves the Wrath of God, and his abode is Hell; what an evil destination it shall be!

17. So you did not slay them, but God slew them, nor did you throw (the dust), but God threw it so that He might test the believers by a gracious trial from Him; verily God is all-Hearing, all-Knowing.

18. This (is the cause) and that God frustrates the crafty plans of the infidels.

19. (Know, O infidels) if you demanded a victory, then indeed the victory (of the Muslims) has come to you, and if

you desist (from attacking the faithful), it will be better for you; if you return (to attack), We also shall return (to assist the believers), and your forces shall never avail at all, though they may be many, and know that God is with the believers.

20. O you who believe! Obey God and His Prophet (Muhammad), and do not turn away from him while hearing him speak.

21. Do not be like those who said: "We heard," while they did not listen.

22. Verily the vilest of animals in God's view are the deaf and dumb who do not understand.

23. Had God found any good in them, indeed He would have made them listen, and even if He made them listen, they would turn back swerving aside.

24. O you who believe! Respond to God and to His Prophet (Muhammad) when He calls you to that which gives life, and know that God (always) gets between man and his heart, and that it is to Him you shall all be ultimately gathered.

25. And guard yourselves against an affliction which may smite not only those who committed injustice among you in particular (but all of you), and know that God is severe in the requital (of evil);

26. Remember when you were few and deemed weak in the earth, fearing that people might kidnap you by force, but He sheltered you, strengthened you with His aid, and provided you of the good things (of sustenance) that you may give thanks.

27. O you who believe! Do not be unfaithful to God and the Prophet (Muhammad), nor be unfaithful to the trusts with you while you know.

28. And know that your wealth and your children are a temptation, and that with God is a mighty reward.

29. O you who believe! If you fear God, He will grant you a distinctive (standard), and remove from you all your sins and forgive you, God is the Lord of mighty grace.

30. When the disbelievers plotted against you to imprison you, or slay you, or drive you away, they devised plans, and God too had a plan; God is the best of planners.

31. Remember how when Our Signs are recited to them,

they say: "Indeed we have heard; if we please, we could say the like of this (Qur'an); it is nothing but the tales of old."

32. And remember when they said: "O God! If this (Qur'an) is the truth from You, then rain upon us stones from heavens, or inflict upon us a painful chastisement."

33. But God is not to chastise them while you are among them, nor is God to chastise them while they still seek forgiveness.

34. And what plea do they have that God should not chastise them while they obstruct (men) from the Sacred Mosque, and they are not its guardians? Its guardians are only those who guard themselves (against evil), but most of them do not know.

35. Their prayer near the (Sacred) House (of God) is nothing but the whistling and clapping of hands; taste then the chastisement for what you were disbelieving.

36. Verily those who disbelieve spend of their wealth to obstruct people from the way of God, so when they spend it (in the end), it shall be against them (a matter of) regret, and they shall be overcome, and those who disbelieve shall be driven to Hell.

37. That God might distinguish the impure from the pure, and put the impure, some of it upon the other, and pile it up together, then cast it into Hell; these are the losers.

38. Tell those who disbelieve that if they desist, their past will be forgiven, and if they return (to their disbelief), then indeed what has already passed against the ancients shall pass against them too.

39. And fight them until there is no more mischief, and the religion is wholly God's; but if they desist, then verily God sees all that they do.

40. And if they turn back, then know that God is your Lord; the Most Excellent Lord, and the Most Excellent Helper.

41. And know (O believers!) that whatever you acquire, a fifth of it is for God, the Prophet, the (Prophet's) near relatives, the orphans, the needy, and the wayfarers, if you believe in God and in what We revealed to Our Servant (Muhammad) on the Day of Distinction, when the two parties met; God has power over all things.

42. (Remember) when you were on the near side (of the

valley), and they were on the farthest side thereof, while the caravan (of the enemy) was in a ground lower than yours, had you mutually made an appointment, you would certainly have failed in its fulfillment, but (you were made to meet) in order that God might enact a matter which was destined to be done, that he who perishes may perish after a clear proof, and he who lives may live after a clear proof; verily God is all-Hearing, all-Knowing.

43. And (remember) when He showed them to you in your dream as few; had He shown them to you many, you would certainly have become disheartened, and you would certainly have disputed in the matter, but God saved you; verily He knows what is in your hearts.

44. And (remember) when He showed them to you, when you met, as few in your eyes, and He reduced you to appear as few in their eyes, so that God might enact the matter which had been destined to be, and to God alone will all matters return.

45. O you who believe! When you meet a party (contingent of infidels), then be firm and remember God much, so that you may be successful.

46. Obey God and His Prophet (Muhammad), and do not fall into disputes, for then you will be weakened in heart, and your power will depart, and be patient; verily God is with those who are patient.

47. And do not be like those who got out from their homes boastfully to be seen of men, yet they obstruct others from the Way of God, and verily God encompasses what they do.

48. And (remember) when Satan made their (sinful) deeds seem alluring to them, and said (to them): "None among men shall triumph over you today, while I am a protector over you." But when the two parties came face to face with each other, he turned upon his heels and said: "I dissociate myself from you; verily I see what you do not see; and God is severe in punishment."

49. The hypocrites and those in whose hearts there is a disease say: "Their religion has beguiled these (Muslims)." Whoever relies upon God, then God is Almighty, all-Wise.

50. If you could but see when the angels take away the

souls of those who disbelieve, smiting their faces and backs saying: "Taste the torment of the burning Fire.

51. "This is for what your own hands have sent forth." God is not unjust to the servants."

52. (Because they acted) like the people of Pharaoh and those before them; they disbelieved in the Signs of God, so God seized them for their sins; verily God is Strong, severe in punishment.

53. This is so because God does not change any favour He bestows upon people until they themselves change their own selves, and God is all-Seeing, all-Hearing.

54. (Because they acted) like the people of Pharaoh and those before them; they rejected the Signs of their Lord, so We destroyed them for their sins, and We drowned the people of Pharaoh, and all were unjust (tyrants).

55. Indeed the vilest of beasts in God's view are those who disbelieve, for they would not believe (no matter what).

56. Those (O Our Messenger Muhammad) with whom you made a covenant break their covenant every time, and they do not guard themselves (against evil);

57. So when you take them in fighting, scatter them (punitively, making them an example) for those who come after them so that they may remember.

58. And if you fear treachery from people, throw back to them (their covenant) on equal terms; verily God does not love the treacherous ones.

59. And do not let those who disbelieve think that they have excelled (the Muslims); verily they shall not frustrate (God).

60. And prepare against them whatever force you can, and steeds of war at the garrison to frighten thereby the enemy of God and of your own selves and (even) of others besides them whom you do not know but God does, and whatever you spend in the way of God shall be fully repaid to you, and you shall never be dealt with unjustly.

61. But if they incline to peace, then you, too, incline to it, and trust in God; He is all-Hearing, all-Knowing.

62. And if they intend to deceive you, then God suffices for you; He it is Who strengthened you with His help and with the believers.

63. He caused affection between their hearts. Had you spent all that is in the earth, you could not have caused that affection between their hearts, but God caused affection between them; He is Almighty, all-Wise.

64. O Our Prophet (Muhammad)! Let God and the believers who follow you suffice for you.

65. O Our Prophet (Muhammad)! Urge the believers to war; if there are twenty patient ones among you, they shall overcome two hundred (infidels), and if there are a hundred (such ones), they shall overcome a thousand disbelievers, for they are people who do not understand.

66. For the moment God has decreased your burden, and He knows that in you there is a weakness; if there are a hundred patient ones among you, they shall overcome two hundred (infidels), and if there are a thousand, they shall overcome two thousand (infidels) with God's permission; God is with those who are patient.

67. It does not befit a prophet (of God) to keep captives unless he has fought (the infidels in war) in the world; you desire the frail goods of this world, while God desires (for you) the hereafter; God is Almighty, all-Wise.

68. Had it not been for an Ordinance from God that had already gone before, surely a great chastisement would have afflicted you for what you took.

69. Eat then of what you acquired in war, of things that are lawful and good, and fear God; verily God is oft-Forgiving, Merciful.

70. O Our Prophet (Muhammad)! Say to the captives in your hands: "If God knows any good in your hearts, He will give you better than what has been taken away from you, and He will forgive you; indeed God is oft-Forgiving, Merciful."

71. If they intend to be unfaithful towards you, so indeed have they been unfaithful to God before, but He gave you power over them, and God is all-Knowing, all-Wise.

72. Verily those who believed, migrated, and strove with their possessions and lives in the way of God, and those who sheltered and helped, are guardians of one another; those who believed and did not migrate, you are not their guardian until they migrate, and if they seek help from

you in (any matter of) religion, then it is incumbent upon
you to help them save against people between whom and
you there is a covenant; God sees all that you do.

73. Some of those who disbelieve are guardians of others; unless you do this, there will be discord in the earth and
a great mischief.

74. Those who believed, migrated, and strove in the way
of God, and those who sheltered and helped, are truly believers, for them is forgiveness and an honourable provision.

75. And those who believed later, migrated and strove
with you, are of you; blood relatives are nearer to each
other in the Book of God; verily God knows everything.

Repentance
(Baraah)

1. (This is a declaration of) immunity from God and
His Prophet (Muhammad) to the idolaters with whom you
have a covenant.

2. So go about in the world for four months, and know
that you are not frustrating God, and that God brings shame
to the infidels.

3. And an announcement from God and His Prophet to
the people on the day of the great pilgrimage, that God is
immune (from any obligation to) the idolaters, and (so is)
His Prophet; therefore, if you repent, it will be for your own
good, and if you turn back, then know that you are not
frustrating God, and announce (O Our Messenger
Muhammad) a painful chastisement to those who disbelieve.

4. Except those (with whom) you have entered into a
pact, from the idolaters who thereafter did not fail you in
aught and have not backed anyone against you, so fulfill
their pact to the end of their term; God loves those who
guard themselves (against evil).

5. When the sacred months are past, then slay the idolaters wherever you find them; seize them and besiege them,
and wait for them in every ambush. If they repent, establish
prayer, and pay zakat, leave their way free to them; God is

the oft-Forgiving, the Merciful.

6. If any of the idolaters seeks protection from you, grant him protection till he hears the Words of God, then convey him to his place of safety; this is so because they are people who do not understand.

7. How can there be any covenant to the idolaters with God and His Messenger except for those with whom you made a covenant at the Sacred Mosque? So long as they stand true to you, then you too be true to them; God loves those who guard themselves (against evil).

8. How can there be any alliance since if they overcome you, they will regard no tie nor covenant? They allure you with sweet words while their hearts are averse (to you), and most of them are transgressors.

9. They have bartered the signs of God for a miserable price, so they turn others away from His Way; evil is what they do.

10. In case of a believer, they pay no regard to any tie, nor to any covenant, and these are they that transgress the limits.

11. But if they repent and establish (regular) prayer, and pay zakat, then they are your brethren in faith, and We explain the signs for people who understand.

12. If they violate their oaths after their covenant, and revile your religion, then fight the leaders of infidelity; there is no oath for them so that they may desist.

13. Will you not fight the people who violated their oaths and plotted to expel the Messenger, having attacked you first? Do you fear them, whereas God is the most deserving that you should fear, if you are believers?

14. Fight them so that God may chastise them by your hands, put them to shame, help bring victory over them, and heal the injured breasts of the believers.

15. He removes the rage of the hearts, and God turns (Merciful) to whomsoever He pleases; God is all-Knowing, all-Wise.

16. Or do you think (O believers) that you will be left alone while God does not yet know those of you who strove and did not take anyone as intervener besides God, His Messenger, and the believers? God is fully aware of all that

you do.

17. It is not for the idolaters to maintain the mosques of God, while they themselves indict their own souls with infidelity. These it is whose deeds are vain, and in the Fire shall they forever abide.

18. Only he shall maintain the mosques of God that believes in God and the Last Day, establishes prayer, pays zakat, and fears none save God; so these it may be that are rightly guided.

19. Do you make the serving of water to the pilgrims and maintenance of the Sacred Mosque equal to (the deeds of) one who believes in God and the last day and strives in God's Way? They are not equal in God's view, and God does not guide the unjust people.

20. Those who believed (in God), migrated and strove in God's Way with their possessions and lives, are the highest in rank in God's view, and only those shall achieve salvation.

21. Their Lord gives them glad tidings of mercy from Him and (His) pleasure, and of gardens wherein lasting bounties are theirs (from their Lord),

22. Abiding therein forever; with God is a great reward.

23. O you who believe! Do not take your fathers or brothers for friends if they favour infidelity over faith, and whosoever of you makes friends with them, then he shall be of the unjust ones.

24. Say (O Our Messenger Muhammad): "If your fathers, sons, brethren, kindred, wives, possessions you have acquired, trade the recess of which you fear, the dwellings you delight therein.., are dearer to you than God and His Messenger, and the striving in His Way, then wait till God brings about His Command; God does not guide people who transgress."

25. Certainly God helped you in many [battle]fields, and on the day of Hunayn when you rendered your great numbers futile and availed you nothing, and the earth was straitened against you although it is spacious, then you turned back retreating.

26. Then God sent down His Tranquility (sakina) upon His Messenger and the believers, and He sent down hosts

which you did not see, and (thereby) chastised those who disbelieved; that is the recompense of the infidels.

27. Then God will turn Merciful after this to whomsoever He pleases, and God is the oft-Forgiving, most Merciful.

28. O you who believe! Indeed the idolaters are unclean, so they shall not approach the Sacred Mosque after this year. If you fear poverty, then God will soon enrich you through His Grace if He pleases; God is all-Knowing, all-Wise.

29. Fight those who do not believe in God nor in the Last Day, nor prohibit what God and His Prophet have prohibited, nor follow the religion of truth, of those who have been given the Book, until they pay the jizya (tributary tax) and remain subdued.

30. The Jews say: "Ezra is the son of God," while the Christians say: "The Messiah is the son of God." These are words coming out of their mouths; they only echo the saying of those who disbelieved before. God fights them; how they turn away!

31. They take their divines and monks as lords besides God, and also the Messiah son of Mary, while they were commanded to worship God, the Only One; there is no god but He; pure is He and Exalted from what they associate with Him.

32. They intend to put out the light of God with their mouths, while God disdains (everything) save that He perfects His light, though the infidels may detest it.

33. He it is Who sent His Prophet with guidance and the religion of truth that He might make it prevail over all other religions, though the polytheists may detest it.

34. O you who believe! Indeed many divines and monks eat away the properties of men through their falsehood, and obstruct others from the Way of God; announce a painful chastisement to those who hoard up gold and silver and do not spend it in God's way;

35. On the Day (of Judgment), it shall be heated in the fire of Hell, then their foreheads, sides, and backs shall be branded therewith, while it is said to them: "This is what you hoarded up for yourselves; taste then what you hoarded."

36. Indeed the number of months with God is twelve in God's Book (since) the Day He created the heavens and the earth. Of them, four are sacred; that is the established religion; so, do not be unjust therein to your own selves, and fight the polytheists altogether, even as they fight you altogether, and know that God is with the pious.

37. Indeed the postponing (of a prohibitive month) is only an addition to infidelity, with which those who disbelieve go astray; they allow it one year and forbid it another, that they may adjust the number of months God has deemed forbidden, thus they allow what God has forbidden; the evil of their deeds has been made fair-seeming to them. God does not guide the infidel people.

38. O you believe! What ails you that you heavily incline to earth when it is said to you: "Go forth (to fight) in the Way of God" ? Are you contented with the life of this world instead of the hereafter? What is the provision of the life of this world compared to the hereafter? Indeed the provision of the life of this world compared to the hereafter is but a trifling.

39. Unless you go forth, He will chastise you with a painful chastisement, and He will put in your place people other than you, and no harm will you do unto Him; God has power over all things.

40. If you do not help him (the Prophet), it does not matter, for indeed God helped him when those who disbelieved expelled him. He was the second of two. When they both were in the cave, he said to his companion: "Do not worry; God is with us." So God sent down tranquility upon him, and strengthened him with hosts (of angels) you did not see, and made the word of those who did not believe abased, and the Word of God exalted to the heights; indeed God is the Almighty, the all-Wise.

41. Go forth (with) light and heavy equipment, and strive in the way of God with your possessions and lives; this is better for you, if you only know.

42. Had there been any immediate gain, and the journey made easy, certainly they would have followed you, but the distance was too long for them; yet they still swear by God saying: "Had we been able, we would surely have

gone with you." They cause their own souls to perish, and God knows that they certainly are liars.

43. God forgives you (O Our Messenger Muhammad)! Why did you give them leave (to stay behind) until those who spoke the truth became manifest to you and you had known the liars?

44. Those who believe in God and the Last Day do not ask leave of you (to be exempted) from striving with their wealth and lives, and God knows who is pious.

45. Only those who do not believe in God and the Last Day ask leave of you (to be exempt), and their hearts are in doubt, hence in their doubt are they tossed to and fro.

46. Had they (really) intended to go forth, they would certainly have made preparations for it, but God was averse to their going forth, so He withheld them, and it was said to them: "Sit (inactively) with those who stay behind."

47. Had they gone forth with you, they would not have added (to your strength) aught save mischief, and they would have certainly hurried about (to and fro) amidst you, sowing dissensions amidst you, and among you there are those who hearken to them, and God knows the unjust.

48. Certainly they sought dissension before they upset matters for you, until the truth came and the decree of God prevailed, though they were averse thereto.

49. Among them there is (many) a man who says: "Exempt me, and do not try me." Surely have they already fallen into trial and Hell encompasses the infidels.

50. If any good befalls you, it grieves them, and if any hardship afflicts you, they say: "Indeed we have taken care of our affair before," and they turn away and they rejoice.

51. Say (O Our Messenger Muhammad): "Never shall anything afflict us save what God has decreed for us; He is our Lord, and on God should the believers rely."

52. Say: "Should await for us aught but one of the two excellent things (victory or martyrdom)? And we can expect for you that God will afflict you with a chastisement from Himself or from our hands. Then wait, we too will wait with you."

53. Say: "Spend willingly or reluctantly; it shall never be accepted from you, for you are a transgressing people."

54. Nothing hinders the acceptance of their offerings save that they reject God and His Messenger (Muhammad), and they come only sluggishly to prayer, and only reluctantly do they contribute.

55. Therefore let not their wealth nor children amaze you. Indeed God intends only to torment them with these (things) in the life of this world, and that their souls depart disbelievers.

56. They swear by God that they are surely of you, whereas they are not of you, but are in fact afraid (of you).

57. If they could find a refuge, or caves, or a place to enter (to hide) therein, they would certainly have turned themselves to it, rushing thereto (in haste).

58. And of them are those who blame you with regard to the (distribution of) alms; if they are given from it, they are pleased, and if they are not, behold! They are enraged.

59. If only they were contented with what God and His Messenger had given them and said: "God is sufficient for us! Soon will God give us of His Grace and His Messenger too; to God alone do we all turn (in hope)."

60. Indeed alms are only for the poor, the needy, the workers (administrating poor-rates), those whose heart's alliance is sought, (the ransoming of) the captives, those in debt, the (promotion of the) Way of God, and the wayfarer, a duty ordained by God, and God is all-Knowing, all-Wise.

61. Among them are those who hurt the Prophet (Muhammad) and say: "He is all ears (i.e. believes everything he hears)." Say (O Muhammad): "He listens to what is best for you; he believes in God and has faith in the believers, and is a mercy to those of you who believe." For those who hurt the Prophet of God is a grievous chastisement.

62. They swear by God to you that they might please you, and God and His Prophet (Muhammad) have a greater right that they should please Him, if they are believers.

63. Do they know that the fire of Hell is for whoever opposes God and His Prophet (Muhammad), to abide for-ever therein? That is the grievous abasement.

64. The hypocrites fear lest a sura should be sent about them declaring openly to them what is really in their hearts. Say: "You scoff! Indeed God brings forth what you fear."

65. If you question them, they will surely say: "We were only discoursing and jesting." Say: "At God, His signs and His Messengers do you scoff?"

66. Do not make excuses; indeed you have denied after believing. If We pardon a party of you, We will chastise another, for surely they are the guilty ones.

67. Hypocrite men and women are one from another; they enjoin evil and forbid good, withholding their hands (from spending in the Way of God). They have forsaken God, so He has forsaken them; verily, the hypocrites are the transgressors.

68. God has promised the hypocrite men and women, and the disbelievers, the fire of Hell to abide therein; it suffices them. God has cursed them, and for them is the everlasting chastisement.

69. (O hypocrites! You are) like those (who flourished) before you; they were stronger than you in might, and more abundant in wealth and offspring; so they enjoyed their portion; thus have you enjoyed your portion as those before you enjoyed theirs, and you indulge in vain discourses just as those (before you) indulged. These are those whose works have come to naught in this world and the hereafter, and these are the losers.

70. Did the news of those before them not come to them? (News) of Noah and 'Ad and Thamud, the people of Abraham, the inhabitants of Midian, and the cities overthrown? Their Messengers came to them with clear proofs (of their truthfulness). Thus it was not God who did injustice to them, but they were unjust to their own souls.

71. Believing men and women are guardians of one another; they enjoin good and forbid evil, establish (regular) prayer and pay zakat, and obey God and His Prophet (Muhammad). God shall bestow on these His mercy; God is Almighty, all-Wise.

72. God has promised the believing men and women gardens beneath which rivers flow to abide therein forever, and excellent mansions in the gardens of Eden. But the good-will of God is the greatest; that is the grand achievement.

73. O Our Prophet (Muhammad)! Strive hard against the

infidels and the hypocrites, and be firm with them, and their abode shall be Hell, and what an evil destination it is!

74. They swear by God that they did not utter (what they are charged with, although) they did indeed utter the word of infidelity, and they disbelieved after their (embracing) Islam. They plotted what they could not achieve, and they only sought revenge because God and His Prophet had enriched them by His Grace. If they repent, it will be good for them, and if they turn back, God will chastise them with a painful chastisement in this world and the hereafter; there shall be neither protector for them on earth nor helper.

75. Of them are those who made a Covenant with God: "If He grants us out of His Grace, we will certainly give charity and we will certainly be of the righteous."

76. But when He did grant them out of His Grace, they became niggardly therewith, and they turned back, averse.

77. So in consequence, He has effected hypocrisy in their hearts till the day when they meet Him, because they had failed to fulfill their promise to God, and because they used to lie (continuously).

78. Do they not know that God knows their hidden thoughts and their secret whisperings, and that God is the Great Knower (of everything unseen)?

79. God will scoff at those who traduce the free givers of charity among the believers, and those who find nothing (to give) but their hard earnings, scoffing thereat, and for them shall be a painful torment.

80. Seek (O Our Messenger Muhammad) forgiveness for them, or do not seek it; it will be the same; even if you seek forgiveness for them seventy times, God will never forgive them. This is so because they disbelieved in God and His Prophet (Muhammad), and God does not guide the transgressing people.

81. Those left behind (in the expedition of Tabuk) were delighted for their sitting (inactive) behind God's Prophet, and they were averse from striving in God's Way with their wealth and lives, and they said (to the others): "Do not go in the heat." Say: "The fire of Hell is fiercer in heat," if only they could understand.

82. They, therefore, shall laugh little and weep much as a

recompense for what they used to earn.

83. So if God brings you back to a party of them, then they seek your permission to go forth, say: "You shall never go forth with me, and you shall never fight an enemy with me; you chose to sit (idle) the first time, so sit (now also idly) with those who stay behind."

84. And do not pray at all for any of them that dies, and never stand at his grave, for they disbelieved in God and His Prophet, and they died wicked.

85. Let not their wealth nor offspring impress you; God only wishes to chastise them with these in this world, and that their souls should depart infidel.

86. Whenever a sura is revealed (enjoining) that (they should) believe in God and strive hard along with His Prophet, those with abundant means seek your permission and say: "Leave us (behind); we may be with those who sit (at home)."

87. They prefer to be with those (women, children and the sick) who stay behind, for a seal has been set on their hearts; therefore, they do not understand.

88. But the Messenger and those who believe with him strive hard with their wealth and lives. For these are all the good things, and these are the successful ones.

89. God has prepared for them gardens beneath which rivers flow to abide therein forever; that is the great achievement.

90. The dwellers of the desert came with excuses that permission might be given to them, and those who lied to God and His Messenger sat (at home); a grievous chastisement shall shortly reach them.

91. There shall be no blame on the weak, nor the sick, nor those who do not find any to spend so long as they are sincere to God and His Messenger. And against the doers of good there is no way (to claim), and God is oft-Forgiving, Merciful.

92. Nor is it on those who came to you to provide them with mounts, and when you said to them: "I do not find any means to transport you," they went back with their eyes overflowing with sorrowful tears that they did not find any means to spend (in the cause).

93. Indeed the way (to charge) is only against those who

seek your permission (to stay behind) while they are rich, preferring to be with the women, the children, and the sick who remain behind, not knowing (what rewards they miss).

94. They will make excuses to you when you return to them (after the expedition). Say (O Our Messenger Muhammad): "Make no excuses (now), by no means will we believe you. Indeed, God has informed us of the truth about you. Now will God behold your doings and (also) His Prophet, then shall you be returned to the Knower of everything hidden and manifest, then you will be informed of all that you were doing."

95. They will swear to you by God, when you return to them, that you may turn aside from them; so turn aside from them; they are unclean, and their abode is Hell, a recompense for what they earned.

96. They will swear to you that you may be pleased with them, but (even) if you are pleased with them, God is not pleased with wicked people.

97. The Arabs (of the desert) are very hard in infidelity and hypocrisy, and more inclined not to know the limits which God has revealed to His Prophet, and God is all-Knowing, all-Wise.

98. And of the Arabs (of the desert) are those who believe in God and the Last Day and deem what they spend to (be means to) approach God and the blessings of the Messenger. Indeed it shall be the means of approach for them; soon shall God admit them into His mercy; God is oft-Forgiving, Merciful.

99. And among the (rustic) Arabs (of the desert) are those who believe in God and the Last Day and deem what they spend to (be the means to) approach God and the blessings of the Messenger. Indeed it shall be the means of approach for them; soon shall God admit them into His mercy; verily God is oft-Forgiving, Merciful.

100. As for the foremost, the first of the muhajirun and the ansar, and those who followed them in goodness, God is well-pleased with them and they with Him, and He has prepared for them gardens beneath which rivers flow to abide therein forever. That is the great achievement.

101. Of those who are around you of the Arabs (of the

desert) there are hypocrites, and from the inhabitants of Medina also are stubborn in hypocrisy; you do not know them, We know them; twice will We chastise them, then shall they be turned to a grievous torment.

102. And others have confessed their faults: they have mixed a good act with an evil one; God may turn to them (in mercy); God is oft-Forgiving, the Merciful.

103. Take alms out of their wealth to cleanse them and purify them thereby, and pray for them; your prayer is an assurance of peace for them. God is all-Hearing and all-Knowing.

104. They do not know that God accepts repentance from His votaries and appreciates alm-giving, and God is oft-Returning (to mercy), the Merciful.

105. And say to them: "Act as you will; God beholds your deeds, and so do His Messenger and the Believers, and then you shall be brought back to the Knower of the hidden and the manifest; it is then that He will inform you of all that you were doing."

106. And others are made to await God's Command, whether He will chastise them or return (in mercy) to them. God is all-Knowing, all-Wise.

107. Those who built a mosque to cause harm (to the faithful), causing infidelity and effecting disunion among the faithful, and an ambush to him who warred against God and His Messenger before, indeed swore (saying): "We desired naught but good;" and God bears witness that they are liars.

108. Never should you stand therein (to pray). Surely a mosque founded on piety from the very first day deserves more that you should stand therein (for prayers); therein are men who love to be purified. And God loves the purified ones.

109. Is he, therefore, who has laid his foundation on the fear of God and (His) Goodwill better or the one who lays his foundation on the brink of a crumbling hollow bank, so it crumbles down with him into the fire of Hell? God does not guide the unjust people.

110. The building which they built will not cease to be a source of disquiet in their hearts until their hearts are cut

into pieces; God is all-Knowing, all-Wise.

111. Indeed God has purchased from the faithful their lives and possessions for theirs (in return) is the Garden (Paradise). They fight in God's way, and they slay and are slain; (this is) a promise binding on Him in the Torah and the Evangel and the Qur'an; who is more faithful to his Covenant than God? Rejoice, therefore, in the bargain that you have transacted, and that is the great achievement.

112. (These are) they who turn to God (seeking forgiveness), who worship Him, praise Him, fast, bow down, prostrate themselves (in prayers), enjoin what is good and forbid what is evil, and keep (themselves) in God's (ordained) limits; therefore proclaim the glad tidings to the believers.

113. It is not for the Prophet nor the believers to seek forgiveness for the idolaters, even though they may be their near of kin, after it has been declared (clearly) to them that they are the inmates of the flaming Hell[fire].

114. Nor was Abraham's seeking forgiveness for his father other than a promise he had made to him; but when it became clear to him that he was an enemy to God, he declared himself clear of him; Abraham was very tender-hearted, patient.

115. Nor is it for God to lead people astray after guiding them (aright). He even makes it clear to them what they should abstain from; indeed God knows all things.

116. God's is the Kingdom of the heavens and the earth; He brings to life and He causes death, and there is no guardian nor helper for you besides God.

117. Surely God has turned in mercy to the Prophet and the muhajirun and the ansar who followed him in the hour of distress, after the hearts of a party of them had nearly swerved (from duty); but He turned to them (also in mercy). Indeed to them He is Compassionate, Merciful.

118. And (also) on the three who were left behind: when the earth became straitened on them, notwithstanding its spaciousness. Even their souls were straitened, (so much so) that they thought that there was no refuge from God but to Him; then He turned to them in mercy that they might turn (to Him). Indeed God is oft-Returning (to mercy), the Merciful.

119. O you who believe! Fear God and be (always) with the truthful.

120. It was not for the people of Medina and those around them of the dwellers of the desert to stay away behind the Prophet of God, nor to perfect their lives to his. This is so because thirst does not afflict them nor fatigue nor hunger in God's way, nor do they tread a path which enrages the infidels, nor do they receive from the enemy (any injury) but on account of its being reckoned to their credit a deed of righteousness. Indeed God does not suffer the reward of the doer of good to go in vain.

121. Nor do they spend anything (in the way of God), small or big, nor do they cut across a valley, but is recorded to their credit, that God may reward them with better than what they were doing.

122. Nor is it for the faithful that they should go forth (to war) all together; why should not then a company from every party of them go forth that they may acquire (proper) understanding in religion, and that they may warn their people when they return to them so that they may be cautious?

123. O you who believe! Fight those infidels near to you and let them find firmness in you, and know that God is with the pious.

124. Whenever a sura is revealed, some of the hypocrites ask (one another in ridicule): "Which of you has this (sura) increased in faith?" As for those who believe, it strengthens them in faith, and they rejoice thereat.

125. As to those in whose hearts there is a disease, it only increases their uncleanliness, and they shall die infidels.

126. They do not see that they are tried once or twice in every year, yet they do not turn (to God), nor do they remember.

127. Whenever a sura is revealed, they cast glances at one another (saying): "Does he (the believer) see anyone of you?" Then they turn away. God has turned their hearts away because they are people who do not understand.

128. Indeed, a Messenger has come to you from among yourselves; grievous to him is your falling into distress, so-

licitous regarding your welfare; towards the faithful he is compassionate and merciful.

129. But if they turn away, Say: "God suffices me. There is no god but He. On Him do I rely, and He is the Lord of the great Throne."

Jonah
(Younus)

In the name of God, the Beneficent, the Merciful.

1. Alif, Lam, Ra. These are verses of the Book of the all-Wise.

2. Is it a wonder for the people that We revealed to a man from among themselves, saying: "Warn mankind and bear glad tidings to those who believe, that there is a footing of firmness with their Lord"? But the infidels say: "Indeed this is an obvious sorcerer."

3. Your Lord is indeed God Who created the heavens and the earth in six days (periods) and is firmly established on the Throne. He regulates everything; no intercessor can there be except with His leave. This is God, your Lord; therefore, worship Him (alone). Will you not then mind?

4. To Him shall all of you return; it is the promise of God in truth. Indeed, (it is only) He Who begins the creation then causes it to return, that He may with equity recompense those who believe and do good deeds. And for those who disbelieve shall be the drink of boiling fluids and a painful chastisement for their disbelief.

5. He is (the One) Who made the sun a radiation and the moon a light, and measured stations for it that you might know the number of years and the reckoning (of time); God created all this only for truth; thus does God make His signs manifest for people who understand.

6. Indeed in the variation of the night and the day, and all that God has created in the heavens and the earth, are sure signs for people who guard (themselves) against evil.

7. Those who do not hope to meet Us (on the Day of Judgment) and are pleased with the life of this world and are satisfied therewith, are the ones who are heedless of Our signs.

8. Their abode is but the Fire, (a punishment) for what they earned.

9. God guides those who believe and do good deeds to their (true) faith; beneath them rivers will flow in the gardens of bliss.

10. Their cry therein (shall be): "Glory be to You, O God!" and their greetings in it (will be): "Peace!" and the last of their cry (will be) that "Praise be to God, Lord of the Worlds."

11. If God were to hasten to men the evil (they have earned) as they would fain hasten on for (their) good, surely their doom would have been decreed to them. But We leave those who do not hope to meet Us (on the Day of Judgment) in their contumacy, blindly wandering (bewildered).

12. When affliction touches a man, he cries to Us whether lying, sitting, or standing; but when We remove his affliction, he passes on as though he had never called unto Us on account of the affliction which touched him; thus to the transgressors is made alluring what they do.

13. Indeed We did destroy generations before you upon committing wrong, and after Messengers had come to them with clear signs, but they would not believe. Thus do We recompense the guilty people.

14. Then We made you their successors in the land so that We might see how you act.

15. When Our clear signs are recited unto them, those who do not hope to meet Us say: "Bring a Qur'an other than this, or change it." Say: "It is not for me to change it as I please; I follow naught but what is revealed to me. Indeed, I fear the chastisement of a great day if I disobey my Lord."

16. Say: "If God had so pleased, I would not have recited it to you, nor would He have taught it to you. Indeed, I have lived among you an age before it. What then do you (still) not understand?"

17. Who then does more wrong than he who forges a lie against God or belies His signs? The guilty ones do not succeed.

18. They worship besides God what can neither hurt nor profit them, and they say: "These are our intercessors with God." Say: "Do you imagine that you inform God of what He does not know in the heavens and in the earth?" Glory be

to Him and Exalted is He far above what they associate (with Him).

19. Mankind was one community, but they later differed; had no word (of decree) already gone forth from your Lord, it would have been decided between them in respect of what they differed therein.

20. They say: "Why is a sign not sent to him from his Lord?" Say: "Indeed, the unseen is only for God, therefore wait; verily I am (also) with you waiting."

21. When We make people taste of (Our) mercy after an affliction has touched them, lo, they devise plots against Our signs. Say: "God is quicker in devising." Verily Our Messengers write down all what you devise.

22. He it is Who enables you to travel by land and sea; so when you board ships; they sail in a favourable breeze, rejoicing thereat, (and when) a violent gale comes to them, and the billows surge in on them from all sides, they think that they are encompassed therewith, then they cry praying to God, professing sincerity to Him in faith, saying: "If You (Lord) deliver us from this, we shall indeed be grateful."

23. But when He delivers them, behold, they rebel in the earth unjustly. O mankind! Your rebellion is against your own selves, a provision for the life (only) of this world, then to Us shall be your return, then shall We inform you of what you were doing.

24. The likeness of this world's life is only as water which We send down from the sky; by its mingling the produce of the earth grows, of which men and cattle eat, until, when the earth puts on its golden raiment and becomes ornamented, its people deem that they have power (of disposal) over it, suddenly comes Our command to it by night or by day, then We render it reaped, as though it had not existed the day before. Thus do We explain the signs in detail for people who reflect.

25. God calls (you) to the abode of peace and guides whomsoever He pleases to the Right Path.

26. For those who do good deeds is an excellent reward and more (than this awaits them). No darkness shall cover their faces nor shall ignominy (befall them); these are the dwellers of the Garden; in it shall they forever abide.

27. The recompense for the evil of those who have earned evil is the like thereof; ignominy shall come upon them; from (the Wrath of) God they shall have no protector; as if their faces have been covered with pieces of the (pitch) dark night; these are the inmates of the Fire; in it shall they abide forever.

28. On the Day (of Resurrection), when We gather them all together, We will then say to those who associated others (with Us): "Keep where you are, you and your associated gods." Then We shall separate them, one from the other, and their associate gods shall say (to them): "It was not us that you worshipped.

29. "God, therefore, is sufficient witness between us and you (that) we were certainly unaware of your worship (of us)."

30. There shall every soul realize what it has sent before, and they shall be brought back to God, their True Lord, and what they fabricated will vanish from them.

31. Say: "Who provides you with sustenance from the sky and the earth? Or who controls your hearing and sight? And who brings forth the living from the dead, and the dead from the living? And who administers all affairs?" They will then say: "(It is none but) God." Then say: "Will you not then fear God?"

32. Then this is God, your True Lord; what is apart from truth but error; whereto then are you turned away?

33. Thus is the word of your Lord that proved true against those who transgress, for they do not believe.

34. Say (O Our Messenger Muhammad): "Of your associates, is there anyone who can originate the creation then repeat it?" Say: "God alone does, in fact, originate the creation and repeat it; whereunto are you then inclined away?"

35. Say: "Of your associates, is there any who can guide to the truth?" Say: "It is God alone Who guides to the truth; is then He Who guides to truth more worthy to be followed or is it that who himself does not go aright unless he himself is guided? What then has befallen you? How (ill) do you judge?"

36. Most of them do not follow (anything) but (their own) conjecture; surely conjecture cannot avail anything

against the truth; verily God knows all that they do.

37. This Qur'an is not to be forged by anyone besides God, but it is a confirmation of (the Scriptures) that went before it and (the clearest) explanation of the Book; there is no doubt therein, it is from the Lord of the Worlds.

38. Or do they say: "He (Prophet Muhammad) has forged it"? Say: "Bring then a sura it and call for (your aid) whomsoever you can besides God if you be truthful."

39. Nay! They rejected that which they did not comprehend with knowledge and whose explanation did not come to them; even thus did those before them deny; see then what the end of the unjust ones was.

40. Of them is he who believes in it, and of them is he who does not believe in it; your Lord knows the mischief-makers.

41. If they reject you, say: "For me are my deeds, and for you yours; you are clear of what I do, and I am clear of what you do."

42. Of them are those who hearken to you. Can you make the deaf hear though they do not understand?

43. And of them are those who look at you. Can you guide the blind though they do not see?

44. God does not do any injustice to people, but people do injustice to their own selves.

45. On the day (of Resurrection) when He gathers them as though they had not tarried but an hour of the day, they will recognize each other. Indeed, those who rejected the meeting with God and were not guided aright will perish.

46. If We let you behold something of (Our wrath) that We warn them against or (before that) We take you to Ourselves, (even) then to Us is their return, then God is a Witness to all that they do.

47. For every people there was a messenger, and when their messenger (was sent), the matter between them was decided with equity, and they shall not (in the least) be wronged.

48. They say: "When will this promise come to pass, if you are truthful?"

49. Say: "I do not have for myself any harm, nor any benefit, except what God pleases. To every people is an ap-

pointed term; when their term comes, they shall neither retard even an hour, nor go before it."

50. Say: "Do you see if His chastisement comes upon you by night or by day, what then is there of it that the guilty hasten for?"

51. Is it (only) when it comes to pass that you will believe in it? Now do you believe when you have been (challenging it) and hastening it on?

52. Then it shall be said to those who had been unjust: "Taste the abiding punishment! Would you (then) receive other than what you have wrought?"

53. They ask you: "Is that true?" Say: "Aye! By my Lord: verily, it is the truth; you will not escape (His wrath)."

54. If every soul that has done injustice had all that is in the earth, it would assuredly ransom itself therewith; they will proclaim their repentance when they behold the doom, and it shall be decided between them with justice, and they shall not be dealt with unjustly.

55. Be it known that God's is what is in the heavens and the earth. Be it (also) known that God's promise is true, yet most of them do not know.

56. He grants life and causes death, and unto Him (alone) shall you all return.

57. O mankind! Indeed an exhortation has come to you from your Lord, and a cure for (the diseases) that are in your hearts, a guidance and mercy for the believers.

58. Say (that) in the Grace of God and in His Mercy, in that they should rejoice; it is better than (the wealth) that they gather.

59. Say: "See what (things) of sustenance God has sent down for you, then you made something of it unlawful and (something) lawful." Say: "Has God permitted you or have you forged a lie against God?"

60. What do those who forge lies against God think of the Day of Resurrection? God is the Lord of Grace for mankind, but most of them do not give thanks.

61. You are not (engaged) in any affair, nor do you recite any part of the Qur'an, nor are you doing any deed but We Witness over you when you are engrossed therein. And even the weight of an atom does not lie concealed from your

Lord in the earth or in the heavens, nor anything less than that nor greater but it is (recorded) in a clear book.

62. Be it known that there shall be no fear on the friends of God, no shall they grieve;

63. (For) they believed and guarded themselves against evil;

64. For them are glad tidings in the life in this world and in the hereafter; the promise of God suffers no change; that is the great achievement.

65. Do not let their discourse grieve you, Glory is wholly God's; He is the all-Hearing, the all-Knowing.

66. Be it known that God's is whatever in the heavens and the earth; those who call unto others besides God do not really follow any associates (of God); they do not follow anything but (their own) conjecture, and they simply lie.

67. He it is Who made for you the night to rest therein, and made you the sight-giving day. Surely there are signs in it for people who hearken.

68. They say: "God has taken a son (to Himself)!" Glory be to Him! He is the self-Sufficient; His (exclusively) is whatever in the heavens and in the earth; you have no authority for this. Do you say against God what you do not know?

69. Say: "Indeed, those who forge a lie against God never succeed."

70. A provision (there will be only) in this world, then to Us (only) is their return, then shall We make them taste severe chastisement for what they disbelieved.

71. Recite to them the story of Noah when he said to his people: "O my people! If my stay and my reminding (you) of the signs of God be hard on you, yet on God do I rely; muster, therefore your designs, and (gather) your false gods; then do not let your designs be dubious, then pass your sentence on me and give no respite.

72. "But if you turn back, then I did not ask any recompense from you; my recompense is only (expected) from God, and I am commanded to be of those submitted to God (Muslims)."

73. But they rejected him, so We delivered him and those with him in the ark, and We made them successors, and We drowned those who rejected Our signs; see then what the

end of the warned ones was!

74. Then We raised up after him messengers to their (respective) people; they came to them with clear evidences, but they would not believe in what they had rejected before. Thus do We seal up the hearts of the transgressors!

75. Then We sent after them Moses and Aaron to Pharaoh and his chiefs with Our signs (miracles), but they showed arrogance and were guilty people.

76. So when the truth came to them from Us, they said: "Indeed, this is (but) clear sorcery."

77. Moses said: "Do you say (this) of the truth when it has come to you? Is it sorcery? Sorcerers do not succeed."

78. "Have you come to us to turn away from (the faith) that we found our fathers doing, and that for you two (only) may be the greatness in the land? But we are not believers in (either of) you."

79. Pharaoh said: "Bring me every sorcerer (thoroughly) skilled."

80. When the sorcerers came, Moses said to them: "Cast down what you have to cast."

81. So when they cast down (their rods and cords), Moses said (to them): "What you have brought is sorcery; God will presently make it naught; indeed, God voids the work of the mischief-makers."

82. God will prove the truth to be the truth by His Word, though the guilty ones are averse (to it).

83. But none believed in Moses except the posterity of his people, in spite of the fear of Pharaoh and their chiefs, lest he should torment them; surely Pharaoh was mighty in the land; verily he was extravagant.

84. Moses said: "O my people! If you (really) believe in God, then on Him (alone) rely, if you submit (to God)."

85. Then they said: "On God (alone) do we rely! Lord! Do not subject us to a trial from the unjust people.

86. "And deliver us by Your mercy from the disbelieving people."

87. We revealed to Moses and his brother: "Take for your people houses to abide in Egypt, and make your houses places of worship, and establish (regular) prayers, and give glad tidings to the believers."

88. Moses (prayed): "O Lord! Indeed You have given Pharaoh and his chiefs splendour and riches in the life of this world, (is it) O Lord so that they might lead (people) astray from Your Path? O Lord! Destroy their riches and harden their hearts so that they will not believe until they see the painful chastisement."

89. He said: "Indeed, the prayer of both of you (Moses and Aaron) is accepted. Keep then fast to the Right path and do not follow the path of those who do not know."

90. We caused the children of Israel to pass (safely) through the sea, then Pharaoh and his hosts chased them in rebellion and hostility. When drowning overtook him, he (cried saying): "I believe that there is no god but (He) in Whom the children of Israel believe, and I submit (to God)."

91. Now! You disobeyed before, and you were among the mischief-makers!

92. But this day We shall save you in your body so that you may become a sign (of Ours) to those who come after you! Yet many are heedless to Our signs."

93. Indeed We lodged the children of Israel (in) a true lodging, and provided them with good things (for their sustenance); but they did not differ until the knowledge had come to them; your Lord will judge on the Day of Resurrection in what they had disagreed.

94. But if you are in doubt about what We have sent down to you, ask those who read the Book (sent) before you. Indeed, the truth has come to you from your Lord, so do not entertain any doubt.

95. Nor be of those who rejected the signs of God (for) then you should also be of the losers.

96. Indeed, those against whom the Word of your Lord has proved true will not believe,

97. Even if every (sort of) sign comes to them, until they witness the grievous chastisement.

98. Why then was there no town that believed, so its faith should have availed it, except the people of Jonah? When they believed, We removed from them the torment of ignominy in the life of the world and provided them (with comfort to enjoy it) for a fixed while.

99. Had (your Lord) pleased, surely all those who are on

the earth would have believed; will you then compel people against their will to become believers?

100. It is not for any soul to believe except by God's permission; while He casts uncleanliness (of infidelity) on those who do not use (their) common sense.

101. Say: "Observe what is in the heavens and the earth," but signs and warnings do not avail people who do not believe.

102. Do they then wait for (anything) but the like of the days of those who passed away before them? Say: "Wait then; verily I too am waiting with you."

103. We shall ultimately deliver Our messengers and those who believe; even so it is binding on Us (that) We deliver the believers.

104. Say: "O people! If you are in doubt about my religion, then (know that) I do not worship those whom you worship besides God; (I only) worship God Who takes you away (from this world), and I am (commanded) to be of the believers."

105. And say: "Set your face towards religion uprightly and do not be polytheists.

106. "And do not call (anyone) besides God, that which neither benefits you nor harms you; if you do, then (beware!) you will be of the unjust ones."

107. Should God afflict you with any harm, none can remove it but He, and if He wills any good to you, none can repel His Grace; He brings it to whomsoever He pleases of His servants; He is the oft-Forgiving, the Merciful.

108. Say: "O people! Indeed the truth (Qur'an) has come to you from your Lord: therefore whosoever receives the guidance, he receives guidance for his own good; whosoever strays, most surely he strays to its detriment; I am not a custodian over you."

109. And (O Our Messenger Muhammad): Follow what is revealed to you and forbear till God grants (His) Judgment; He is the best of all judges.

Hud

In the name of God, the Beneficent, the Merciful.

1. Alif, Lam, Ra. (This is) a Book whose verses are firmly arranged (together) then separated (in revelation), from the all-Wise, the all-Aware.

2. That you should not worship (anyone) but God; verily I am a warner for you from Him, and a bearer of glad tidings;

3. And (to preach to you): "Seek the forgiveness of your Lord, then turn to Him repentant; He will provide you with a goodly provision to an appointed term, and bestow His grace upon everyone of merit; if you turn back, then verily I fear for you the torment of a great day.

4. "Unto God is your return, and He has power over all things."

5. Behold! They fold up their hearts that they may conceal (their infidelity) from Him. Behold! When they put their garments as a covering, He knows (all) that they conceal, and all that they reveal; verily He knows (the inmost secrets) of the hearts.

6. There is no moving creature on earth but on God is its sustenance, and He knows its resting-place and its repository; all is in the manifest Book.

7. It is He Who created the heavens and the earth in six days-and His Throne was on the water-that He might try you, which of you is best in conduct, and if you (O Our Messenger Muhammad) say: "You shall surely be raised up after death," surely will those who disbelieve say: "This is (nothing) but open sorcery."

8. If We hold back from them the torment until a reckoned time, they will surely say: "What holds it back?" Beware! On the day it comes to them, it shall not be turned away from them, and that which they used to scoff at will encircle them.

9. If We make man taste mercy from Us, (and) then take it from him; verily he is despairing, ungrateful.

10. If We make him taste (Our) favours after distress has afflicted him, he will surely say: "The evils have (all) gone away from me." Indeed he is joyous, boastful,

11. Except those who forbear and do good deeds; for these there is forgiveness and a great recompense.

12. So perchance you may (be inclined) to give up a part of what is revealed to you, and your breast becomes straitened by it lest they should say: "Why has a treasure not been sent down to him or an angel come with him?" You are but a warner, and God is the Custodian over all things.

13. Or do they say that he has forged it? Say: "Bring then ten surahs like it forged, and call (to your aid) whomsoever you can besides God, if you are truthful."

14. If they do not answer you, know then that this (Qur'an) is revealed (only) by God's knowledge, and that there is no god but He! Will you then submit?

15. We shall pay whosoever desires the life and pomp of this world (the recompense for) their deeds therein; they shall suffer no loss.

16. These are they for whom there is nothing in the hereafter but the Fire, and vain shall be all that they wrought in it, and vain shall be all what they were doing.

17. Can they be like the one who has a clear proof from his Lord and a witness follows him from Him, and he is preceded by the Book of Moses, a guide and a mercy (testifying to it)? These believe in it, and whosoever of the parties (of idolaters) disbelieves in it, the Fire is the promised place; so, do not be in doubt about it; verily it is the truth from your Lord; but most people do not believe.

18. Who is more unjust than he who forges a lie against God? These shall be presented before their Lord, and the witnesses shall say: "These are those who lied against their Lord." Now verily the curse of God is on the unjust.

19. Those who hinder (others) from the path of God and seek to make it (look) crooked, disbelieving in the hereafter,

20. These shall in no way frustrate (God's design) on earth, nor shall there be any protecting friends for them besides God. The torment shall be doubled for them; they could not bear to hear, nor could they see.

21. These are they who have lost their lives, and what they invented in their minds have deserted them.

22. They are the very ones who in the Hereafter will

surely be the greatest losers.

23. Those who believe and do good deeds, humbling themselves before their Lord, are the dwellers of Paradise, they will (forever) abide therein.

24. The two parties are like the blind and the deaf, and those with sight and with hearing. Are the two equal in their likeness? Will you not then take heed?

25. Indeed We sent Noah to his people (and he said to them): "I am a clear warner for you,

26. "That you shall not worship (anyone) but God; verily I fear for you the chastisement of a painful day."

27. Then the chiefs of those who disbelieved from among his people said: "We only see in you a man like ourselves, and we do not see that any has followed you except those who are the lowest (in social status) of us (those who act) on first impressions; nor do we see in you any excellence over us; nay, we deem you liars."

28. He said: "O my people! Do you think that if I have with me clear proof from my Lord, and He has bestowed on me mercy from Himself, that it has been made obscure to you (through your ignorance) that we shall compel you to (accept) it even though you are averse to it?

29. "And, O my people! I do not ask of you any wealth in return for it; my reward is exclusively with God, and I shall not drive away those who believe; verily, they shall meet their Lord. But I see you a people (who act) ignorantly.

30. "And, o my people! Who will help me against God if I drive them away? Will you not then take heed?

31. "I do not say to you that with me are the treasures of God, and I do not know the unseen, nor do I say that I am an angel, and I do not say about those whom your eyes hold in contempt that God will never bestow on them any good. God knows best what is in their hearts, for verily then I should be among the unjust."

32. They said: "O Noah! Indeed you have disputed with us and you have prolonged the dispute with us, now bring us what you have threatened us with, if you are among the truthful."

33. He said: "Indeed, God will bring it to you only if He wills, and by no means shall you prevail against Him.

34. "My good advice will not avail you, if I intend to give you good advice, if God wills that He should leave you to stray. He is your Lord, and to Him shall you be returned."

35. Or they say: "He (Muhammad) has forged it (Qur'an)." Say: "If I have forged it, my guilt shall fall on me, and I am free of your guilt."

36. It was revealed to Noah that "Never will any of your people believe except those who have already believed; therefore, do not grieve for what they do.

37. "And make an ark under Our eyes and revelation, and do not plead with Me about the unjust; verily they shall be drowned."

38. He began making the ark, and whenever the chiefs of his people passed by him, they mocked at him. He said: "If you mock at us, verily we too shall mock at you, even as you mock at us.

39. "Soon shall you know on whom a torment which will disgrace him descends, and upon whom (ultimately) a lasting torment falls."

40. When Our command came, and water gushed forth out of the oven, We said: "Carry (O Noah) into it a pair, a male and a female, of each kind, and your family, except those on whom the sentence has already been passed, and those who believe." There were only a few who believed with him.

41. He (Noah) said: "Embark upon it. In the name of God its sailing and its anchorage shall be! My Lord is oft-Forgiving, most Merciful."

42. It (ark) moved on with them amid waves (towering) like mountains, and Noah called out to his son, who was aloof: "O my son! Embark with us and do not be with the disbelievers."

43. He said: "I will betake myself to a mountain that shall secure me from the water." He (Noah) said: "There is no protector today from God's decree but he (of whom) He has mercy," and a wave passed between them, so he was among the drowned.

44. It was said: "O earth! Swallow down your water, and O sky! Withhold (your rain);" the water abated, and the decree was fulfilled, and it rested on (Mount) al-Judi, and it

was said: "Away with the unjust people!"

45. Noah cried to his Lord and said: "Lord! My son is of my family, and verily Your promise is true, and You are the most just of judges."

46. He said: "O Noah! Indeed, he is not of your family; his conduct is not righteous; therefore, do not seek of Me that of which you have no knowledge; verily I admonish you lest you should be of the ignorant."

47. He said: "O Lord! I seek refuge in You from asking You that of which I have no knowledge. Unless You forgive me and have mercy on me, I shall be of the losers."

48. It was said: "O Noah! Debark with peace from Us and blessings on you and on the people that will spring from those with you, and there shall be (other) people whom We shall afford provisions, then a painful torment shall afflict them from Us."

49. These are (some) of the tidings of the unseen which We reveal to you (O Our Messenger Muhammad); you did not know them yourself nor your people before. Be, therefore, patient; verily the end is (only) for the pious ones.

50. To (the people of) Ad (We sent) their brother Hud. He said: "O my people! Worship (the only) God, you have no god other than He; you are but forgerers.

51. "O my people! I do not ask you any recompense for it; my recompense is only with Him Who created me. Do you not then understand?

52. "And O my people! Ask forgiveness of your Lord and turn repentant unto Him; He sends clouds on you pouring down abundant rain, and He adds strength to your strength. Do not turn back as guilty ones."

53. They said: "O Hud! You have not brought us any clear sign (of your truthfulness) and we will not desert our gods on account of your words, nor are we believers in you!

54. "We say nothing but that some of our gods have smitten you with evil." He said: "I call God to witness, and you also witness that I am clear of what you associate-

55. "Besides Him, and then conspire against me, all of you, and give no respite.

56. "Indeed I rely on God, my Lord and your Lord; there is no living creature but that He holds it (in His control) by its

forelock; verily my Lord is on the Right Path.

57. "But if you turn back, then indeed I have conveyed to you that which I have been sent, and my Lord will make people other than you succeed you, and you cannot do harm to Him in any way at all; verily my Lord is the (ever) protecting (over all things)."

58. When Our decree came to pass, We delivered Hud and those who believed with him by a mercy from Us, and We delivered them from a (very) severe torment.

59. This was (the people) of Hud; they denied the signs of their Lord and disobeyed His messengers, and followed the bidding of every insolent tyrant.

60. They were followed in this world by a curse, and on the Day of Resurrection too. Behold! Verily (the people of Ad) disbelieved in their Lord. Away with the people of Hud.

61. To the (people of) Thamud We sent their brother Salih. He said: "O my people! Worship (none but the only) God. You have no god other than He; He raised you from the earth and has given you to flourish therein; therefore, ask forgiveness of Him, then turn repentant to Him. Indeed my Lord is (ever) nigh."

62. They said: "O Salih! Indeed you were amongst us in whom (our) hopes were centered before this. Do you (now) forbid us from worshipping what our fathers worshipped? We are in a disquieting doubt about that to which you call us."

63. He said: "O my people! Do you not see if I am on a clear guidance from my Lord and He has granted me mercy from Himself: who would help me against God had I disobeyed Him? Indeed you would then increase my lot nothing but loss.

64. "O my people! This is God's she-camel for you a sign (of my truthfulness); therefore, leave her to (freely) pasture on God's earth and do not touch her with any harm, for then a ready torment will overtake you."

65. Yet they hamstrung her. Then he said: "Enjoy (yourselves) in your abode for three days; that is a promise not to be belied."

66. When Our decree came (to pass), We delivered Salih and those who believed with him by mercy from Us, and

(We delivered them) from the ignominy of that day; verily your Lord is the all-Strong, the Almighty.

67. The (mighty) blast seized those who were unjust, so they became in their homes motionless corpses,

68. As though they never dwelt therein. Behold! (The people of) Thamud disbelieved in their Lord. Away with (the people of) Thamud.

69. Indeed Our messengers (angels) came to Abraham with glad tidings, saying: "Peace!" (Abraham) answered: "Peace," not delaying to bring a roasted calf.

70. But when he saw that their hands did not extend towards it, he mistrusted them and conceived fear of them. "Do not fear us," they said; "We are sent to Lot's people."

71. His wife was standing by; she laughed, then We bestowed upon her the glad tidings of Isaac and after him Jacob.

72. She said: "O woe unto me! Shall I bear a son (now that) I am (extremely) old? This indeed is amazing!"

73. They said: "Do you wonder at the decree of God? God's mercy and His blessings be upon you, O people of the House! Indeed He (alone) is Praiseworthy, all-Glorious!"

74. When the awe had gone away from Abraham and the glad tidings came to him, he began pleading with Us (on behalf of) the people of Lot.

75. Indeed Abraham was indeed forbearing, compassionate, oft-returning (to God).

76. "O Abraham! Forsake this! Indeed the decree of your Lord has come to pass, and verily to them a torment shall come (that is) irreversible."

77. When Our messengers (angels) came to Lot, he was grieved for them and felt his arm straitened to protect them and said: "This is a distressful day."

78. His people came rushing to him, for aforetime they did evil deeds. "O my people! These are my daughters; they are purer for you, so guard yourselves against (the punishment of) God, and do not disgrace me regarding my guests. Is there anyone among you whose mind is sound?"

79. They said: "Indeed you know that we have no need for your daughters, and you very well know what we intend (to do)."

80. He said: "Would that I had strength to resist you or betake myself to a strong supporter."

81. They said: "O Lot! Verily we are messengers from your Lord! They shall never reach you! So, depart with your people while a part of the night remains, and let none of you turn back-save your wife. Surely what befalls them shall befalls her too; their appointed time is surely the morning; is not the morning nigh?"

82. So when Our decree came to pass, We turned their towns upside down and rained on them hard stones of baked clay, (spreading) layer on layer,

83. Marked (for punishment) with your Lord; nor are their ruins distant from the unjust ones.

84. To (the people of) Midian (We sent) their brother Shu'ayb. He said: "O my people! Worship God (alone); you have no god other than Him, and do not give short measure and weight; verily I see you in prosperity, and verily I fear for you the torment of an all-Encompassing Day.

85. "And O my people! Give full measure and (correct) weight in justice, and do not defraud people of their things, and do not act corruptly in the earth, making mischief therein.

86. "That which is left by God to you is good for you, if you are believers, but I am not a keeper over you."

87. They said: "O Shu'ayb! Does your religion enjoin you that we should forsake what our fathers worshipped or that we (should forsake to) do with our property what we please? Forsooth you are the one forbearing, the right-minded."

88. He said: "O my people! Do you not see if I am on a clear sign (guidance) from my Lord, and (He) has provided me from Himself with sustenance (pure and) good, and that I do not desire that in opposition to you I betake myself to that from which I forbid you? I desire naught but the reform of what I am able to do, my guidance is with none but God; on Him (alone) do I rely, and to Him (alone) do I turn (for aid).

89. "And, O my people! Do not let your opposition to me cause you to sin lest befalls you that which is like what befell the people of Noah, or the people of Hud, or the people

of Salih; nor the people of Lot are far off from you.

90. "Ask forgiveness of your Lord, and turn to Him (repentant); verily my lord is all-Merciful, Loving, Kind."

91. They said: "O Shu'ayb! We do not understand much of what you say, and most surely we see you weak amongst us, and were it not for your family, we would surely have stoned you, and you are not powerful against us."

92. He said: "Is my family more esteemed by you than God? And you cast Him behind your backs neglectfully? Indeed, my Lord encompasses all that you do.

93. "And O my people! Act according to your ability; I, too, am acting; soon will you come to know on whom comes the torment that will disgrace him, and who it is that lies and watches; verily, I, too, am watching with you."

94. When Our decree came to pass, We delivered Shu'ayb and those who believed with him by mercy from Us, and the (mighty) blast overtook those who did injustice so they became in their homes motionless corpses,

95. As though they had not dwelt therein. Behold! Away with (the people of) Midian, even as (the people of) Thamud were cast away.

96. Indeed We sent Moses with Our signs, and an authority (which was) manifest,

97. To Pharaoh and his chiefs, but they followed the bidding of Pharaoh, (though) the bidding of Pharaoh was not a right directive.

98. He shall lead his people on the Day of Resurrection, and bring them down to the Fire; but woeful will be the leading and the place led to.

99. They are followed by a curse in this (life) and also on the Day of Resurrection, and woeful is the gift which shall be given (to them).

100. This is of the account of the communities We relate to you (O Our Messenger Muhammad). Of them some are standing and some have been mown down (by the passage of time).

101. We did no injustice to them; they were unjust to their own selves; so, their gods, whom they invoked besides God, did not avail them aught when the decree of your Lord came to pass; they did not add (aught to their lot but

perdition).

102.   Such is the grasp (of the punishment) of your Lord when He grasps the towns while they are unjust. Indeed His retribution is painful, severe.

103.   Verily, in this there is a sign for him that fears the chastisement of the hereafter. This is a day for which mankind shall be gathered together, and this day shall be witnessed (by all).

104.   We do not delay it except to an appointed term.

105.   When it approaches, no soul shall speak but by His leave; then (some) of them shall be wretched and some blessed.

106.   As for those who shall be doomed, these shall be (hurled) into the Fire; for them shall be sighing and groaning therein.

107.   They shall abide therein so long as the heavens and the earth endure, except that which your Lord wills. Surely your Lord is the (Mighty) Doer of whatsoever He pleases.

108.   As for those who will be blessed, they shall be in the garden (Paradise) abiding therein so long as the heavens and the earth endure, except that which your Lord wills; (it will be) an unceasing gift.

109.   Be, therefore, in no doubt concerning what these people worship; they worship just as their fathers worshipped before, and verily We will pay them back in full their due share without any rebate.

110.   Indeed We bestowed the Book unto Moses, but variance was created in it; had no word gone forth from your Lord, the matter would surely have been decided between them, and verily they are in doubt (about the Qur'an which is) disquieting (to them).

111.   Indeed to all will your Lord pay back in full their recompense for all their deeds; verily He is fully aware of all that they do.

112.   Stand then fast (O Our Messenger Muhammad) on the Right Path as you are commanded (by your Lord), and also he who has turned (to God) with you, and (O men) do not be inordinate. Indeed He well sees whatever you do.

113.   Do not incline to those who act unjustly lest the Fire should touch you, for there is no protector for you be-

sides God, nor shall you be helped.

114. Establish prayer in the two ends of the day, and at the approaches of the night. Indeed the good deeds take away the evil ones; this is a reminder for the (believers who are) mindful (of their Lord).

115. Be patient, for verily God does not suffer the recompense of the righteous ones to be lost.

116. But why were not there any generations before you, those endowed with understanding, forbidding mischief on earth, except a few of those whom We delivered from among them? Those who did injustice followed what they were made to enjoy (of the plenty), and they were guilty.

117. Nor was your Lord to destroy communities unjustly while their people were righteous.

118. Had your Lord willed, He would certainly have made mankind a single (unified) nation, but they will never cease to differ,

119. Except he on whom your Lord has had mercy, and for this did He create them; the promise of your Lord is fulfilled: I will certainly fill Hell with the jinn and man altogether.

120. All that We relate to you of the accounts of the messengers is to confirm your heart therewith. The truth has come to you in this, and an admonition and a reminder to the believers.

121. Say (O Our Messenger Muhammad) to those who do not believe: "Act as you wish; verily we, too, shall act,

122. "And wait! For verily we, too, shall wait;

123. "And God's is the unseen (worlds) of the heavens and the earth, and to Him (only) is the whole affair returned, so worship Him and rely (only) on Him; your Lord is not heedless of what you do."

Joseph
(Yousuf)

In the name of God, the Beneficent, the Merciful.

1. Alif, Lam, Ra. These are the verses of the Book (which makes the truth) manifest.

2. Verily We have sent it down, the Arabic Qur'an, so that you may understand.

3. We narrate to you (O Our Prophet Muhammad) the most excellent of narratives by (means of) what We have revealed to you, this Qur'an; though before this you were unaware.

4. Joseph said to his father (Jacob): "O my father! Verily I saw (in a vision) eleven stars, the sun, and the moon, all prostrating to me."

5. He (Jacob) said: "O my son! (Beware!) Do not relate your dream to your brothers lest they should plot against you a (wicked) plot. Verily Satan is an open enemy to man.

6. "And thus will your Lord choose you and teach you the interpretation of sayings (visions), and perfect His Grace unto you and the children of Jacob even as He perfected it to your [fore]fathers aforetime, Abraham and Isaac. Verily your Lord is all-Knowing, all-Wise."

7. Indeed, in (the accounts of) Joseph and his brothers there are signs for the inquirers.

8. They said: "Surely Joseph and his brother are dearer to our father than we are, though we are a bigger group. Verily our father is in manifest error.

9. "(So) slay Joseph! Or cast him out to some (other) land, so that to you (exclusively) will be the attention of your father, and you may be after that a righteous people."

10. A speaker among them said: "Do not slay Joseph but throw him into the bottom of the well, perhaps some wayfarers may take him up, if you must do it."

11. They said: "O our father! What causes you not to trust us regarding Joseph? Verily, we are his well-wishers.

12. "Send him with us tomorrow so that he may enjoy himself and play, and we will surely be his guards."

13. He said: "It certainly saddens me that you should take him away, and I fear the wolf might devour him while you are inattentive to him."

14. They said: "If the wolf were to devour him while we are (such a large group), verily then we should be losers."

15. So when they had gone with him and agreed to put him in the bottom of the well, We revealed to him (to Joseph, saying): "You will (one day) most surely tell them of

this deed of theirs while they cannot recognize (you)."

16. And they came to their father at nightfall weeping.

17. They said: "O our father! Verily we went racing and left Joseph by our belongings, then a wolf devoured him, but you will not believe us, even if we are truthful."

18. They came with his shirt (stained) with fake blood. He said: "Nay! You have beguiled your (guilty) selves into something, yet (my course is) patience, and God is He Whose aid is sought against what you describe."

19. There came a caravan, and they sent their water drawer and he let down his bucket. He said: "O good news! This is a youth!" And they concealed him as an article of merchandise, and verily God was the Knower of all that they were doing.

20. And they sold him for a paltry price, a few counted dirhams, and they had no interest in him.

21. And the Egyptian who purchased him said to his wife: "Give him an honourable place, maybe he will benefit us, or maybe we will adopt him as a son." Thus did We establish Joseph in the land (Egypt) and that We may teach him the interpretation of events (seen in visions). Indeed God is Predominant over his affairs, though most people do not know.

22. When he (Joseph) attained his prime (maturity), We bestowed upon him authority (prophethood) and knowledge, and thus do We recompense those who do good deeds.

23. She, in whose house he was, sought to seduce him from his (pure) self, and she (even) locked the doors and said: "Now come!" He said: "(I seek) God's refuge! Verily He is my Lord! He made my abode good; verily the unjust ones do not prosper."

24. Indeed she longed for him, and he (also) would have longed for her, had he not seen the evidence of his Lord. Thus it was that We might turn away from him (all) evil and shameful deeds; verily he was (one) of Our (true) servants.

25. They both raced to the door, and she rent his shirt from behind, and they met her husband at the door. She said: "What is the punishment for the one who intends to commit an evil act to your wife save that he be imprisoned or painfully tormented?"

26. He (Joseph) said: "(But) she sought to seduce me from

my (pure) self." A witness of her own household testified: "If his shirt is rent from the front, she speaks the truth while he lies,

27. "But if his shirt is rent from behind, then she lies while he is the truthful one."

28. So when he (husband) saw the shirt rent from behind, he said: "Verily it is a guile act of you women! Verily your guile is great!

29. "O Joseph! Leave this affair, and you (wife) ask forgiveness for your sins; verily you are of the guilty (ones)."

30. The women in the city said: "The wife of the great al-`Aziz (chief) seeks to seduce her slave from his (pure) self. Verily he has affected her deeply with love. Verily we see her in manifest error."

31. When she heard of their scheming talk, she sent (inviting) them, and she prepared for them a repast, and, giving each one of them a knife, she called (on Joseph saying): "Come out to them." So when they saw him, they extolled him, and (in their amazement) cut their hands and said (amazingly): "Hasha lillah" (imperfection is far from God)! This is not a mortal; this but a noble angel!"

32. She said: "This is he about whom you blamed me, and indeed I sought to seduce him from his (pure) self, but he strongly abstained from committing sins, and (now) if he does not do what I bade him, he shall certainly be imprisoned, and he shall certainly be of those debased!"

33. He said: "O Lord! Prison is dearer to me than that to which they invite me, and if You do not turn their guile away from me, I may yield to them and become of the ignorant ones."

34. His Lord, thereupon, heard (his prayer), and He turned their guile away from him. Verily He is the all-Hearing, the all-Knowing.

35. Then it occurred to them (even) after they had seen the signs (of his innocence), that they should imprison him for some time.

36. Two youths entered with him the prison. One of them said (to Joseph): "Verily I saw myself (in a vision) pressing wine." The other said: "I saw myself (in a vision) carrying bread on my head and birds were eating thereof. Inform us

of its interpretation. Verily we see you as one who does good deeds."

37. He (Joseph) said: "There shall not come to you any food with which you are fed but I inform you both of its interpretation before it even reaches you. This is of what my Lord has taught me. Verily I have forsaken the religion of people who do not believe in God, and are disbelievers in the hereafter.

38. "And I follow the religion of my fathers Abraham, Isaac and Jacob, and it is not (lawful) for us to associate aught with God. This is by God's Grace upon us and on mankind but most people do not give thanks.

39. "O my fellow inmates! Are (many) gods differing from each other better, or God, the One, the all-Dominant?

40. "You only worship besides Him (mere) names which you have named, you and your fathers. God has not sent down for them any authority; there is no judgment but God's. He has bidden that you worship none but Him. This is the right religion, but most people do not know.

41. "O my fellow inmates! As to one of you, he will pour out wine for his lord to drink; as for the other, he shall be crucified, so much so that the birds shall eat from his head. The matter about which you two inquired is thus decreed."

42. He said to him of the two whom he knew would be delivered: "Mention me to your lord." But the devil caused him to forget mentioning him to his lord, so he remained in prison a few years.

43. The king said: "In truth, I saw (in a vision) seven fat kine devoured by seven lean ones, and seven green ears and others dry. O chiefs, explain to me (the meaning of) my dreams, if you can interpret a dream."

44. They said: "Confused dreams (are these)! We do not know the interpretation of such (confused) dreams."

45. One of the two who had been released remembered, even after a long time, and said: "I will expound to you its interpretation, so let me go (to the prison)."

46. "Joseph! O truthful one! Expound to us (the implication of) seven fat kine devoured by seven lean ones, and seven ears green and (seven) others dry, so that I may return to the people and they may know."

47. He said: "You shall sow for seven years as usual, but you should leave that which you reap in its ears except a little, of which you eat.

48. "Then shall come after that seven years of hardship (famine), which shall eat away all that you laid by beforehand for them except a little of what you preserved.

49. "Then people after that will have abundant rain, and in having it they will press wine."

50. The king said: "Bring him to me!" So when the messenger came to him, he (Joseph) said: "Go back to your lord and ask him what the matter with the women who cut their hands is; verily my Lord knows their guile."

51. The king said (to the women): "What was the matter with you when you sought to seduce Joseph from his (pure) self?" The women said: "Hasha lillah (far from God is every imperfection); we do not know of any evil (charge) against him!" The wife of al-Aziz said: "Now the truth has become manifest. I sought to seduce him from his (pure) self, and verily he is a truthful one!"

52. Joseph said: "This inquiry I caused that he might know that I have not been unfaithful in his absence, and that God does not guide the guile of the unfaithful ones.

53. "I do not exculpate myself. Verily (one's) self is wont to bid to evil except such as my Lord has had mercy on. Verily, my Lord is oft-Forgiving, all-Merciful."

54. The king said: "Bring him to me. I will choose him for my own service." So when he had spoken to him, he (king) said: "Verily you are henceforward in our own presence (honourably) accommodated, trusted!"

55. He said: "Set me (in authority) over the treasuries of the land; verily I am a (faithful) keeper, knowing well (its management)."

56. Thus did We establish Joseph in the land, to take possession therein as he pleased. We bestow Our mercy on whomsoever We will, and We do not waste the recompense of the doers of good.

57. Certainly the recompense of the hereafter is (much) better for those who believe and guard (themselves) against evil.

58. Joseph's brothers came and they entered, and he knew

them but they did not recognize him.

59. When he had furnished them with their provision, he said to them: "Bring me a brother of yours from your father; do not you see that I give full measure, and that I am the best of hosts?

60. "But if you do not bring him to me, then there shall be no measure for you with me, nor shall you (even) come near me."

61. They said: "We will seek to get him from his father, and we shall certainly do so."

62. He said to his servants: "Put their goods into their saddle-bags so that they may perceive it when they return to their family, perchance they might come back."

63. So when they returned to their father, they said: "O our father! The measure is denied to us. So send with us our brother, so that we may get the measure, and we will certainly guard him (well)."

64. He said: "Can I trust him to you except as I entrusted his brother to you aforetime? But God is the Best Guard and He is the Most Merciful of the merciful ones."

65. When they opened their belongings, they found their goods returned to them. They said: "O father! What (more) can we desire? Our goods have been returned to us, and we will bring more for our family and guard our brother, and we shall have in addition the measure of a camel (load)! This is (only) an easy measure."

66. (Jacob) said: "Never will I send him with you until you pledge a firm covenant in God's name that you will most surely bring him back to me, unless you are completely surrounded." When they pledged a covenant to him, he said: "(There is) God over all that we say, a Guardian-Witness.

67. He said: "O my sons! Do not enter through one gate, but rather enter through different gates, and I cannot avail you aught against God. The judgment is only God's. On Him do I rely, and on Him (alone) let the reliants rely."

68. When they had entered as they were bidden by their father, it did not avail them aught against (the decree of God); but (it was only) a desire in Jacob's heart which he satisfied, and verily he was endowed with knowledge for

We had taught him, though most people do not know.

69. When they entered unto Joseph, he lodged his brother (Benjamin) with himself (privately) and said: "I am your brother; therefore, do not grieve at what they do."

70. When he had furnished them with their provisions, the drinking cup was placed in his brother's saddlebag. Then a caller cried out: "O you of the caravan! Verily you are thieves!"

71. They said, while turning to them, "What is that which you miss?"

72. He said: "We miss the king's drinking cup and whosoever brings it shall have a camel load, and I am in charge of it."

73. They said: "By God! You know that we did not come to make mischief in the land, nor are we thieves."

74. They said: "But what shall be the punishment for this, if you (are proven to) be liars?"

75. They said: "The punishment for it shall be that he in whose bag it is found shall himself be (held as bondman) in penalty for it. Thus do we punish the wrong-doers."

76. Then he (Joseph) began (the search starting) with their sacks before that of his brother, then he drew it out of his brother's sack. Thus did We plan for Joseph; it was not (lawful) that he should take his brother under the king's law unless God willed it. We raise the degrees (of wisdom and knowledge) of whomsoever We will and above everyone endued with knowledge is the all-Knowing.

77. They said: "If he steals, indeed, a brother of his stole before." But Joseph kept it a secret to himself, and he did not disclose it to them. He said: "You are in an evil condition, and God knows best what you allege."

78. They said: "O al-Aziz! His father is very old; so, take one of us in his place. Verily we see you do good unto others."

79. He said: "God protect us that we should seize (anyone) other than him with whom we found our property, for verily we would then be among the unjust ones."

80. When they despaired of (moving) him, they retired whispering (to each other). The eldest among them said: "Do you not know how your father took a (firm) covenant

from you in God's name, and how you failed about Joseph aforetime? So, I will never leave this land until my father permits me or God decides for me; He is the best of judges.

81. "Return to your father and say: `O father! Verily your son committed theft; we bear no witness but to what we have known, and we could not guard against the unseen.

82. "And inquire in the town in which we were and the caravan with which we proceeded, and verily we are truthful.'"

83. He said: "Nay! You have contrived a (suitable) story for you; so (my course is) comely patience; maybe God will bring them to me all together; verily He is all-Knowing, all-Wise."

84. He turned away from them and said: "Alas! My grief for Joseph!" And his eyes were whitened with grief, and he was a repressor (of grief).

85. They said: "By God! You will not cease to remember Joseph until you are (seriously) ill or (until) you perish."

86. He said: "I only complain about my distress and grief to God, and I know from God what you do not.

87. "O my sons! Go and inquire about Joseph and his brother, and do not despair of God's mercy. Verily, only the disbelieving people despair of God's mercy."

88. So they came unto him and said: "O al-Aziz! Distress has touched us and our family, and we have (now) come only with scanty capital; so, give us full measure and bestow charity on us. Verily God rewards the charitable ones."

89. He said: "Do not you know what you did to Joseph and his brother when you were ignorant (of the consequences)?"

90. They said: "Are you indeed Joseph?!" He said: "Indeed I am Joseph, and this is my brother; in truth God has been gracious to us. Verily he who practices piety and is patient (is always rewarded), for verily God does not waste the reward of those who do good."

91. They said: "By God! God has indeed favoured you over us, and we were certainly guilty."

92. He said: "(There shall be) no reproof against you (from) this day (on); may God forgive you, and He is the Most Merciful of the merciful (ones).

93. "Take my shirt and cast it on my father's face and he shall thus recover his sight, and bring me all your family."

94. When the caravan with Joseph's shirt had left (Egypt), their father (even there in his place) said: "I feel the smell of Joseph, if you do not think that I dote."

95. They said: "By God! Verily you are in your error."

96. So when the bearer of glad tidings came, he cast it (the shirt) on his (Jacob's) face, and (forthwith) eye-sight returned to him. He said: "Did I not tell you that I certainly know from God what you do not?"

97. They said: "O father! Ask forgiveness for our sins; verily, we are guilty."

98. He said: "Soon will I ask forgiveness for you from my Lord: Verily He is the oft-Forgiving, Most Merciful."

99. When they entered in the presence of Joseph, he accommodated his parents with himself and said: "Enter Egypt, if God wills, (all of you) in security."

100. He raised his parents to the throne, and they fell down to him prostrating. He said: "O father! This is the interpretation of my dream of aforetime! Indeed, my Lord has made it come true, and indeed He was kind to me when He took me out of the prison and brought you from the desert (into this town to me), after Satan had sown dissension between me and my brothers. Verily my Lord is Benign to whomsoever He wills. Verily, He is all-Knowing, all-Wise.

101. "O Lord! Indeed You have given me of the dominion and taught me the interpretation of events (visions). O Originator of the heavens and the earth! You (alone) are my guardian in this world and the hereafter; cause me to die a Muslim (submitting to You) and join me with the righteous."

102. This is of the unseen which We reveal to you (O Our Messenger Muhammad), nor were you present with them when they resolved their affair, or when they were devising their plans.

103. Yet most people do not believe (it), though you desire it.

104. You do not ask of them a recompense for it; (it) is none other than an admonition to (all) the worlds (of creation).

105. How many a sign in the heavens and the earth

whereby they pass and turn away therefrom?

106. Most of them do not believe in God except the polytheists.

107. Then do they feel secure when an overwhelming chastisement comes to them from God or (that) the hour suddenly comes to them while they are unaware?

108. Say (O Our Messenger Muhammad): "This is my way; I invite (all of you) with clear sight to God, (which) I and he that follows me (possess). Glory be to God, and I am not one of the polytheists."

109. We did not send (messengers) before you but (they were) men to whom We revealed from (among) the people of the towns. Do they not travel in the land so that they may see what the end of those before them has been? Certainly the abode of the hereafter is the best for those who guard themselves (against evil). Do you not then understand?

110. Till when the messengers despaired and deemed that they were indeed belied, Our help came to them, and We delivered whomsoever We willed, and Our wrath is not warded off from the guilty people.

111. Indeed, in their stories is a lesson for men of understanding. It is not a tale which has been forged, but it is a confirmation of what went before, a detailed exposition of all things and a guide and mercy to people who believe.

The Thunder
(ar-Ra'd)

In the name of God, the Beneficent, the Merciful.

1. Alif, Lam, Mim, Ra. These are the verses of the Book, and that which has been revealed to you from your Lord is the truth, but most people do not believe.

2. God it is Who raised the heavens without any pillars that you see, then firmly established Himself on the Throne (of absolute authority), and made the sun and the moon subservient (to His Will); each runs its course to a time appointed (for it); He regulates the affair. He explains the signs so that you may be certain about meeting your Lord.

3. He it is Who spread out the earth and made in it firm mountains and flowing rivers; and of all fruits. He has made

in it in pairs, two (male and female) kinds; He causes the night to enshroud the day; verily in this there are signs for people who reflect.

4. In the earth are tracts, side by side, and gardens of vine, corn fields, and palm trees having one root and (others) having many, (although) they are all watered with one (and the same) water. Yet some We make more excellent than others in taste. Verily in this there are signs for people who understand.

5. If you wonder, then wondrous is their saying: "When we are dust, would we then surely be (returned) in a new creation?" These are they who disbelieve in their Lord, and these shall have collars (of servitude) around their necks, and they are the companions of the Fire, in it shall they forever abide.

6. They ask you to hasten on the evil (chastisement) before the good, and (although) indeed exemplary punishments have come to pass before them. Your Lord is indeed the Lord of forgiveness to people despite their injustice; verily your Lord is severe in requital.

7. Those who disbelieve say: "Why has no sign been revealed to him (Muhammad) from his Lord?" Verily you are a warner and a guide to every nation.

8. God knows what every female bears, and that which the wombs fall short (of completion), and that in which they increase; and of everything (there is) with Him a measure,

9. Knower of the unseen and the seen, the great, the Most Sublime.

10. Alike (to him) among you is he who conceals (his) speech or speaks aloud, and he who hides himself by night and goes forth by day.

11. For him there are (angels) following one another, before him and behind him, guarding him by God's command; verily God does not change the condition of people until they change what is in themselves; when God decrees to punish any people, there is none to repel His punishment; there is none besides Him to protect.

12. He it is Who shows you the lightning causing fear and hope, and He raises the laden clouds.

13. Thunder glorifies Him with praise, and the angels too

in awe for Him; and He sends the thunderbolts and smites with them whomsoever He wills; and yet they dispute concerning God while He is Mighty in prowess!

14. To Him (alone) the true prayer is due, and those to whom they pray besides Him give no answer, yet (they are) like one who stretches his two hands to water that it may reach his mouth, but it will not reach it, and the prayer of the infidels does nothing but goes far astray.

15. Whatever is in the heavens and the earth prostrate to God (alone) willingly or by constraint; so do their shadows also at morn and in the eve.

16. Say (O Our Messenger Muhammad): "Who is the Lord of the heavens and the earth?" Say: "God!" Say: "Do you still take guardians besides Him that can do neither benefit nor harm to their own selves?" Say: "Are the blind and the seeing alike? Or can darkness and light be akin? Or have they made partners to God who have created (any) creation like His, so that what is created has become confused to them?" Say: "God (alone) is the Creator of all things, and He is the (only) One, the all-Dominant, the Almighty."

17. He sends down water from the heavens, then the valleys flow according to their measure, and the torrent bears along the swelling foam, (mounting to the surface); and a scum like it arises from what they melt in the fire for the sake of (making) ornaments or (necessary) implements. Thus does God compare truth and falsehood. Then as for the scum, it passes away as a worthless thing; as for that which benefits people, then it remains in the earth. Thus does God set forth parables -

18. For those who respond to (the call of) their Lord are good things; (as for) those who do not respond to Him, even if they had all that is in the earth and the like thereof with it, they would certainly offer it for a ransom; for them shall be a terrible reckoning, and their abode is Hell, and what a wretched resting place it will be!

19. Is then he who knows that which has been revealed to you from your Lord is the truth like him who is blind? Will only those endowed with understanding bear it in mind?

20. Those who fulfill the covenant of God and do not break their pledge,

21. Those who join together what God has bidden to be joined, fear their Lord, and dread the terrible reckoning,

22. Those who are patient, seeking the pleasure of their Lord, establishing prayer, spending (benevolently) of what We have provided them with, secretly and openly, and warding off evil with good deeds; for these is the (happy) attainment of the eternal abode,

23. The garden of perpetual bliss which they will enter, and also the righteous among their parents, spouses, and offspring; and the angels shall enter unto them from every portal,

24. (Saying): "Peace be unto you for what you patiently persevered! (And now) how excellent the sequel of the eternal abode is!"

25. Those who break the covenant with God after it is pledged, and rend asunder what God has bidden to be joined, and make mischief in the land, theirs shall be the curse, and theirs shall be the terrible abode.

26. God grants abundant sustenance to whomsoever He pleases, and straitens it (similarly). They rejoice in the life of this world as against the hereafter, but (only some) means (of temporary enjoyment).

27. Those who disbelieve say: "Why is no sign revealed to him from his Lord?" Say: "Verily God leaves to stray whomsoever He wills, and He guides to Himself whomsoever turns to Him (seeking His Way)."

28. The hearts of those who believe are set at rest through remembering God; certainly through remembering God (only) are hearts set at ease.

29. (For) those who believe and do good deeds a great bliss shall be theirs, and a beautiful place of return.

30. Thus did We send you (O Our Messenger Muhammad) to people before whom other people have passed away, that you might recite to them (the Qur'an) which We have revealed to you while they deny the Beneficent (God). Say: "He is my Lord; there is no god but He; on Him (only) do I rely, and to Him (alone) is my return."

31. Even if there were a Qur'an by which the mountains were made to move, or the earth cloven asunder, or the dead made to speak thereby; nay! The command is wholly

God's. Do not those who believe yet know that if God willed, He would certainly guide all people? Those who disbelieve, it will not cease to strike them for what they do, a torment, or it will settle close to their abodes, until the promise of God comes to pass; verily God does not fail His promise.

32. Indeed the messengers before you were ridiculed, but I gave a respite to those who disbelieved, then I seized them. How then was My requital?

33. Is He then who stands (presently) over every soul (and knows) what it does (like one who does not)? Yet they ascribe partners to God! Say (O Our Messenger Muhammad): "Name them!" Is it that you inform Him of what He does not know on earth, or is it (just) a show of words? Nay! But their contrivance is made to appear fair seeming to those who disbelieve, and they are kept back (thereby) from the (right) Path; and whom He (God) leaves to stray, for him there shall be no guide.

34. For them is a torment in the life of this world, and surely the torment of the hereafter is more grievous, and for them there shall be no protector against God.

35. The similitude of the Garden (of bliss) promised to the righteous is that rivers flow beneath it; its fruits are everlasting, and its shade too. This is the requital of those who guard (themselves) against evil, and the requital of the disbelievers is the Fire.

36. Those to whom We have given the Book rejoice at what has been revealed to you, and of the clans are some who deny a part thereof. Say: "Verily, I am commanded that I should serve (only) God; I associate none with Him; I only invite you (all) and to Him (only) is my return."

37. Thus have We sent it (Qur'an, a true) authority in Arabic, and if you follow their (vain) desires after what has come to you of the knowledge, there shall be none for you besides God for a guardian or protector.

38. Indeed We sent messengers before you and We appointed for them wives and offspring, and it is not for a messenger to bring a sign (miracle) but by God's permission; for every term there is a prescribed Book.

39. God effaces (of it) whatever He pleases and (similarly) confirms (what he wills); with Him is the mother (basic

source) of the Book.

40. We will either show you a part of what We promised them, or take your soul to Ourselves (it makes no difference), for verily on you is (incumbent) to deliver the Message, and on Us is calling them to account.

41. Do not they see that We come unto their land and (gradually) reduce its borders? God pronounces a doom; there is none to reverse His command, and He is swift in reckoning.

42. Indeed those before them devised plots, but God's is all planning; He knows what every soul earns and soon will the disbelievers know to whom the sequel of the eternal abode belongs.

43. Those who disbelieve say: "You are not sent (by God)." Say (O Our Messenger Muhammad): "God, and those who are endowed with the knowledge of the Book, suffice for witnesses between me and you."

Abraham
(Ibrahim)

In the name of God, the Beneficent, the Merciful.

1. Alif, Lam Ra'. (This is) a Book which We have revealed unto you so that you may bring people forth from utter darkness into light by their Lord's permission, (and bring them) to the way of the Mighty, the Praised One,

2. God, to Him belongs whatever is in the heavens and in the earth, and woe unto the unbelievers on account of the severe chastisement,

3. Those who love this world's life more than the hereafter and turn away from God's path and desire to make it (look) crooked; these are in a great error.

4. We did not send any apostle but speaking the language of his people, so that he might explain to them clearly, then God makes whom He pleases err, and He guides whom He pleases, and He is the Mighty, the Wise.

5. Certainly We sent Moses with Our communications, saying: "Bring your people forth from utter darkness into the light and recount to them the days of God; most surely there are signs in this for every patient, grateful one."

6. Moses said to his people: "Remember God's favour unto you when He delivered you from Pharaoh's people who subjected you to severe torment, slaying your sons and sparing your women, and in this there was a great trial from your Lord,

7. "And your Lord made it known: `If you are grateful, I will certainly grant you more, and if you are ungrateful, My chastisement is truly severe.'"

8. And Moses said: "If you, as well as all those on earth, are ungrateful, God most surely is self-Sufficient, Praised."

9. Has not the account of those before you, the people of Noah, Ad and Thamud, and those after them, reached you? None knows them but God. Their apostles came to them with clear arguments, but they thrust their hands into their mouths and said: "Surely we deny that with which you are sent, and most surely we are in serious doubt regarding what you invite us to."

10. Their apostles said: "Is there doubt about God, Maker of the heavens and the earth? He invites you to forgiveness of your sins and a respite till an appointed term." They said: "You are no more than a mortal like us; you only wish to turn us away from what our fathers used to worship. Bring us, therefore, some clear proof."

11. Their apostles said to them: "We are but mortals like you, yet God bestows His favours upon whomsoever He pleases of His servants, and it is not for us that we should bring you a proof except by God's permission; and upon God (alone) should the believers rely.

12. "And what reason do we have that we should not rely on God? He has indeed guided us in our ways, and we would certainly bear patience with your persecution of us; and on God (alone) should those who seek reliance depend."

13. Those who disbelieved said to their apostles: "We will most certainly drive you out of our land, or else you should come back into our religion." So their Lord revealed to them: "We will most surely destroy those who are unjust,

14. "And most certainly We will settle you (apostles) in the land after them; this is for him who fears standing in My presence and who heeds My threat."

15. And they asked for judgment and every obstinate

transgressor was disappointed:

16. Beyond him is Hell, and he shall be given festering water to drink;

17. He shall drink it little by little and shall not be able to swallow it; and death will approach him from all sides; yet he shall not die but face a vehement torment:

18. The similitude of those who disbelieve in their Lord: their deeds are like ashes on which the wind blows hard, on a stormy day; they shall have no power over anything of what they have earned; this is the straying (from the Right Path).

19. Do not you see that God created the heavens and the earth in truth? If He so wills, He can take you away and bring (in your place) a new creation.

20. And this is not difficult for God at all.

21. And they shall come forth before God altogether, then the weak shall say to those who were haughty: "Verily we were your followers, so can you avert any part of the chastisement of God from us?" They will say: "Had God guided us, we too would surely have guided you. It is the same to us (now) whether we implore impatiently or we are patient; there is no way to escape."

22. Satan shall say after the affair is decided: "Verily God promised you the promise of truth, and I gave you promises but failed to keep them; and I had no authority over you except I called you and you responded to me; so, do not blame me but (rather) blame your own selves. I cannot be your helper (now), nor can you be mine. Verily I disbelieved in your making me a partner with God from before. Surely for the unjust ones there is a painful chastisement."

23. Those who believe and do good deeds will be admitted into gardens beneath which rivers flow to abide therein by their Lord's permission; their greeting therein will be: "Salam! (peace)."

24. Do not you see how God sets forth a comparison of a goodly word (being) like a goodly tree whose root is firmly fixed and whose branches (stretch up) into the sky,

25. Yielding its fruit in every season by its Lord's permission. And God sets forth comparisons (like this) for people so

that they may reflect.

26. The similitude of an evil word is like an evil tree whose roots lie on the surface of the earth; it has no stability.

27. God strengthens those who believe with the confirmed words in the life of this world and in the hereafter, and God leaves the unjust ones to stray; God does what He pleases.

28. Have you seen those who have changed God's bounties by ingratitude, and caused their people to halt in the abode of perdition?

29. Hell! They shall enter into it; and an evil place (it is) to stay in!

30. And they set up (idols as) equals to God that they might lead people astray from His path. Say: "Enjoy (your pleasures for a while), for your return is to the Fire."

31. Tell My servants who believe in Me that they should establish prayer and spend (charity) secretly and openly out of what We have given them before the day comes when no bargaining nor befriending shall take place.

32. God is He Who created the heavens and the earth, and sent down water from the heavens, then brought forth fruit therewith as sustenance for you; and made the ships usable to you that you may sail in the sea by His command, and subjected the rivers to you.

33. He has made the sun and the moon pursuing their (respective) courses; and He has made the night and subjected the day to you,

34. And He gives you of everything that you ask Him, and if you (try to) compute God's bounties, you will not be able to do so; indeed man is very unjust, ungrateful.

35. Abraham said: "Lord! Make this city secure, and keep me and my sons away from worshipping idols,

36. "Lord! Verily they have led many people astray; so, whosoever follows me is surely of me, and whosoever disobeys me, then verily You are the oft-Forgiving, Most Merciful.

37. "Lord! Indeed I have housed a part of my offspring in a barren valley near Your Sacred House, O Lord, that they may establish prayer; therefore, make the hearts of some people yearn to them, and provide them with fruits that they

may be grateful.

38. "Lord! Verily You know what we hide and what we openly declare, nothing in the earth nor in the heavens is hidden from God.

39. "To God, Who has granted me Ishmael and Isaac in my old age, belongs all praise. O Lord! Accept the supplication!

40. My Lord! make me keep up prayer and from my offspring (too), O our Lord, and accept my prayer:

41. "O Lord! Forgive me and my parents and the believers on the day when the reckoning shall be set up!"

42. Do not think God to be heedless of what the unjust ones do. He only gives them a respite to a day when eyes shall be fixed open (in terror),

43. (As they come) running on with horror, their heads upraised, their glance not returning to them, and their hearts blank.

44. And warn people of the day when chastisement comes to them. It is then that those who did injustice will say: "O Lord! Grant us a respite for a yet short term so that we may respond to Your call and follow the messengers." Did you not used to swear aforetime that there would be no extinction for you?

45. And you dwelt in the abodes of those who did injustice to their own selves, and it was made clear to you how We dealt with them, and We set forth parables for you.

46. And indeed they devised their plots, but all their plots were within the view of God, even if their plot had been such (a powerful one) as to move mountains thereby.

47. And do not think that God will fail His messengers in His promise; verily God is Mighty, Lord of Retribution.

48. On the day when the earth changes into a different earth, and (so will) the heavens too, and all men shall be marshaled forth to God, the One, the Vanquisher,

49. And you will see the guilty (ones) on that day bound together in chains;

50. Their garments (shall be) of pitch and their faces covered with fire,

51. So that God may recompense each soul according to what it earned; verily God is swift in reckoning.

52. This is a clear message for mankind, so that they may be warned thereby, so that they may know that He is the One God, and that men of understanding may take heed.

The Rocky Tract
(al-Hijr)

In the name of God, the Beneficent, the Merciful.

1. Alif, Lam, Ra. These are the verses of the Book and (of) a Qur'an that makes (matters) clear.

2. Often those who disbelieve wish that they were Muslims.

3. Leave them (O Our Prophet Muhammad) eat and enjoy themselves and hope may beguile them, for soon they will know.

4. We did not destroy any town but it (already) had a fixed term.

5. No people can hasten on their doom, nor can thy delay it.

6. They say: "O you to whom the Reminder (Qur'an) has come down, verily you are insane.

7. "Why do you not bring the angels to us if you are truthful?"

8. We only send down the angels with truth, and they would not be then given any respite.

9. Verily, We have revealed the Reminder and indeed We will be its Guardian.

10. Indeed We sent (prophets) before you among the people of former times,

11. No messenger came to them but they used to mock (at him).

12. Even so do We cause it to traverse into the hearts of the guilty;

13. They do not believe in it; and indeed the example of former times has already gone before.

14. Even if We open to them a gateway to heaven, that they may continuously ascend into it,

15. Certainly they would say: "(It is) only that our eyes have been intoxicated rather we are people bewitched."

16. Indeed We have made constellations in the heavens, and We have beautified them for the beholders.

17. We have guarded it from every accursed Satan,

18. Except he who (tries to) eavesdrop; a visible flame pursues him.

19. We have spread the earth out and cast thereon firm mountains, and We caused everything to grow therein,

20. We have made means of sustenance therein for you and for other (creations).

21. There is not a thing but its treasures are with Us, and We do not send it down but in a known measure.

22. We send the winds fertilizing, then (We) send down water from heaven; thus do We give it to you to drink, but it is not you who store it.

23. Verily We alone cause life and death, and We alone are the Heirs.

24. Indeed We know those eager to be foremost among you, and We know those who like to lag behind.

25. And verily your Lord will gather them together; verily He is all-Wise, all-Knowing.

26. Indeed We created man of sounding clay, of black mud moulded into shape.

27. And the jinn We created before of intensely hot (smokeless) fire.

28. Remember when your Lord said to the angels: "Verily I shall create man of the essence of black mud fashioned into shape.

29. "So when I complete him and breathe My spirit into him, you should fall down to him prostrating."

30. So all the angels prostrated in obeisance,

31. Except Iblis; he refused to be with those who prostrated.

32. He (God) said: "O Iblis! What hinders you from joining those who prostrate?"

33. He said: "I am not one who prostrates in obeisance to man whom You created of the essence of black mud fashioned into shape."

34. He (God) said: "Then get out of it, for verily you are driven away accursed,

35. "And verily My curse will be on you till the Day of

Judgment."

36. He said: "Lord! Give me a respite till the day when they are raised."

37. He (God) said: "Then indeed you will be of those who are given respite,

38. "Till the day of the appointed time."

39. He said: "Lord! Because You have left me to stray, I will certainly make error attractive to them on earth, and I will certainly cause them all to stray,

40. "Save Your (devoted) servants among them, the sincere ones."

41. He (God) said: "This is a right way to Me,

42. "Verily there shall be no authority for you over My devoted servants, except those who deviate and follow you,

43. "And I will certainly promise that Hell shall be the abode for all of them,

44. "It (Hell) has seven gates; for each (gate) shall be a separate party (of the sinners) assigned.

45. "Verily the pious shall be in the midst of gardens and fountains,

46. ("While the angels say:) `Enter in peace and security,'

47. "We will root out whatever rancor is in their hearts; (they shall be) as brothers, on couches facing each other.

48. "No weariness shall touch them therein, nor will they ever be cast out of it."

49. Announce to My servants that verily I am the oft-Forgiving, the Merciful,

50. And that My chastisement is the most painful one,

51. Inform them of Abraham's guests;

52. When they entered unto him, they said: "Peace." He said: "Verily we are apprehensive of you!"

53. They said: "Do not be afraid! Verily we bear to you glad tidings of a son endowed with knowledge."

54. He said: "Do you bear to me glad tidings (of a son) while old age has touched me? Of what do you then bear glad tidings to me?"

55. They said: "We bear glad tidings to you in truth; so, do not despair."

56. He said: "And who despairs of the mercy of his Lord

other than those who have gone astray?"

57. He said: "What is your business, then, O messengers (of God)?"

58. They said: "Verily we are sent to a guilty people,

59. "Except the family of Lot; verily we shall deliver them all,

60. "Except his wife; we are certain that she shall be among those who remain behind (condemned)."

61. So when the messengers came to the family of Lot,

62. He (Lot) said: "Verily you are people whom we do not know."

63. They said: "Nay! We come to you with that in which they have been doubting,

64. "We come to you with the truth, and we certainly are truthful.

65. "So go forth with your followers during a portion of the night, and do not lag behind them, and let none of you turn back; and go forth whither you are bidden."

66. We revealed to him this decree (of Ours) that these people would be eradicated in the morning.

67. Then the people of the town came rejoicing.

68. He said: "Verily these are my guests; therefore, do not disgrace me;

69. "Fear (the punishment of) God, and do not put me to shame."

70. They said: "Have we not forbidden you against (protecting) anyone?"

71. He said: "These are my daughters (you may wed them) if you must do (such thing)."

72. By your life, (O Our Prophet Muhammad), they were certainly intoxicated, wandering, bewildered.

73. So the (violent) blast seized them before dawn.

74. Thus did We turn it (city) upside down, and a rain of stones of baked clay poured down on them.

75. Verily in this are signs for those who carefully scrutinize.

76. Verily it is on a path that (still) stands;

77. Verily in this there is a sign for the believers.

78. And verily the inhabitants of the thicket too were most surely unjust ones.

79. We inflicted retribution on them, and indeed they are both on a path that is (still) open.

80. Indeed the inhabitants of al-Hijr (stone-carved homes) rejected the messengers;

81. We brought Our signs to them, but they turned away therefrom.

82. And they hewed habitations out of the mountains and felt secure.

83. So the (violent) blast seized them in the morning,

84. What they had earned was of no avail to them.

85. And We did not create the heavens and the earth and what is between them but in truth; and verily the Hour (of reckoning) is certain to come; so, (O Our Prophet Muhammad) forgive (people) with grace.

86. Verily, your Lord is He, the Creator, the all-Knowing.

87. Indeed We have given you the seven much repeated (verses) and the Great Qur'an.

88. Do not stain your eyes (covetously) at what We have provided married couples among them with, to enjoy, and do not grieve for them, and be kind unto the believers.

89. Say: "Verily, I am the open warner (from God)."

90. Just as We sent down on those who were divisive,

91. Those who broke up the Qur'an into parts.

92. So, by your Lord, We shall certainly question them all,

93. As to what they used to do.

94. Therefore, openly declare (O Our Prophet Muhammad) what you are bidden, and turn away from the polytheists.

95. Verily We are sufficient for you against the scoffers,

96. Those who set up with God another god, soon shall they come to know.

97. Indeed We know that your breast straitens at what they say;

98. But celebrate the praise of your Lord, and be of those who prostrate themselves (to God) in obeisance,

99. And worship your Lord until what is certain comes to you.

The Bee
an-Nahl

In the name of God, the Beneficent, the Merciful.

1. The decree of God comes; therefore, do not (seek to) hasten it. Glory be to Him and Exalted is He above what they associate with Him.

2. He sends down the angels with the Spirit by His own decree on whomsoever He pleases of His servants (saying): "Warn (mankind) that there is no god but I; therefore, fear Me."

3. He created the heavens and the earth with the truth; Exalted is He above what they associate (with Him).

4. He created man from a drop of sperm, and, behold, he is an open disputer.

5. He created cattle for you, wherein is warmth and many gains, and you eat thereof.

6. There is comeliness in them for you when you drive them (home) and when you lead them forth (to pasture).

7. They bear your loads to lands which you could not otherwise reach but with distress; verily your Lord is Compassionate, Merciful.

8. (He made) horses and mules and donkeys that you might ride upon them, and as finery; and He creates what you do not know.

9. It rests upon God to make the straight Way, and among them are deviating ones; if He pleases, He would certainly guide you all aright.

10. He it is Who sends down water from the heavens for you; from it you drink, and by it trees grow, on which you pasture your cattle.

11. With this He produces corn for you, olives, palm trees, grapes, and all fruits; verily there is a sign in this for people who reflect.

12. He has made the night and the day, the sun and the moon, of use to you, and the stars have been made of service by His decree; verily there are signs in this for people who understand.

13. What He has produced in the earth of varied hues, verily there is a sign in this for people who are mindful.

14. He it is Who made the sea of service that you might eat fresh (fish) meat from it and take out therefrom ornaments which you wear from it; and you see the ships cleaving through it, and that you might seek of His Grace, and that you might offer thanks.

15. He has cast great mountains (standing firm) in the earth lest it may shake with you, and rivers and roads that you may be guided aright.

16. And landmarks (too), and by stars are they guided.

17. Then is He who creates like that who does not? Will you not then consider?

18. If you would count God's bounties, you would not be able to compute them; verily God is oft-Forgiving, Most Merciful.

19. God knows what you hide and what you reveal.

20. Those whom they call on besides God do not create anything, while they are themselves created.

21. (They are) dead, not living, and they do not have knowledge as to when they will be raised.

22. Your God is One God; the hearts of those who do not believe in the hereafter do not acknowledge (the truth), and they are arrogant people.

23. Of course God knows what they hide and what they reveal; verily He does not love arrogant people.

24. When it is said to them: "What is it that your Lord has revealed?" They said: "The legends of the ancient."

25. So they shall bear their burden entirely on the Day of Judgment, and also the burdens of those whom they led astray without knowledge. Behold! Evil is what they bear.

26. Indeed those before them plotted, and then (the Wrath of) God came (and destroyed) their buildings from the foundations, and the roof fell over them, and the torment came to them from where they did not perceive.

27. Then on the Day of Resurrection He will bring them to disgrace and say: "Where are My partners about whom you have been disputing?" Those who have are endowed with knowledge will say: "Verily, the disgrace this day and the evil is upon the unbelievers."

28. (They are) those whose life the angels terminate while they behave unjustly to their own selves; then they will offer

submission (saying): "Aye! Indeed God well knows what you were doing.

29. "Therefore enter the gates of Hell to stay therein; woeful indeed will be the abode of the haughty people!"

30. It is said to those who guard themselves against evil: "What is that which your Lord has revealed?" They say: "Good." There will be good in this world for those who do good, but indeed the abode of the hereafter is better, and excellent indeed is the abode of those who guard themselves (against evil).

31. Gardens of eternity: they shall enter therein, rivers flowing beneath them; they shall have whatever they desire. Thus does God reward those who guard themselves (against evil).

32. Those whom the angels take away in state of goodness while receiving them (the angels) will say: "Peace be on you; enter the Garden, for what you have done."

33. Do they waiting till the angels to come to them, or the Decree of your Lord is passed? Thus did those before them behave, and God was never unjust to them; they were unjust to their own souls.

34. So the evil results of their deeds afflicted them, and that which they were scoffing at encompassed them.

35. They who associated (others with God) say: "Had God willed, we would have worshipped naught besides Him, (neither) we nor our fathers; nor would we have forbidden anything without a decree from Him." So did those before them say. Should the messengers then do anything other than clearly convey the message?

36. Indeed We raised in every nation a messenger (who said): "Worship God (only), and stay clear of the worship of every kind of idol (taghut)." So among them were some whom God guided, and among them were others on whom error was confirmed. Therefore, travel throughout the world and see what the end of those who rejected (Us) has been.

37. (Even) if you strongly wish for their guidance, yet verily God does not guide those whom He leaves to stray, nor shall they have anyone to aid.

38. They swear by God, with the strongest of their oaths, that God will not raise those who die. Nay! It is a promise

binding upon Him in truth, yet most people do not know.

39. (They will be resurrected) so that He may manifest to them that about which they differed, and so that those who disbelieved may know that they were liars.

40. Indeed, Our Word for a thing, when We will, is that We say: "Be," and it is.

41. Those who migrate in (the cause of) God after being oppressed, We will certainly give them good in this world, and certainly the reward in the hereafter is much greater, if they only know.

42. Those who endure patiently and rely on their Lord (alone),

43. We sent nothing before you except men (as Our messengers). We revealed to them; so, ask those who remember (God often) if you do not know.

44. (We sent them) with indisputable evidence and scriptures, and We revealed the Zikr (Qur'an) to you so that you might clarify to mankind what has been revealed to them, perhaps they will reflect.

45. Can they who devise evil stratagem ever feel secure by the earth swallowing them (concealing them) from God's torment coming from where they cannot know?!

46. Or that He may seize them while they move around?! They shall never frustrate (God's Decree).

47. Or that He may seize them by a slow destruction? Indeed your Lord is Compassionate and all-Merciful.

48. Or can they not see that God has created everything, that its shadow turns right and left, prostrating in obeisance to God, lying abased?

49. Whatever is in the heavens and the earth, the angels, the beasts, all prostrate in obeisance to God, showing no sign of naughtiness.

50. They fear their Lord (Who is ever) above them and do what they are commanded.

51. God has said: "Do not take two gods. Indeed there is only One God; so, Me (alone) should you fear."

52. Everything in the heavens and the earth belong to Him, and to Him (only) should there be constant obedience. Will you then fear any other than God?

53. Whatever bounty with you is from God; then when

distress touches you, you cry unto Him for help.

54. Yet when He removes the distress from you, lo, some of you associate others with their Lord;

55. That they may deny what We have given them. Then enjoy yourselves (for the time being); for soon will you come to know.

56. They set aside for what they do not know a portion of that with which We have provided them. By God! You shall be questioned about what you have been forging.

57. They ascribe daughters to God. Glory be to Him. And for themselves they only have a wishful thinking.

58. When a daughter is announced to one of them, his face becomes darkened, and he is filled with wrath.

59. He hides himself from people because of the "evil" of what is announced to him; (pondering whether) he should "disgracefully" keep her or bury her alive in the ground. Behold how evil their judgment is.

60. The attribute of evil applies to those who do not believe in the hereafter, and the highest attribute belongs to God, for He is the Mighty, the Wise.

61. If God were to punish people for their iniquity, He would not leave a single moving being (on earth), but He gives them respite until an appointed term; so when their doom comes, they shall not (be able to) delay it even an hour, nor shall they bring it on before its appointed time.

62. They assign to God what they themselves hate, and their tongues ascribe the deceit that they shall have all good things. There shall inevitably be the Fire for them, and they shall be sent ahead to it.

63. By God! Indeed, We sent messengers to people before you, but Satan made their deeds fair-seeming to them, so he is their guardian today, and for them there shall be a grievous chastisement.

64. We did not reveal the Book to you (O Our Prophet Muhammad) except that you may explain to them that about which they differ, and as a guidance and a mercy for those who believe.

65. God has sent down water from the heavens, then He enlivens the earth therewith after its death; verily in this there is a sign for people who listen.

66. For you there is in the cattle a lesson; We give you to drink what is in their bellies from betwixt the chyme and the blood pure milk, easy and palatable for those who drink it.

67. And of the fruits of the date palms, and grapes-you obtain from them both drinks of intoxication and goodly substance; verily in this is a sign for people who understand.

68. Your Lord revealed to the bee saying: "Make hives in the mountains and in the trees and in what they build,

69. "Then eat of all the fruits and walk in the ways of your Lord submissively." There comes out from within it a drink of various shades of colour, therein is healing for men; verily in this is a sign for people who reflect.

70. God has created you, then He shall take you away, and among you is he who is taken back to the meanest state of life, so (much so) that he knows nothing after once having had knowledge. God is all-Knowing, all-Powerful.

71. God has favoured some of you over others in the provision of sustenance. Now those who have been more favoured do not give their sustenance to those whom their right hands possess so that they may be equal therein. Is it then the bounty of God which they deny?

72. God has blessed you with wives from among your own selves, and has granted you sons and grandchildren by your wives and sustained you with good things. Is it then in falsehood that they believe, and in the bounty of God that they disbelieve?

73. Do they worship others than God that have no control over any sustenance for them in the heavens and the earth, having no power at all?

74. So do not coin any similitude for God; verily God knows (everything) while you do not.

75. God sets the example of the two men: one is a slave, the property of another; he has no power over anything, while the other is that whom We have Ourselves sustained with a goodly sustenance from which he spends privately and publicly. Are they both equal? All praise is God's! Yet most of them do not know (this much).

76. God sets forth the parable of two men: one of them is

dumb, unable to do anything; he is a burden even to his master; wherever he sends him, no good comes out of him. Can he be equalled to that who enjoins justice and he himself is on the Straight Path?

77. To God belongs the unperceivable of the heavens and the earth; and the matter of the Hour (of judgment) is but like the twinkling of the eye, or even more nigh; verily God has power over all things.

78. God has brought you forth from the wombs of your mothers - you knew nothing - and He gave you hearing, sight and heart, so that you might give thanks.

79. Do they not remark the birds held poised in the sky? Nothing holds them but God; verily in this are signs for people who believe.

80. God has made houses for you, a place of rest, and He has made houses (tents) from the skins of cattle for you which you find so light to carry on the day you depart and the day you camp, and of their wool, fur and hair, are goods of convenience and provision for a time.

81. God has made (some) of the mountains places of refuge for you, and He has made for you garments to protect you against the heat, and coats of mail to protect you in your fighting. Thus He completes his bounties unto you so that you may submit (to Him in appreciation).

82. But if they turn away from you, then only the delivering of Our clear message is incumbent upon you.

83. They recognize the bounties of God, yet they deny them, and most of them are unbelievers.

84. One day, We shall raise from among every nation a witness, there shall be no permission then for those who disbelieve (to make excuses), nor shall they be permitted to solicit amends.

85. When those who act unjustly see the torment, it shall not be lightened for them, nor shall they be given respite.

86. When those who associate (others with God) see those they associated (with Him), they shall say: "Lord! These are the ones we associated (with You) whom we called besides You!" But they will throw their word back to them and say: "Indeed, you are liars!"

87. They shall tender submission to God on that day; and

what they were forging shall fail them.

88. (As for) those who disbelieve and hinder people from the way of God, We shall increase their share of torment, for they were causing mischief.

89. One day, We shall raise a witness in every people from among themselves, and bring you (O Our Prophet Muhammad) as a witness over all, and We have revealed unto you the Book, explaining everything, a guidance, mercy, and glad tidings to those who submit themselves (to God).

90. God enjoins justice and benevolence (to others) and giving to kindred, and forbids lewdness and evil and rebellion. He exhorts you that you may take heed.

91. And fulfill the covenant of God when you have pledged (to fulfill it), and do not break the oaths after ratification thereof, when you have consented that God is a surety over your covenant; indeed God knows whatever you do.

92. And do not be like her who unravels her yarn, splitting it up into thin filaments, after she has made it strongly spun; you take your oaths as a means of deceit between you because one nation is more numerous than the other. Verily God only tries you by this; and most surely he will make clear to you on the Day of Judgment concerning that about which you differed.

93. Had God willed, He would surely have made you all a single nation, but He leaves to err whomsoever He pleases and guides whomsoever He pleases; you will certainly be questioned about what you were doing.

94. Do not take your oaths as means of deceit between you, lest a foot should slip after being firmly fixed, and you taste evil on account of hindering others from God's Way; and there would be a great torment for you.

95. Do not sell the Covenant of God for a mean price, for verily with God is that which is better for you, if only you knew.

96. What is with you passes away, and what is with God is everlasting; We shall certainly give those who exercise patience their (just) recompense with the best of what they were doing.

97. Whosoever did good, whether male or female, being

a believer, then We shall certainly make them live a good and pure life. We shall certainly give them their (just) recompense with the best of what they were doing.

98. When you recite the Qur'an, seek refuge with God against Satan the accursed.

99. Indeed there is no authority for him over those who believe and rely on their Lord;

100. Indeed, his authority is only over those who befriend him and those who associate others with God.

101. When We change one sign for another, and God knows best what He sends down, they say: "You (Muhammad) are only a forgerer." Nay! Most of them do not know.

102. Say (to the believers, O Our Prophet Muhammad): "The Holy Spirit has brought it down from your Lord in truth, that it may strengthen (the faith of) those who believe, and as a guidance and glad tidings to those who submit (to God)."

103. Indeed We know that they say: "It is only a man that teaches him." The tongue of him whom they (falsely) hint at is non-Arabic, while this language is (pure and) clear.

104. Those who do not believe in the signs of God, God does not guide them; for them there shall be a painful torment.

105. Verily, only those who do not believe in the signs of God forge, and these are the liars.

106. He who disbelieves in God after having believed, save he who is compelled while his heart remains steadfast with respect to his faith, and he who opens his breast for disbelief, on these is God's Wrath; for them there shall be a great torment.

107. This (is so) because they prefer the life of this world to the hereafter, and because God does not guide the unbelieving people.

108. These are those on whose hearts God has set a seal, and on their hearing and sight (as well), and these are the heedless (ones).

109. There is no doubt that in the hereafter they will be the losers.

110. Then verily your Lord, to those who migrate after

being persecuted, then they struggled hard and exercised patience, verily your Lord after that is oft-Forgiving, Most Merciful.

111. (Remember) the day when every soul shall come pleading for itself, and every soul shall be recompensed fully for what it has done, and they will not be dealt with unjustly.

112. God sets down an example: a town safe and secure, its sustenance comes to it in abundance from every side, then it becomes unappreciative of the bounties of God; so God makes it taste extreme hunger and dire fear for the evil its inhabitants committed.

113. Certainly a messenger came to them from among themselves, but they rejected him, so a torment seized them for they were behaving unjustly.

114. So eat of what God has provided for you lawful and good things, and offer thanks for God's bounty if you adore Him.

115. He has made forbidden to you what dies of itself, the blood and flesh of pigs, and that over which any name other than God's has been invoked; but whosoever is forced by necessity (to partake thereof), not desiring nor wilfully transgressing the limit, then verily God is oft-Forgiving, Most Merciful.

116. Do not utter falsehood concerning what qualify (as pure or impure), saying: "This is lawful and this is forbidden," to forge a lie against God; verily those who forge a lie against God do not succeed.

117. There is very little enjoyment, and there is a painful torment.

118. To those who were Jews We had forbidden from before what We have already related to you; and We did not do them any injustice, but they were unjust to their own selves.

119. Yet verily your Lord, to those who commit evil in ignorance and turn (repentant) after that and make amends, is oft-Forgiving, Most Merciful.

120. Abraham was an Imam, devoutly obedient to God, upright; he was not a polytheist.

121. (He was) grateful for His bounties; He chose him

and He guided him on the Right Path.

122. We gave him good in this world, and verily in the hereafter he will surely be among the righteous ones.

123. So We revealed to you (O Our Prophet Muhammad) that you follow the religion of Abraham, the upright, and he was not a polytheist.

124. The Sabbath was ordained only for those who differed about it; and verily your Lord will judge between them on the Day of Judgment concerning that about which they used to differ.

125. Call to the way of your Lord with wisdom and kind exhortation, and dispute with them in the manner which is the best; verily your Lord knows best who has gone astray from His Path, and He knows best those who are rightly guided.

126. If you punish, then punish as you were afflicted; but if you show patience, it will certainly be best for those who bear patiently.

127. Be patient (O Our Prophet Muhammad), and your patience is only by (the help of) God; do not grieve for them, and do not be distressful at what they devise.

128. Verily God is with those who guard (themselves against evil) and those who do good (unto others).

The Children Of Israel
(Bani Isra'il)

In the name of God, the Beneficent, the Merciful.

1. Glory be to Him Who carried His servant (Muhammad) by night from al-Masjid al-Haram (Ka'ba) to the farthest mosque (al-Masjid al-Aqsa) whose precincts We have blessed, that We may show him of Our signs; verily He is the all-Hearing, the all-Seeing.

2. We bestowed the Book upon Moses and made it a guidance for the children of Israel, (saying): "Do not take any other than Me as Guardian."

3. (They were) the offspring of those whom We carried with Noah (in the ark); verily he (Noah) was a grateful servant.

4. We declared to the children of Israel in the Book: "You

will certainly make mischief in the land twice, and you will certainly be elated with great arrogance.

5. "So when the promise of the first of the two periods of mischief came (to pass), We sent Our servants over you with terrible prowess, so (much so that) they went around from house to house, and it was a warning completely fulfilled.

6. "Then We gave you back (the opportunity) to prevail over them, and We aided you with wealth and offspring and made you a numerous host.

7. "If you do good deeds, you do it for your own selves, and if you do evil it is (likewise) against your own selves; so when the second promise came (to pass), We roused your enemies so that they might sadden your faces, and that they might enter the Mosque as they entered it the first time, and destroy whatever they conquered with total destruction.

8. "It may be that your Lord will have mercy on you, but if you return (to disobedience), We shall return (to chastisement), and We have made Hell a prison for the unbelievers."

9. Verily, this Qur'an guides to that which is the most upright, and announces glad tidings to the believers who do good deeds that they shall have a great reward.

10. For those who do not believe in the hereafter We have prepared a painful torment.

11. Man prays for evil as he should pray for good; and man is ever hasty.

12. We have made the night and the day two (of Our) signs, then We cause the Sign of the night to be an extinguishing, and We make the Sign of the day sight-giving that you may seek grace from your Lord, and that you may know the number and the count of years; and We have explained everything in detail.

13. We have caused every man's destiny to cling to his neck, and We shall bring forth to him on the Day of Resurrection a book which he will find wide open.

14. (It will be said to him): "Read your book; your own self suffices today as a reckoner against you."

15. Whosoever is guided to the right way is verily (earning) for his own self; and whosoever goes astray, verily he

strays against his own self. And the bearer of a burden shall not bear the burden of another; and We do not chastise people until We raise a messenger (among them).

16. When We intend to destroy a town, We send Our commandment to those of its people who lead easy lives (to obey Us), and yet they transgress in it; then the word proves true against it, so We destroy it a complete destruction.

17. How many nations after Noah have We destroyed? And your Lord is sufficient, with regard to the sins of His servants, Knowing and seeing.

18. Whosoever desires that which passes hastily (life), We hasten for him therein what We please for whomsoever We will, then We provide Hell for him; he shall enter it despised, driven away.

19. Whosoever desires the hereafter and strives for it with a (sincere) striving, and he is a believer, the striving of these shall find favour.

20. All (of them) We aid, these as well as those, out of the bounty of your Lord; and the bounty of your Lord is not restricted.

21. Behold how We caused some of them to excel others; and surely the hereafter is much greater in degrees, and greater still in respect of excellence.

22. Do not associate with God any other gods, lest you should sit despised, destitute.

23. (Your Lord) has commanded that you shall not serve any but Him, and that you shall do goodness to your parents, should either or both of them reach old age; do not utter any word of displeasure to them; do not chide them, and speak to them kind words.

24. Lower for them the wing of humility out of compassion and say: "Lord! Have mercy on them as they cherished me when I was little."

25. Your Lord knows best what is in your hearts; if you are righteous, then verily He is oft-Forgiving.

26. Give to the near of kin his due, and to the needy and the wayfarer too; and do not squander wastefully.

27. Verily the squanderers are the brethren of the devils, and Satan is ungrateful to his Lord.

28. If you turn away from them, seeking mercy from

your Lord, which you hope for, then speak kindly to them.

29. Do not let your hand be shackled to your neck, nor stretch it forth to extremes (in spending), lest you should thereafter sit blamed, destitute.

30. Verily your Lord extends sustenance to whomsoever He wills, and He measures it (justly); verily He is Aware of His servants, Seeing.

31. Do not kill your children even for fear of want. We sustain them and your own selves too; verily killing them is a great sin.

32. Do not approach adultery; indeed, it is a shameful act, and an evil way.

33. Do not kill anyone whose killing God has forbidden except for a just cause; and whoever is slain unjustly, then We have indeed given his heir authority, but let him not exceed the limits of slaying; verily he is aided (by God).

34. Do not approach the property of an orphan except in a way that is good, until he attains his maturity and you fulfill (your) promise; verily there shall be questioning concerning every promise (made).

35. Give full measure when you measure out and weigh with a correct balance; this is good and most fair in the end.

36. Do not pursue that of which you have no knowledge; verily the hearing, the sight, and the heart shall all be questioned about it.

37. Do not walk on the earth exuberantly; for you cannot rend the earth nor reach (the heights of) the mountains stretching.

38. All this-the evil of it-is hateful to your Lord.

39. This is some of the wisdom which your Lord has revealed to you, and do not set up with God any other god lest you should be cast into the Fire, blamed and outcast.

40. Has your Lord then preferred to give you sons, and daughters (for Himself) from among the angels? Verily, you utter monstrous statements.

41. Indeed We have displayed (the warnings) in this Qur'an that they might take heed; but it increases nothing in them save aversion.

42. Say (O Our Prophet Muhammad): "If there were with Him any other gods, as they say, then certainly they would

have been able to seek a way against the Lord of the Throne.

43. Glory be to Him and Exalted is He far above what they say. He is the Sublime, the Great.

44. The seven heavens and the earth and all those in them glorify Him, and there is nothing which does not call forth His praise, but you do not understand their glorifications; verily, He is the Forbearing, the oft-Forgiving.

45. When you (O Our Prophet Muhammad) recite the Qur'an, We set a hidden veil between you and those who do not believe in the hereafter.

46. We have put coverings on their hearts lest they should understand it, and in their ears a heaviness, and when you mention your Lord alone while (reciting) the Qur'an, they turn their backs in aversion.

47. We know best what they can hear when they hearken to you when they are whispering secretly apart, when the unjust say: "You are following only a bewitched man."

48. Behold (O Our Prophet Muhammad) what comparisons they coin for you; for they have gone (so far) astray that they cannot find the right way.

49. They say: "When we become (mere) bones and the dust of decay, then shall we really be raised a new creation?"

50. Say (O Our Prophet Muhammad): "Even if you become stones or iron,

51. "Or any other creature which seems in your minds to be harder (to resurrect)." But they will say: "Who will cause us to return?" Say: "He Who created you first." Then they will wag their heads at you and say: "When will that be?" Say: "Maybe it is nigh."

52. On the day when He calls you forth, and you will respond with His Praise, and you will think that you tarried (in your graves) but a short while.

53. Tell My servants that they should utter (only) that which is best. Verily Satan sows dissension among them; verily Satan is an open enemy to man.

54. Your Lord knows you best. If He wills, He grants you His mercy, and if He wills, He chastises you; and We did not send you to be a guardian over them.

55. Your Lord knows best all those who are in the heavens and the earth; and indeed We have exalted some proph-

ets over (others), and We gave David the Psalms (Zabur).

56. Say: "Call those whom you fancy (to be gods) other than Him: they shall have no power to move distress from you nor alter it."

57. Those whom they call upon to seek access to their Lord (to know) which of them is the nearest (to Him); they hope for His mercy, and they fear His chastisement; verily, the chastisement of your Lord is to be dreaded.

58. There is no town which We shall not destroy before the Day of Judgment, or chastise with a severe chastisement; that is written in the Book.

59. Nothing hinders Us from sending signs save that the ancient rejected them; and We gave Thamud the she-camel, an open sign, but they did injustice to her; and We only send signs to warn (people).

60. Behold! We said to you: "Verily, your Lord encompasses mankind," and We only caused the vision which We showed you a trial for people, and (similarly) the accursed tree in the Qur'an, and We cause them to fear, yet it increases nothing in them but their grievous transgression.

61. Behold! We said to the angels: "Prostrate to Adam." All prostrated except Iblis. He said: "Am I to prostrate to him whom You have created of clay?"

62. He said: "Do you see this one whom You have honoured above me? If you grant me a respite until the Day of Judgment, I will bring his posterity under my sway except a few."

63. He said: "Begone! But whosoever of them follows you, then verily Hell is your full recompense!

64. "And tear away whomsoever of them you can with your voice, and bring against them your cavalry and infantry, and partake with them in their riches and children, and make promises to them." But Satan promises them only deception.

65. "Verily (as for) My servants, you shall not have any authority over them, and your Lord suffices (for their) guardian."

66. Your Lord is He who sails the ships for you in the sea that you might seek of His grace; verily, He is ever to you the Most Merciful.

67. When any distress touches you in the sea, away go those whom you invoke save He; yet when He brings you safely to the land, you turn away (from Him); and man has ever been ungrateful.

68. Do you then feel against His causing a part of the earth to be swallowed up or He sends against you a violent shower of stones, then you shall find no protector for you (besides Him)?

69. Or do you feel secure against His taking you back into it (sea) another time, then sending a fierce gale on you and drowning you for what you disbelieved? Then you will find no helper against Us.

70. Indeed We have honoured the children of Adam, and We transport them in the land and in the sea, and We provide them with sustenance of good things, and We have exalted them over most of those We have created with a high degree of preference.

71. Remember the Day when We will summon every nation with their leader (imam); then those given their books in the right hand shall read their books, and they shall not be dealt with (even) a whit unjustly.

72. But whosoever is blind in this (life), he shall also be blind in the hereafter, and more erring from the way.

73. And verily they had been conspiring to turn you away from that which We have revealed to you, then they would surely have taken you as a friend.

74. If it were not (for the fact) that We had firmly established you, you would surely have been close to inclining a little towards them.

75. In that case, We would surely have caused you to taste a double (torment) in this life, and a double (torment) after death, and then you would not have found anyone to help you against Us.

76. They had been conspiring to unsettle you from the land, that they might drive you out of it, but then they would have tarried (therein) after you.

77. This was Our way with those of Our messengers whom We sent before you, and you shall not find any change in Our way.

78. Establish prayer (regularly) from sunset till the dark-

ness of the night, and the recital at dawn; verily the recital at dawn is witnessed.

79. And (in a part) of the night, awake from sleep for performing the prayer, as a supererogation for your own good, perchance your Lord will bring you to a praised position.

80. And say: "Lord! Cause me to enter by an entrance of truth, and cause me to go out by an exit of truth, and grant me an authority from You to assist (me)."

81. And say: "Truth has come and falsehood has vanished; verily falsehood is doomed to vanish."

82. We revealed in the Qur'an (gradually) that which is a healing and a mercy to the believers, but it increases the unjust nothing but perdition.

83. When We bestow Our bounties on man, he turns aside and distances himself, and when any evil touches him, he is despondent.

84. Say (O Our Prophet Muhammad): "Everyone acts according to his own manner; thus your Lord best knows who (among you) is the best guide to the right way."

85. They ask you about the spirit. Say: "The spirit is from the command of my Lord, and you have been given only a little portion of knowledge."

86. If We wish, We would certainly take away that which We revealed to you, then you would not find anyone to plead on your behalf,

87. Save (for) the mercy from your Lord; verily, His grace unto you is great.

88. Say: "(Even) if men and the jinn come together to bring the like of this Qur'an, they will not (be able to) bring the like of it, even if some of them were to be helpers to each other."

89. Indeed We have explained to people in this Qur'an every (kind of) parable, yet most of them ungratefully turn away therefrom.

90. They said: "We will never believe in you until you cause a spring for us go gush forth from the ground.

91. "Or (show us) a garden of date-palms and grapes, and that you can cause rivers to flow gushing forth in their midst.

92. "Or cause the heavens to fall upon us in pieces, as you assert, or bring God and the angels (to vouch for you) face to face (with us);

93. "Or (show us that) you have a house of gold, or ascend into the heavens; and we shall never believe in your ascending until you cause a book to be sent down to us, that we may read it." Say (O Our Prophet Muhammad): "Glory be to my Lord! Am I but a man (sent by God as a) messenger?"

94. Nothing prevented people from believing when the guidance came to them except that they said: "Has God sent a man (like us as) His messenger?"

95. Say: "If there were angels walking on earth settled (there) in security, surely We would have sent down an angel to them from heaven, as a messenger."

96. Say: "God suffices as witness between me and you; verily He is Aware, Seeing."

97. Whomsoever God guides is rightly guided; and whomsoever He leaves to stray, you shall never find any guardian for him other than God; We shall gather them together on the Day of Resurrection on their faces, blind, dumb and deaf; their abode shall be Hell-as it abates. We shall increase the blaze for them.

98. This is their recompense; for they disbelieved in Our signs, and they said: "When we become (mere) bones and the dust of decay, then shall we still be raised in a new creation?"

99. Do they not see that God, Who created the heavens and the earth, is certainly able to create the like of them, and He has decreed for them a term in which there is no doubt? But the unjust turn away (from it) to deny it.

100. Say: "If you were to own the treasures of the mercy of my Lord, then you would certainly withhold them for fear of spending them, and man is ever niggardly."

101. Indeed We bestowed upon Moses nine clear signs; so, ask the children of Israel. When he came to them, Pharaoh said to him: "Verily, I deem you bewitched.

102. "Indeed, you know that none has sent these down." He said: "The Lord of the heavens and the earth has penetrating insights, and I think you, Pharaoh, are surely doomed

to perdition."

103.   He resolved to stir them up to depart from the land, so We drowned him (Pharaoh) and those with him all together.

104.   We said after that to the children of Israel: "Abide in peace in the land, but when the later promise comes, We shall bring you all together."

105.   In truth We have sent it down, and in truth it has come down; and We did not send you (Muhammad) except as a bearer of glad tidings and a warner.

106.   And it is a Qur'an which We have divided (into chapters) so that you may recite it to people at intervals, and We have revealed it gradually, in portions.

107.   Say (O Our Prophet Muhammad): "Believe in it or do not; verily, those who are (already) given the knowledge from before it, they fall down on their faces prostrating (to God) in obeisance."

108.   They say: "Glory be to our Lord! Verily the promise of our Lord was (a certainty) to be fulfilled."

109.   And they fall down on their faces weeping and it increases their humility.

110.   Say: "Call upon God, or call upon ar-Rahman (the Beneficent); whichever you call upon, to Him belong the best names. And do not say your prayer too loudly, and do not say it too softly either, but seek a middle course between these two (extremes)."

111.   Say: "All praise is due to God Who has not taken a son, and Who has no partner in the Kingdom (of heaven), and there is no helper for Him against any humility; and proclaim His greatness magnifying (His glory)."

The Cave
(al-Kahf)

In the name of God, the Beneficent, the Merciful.

1.   All praise belongs to God Who revealed the Book upon His servant, causing no crookedness therein;

2.   Straight, that he might warn of a severe punishment from Him, and give glad tidings to the believers who do good deeds that theirs shall be a good recompense,

3. Wherein to abide forever.

4. And that he might warn those who say: "God has taken a son to Him."

5. They have no knowledge of it, nor did their fathers; grievous is the word that comes out of their mouths. They speak nothing but a lie,

6. Then maybe you will wear yourself out with grief if they do not believe in this announcement.

7. Verily We have caused whatever is in the earth to be an embellishment for it, that We may test them as to which of them is best in behaviour;

8. Indeed We will make whatever is on it bare, barren ground.

9. Or do you think that the fellows of the Cave and the Inscription (ar-Raqim) were a wonder of Our signs?

10. When the youths sought refuge in the cave, they said: "Lord! Grant us mercy from You and provide a right course for us in our affairs."

11. Then We set a seal on their ears for a number of years in the cave.

12. Then We raised them up that We might know which of the two parties was best able to reckon the duration of their stay.

13. We relate to you their story in truth; indeed, they were youths who believed in their Lord, and We increased them in guidance.

14. We strengthened their hearts with steadfastness when they stood up; they then said: "Our Lord is the Lord of the heavens and the earth; never will we ever call on any god other than Him, for indeed we should then have uttered an extravagance.

15. "These our people have taken gods other than Him; why do they bring no clear authority in their support? Who is there more unjust than he who forges a lie against God?"

16. (They were told): "When you have left them and what they worship besides God, betake yourselves for a refuge to the Cave; your Lord will extend His mercy to you and will provide for you a way to ease in your affair."

17. You could see the sun, when it rose, move away from their cave to the right, and when it sets it leaves them to the

left, while they were in the cleft thereof; this is one of the signs of God. Whomsoever God guides is rightly guided, and whomsoever He leaves to stray, you shall never find for him anyone to guide (to the right path).

18. You would have deemed them awake while they were asleep. And We turned them to the right and the left, and their dog lay stretching out his paws at the entrance. Had you seen them, you would surely have turned away frightened, and you would surely have been filled with awe.

19. Thus did We raise them that they might question each other. One of them asked: "How long have you tarried (here)?" They said: "We have tarried a day or part of a day." (others) said: "Your Lord (alone) knows best how long you have tarried (here); so, send one of you with this silver coin of yours to the city, and let him see which has the purest food, then let him bring provision to you from it, and let him behave with civility, and do not make yourselves known to anyone.

20. "Surely if they come to know about you, they will stone you, or force you to return to their creed, and then you will never succeed."

21. And thus did We cause them to come across them that they might know that God's promise is true, and that there is no doubt about the Hour. When they disputed among themselves regarding their affair, they said: "Build a monument over them. Their Lord knows them best." Those (believers) who prevailed in their affairs said: "Certainly we will raise a mosque over them."

22. They will say: "Three; the fourth of them was their dog." (Others) will say: "Five; the sixth of them was their dog," guessing about the unperceivable; and yet others say: "Seven; and the eighth of them was their dog." Say (O Our Prophet Muhammad): "My Lord knows best their number; none but a few know them;" therefore, do not dispute about them save in outward contention, and do not ask any about them."

23. Do not say about anything: "I will certainly do it tomorrow."

24. But only say: "If God will," and remember your Lord when you forget and say: "Maybe my Lord will guide me

nearer than this to the right (way)."

25. They stayed in the Cave three hundred years and nine more.

26. Say: "God (alone) knows best how long they stayed. To Him belongs what is unperceivable in the heavens and the earth; how clear His sight and hearing are! They have no guardian apart from Him, and He does not share anyone in His Sovereignty."

27. Recite what has been revealed to you of the Book of your Lord; none shall change His Word. And you shall not find any refuge other than Him.

28. Restrain yourself with those who call unto their Lord morning and evening, seeking to please Him, and do not let your eyes turn away from them, aspiring the pomp of the life of this world. And do not obey that whose heart We have made unmindful of remembering Us, and who follows his inclination, and his case is transgressing all limits.

29. Say: "The truth is from your Lord; so whoever chooses to believe, let him believe, and whoever elects to disbelieve, let him disbelieve." Verily We have prepared a Fire for the unjust ones; its canopy will encompass them, and when they cry for water, they shall be given water like molten brass which will scald their face; how wretched will the drink be, and how ill a resting place it is!

30. As to those who believe and do good deeds, We surely do not waste the recompense for any deed of righteousness.

31. For these are gardens of eternity beneath which rivers flow; they shall be adorned therein with bracelets of gold, and they shall wear green robes of fine silk, and thick brocades woven with gold, reclining therein on raised couches. What a blissful recompense, and how goodly a resting place!

32. Strike for them the similitude of two men; We provided for one of them two gardens of grape-vines, and We surrounded them with date-palms, and We placed corn fields in their midst.

33. Each garden brought forth fruit, failing nothing of it, and We caused a river to gush forth in their midst.

34. He had fruits (in abundance), and he said to his com-

panion, conversing, "I am greater than you in wealth, mightier in (the following of) men."

35. He entered his garden being unjust to his own self saying: "I do not think that this will ever perish,

36. "And I do not think that the Hour will ever come, and even if I am returned to my Lord, I will certainly find a better resort than this."

37. His companion, conversing with him, said: "Do you disbelieve in Him that created you from dust, then from a sperm-drop, then fashioned you (into) a complete man?

38. "As for me, God is my Lord, and I do not associate any with my Lord.

39. "And why did you not say, when you entered your garden, `(It is) as God willed; there is no power but with God'? If you perceive that I am less than you in wealth and children,

40. "Maybe my Lord will grant me better than your garden, and He may send on it a thunderbolt from heaven, that it becomes in the morning a barren and flat earth?

41. "Or its water becomes trapped under the ground, so that you are never able to find it."

42. His fruit was encircled (by destruction), so in the morning he was wringing his hands for what he had spent in it, and it lay on its trellises. He said: "Alas! Would that I had not associated anyone with my Lord!"

43. He had no force to help him other than God, nor could he help his own self.

44. Here protection is only from God, the True (One); He is the best to reward and to requite.

45. Set forth for them the similitude of the life of this world: it is like the water which We send down from heaven; the herbage of the earth mingles with it, then it becomes dry chaff which the winds scatter; God has power over all things.

46. Wealth and children are the adornments of the life of this world; and the ever-abiding good deeds are best in the eyes of your Lord in (earning) rewards, and best as hopes (of His mercy).

47. One day We shall cause the mountains to pass way, and you will see the earth a levelled plain, and We shall gather

them then, leaving none behind.

48. And they shall be brought forth before your Lord in ranks; (and they shall be told): "Now you have come to Us as We created you at first; nay, you supposed that We had never appointed a fulfillment (of Our promise) to you."

49. (When) the Book is set in place, you will then see the guilty fearful of what is (recorded) therein; and they will say: "Woe unto us! What a book this is! It leaves nothing (of our sins) unrecorded, be it small or big, without enumerating (each one of) them!" And they will find whatever they did present (in it), and your Lord does not deal unjustly with anyone.

50. When We said to the angels: "Prostrate before Adam," they all prostrated save Iblis; he was of the jinn, and he transgressed the command of his Lord. "Would you then take him and his progeny as friends rather than Me, and they are enemies to you?! How evil an exchange that is!

51. I did not call them to witness the creation of the heavens and the earth, nor the creation of their own selves, nor am I one who takes those who lead people astray as my helpers.

52. One Day, He shall say: "Call on those whom you thought to be My partners." They will call on them, but they will not listen to them, and We will set a valley of perdition between them.

53. The guilty ones shall see the Fire, and apprehend that they are falling into it, and they will find no escape therefrom.

54. Indeed We have displayed for mankind in this Qur'an every kind of similitude, but man is the most disputing of all beings.

55. What prevents people from believing, when guidance comes to them, and from praying for their Lord's forgiveness, except that what happened to the ancients should overtake them (too), or that (they ask that) the chastisement of the peoples of yore come face to face with them?

56. We only send messengers as bearers of glad tidings and warners, and those who disbelieve dispute in falsehood, that they may refute the truth with it, and they take My signs and that by which they have been warned for a jest.

57. Who is more unjust than that who is reminded of the signs of his Lord then he turns away from them and forgets what his two hands have sent forth? Verily We have caused veils over their hearts lest they should understand it, and in their ears a heaviness, and if you call them to guidance, they will never be rightly guided at all.

58. But your Lord is oft-Forgiving and Lord of mercy. Were He to seize them for what they have earned, surely He would hasten for them the chastisement; but for them is a tryst from which they shall never find a refuge.

59. We destroyed these towns when their inhabitants committed iniquities; but We had an appointed time for their destruction.

60. Behold! Moses said to his young servant: "I will not give up till I reach the junction of the two rivers, even if I go on for years."

61. So when they reached the junction of the two rivers, they forgot their fish, and it took its way into the sea, burrowing.

62. But when they had gone (some distance), he said to his youth: "Bring us our morning meal; indeed we have encountered weariness from this journey."

63. He said: "Did you see (what happened) when we took refuge on the rock, then verily I forgot the fish, and nothing made me forget to mention it but Satan; and it took its way into the sea? What a wonder!"

64. He said: "That is what we were seeking!" So they retraced their steps.

65. Then they found one of Our servants whom We had vouchsafed mercy from Us, and We had taught him knowledge from Ours.

66. Moses said to him: "Shall I follow you on condition that you teach me of the (higher) truth you have been taught?"

67. He said: "You certainly cannot bear patiently with me.

68. "How can you be patient about that of which you do not have full knowledge?"

69. He said: "You will find me patient, if God will, and I shall not disobey you in any matter."

70. He said: "If you follow me, do not ask me about any-

thing until I mention it to you myself."

71. Then they set off until they embarked in a boat, and he made a hole in it. (Moses) said: "Did you make a hole in it to drown its crew? Indeed you have done a strange thing."

72. He said: "Did I not tell you that you cannot bear patience with me?"

73. He (Moses) said: "Do not chide me that I forgot, and do not constrain me to a difficult thing in my affair."

74. Then they went on until they met a boy and he slew him. He said: "You slew an innocent person, not (in retaliation) for someone (he had slain)? Indeed you have done a horrible thing!"

75. He said: "Did I not tell you that you could not bear with me patiently?"

76. He said: "If I ever ask you about anything else after this (incident), then do not suffer me to remain in your company; then indeed you shall have found an excuse in my case."

77. Then they went on until they came to the people of a town. They asked its people for food, but they declined to receive them as guests; then they found in it a wall about to fall. He set it upright. He said: "If you had wished, you might surely have taken a wage for it."

78. He said: "This shall be the parting point between me and you. Now I will acquaint you with the real meaning of what you could not bear patiently with me.

79. "As for the boat, it belonged to some poor men who plied in the sea, and I intended that I should damage it, for there was a king after them who seized every boat by force.

80. "As for the boy, his parents are believers, and we feared that he should grieve them by rebellion and disbelief;

81. "So we desired that their Lord would instead bless them with one better than him in purity and closer in affection.

82. "As for the wall, it belongs to two orphan boys in the city. Underneath it is a treasure (intended) for them, and their father is a righteous man; so, your Lord willed that they should attain their maturity and take out their treasure as a mercy from Him; I did not do it of my own will. This is the

real meaning of that which you could not bear patiently."

83. They ask you about Dhul-Qarnayn (Double Horns). Say: "I shall recite to you something about him."

84. Verily We made him mighty in the world, and We gave him means of access to everything.

85. So he followed a route,

86. Until, the sun having set, he reached a place and found it setting in a black muddy pool, and he found people by it. We said: "O Dhul-Qarnayn! Either chastise them, or treat them with kindness."

87. He said: "As to him who is unjust, we shall chastise him, then he will be returned to his Lord, and He will chastise him with a grievous chastisement.

88. "As for him who believes and does good deeds, his shall be a goodly recompense, and his task shall be easy since we order it by our command."

89. Then he followed an easy route,

90. Until he reached the place where the sun rises. He found it rising on people for whom We had not provided any shelter from it.

91. Even so; and indeed We had full knowledge of whatever was with him.

92. Then he followed a route,

93. Until he reached a place between two mountains. He found on one side people who could scarcely understand a word.

94. They said: "Truly Gog and Magog cause mischief in the land. Shall we collect for you the (necessary) resources (from among ourselves) so that you may raise a barrier between us and them?"

95. He said: "The power in which my Lord has established me is better; so, help me only with the strength (of labourers). I will make a barrier between you and them.

96. "Bring me blocks of iron." When it filled the space between the mountain sides, he said: "Ply your bellows." Having made it red-hot with fire, he said: "Bring me molten brass that I may pour over it."

97. So they could not scale it, nor could they dig a hole therein.

98. He said: "This is a (sign of) mercy from my Lord; but

when the promise of my lord comes to pass, He will level it, and my Lord's promise is (always) true."

99. On that day, We will let them dash against one another, and the trumpet will be blown; then We will gather them all together.

100. And on that day We will present Hell to the disbelievers, fully exposed to their view,

101. Those whose eyes were under a veil against My reminder, and who could not bear to hear.

102. Do those who disbelieve think that they can take My servants as their guardians besides Me? In truth We have prepared Hell for the infidels to be entertained (therein).

103. Say (O Our Prophet Muhammad): "Shall We acquaint you with the greatest losers?"

104. "They are those whose efforts are lost in the life of this world, while they deem that they were acquiring good by their deeds.

105. "Those are the ones who disbelieved in the signs of their Lord, and in the meeting with Him; their deeds, therefore, shall be in vain, and He shall assign no weight for them on the Day of Resurrection."

106. Thus Hell is the recompense for what they disbelieved and held My signs and messengers with scorn.

107. Verily those who believe and do good deeds shall be entertained with the gardens of Paradise,

108. Abiding therein, desiring not to be removed therefrom.

109. Say (O Our Prophet Muhammad): "Should the sea become ink (to write) the words of my Lord, it would certainly be exhausted before my Lord's words are exhausted, (and) even if We bring the like of it to replenish."

110. Say: "I am only a man like you. It is revealed to me that your God is One God; therefore, whosoever desires to meet his Lord, let him do good deeds, not associating any in the worship of his Lord.

Mary
(Maryam)

In the name of God, the Beneficent, the Merciful.

1. Kaf; Ha; Ya; 'Ayn; Sad.

2. (This is) a recital of the mercy of your Lord to His servant Zachariah,

3. When he called unto his Lord in a low voice,

4. He said: "Lord! Verily my bones are weakened, and my head glistens with white hair; but I have never been unblessed in my supplication to you, O Lord!

5. "And verily I fear my kindred after me, and my wife is barren; so, grant me from Your an heir,

6. "Who shall inherit me and the family of Jacob. And make him, Lord, one with whom You are well-pleased."

7. "O Zachariah! Verily We convey to you the glad tidings of a son. His name shall be John (Yahya), and We have never given this name to anyone before."

8. He said: "Lord! How can I have a son when my wife is barren, and indeed I have reached extreme old age?"

9. He said: "So shall it be. Your Lord says it is easy, for indeed I created you aforetime when you were nothing."

10. He said: "Lord! Vouchsafe me a sign." He said: "Your sign is that you shall not speak to people for three nights, though sound (in health)."

11. Then he went out of the sanctuary to his people and signaled to them that they should glorify (God) morning and eve.

12. "O Yahya! Hold the Book fast!" We granted him judgment while still a child;

13. And compassion from Us and purity, and he was one who guarded himself (before God),

14. And he was dutiful to his parents, neither insolent nor disobedient.

15. Peace be on him the day he was born, the day he dies, and the day he is raised to life again.

16. And mention in the Book Mary (too), when she withdrew herself from her family to an eastward place.

17. Then she took a veil (to cover herself) from them; then We sent her Our Spirit, who appeared to her as a man

sound (in form).

18. She said: "Verily I take refuge in the Beneficent from you, if you are God-fearing."

19. He said: "I am only a messenger from your Lord to give you (the glad tidings of) a purified son."

20. She said: "How can I have a son while no man has touched me, nor have I been unchaste?"

21. He said: "So shall it be. Your Lord says: `It is easy for Me, and that We may make him a sign to people, and a mercy from Us. It is a matter (already) decreed.'"

22. So she conceived him and retired to a remote place.

23. And the birth-pangs forced her to betake herself to the trunk of a palm-tree. She said: "Oh! Would I had died before this and become a thing totally forgotten!"

24. The one who was beneath her then called out to her: "Do not grieve. Verily your Lord has set a stream beneath you;

25. "So shake yourself towards the trunk of the palm tree: it will drop dates fresh and ripe upon you;

26. "Then eat and drink, and cool your eye. Then if you see any man, say: `Verily I have vowed a fast to the Beneficent, and I shall speak to no man today.'"

27. She came with him to her people carrying him. They said: "O Mary! You have surely done something strange (unexpected of you)!

28. "Sister of Aaron! Neither your father was a bad man, nor was your mother unchaste."

29. She then pointed to him. They said: "How can we speak to a child in the cradle?"

30. He said: "Verily I am God's servant; He has given me a Book and made me a prophet.

31. "And He has made me blessed wherever I may be, and He has enjoined on me prayer and zakat as long as I live,

32. "And (to be) dutiful to my mother, and He has not made me insolent, unblessed.

33. "And peace be upon me the day I was born, the day I die, and the day I am raised to life again."

34. This is Jesus son of Mary; a statement of the truth about which they dispute.

35. It is not for God that He should take to Himself a son. Glory be to Him. When a matter is decreed, He only says to it "Be!" and it is.

36. "Indeed, God is my Lord and your Lord; so, serve (only) Him; this is the Right Path."

37. Then the sects disputed among themselves, and woe to those who disbelieved on account of a great day.

38. How clearly shall they hear, and how clearly shall they see, on the day when they come (back) to Us! The unjust this day are in manifest error.

39. Warn them against the intense regret, when the matter is decreed; they are (now) heedless, disbelieving.

40. Verily We inherit the earth and those who are upon it and to Us shall they all be returned.

41. And mention in the Book (Qur'an) Abraham; verily he was a man of truth, a Prophet (of Ours).

42. He (Abraham) said to his father, "O father! Why do you worship that which does not hear, nor see, nor does it avail you in aught?

43. "O father! Indeed it has come to me of the knowledge that which has not come to you; so follow me: I shall guide you on the Straight Path.

44. "O father! Do not worship Satan; verily Satan was disobedient to the Beneficent (God).

45. "O father! Verily I fear a chastisement shall touch you from the Beneficent (God) should you befriend Satan."

46. Said he, "Do you incline against my gods, O Abraham?! If you do not desist, I will certainly stone you; begone from me for a long while..."

47. He (Abraham) said, "Peace be on you! I shall pray my Lord to forgive you; verily He is most gracious unto me.

48. "I withdraw from you all and from what you call upon other than God, and I call upon only my Lord, haply in my prayer to my Lord I shall not be unblest."

49. And when he withdrew from them and from what they worshipped besides God, We granted him Isaac and Jacob, and each of them We made a prophet.

50. And We granted them of Our mercy and assigned to them a lofty tongue of truthfulness.

51. And mention in the Book (Qur'an) Moses; verily he

was specially chosen, a messenger, and a prophet.

52. And We called upon him from the right side of Mount Sinai and made him draw nigh (to Us) for a communion.

53. And We granted him out of Our mercy his brother Aaron (also) a prophet.

54. And mention in the Book (Qur'an) Ishmael; verily he was ever true to his promise, and he was a messenger, a prophet.

55. And he enjoined upon his family prayers and charity, and he was well-pleasing to his Lord.

56. And mention in the Book (Qur'an) Idris; verily he was a truthful one, a prophet.

57. And We exalted him to a high station.

58. These are the ones upon whom God bestowed His bounties from among the prophets of the posterity of Adam, and of those whom We carried (in the ark) with Noah, and of the posterity of Abraham and Israel, and of those whom We guided and We chose. When the Signs of the Beneficent (God) were rehearsed to them, they fell down prostrating (in obeisance), weeping.

59. But a succession followed after them who neglected the prayers and they followed their lust, so they shall soon meet perdition -

60. Except those who repented and believed and did good dees; these shall enter the garden (Paradise) and they shall not be dealt with unjustly in the least.

61. The Gardens of Eternity which the Beneficent (God) has promised to His servants in the Unseen: for His promise shall come to pass.

62. They will not hear any vain discourse therein but peace, and they shall have their sustenance therein in the morn and in the eve.

63. This is the garden (Paradise) which We shall cause to be inherited by the pious from among Our servants.

64. (The angels say:) "O Messenger of God (Muhammad)! We do not come down except by the command of your Lord. His is whatever before us and whatever behind us and whatever between these! And Your Lord is not forgetful.

65. "The Lord of the heavens and the earth and whatever between them both; so worship Him (alone), and be

steadfast in His worship! Do you know anyone else named with the same name?!"

66. Man says, "What?! When I am dead, shall I be brought forth alive?!"

67. What?! Does man not bear in mind that We created him before when he was naught?

68. So by your Lord! Most certainly We shall gather them together and Satan too; then shall We certainly bring them forth round Hell on their knees.

69. Then shall We pick out from every group among them those who wre more intensely rebellious against the Beneficent (God).

70. And We certainly know best those who deserve most to be burnt therein.

71. And (there is) none among you but shall go down to it; this is of your Lord an (unavoidable) decided Decree.

72. Then We shall save those who guarded themselves against evil, and We shall leave the unjust therein on their knees.

73. When Our clear Signs are rehearsed unto them, those who disbelieve say to those who believe, "Which of the two parties is best in action? And which is the most goodly company?!"

74. How many of the generations before them did We destroy? They were even better equipped and were more glittering to the eye.

75. Say (O Our Messenger Muhammad!): "As to those who are in error, the Beneficent (God) will certainly prolong the span of their lives until they behold what they were promised, be it the chastisement (in this world) or the Doom; then they shall know who is worse placed and who is weakest in forces!"

76. God increases in guidance those who are guided aright; and the everlasting good deeds are best with your Lord in recompense and best in the ultimate return.

77. Have you then seen him who disbelieves in Our Signs and says: "I shall surely be given wealth and children"?

78. Has he got into the knowledge of the unseen?! Or has he taken a promise from the Beneficent (God)?!

79. By no means! We shall write down what he says and

We shall prolong for him the duration of the chastisement.

80. And We shall return all what he spoke of, and he shall come to Us all alone.

81. They have taken gods besides God to give them power and glory!

82. By no means! Soon shall they disavow their worship, and they shall be adversaries against them.

83. What?! Do you not see that We have sent satans against the disbelievers to incite them with an incitement (to sin)?

84. So do not be in haste against them; We only count to them a limited number (of days).

85. On the Day (of Resurrection), We will gather the pious to the Beneficent (God) like the guests of honour.

86. But We will drive the guilty ones to Hell like (the thirsty) herd (to the watering place).

87. They shall have no intercession save that who has taken a promise from the Beneficent (God to do so).

88. And they say, "The Beneficent (God) has taken a son to Him"!

89. Indeed you have put forth a most monstrous thing!

90. The heavens might be burst thereat, and the earth might cleave asunder, and the mountains fall down in fragments -

91. That they should ascribe a son to the Beneficent (God).

92. Nay! It does not behove the Beneficent (God) that He should take (to Him) a son.

93. None of the beings in the heavens and the earth but must come to the Beneficent (God) as a servant.

94. And indeed He has an account of all, and He numbered them with an exact numbering.

95. And each one of them shall come to Him on the Day of Judgment singly.

96. Verily, the Beneficent (God) will bestow love upon those who believe and do good deeds.

97. So have We only made it (Qur'an) easy in your own tongue so that you might give glad tidings thereby to the pious, and to warn thereby people who are contentious.

98. And how many generaions did We destroy before them? Do you find out anyone (anywhere)? Or do you hear

even a whisper of them at all?

Ta Ha

In the name of God, the Beneficent, the Merciful

1. Ta Ha.

2. We did not send the Qur'an to you (O Our Messenger Muhammad!) so that you distress yourself!

3. Save as a Reminder to him who fears God.

4. (It is) a Missive (sent down) from Him Who created the earth and the heavens on high.

5. The Beneficent (God), firm on the Arsh (throne of authority).

6. His is whatever in the heavens and in the earth, and what is between them twain, and what is beneath the lowest of the low below the earth.

7. And if you speak aloud (or whisper), verily He knows all that is secret and whatsoever is yet more hidden.

8. God, there is no god but He; His are all the very Best Names.

9. Has the story of Moses come to you?

10. When he saw a fire, he said to his family, "Tarry here, for verily I perceive a fire; haply I may bring you a brand from it, or I may find at the fire some guidance."

11. So when he came to it (the fire), a voice called: "O Moses!

12. "Verily I am your Lord! So take off your shoes; you are in the sacred valley of Tuwa.

13. "And I have chosen you (for Prophethood), so hearken to what is revealed (to you)!

14. "Verily I (alone) am God; there is no god but I; worship (only) Me, and establish prayer for My Remembrance!

15. "Verily the Hour (of Doom) is sure to come but My design is to keep it hidden, so that every soul may be recompensed with what it endeavours.

16. "Therefore do not let him who does not believe in it, who follows his own vain desires, turn you away from the truth else you should perish.

17. "And what is this in your hand, O Moses?"

18. He said: "This is my staff; I recline on it, and I beat

down leaves with it for my sheep, and for me therein other uses too."

19. He said: "Cast it down, O Moses!"

20. So when he cast it down, lo, it was a serpent running.

21. He said: "Take hold of it, and have no fear, for We shall restore it to its former state.

22. "And place your hand under your armpit, it shall come forth white without any harm, another Sign (miracle),

23. "That We may show you of Our greater Signs (miracles).

24. "Go to Pharaoh! Verily he has transgressed all bounds!"

25. Said he, "Lord! Expand my breast,

26. "And make my task easy for me,

27. "And loosen the knot of my tongue,

28. "(So that) they may understand my speech,

29. "And appoint for me an aide from my family,

30. "Aaron my brother,

31. "Strengthen my back by him,

32. "And associate him in my affair,

33. "So that we may glorify You much,

34. "And remember You much,

35. "Verily You are over-seeing over us."

36. He (God) said: "Granted is your prayer, O Moses!"

37. And indeed We conferred Our favour on you at another time (before),

38. When We revealed to your mother what was revealed,

39. That: "Cast him into a chest, then cast it into the sea, then the sea shall throw him ashore;" there he shall be taken by one who is an enemy to Me and an enemy to him; and I cast down (the garment of) love over you from Me (that everyone may love you); so that you might be brought up under My eyes (as I please):

40. Behold! Your sister went (to Pharaoh's wife) and said: "Shall I show you one who will take care of him?" So We brought you back to your mother so that her eyes might be cooled and she might grieve no more; and you even killed a man (and were perturbed) and We saved you from the grief and We tried you with a heavy trial and then you tar-

ried among the people of Midian, then you came hither as ordained (by Us), O Moses!

41. And I have chosen you for Myself;

42. Go, you and your brother, with my Signs (miracles) and do not slacken either of you in remembering Me.

43. Go both of you to Pharaoh, verily he has transgressed (the bounds).

44. Then speak both of you to him a gentle word, haply he may get admonished or fear (Our retribution).

45. Both (Moses and Aaron) said: "Lord! Verily we fear lest he should hasten with insolence against us or lest he should transgress all bounds."

46. He (God) said: "Fear not, both of you; verily I am with you both; I do hear and see,

47. "So go both of you to him and say: `Verily we are messengers from your Lord; so, send with us the children of Israel and do not torment them! Indeed we have brought Signs (miracles) from your Lord; and peace will be to him who follows the guidance;

48. "Verily, it has indeed been revealed to us that the chastisement shall certainly come upon him who lies and turns back."

49. (Pharaoh) Said: "And who is the lord of both of you, O Moses?"

50. He (Moses) said: "Our Lord is He Who gave to everything its (suitable) form and then (also) guided it aright."

51. (Pharaoh) Said: "What then is the state of the past generations?"

52. He said: "The knowledge thereof is with my Lord in a Book (secured by Him); my Lord does not err, nor does He forget."

53. He Who made the earth for you a bed and made for you paths therein, and sent down from the heavens water; then We have brought forth thereby pairs of plants various (in kinds),

54. Eat and pasture your cattle; verily in this are Signs for those who are endowed with understanding.

55. From the (earth) did We create you, and into it will We return you, and out of it will We bring you forth a second time.

56. And indeed We showed him Our Signs, all of them, but he belied and refused (to believe).

57. Said he: "Have you come to us so that you turn us out of our land by your sorcery, O Moses?!

58. "Then we too will certainly produce before you a sorcery like it, so make between us and you a tryst which we will not fail nor should you, in a place where both (parties) shall have even chances."

59. (Moses) Said: "Your tryst shall be the day of the festival, and let the people be gathered together in the bright of the noon."

60. So Pharaoh turned back and collected his crafts and thereafter he came.

61. Moses said to them: "Woe unto you! Do not forge a lie against God lest He should destroy you by a chastisement; whoever forges a lie shall certainly fail."

62: Then they (magicians) disputed about their affair among themselves, and they kept their talk a secret.

63. (At last) they said: "These two are certainly (expert) sorcerers who intend to drive you out of your land by their sorcery and wipe out your most exemplary tradition!

64. "So muster your plan then come in an (organized) order; and indeed whoever overcomes this day shall gain the upper hand."

65. They said: "O Moses! Either you cast (first) or we shall be the first to cast down."

66. (Moses) said: "Nay! You cast down (first)!" Then lo! Their cords and rods seemed to him by their sorcery as if they were running.

67. Then Moses felt fear within himself.

68. Said We: "Fear not! Verily you shall be the uppermost!

69. "And cast down what is in your right hand; it shall swallow up whatever they have wrought; verily they have wrought by the plan of a sorcerer, and a sorcerer shall never be successful whatever his manner (of skill) may be."

70. Then the sorcerers fell down prostrating and they said: "We believe in the Lord of Aaron and Moses!"

71. (Pharaoh) said: "Do you believe in him before I give you leave? Verily he is your chief (sorcerer) who taught you

sorcery; I shall therefore cut off your hands and your feet on the opposite sides, and I will crucify you on the trunks of palm trees, then you will certainly come to know which of us is more severe in tormenting and more abiding!"

72. They said: "Never shall we prefer you to what has come to us of the clear Signs, to Him Who made us; so, decree whatever you will, for you can decree only about the life of this world,

73. "Verily we do believe in our Lord that He may forgive us our sins and the sorcery you compelled us (to do); and God is the Best and the Most Abiding!"

74. Verily for him who comes to his Lord as a sinner shall be Hell; he shall never die in it nor shall he live.

75. And whosoever comes to Him as a believer, having done good deeds, for them are ranks that are sublime,

76. Gardens of Eternity beneath which rivers flow to abide therein, and such is the recompense of the one who purifies himself (from evil).

77. Indeed We revealed to Moses: "Travel by night with My servants and strike for them a dry path in the sea, and do not fear to be overtaken (by Pharaoh), nor should you fear (drowning)."

78. And Pharaoh followed them with his hosts, and the billows of the seas covered them as they were drowned.

79. And Pharaoh led his people astray and he never guided them aright.

80. O children of Israel! We rescued you from your foe and made a Covenant with you on the right side of the Tur (Mount Sinai), and We sent down to you the manna and quails:

81. Eat of the good things with which We have provided you and do not transgress lest My Wrath should descend upon you, and upon whoever My Wrath descends is certain to perish.

82. And verily I am the Most Forgiving to the one who repents and believes and does good deeds, then he continues to follow the right guidance.

83. (God said:) "But what made you hasten (away) from your people, O Moses?"

84. (Moses) said: "They are close on my track and I has-

tened to you, Lord, so that You might be well-pleased (with me)."

85. (God) said: "Verily We have tried your people in your absence, and the Samiri had led them astray."

86. So Moses returned to his people angry, sorrowful, and said: "O my people! Did your Lord not promise you a goodly promise? Did then the promise seem long to you? Or did you wish that the Wrath from your Lord should descend upon you for violating the tryst with me?"

87. They said: "We did not violate the tryst with you out of our own accord, but we were made to bear the burdens of the ornaments of the people, so we cast them away, and thus did the Samiri suggest."

88. Then he brought forth (from the fire) for them (the image of) a calf, a (mere) body which (also) gave out the lowing sound. Then they said: "This is your god and the god of Moses, except that he (Moses) has forgotten."

89. What?! Do not they see that it could not return to them a word (for an answer) and that it could neither hurt nor benefit them?!

90. And indeed Aaron had said to them before: "O my people! Verily you are tried by it (image) and verily your Lord is the Beneficent (God), so follow me and obey my order."

91. They said: "Never shall we cease worshipping it until Moses returns to us."

92. (Moses) said: "O Aaron! What hindered you when you saw them going astray -

93. "That you did not follow me? Have you then disobeyed my order?"

94. (Aaron) said: "O son of my mother! Do not seize me by my beard nor by my head; I was afraid lest you should say: `You have caused a division among the children of Israel and did not respect my word!'"

95. (Moses) said: "What was your case, O Samiri?"

96. (Samiri) said: "I saw what they did not see, so I took a handful of (the dust) from the track of the Messenger (angel) and flung it (into the image of the calf) for so did my self prompt me (to do)."

97. (Moses) said: "Begone then, verily for you it shall be

in this life to say: `Touch me not'; and (besides this) you have a tryst (of punishment) that will never fail; and (now) look at your god whose worship you kept (so long); certainly we shall burn it then we shall certainly scatter (the ashes) of it into the sea (with a wide) scattering!

98. "Verily your God is only Allah; there is no god but He; He comprehends all things in (His) Knowledge!"

99. Thus do We relate to you (O Our Messenger Muhammad!) of the (historic) accounts of what has passed (of old); and indeed We have given to you from Ourselves a Reminder (Qur'an).

100. Whosoever turns aside from it shall certainly bear on the Day of Resurrection a burden,

101. Abiding therein; while grievous will it be for them on the Day of Resurrection to bear,

102. (On) the Day when the trumpet is blown and We gather the guilty ones, the blear-eyed (terrified) ones.

103. They shall consult among themselves in a low voice (saying): "You tarried but only ten (days)..."

104. We know best what they will say, when the most ideal ones of them in conduct will say: "You tarried but only one day!"

105. And they ask you (O Our Messenger Muhammad!) about the mountains; say, "My Lord will root them up and scatter them away as dust (on the Day of Resurrection),

106. "Then He shall leave it a plain, smooth level,

107. "You shall see in it no crookedness nor unevenness."

108. On that Day, they shall follow the summoner, no crookedness (shall be shown) to him, and low shall be the voices before the Beneficent (God) that you shall hear naught but the light footfall.

109. On that Day, no intercession shall avail anyone save (that of) whom God has permitted and with whose word He is pleased.

110. He knows what is before them and what is behind them, while they do not comprehend it according to their own knowledge.

111. And all faces shall be humbled before the ever-Living, the self-Subsistent God, and indeed disappointed will be

he who bears iniquity.

112. And whosoever does good deeds and he is a believer shall have no fear of injustice (to him) nor of any curtailment (of his dues).

113. Thus have We sent down (to you, O Our Messenger Muhammad!) an Arabic Qur'an and explained therein some of the threats that they may adopt piety or that it may serve to them as a reminder.

114. High above all is God, the King, the self-Existent Truth; and do not hasten (O Our Messenger Muhammad!) with the Qur'an before it is completed to you in revelation, and say, "O my Lord! Increase me in knowledge!"

115. And indeed We had made a covenant with Adam before but he forgot; yet We did not find in him any intention (to disobey Us).

116. When We said to the angels, "Prostrate in obeisance to Adam," they prostrated in obeisance save Iblis; he refused.

117. Then We said: "O Adam! Verily this is an enemy to you and your wife; therefore, let him not drive you both out of the Garden for then you should be put to toil,

118. "For you it is ordained that you shall not be hungry in it, nor shall you be naked.

119. "And that you shall not be thirsty in it, nor shall you feel the heat of the sun."

120. But Satan whispered to him saying, "O Adam! Shall I guide you to the tree of eternity and to a kingdom which never decays?"

121. Then they both ate of it, so their nakedness appeared to them and they both began to cover themselves with the leaves of the garden; and Adam acted not (according to the advice of) his Lord and he strayed.

122. Then his Lord chose him and turned to him and guided him.

123. (And God) said: "Get down hence both of you, all together, one of you (being) the enemy of the other. So guidance will surely come to you from Me, then whoever follows My guidance, he shall not stray nor shall he grieve.

124. "And whoever turns away from mentioning Me, verily his shall be a straitened life, and We shall raise him up

on the Day of judgment blind."

125. He shall say: "Lord! Why have you raised me blind whereas indeed I was seeing (before)?"

126. (God) will say: "Thus (is your recompense) for Our Signs came to you which you ignored, and as such you are forsaken this very Day.

127. "Thus will We reward him who transgresses and rejects the Signs of his Lord, and certainly the torment of the hereafter will be more severe and more lasting."

128. What?! Does it not guide them aright (to know) how many generations We destroyed before them, amidst whose dwellings they (now) walk about? Verily in this are Signs for those (endowed) with understanding.

129. Had not a Word from your Lord gone forth, their punishment would have immediately ensued; and the term (of respite) appointed.

130. So be patient with what they say, and glorify your Lord by praising Him before the rising of the sun and before its setting, and in some hours of the night glorify Him, and during parts of the day, that you may achieve the Pleasure (or your Lord).

131. And do not strain your eyes to that with which We have provided (different) parties of them of the splendour of the life of this world, so that We may try them thereby; for the provision of your Lord is better and more abiding.

132. And enjoin prayer on your followers, and adhere steadily to it, We ask you not for subsistence, but We Ourselves give you subsistence; and the success of the hereafter is for those who guard themselves (against evil).

133. And they say, "Why does he not bring us a Sign from his Lord?" What?! Has not there come to them the clear evidence which were in the former Scriptures?

134. And had We destroyed them with a chastisement before this, they would certainly have said: "Lord! Why did you not send us a Messenger for then we would have followed Your Signs before we were thus humiliated and disgraced?"

135. Say (O Our Messenger Muhammad!): "Every one (of us) is awaiting, so you too wait; then soon you will come to know who have been the followers of the even way and

who has been guided aright."

The Prophets
(al-Anbiya)

In the name of God, the Beneficent, the Merciful

1. Nigh has drawn to people (the day of) their reckoning, yet they heedlessly are turning aside.

2. Every time a new reminder comes to them from their Lord, they hear it, and they get busy in sport.

3. Preoccupied with trifles and discoursing in secret are those who did wrong (saying): "Is this (man) other than a human being like your own selves? What?! Will you then yield to sorcery while you see (it)?!"

4. He said: "My Lord (well) knows (every) word in the heavens and the earth, and He is the all-Hearing, the all-Knowing."

5. Nay! They say: "(These are) medleys of dreams! Nay! He has forged it! Nay! He is a poet; let him then bring us a Sign like the ones that were sent to the former ones (Messengers)."

6. None of the people of the towns which We destroyed before them believed. What?! Will these (now) believe?!

7. And We sent none before you except men to whom We revealed, so ask the people of the Reminder if you do not know.

8. We did not give them bodies which did not eat food, nor were they to abide (in this world) forever.

9. Then We fulfilled to them Our Promise, and We saved them and those whom We willed, and We destroyed the extravagant ones.

10. Indeed We have sent down to you a Book (Qur'an) wherein is your remembrance; what! Do you not then understand?

11. How many a town (the people of) which were iniquitous did We destroy, and We raised up after it another people?

12. So when they felt (the coming of) Our torment, lo, they tried to flee therefrom.

13. (We said): "Flee not but return to that wherein you revelled, and to your dwellings, haply you will be ques-

tioned."

14. They said: "Oh! Woe unto us! Verily we were unjust!"

15. And their cry never ceased till We made them like reaped corn, extinct,

16. We did not create the heavens and the earth and what is between them for sport.

17. Had We intended that We should take amusement, We could certainly have taken it from (the things) with Us, if We would have done it.

18. Nay! We hurl the truth upon falsehood, that it crushes its head, and lo! It vanishes, and woe unto you for what you described (of God).

19. His is whatsoever in the heavens and in the earth; those who are with Him are not proud to worship Him, nor do they get weary.

20. They glorify (Him) by night and by day, and they never intermit.

21. Or have they taken gods from the earth who can raise (the dead)?

22. Had there been in (the heavens and the earth other) gods except God, both (heavens and earth) would have been in disorder; so glorified is God, Lord of the Arsh (throne) from what they attribute (to Him).

23. He is not questioned about what He does, but they shall be questioned.

24. Have they taken besides Him other gods? Say (O Our Messenger Muhammad!): "Bring your proof. This (Qur'an) is the Reminder to those with me, and the Reminder to those before me; nay! Most of them do not know the truth, so they turn aside."

25. And We did not send any Messenger before you (O Our Messenger Muhammad!) but We revealed to him that "Verily there is no god but I; so worship Me (Alone)."

26. And they say: "The Beneficent (God) has taken to Him a son." Glory be to Him! Nay! They are (His) honoured servants.

27. They speak not before He speaks, and they act only on His bidding.

28. He knows what is before them and what is behind

them, and they cannot intercede but for him whom He approves and they, of fearing Him, tremble.

29. And whosoever of them says: "Verily I am god" besides Him, such one We will recompense with Hell; thus do We recompense the iniquitous.

30. Can those who disbelieve not see that the heavens and the earth were one piece, and that We cleft them asunder, and We made of water everything alive? Will they not then believe?

31. And We have made in the earth (lofty) mountains (standing firm) lest it should shake with them, and We have made therein broad highways that they may be guided aright.

32. And We have made the heavens a canopy, well-guarded, and yet they, from its Signs, turn aside.

33. And He it is Who created the night and the day, the sun and the moon, all in their (respective) orbits move.

34. We did not grant any man before you life eternal. What then if you die, will they live forever?

35. Every soul shall have the taste of death; We try you with evil and with good (by the way of) test; and to Us shall you all be returned;

36. When you behold those who disbelieve, they treat you with nothing but ridicule (saying): "Is this the one who speaks of your gods?" while they, at the mention of the Beneficent (God), are themselves disbelievers.

37. Man is made of haste; I shall show you My Signs, so ask Me not to hasten (on).

38. And they say: "When will this promise (of threat) come to pass, if you are truthful?"

39. If only those who disbelieve come to know when they shall not be able to keep off (hell) fire from their faces and backs nor shall they be helped.

40. Nay! But it shall come on them suddenly, and it shall make them confounded, so they shall neither be able to repel it, nor will they be respited.

41. And indeed (some) of the messengers before you were ridiculed too, but those who ridiculed were surrounded by that (very torment) which they had been ridiculing.

42. Say (O Our Messenger Muhammad!): "Who can protect you by night and by day from the Beneficent (God)?"

Nay! They from the remembrance of their Lord turn aside.

43. Or have they gods who can protect them from Us? They have no power to help their own selves, nor shall they ever be protected from Us.

44. Nay! We provided (enjoyment) to these and their fathers until the period grew long for them. What?! See they not that We come to the land, shortening its borders? Shall they then be the prevailing ones?

45. Say (O Our Messenger Muhammad!): "Verily I do but warn you by the revelation (from God);" but the deaf will not hear the call whenever they are warned.

46. And yet if a blast of your Lord's punishment touches them, they will certainly say: "Woe unto us! Verily we had been unjust!"

47. And We shall set up the balances of justice on the Day of Judgment, so no soul shall be dealt with unjustly in the least, and even if there be the weight of a grain of mustard seed, (even that) We will bring it (into account), and sufficient are We as reckoners.

48. Indeed We did grant Moses and Aaron the (Book of) Criterion (between right and wrong), and light and a reminder for the pious -

49. Who fear their unseen Lord, and of the Hour (of doom) they are frightened.

50. This (Qur'an) is a blessed Reminder which We have sent down (to Our Messenger Muhammad). Do you then deny it?

51. And indeed We gave to Abraham his rectitude before, and We did know him well.

52. (Recollect, O Our Messenger Muhammad!) when (Abraham) said to his father and his people: "What are these images to which you (as devotees) cleave?"

53. They said: "We found our fathers worshipping them."

54. He said: "Indeed you and your fathers had been in manifest error."

55. They said: "Have you brought us the truth, or are you of the jesters?"

56. He said: "Nay! Your Lord is the Lord of the heavens and the earth, Who has created them, and I to this am a witness.

57. "And by God, I will scheme against your idols after you go away, turning back."

58. So he broke them into pieces except the chief among them so that they may haply return (to their better judgment).

59. They said: "Who has done this to our gods? Verily this is of the unjust ones."

60. (Some others) said: "We heard a youth speak of them; he is called Abraham."

61. They said: "Then bring him before the eyes of the people that they may bear witness."

62. They said: "Have you done this to our gods, O Abraham?"

63. (Abraham) said: "Nay! The chief of them has done it! It is this (idol)! So ask them, if they can speak at all!"

64. Then they turned to themselves and said: "Verily you yourselves are the unjust ones."

65. Then they were confounded in their heads (and they helplessly said): "You know fully well that these (idols) do not speak!"

66. (Abraham) said: "What! Do you worship then besides God what profits you naught, nor can they do you any harm either?

67. "Fie upon you and upon what you worship besides God! What?! Do you not understand?!"

68. They said: "Burn him and help your gods if you can do (anything at all)."

69. We said, "O fire! Be cool and a (means of) safety for Abraham."

70. And they intended a scheme against him, but We made them the losers.

71. And We delivered him and (also) Lot, (and took them safely) to the land which We have blessed for all nations of the world.

72. And We bestowed upon him Isaac and Jacob as an additional gift, and We made all of them righteous.

73. And We made them leaders guiding (people) by Our Command, and We revealed to them the doing of good, the establishing of prayer, the giving of alms, and (only) Us did they worship.

74. And to Lot We granted wisdom and knowledge, and We delivered him from the town whose people were doing filthy deeds, for they were evil people, perverts.

75. And We admitted him into Our mercy; verily he was of the righteous.

76. (Remember) Noah, when he cried aforetime. We responded to him and delivered him and his companions from the great calamity.

77. And We helped him against his people who rejected Our Signs; verily they were evil people, so We drowned them all.

78. And David and Solomon when they were judging about the cornfield when the sheep of certain people pastured in it by night, and We to their judgment were Witnesses.

79. Then We made Solomon to understand it, and to each one We gave wisdom and knowledge, and We made the mountains and the birds subservient to David, to sing hymns of (Our praise), and We were the doers.

80. And We taught him the art of making the coat of mail for you that you might protect yourselves in your wars; will you then be grateful?

81. And to Solomon (We subjected) the wind blowing violently at his command to the land wherein We had blessed, and We are of all things the Knowers.

82. And of the satans there were those who used to dive for him and to do other work besides that, and We were guardians over them.

83. And (remember) Job (Ayyub), when he cried to his Lord (saying): "Verily distress has touched me, and You are the Most Merciful of the merciful ones!"

84. So We responded to him and We removed that which distressed him and We restored his people to him and even doubled their number as a mercy from Us and a Reminder to the worshippers (of Us).

85. And (remember) Ishmael and Idris and Zulkifl; all were of the patient ones.

86. We admitted them into Our mercy; verily they were of the righteous.

87. And (remember) Jonah (Thul-Nun, i.e. Younus) when

he went in anger and imagined that We would not have power over him; then he cried out from the darkness: "There is no god but You! Glory be to you; verily I was of the unjust ones!"

88. Then We responded to him and delivered him from the distress, thus do We deliver the believers.

89. And (remember) Zachariah when he cried to his Lord: "O Lord! Do not leave me alone (without offspring) though You are the best of heirs!"

90. Then We responded to him and granted him John (Yahya) and cured his wife (of her barrenness); verily they did vie in goodness and did call unto Us with love and reverence and were to Us humbled.

91. And (O Our Messenger Muhammad!) Remember her (Mary) who guarded her chastity. We breathed into her Our Spirit, and We made her and her son a Sign to all peoples.

92. Verily this Brotherhood of yours is a single Brotherhood, and I am your Lord! Therefore worship Me (alone).

93. But they have rent this (Brotherhood) asunder (into sects), and yet to Us shall all of them return.

94. So whosoever shall do good deeds and he is a believer, there shall be no rejection of his endeavour, and verily We will write it down for him.

95. There is a ban on any people of the towns which We destroyed that they shall never return,

96. Until Gog and Magog are let loose, and they shall from every elevation hasten forth.

97. And the true promise shall draw nigh, then lo! The eyes of those who disbelieve shall stare in amazement; (and they shall say): "Woe to us! Indeed we were in heedlessness as to this; nay! We were the unjust ones."

98. Verily you and what you worship besides God shall be the fuel of Hell (fire); to it shall you (surely) come.

99. Had these been gods, they would not have got there, but they shall all abide therein.

100. For them therein shall be groaning, and they shall not hear therein (any other sound).

101. Verily those for whom goodness from Us was sent forth, those from it (Hell) shall be kept away.

102. They will not hear (even) the slightest sound of it

(Hell) and they in what their souls desire shall abide.

103. Grief shall not reach them nor the great terror, and the angels shall meet them (saying): "This is your Day which you were promised."

104. On that Day We will roll up the heavens as the written scroll is rolled up; just as We caused the first creation, so will We start a new one. (It is) a promise binding on Us, verily We were doing it.

105. And indeed We did write in the Psalms (Zabur) after the Reminder (Torah) that My righteous Servants shall inherit the earth.

106. Verily in this (Qur'an) is a message for people who worship (Us).

107. And We did not send you (O Our Messenger Muhammad!) but as a mercy for all the worlds.

108. Say: "It has only been revealed to me that your God is One God; will you then submit (to Him)?"

109. And if they turn back, say: "I have warned you all alike, and I know not whether nigh or far is that which you are promised.

110. "Verily He knows what is spoken aloud and He knows too what you hide.

111. "And I know not haply this (respite) may be a trial for you and a provision until a time."

112. (The Messenger Muhammad, praying) said: "Lord! Judge with the truth, and Our Lord is the Beneficent Whose help is sought against what you (people) ascribe (to Him)."

The Pilgrimage
(al-Hajj)

In the name of God, the Beneficent, the Merciful

1. O people! Fear your Lord! Indeed, the quake of the Hour is terrifying!

2. On the day, when you behold it, every suckling mother shall forsake the babe she had suckled, and every pregnant woman shall lay down her burden, and you shall behold people looking drunk, but they are not drunk; God's chastisement, though, will be terrifying.

3. Among people is he who disputes about God with-

out knowledge, following every rebellious Satan.

4. Against him is decreed that whosoever takes him as his friend, then he shall beguile him and lead him to the torment of the burning Fire.

5. O people! If you are in doubt about the Rising, then We created you from dust, then from a drop of sperm, then from a clot, then from a lump of flesh, wholly formed and (sometimes) partially formed, that We may manifest Our power to you. And We cause what We will to stay in the womb until an appointed term, then We bring you forth infants, that you may reach maturity. And of you is he who is caused to die, and of you is he who is kept to the feeblest age that he knows nothing after having known. You behold the earth dead dry, but when We send down water upon it, it stirs and swells and produces every kind of attractive herbage.

6. This is (so) because God is indeed True, and because He gives life to the dead, and He has power over all things.

7. And that the Hour is coming; there is no doubt therein, and that God will raise those who are in the graves.

8. Among people is one who disputes about God without knowledge or any guidance, or an enlightening book,

9. Turning away haughtily that he may lead people astray from the way of God. For him is a disgrace in this world, and We shall make him taste the punishment of the burning Fire on the Day of Judgment.

10. "This is for what both of your hands had sent before; verily God is not unjust to His servants."

11. Among people is he who worships God on the verge; so, if good befalls him, he is satisfied, and if a trial afflicts him, he turns away, losing both this world and the hereafter; that is the manifest loss.

12. He calls besides God that which does not harm him nor profits him; that is straying far off.

13. He calls upon one whose harm is nearer than his advantage. Evil is his guardian, and it certainly is his companion.

14. Indeed, God will admit those Who believe and do good deeds into gardens beneath which rivers flow. God does what He intends.

15. Whoever thinks that God will never help him in this life nor the hereafter, let him stretch a cord to the heavens, then let him sever it, then see if his device takes away what he is enraged at.

16. We have thus revealed it as manifest signs, so that God may guide whomsoever He pleases.

17. On the Day of Judgment, God will decide between those who believe, those who are Jews, the Sabians, the Christians, the Magians, and the polytheists; verily God is witness over all things.

18. Do you not see that to God prostrates whosoever is in the heavens and the earth, the sun and the moon, the stars and the mountains, the trees and the animals, and many people, too? Whomsoever God disgraces, there is none for him to honour. Indeed, God does whatever He pleases.

19. These are two disputants who dispute about their Lord: As for those who disbelieved, garments of fire shall be cut for them, and boiling water shall be poured over their heads.

20. With it shall be melted whatsoever is in their bellies, and their skins, too.

21. And for them are hooked rods of iron.

22. Every time they intend to get away therefrom, out of anguish, they are turned into it. Taste the torment of the burning Fire.

23. God will admit those who believe and do good deeds into gardens beneath which rivers flow; they shall be adorned therein with bracelets of gold and with pearls, and their clothing therein shall be of silk.

24. For they are guided to goodly words, and they are guided to the path of the Praised One.

25. Those who disbelieve and obstruct the way of God and from the Sacred Mosque which We have made equally for the dweller therein as well as the stranger, and whoever intends to unjustly do wrong therein, We will make him taste a grievous chastisement.

26. Behold! We fixed for Abraham the place of the House, "Associate nothing with Me, and cleanse My House for those who circumambulate and stand in prayer, and bow and prostrate themselves.

27. "And proclaim the hajj to the people. They will then come to you from every remote way, on foot, and on lean camels.

28. "That they may witness advantages for them, and mention the name of God during the appointed days over what He has provided them of livestock quadruped, and then eat of them and feed the poor."

29. Then let them tidy themselves and fulfill their vows, and let them circumambulate the Ancient House.

30. Let (the pilgrimage) be so, and whoever respects the inviolabilities of God, it is best for him with his Lord. The livestock are made lawful to you, save that which has been recited unto you; then shun the pollution of the idols, and shun vain talk,

31. Being upright for God, not associating anyone with Him. Whosoever associates any with God, it is as though he has fallen from heavens and birds snatched him away, or the wind wafted him to a distant place.

32. Let that be. And whoever respects the signs of God, verily it is (a sign) of the piety of the hearts.

33. There are benefits therein for you till a fixed time, and the place of their sacrifice is the Ancient House.

34. We have prescribed a rite for every nation that they may mention the name of God on what He has provided them of the quadruped livestock. Your Lord is One God, so submit to Him, and give glad tidings to the humble,

35. Whose hearts quake when God is mentioned, and those who bear patiently what befalls them, and keep regular prayers, and spend (in God's way) of that with which We have provided them.

36. We made the sacrificial camels for you among the signs of the religion of God. In them there is (plenteous) good for you; so mention the name of God on them, standing in rows, and when they fall down on their sides; eat thereof, and feed the poor who do not ask, and the beggar; thus have We subjected them to you; haply you may give thanks.

37. Neither their meat nor blood reach God, but piety on your part does; thus has He subjected them to you that you might glorify God for having guided you aright, and

give glad tidings to the doers of good deeds.

38. God defends those who believe; verily God does not love anyone unfaithful, ungrateful.

39. Permission is granted to those against whom war is waged (to fight back), for they have been oppressed, and God is well able to help them-

40. They have been expelled from their homes unjustly for saying: "Our Lord is God!" Had God not repelled some people through others, cloisters and churches, synagogues and mosques in which God's name is much mentioned, would have been razed. Indeed God will help him who supports Him; indeed God is strong, mighty.

41. Those who, if We establish them in the land, observe prayer and pay zakat, and enjoin good and forbid evil, and to God belongs the outcome of all affairs,

42. If they reject you (O Muhammad), so did before you the people of Noah and Ad and Thamud,

43. And the people of Abraham and of Lot,

44. And the dwellers of Midian (all rejected), and Moses was also rejected, but I gave a respite to the disbelievers, then I seized them, so how (severe) was my disapproval?

45. How many towns did We destroy, tumbling over their roofs, for their people were unjust? How many wells lie idle, neglected? And yet how many lofty castles stand abandoned?

46. Have they not travelled in the land so that their hearts may understand and ears may hear? Indeed it is not the eyes that are blind; the hearts in the bosoms have indeed become blind.

47. They ask you to hasten the chastisement. God will never fail His promise, and surely a day with your Lord is as a thousand years of your reckoning.

48. How many a city did I respite while it was unjust, then I seized it? And unto Me is the final return.

49. Say: "O people! I am only sent to deliver a clear warning to you."

50. For those who believe and do good deeds is pardon and an honourable provision.

51. Those who strive to invalidate Our signs shall be the inmates of the flaming Fire.

52. We did not send before you any messenger or prophet but when he had a desire, Satan cast vanity into his desire; yet God annuls that which Satan casts, then God establishes His signs; God is all-Knowing, all-Wise.

53. So that He may make that which Satan casts as a trial to those in whose hearts there is a disease, and to those whose hearts are hard; indeed the unjust are in a distant separation,

54. And that those who have been given the knowledge may know that it is the truth from your Lord, so they may believe in it, and may humble their hearts thereto, and God guides those who believe to the Right Path.

55. Those who disbelieve will not cease doubting it until the Hour overtakes them suddenly, or a chastisement of a disastrous day.

56. The Kingdom that day shall belong to God; He will judge between them. Those who believe and do good deeds will be in gardens of bliss,

57. For those who disbelieve and reject Our signs there is a disgraceful chastisement (in store).

58. Those who migrate in the way of God, and are then slain or they die, God will certainly provide them with an excellent sustenance; surely God is the best of providers.

59. He will indeed admit them into an entrance with which they shall be well-pleased; God is the all-Knowing, most Patient.

60. Let that be so, and he who retaliated with the like of what was inflicted upon him, then again he was oppressed, most certainly God will aid him; God is Merciful, Forgiving.

61. That is so because God causes the night to enter into the day, and the day to enter into the night, and because God is all-Hearing, all-Seeing.

62. That is so because God is the Truth, and that what they call upon besides Him is the falsehood, and because God is the Highest, the most Great.

63. Do you not see that God sends down water from the heavens and the earth becomes green? Indeed God is Kind, all-Aware.

64. To Him belongs everything in the heavens and the earth; God is self-Sufficient, worthy of all Praise.

65. Do you not see that God has subjected for you whatsoever is in the earth, and the ships sail in the sea by His command? And He holds back the heavens lest it should fall on earth save with His permission; God is Compassionate, all-Merciful.

66. He it is Who has brought you to life, then He will cause you to die, then He shall bring you to life again; man is surely ungrateful.

67. To every people We have prescribed rites which they shall observe, so they should not dispute with you about the affair, and call unto your Lord; you are on the right course.

68. If they dispute with you, say: "God knows best what you do.

69. "God will judge between you on the Day of Judgment in that wherein you differ."

70. Do you not know that God knows what is in the heavens and the earth? Indeed all is in a record; that is easy for God.

71. They worship besides God that for which He has not sent any authority, and that of which they have no knowledge; there shall be no helper for the unjust.

72. When Our clear signs are recited unto them, you will perceive repugnance on the faces of those who disbelieve. They practically leap upon those who recite Our signs. Say: "Shall I inform you of what is worse than this? God has promised the Fire for those who disbelieve; how evil an ending!"

73. O people! A parable is set forth, so listen to it. Those whom you call upon besides God cannot create a fly, even if they all gather together for it, and should the fly carry away anything from them, they cannot recover it; weak are the invoker and the invoked!

74. They do not measure God with His true measure; God is Almighty, omni-Potent.

75. God chooses messengers from among the angels, and from men; God is all-Hearing, all-Seeing.

76. He knows what is before them, and what is behind them, and to God are all affairs returned.

77. O you who believe! Bow down and prostrate, and

worship your Lord, and do good deeds, haply you may succeed.

78. Strive for God as it behooves you to strive for Him; He has chosen you and laid upon you no hardship in religion, the faith of your father Abraham who named you Muslims before and in this (revelation) that the messenger might be a witness over you, and that you might be witnesses over man. So establish prayer and pay zakat and hold fast to God; He is your Master; He is the best to protect, and the best to help.

The Believers
(al-Mu'minun)

In the name of God, the Beneficent, the Merciful.

1. Successful, indeed, are the believers,

2. Who are humble while offering their supplications,

3. Who keep themselves aloof from vain talk,

4. And who purify themselves by offering zakat;

5. They guard their modesty,

6. Except from their wives or those whom their right hands possess, for then they are not to be blamed.

7. Whosoever seeks beyond that, then they are the ones who transgress all bounds.

8. (Believers are) the ones who honour their trusts and safeguard their pledge,

9. They are keenly mindful of their prayers,

10. They, indeed, are the ones who shall be the inheritors;

11. They shall inherit Paradise, therein they shall (forever) abide.

12. We have surely created man of an extract of clay.

13. Then We placed him as a sperm in a secure resting place.

14. Then We made the sperm a clot, then the clot a lump of flesh, then We made the lump of flesh bones, then We clothed the bones with flesh, then We made it into another creation; so, praised be God, the Best of Creators.

15. Then verily thereafter you (all) shall die.

16. Then you shall certainly be raised on the Day of Judg-

ment.

17. We have surely made above you seven paths (heavens); of none of Our creation are We heedless.

18. We sent down water from the heavens in a (certain) measure, and We caused it to settle in the earth, and We surely are able even to take that away.

19. We grew therewith gardens of date palms and grapes for you, and for you are plentiful fruits therein from which you eat,

20. And a tree grows out of Mount Sinai producing oil and a condiment for those who (wish to) eat,

21. Verily, there is a lesson for you in the cattle: We provide you with milk from what is in their bellies, and there are benefits for you in them in abundance, and of them do you eat.

22. And on them, and on board ships, are you borne.

23. We surely sent Noah to his people and he said: "O people! Worship God (alone); you have no other god besides Him; will you not then guard (yourselves against evil)?"

24. But the chiefs of those who disbelieved from among his people said: "Here is a man like yourselves who intends to exalt himself above you; had God willed, He would certainly have sent angels (instead). We have heard of none of this from our fathers of old;

25. "He is certainly but a possessed man; so, bear with him for some time."

26. He (Noah) said: "Lord! Assist me against their calling me a liar."

27. So We revealed to him: "Make the ark according to Our own insight and inspiration, and when Our command comes, and the water gushes out from the oven, take into it two of each and every pair, and your family, except that regarding whom We had already said a word, and do not plead unto Me on behalf of those who have wronged their own selves, for verily they shall be drowned."

28. When you and all who accompanying you settle (in the ark), say: 'All praise is due to God Who delivered us from the unjust people.'

29. "And say: `Lord! Enable me to disembark at a blessed

landing place, for You are the best of those who (help) disembark.'"

30. In this are sure signs, and We do put people to the test.

31. Then we raised after them another generation.

32. Then We sent them a messenger from among them to "Worship God, for you have no god other than Him; will you not guard (yourselves against evil)?"

33. The chiefs among his people who disbelieved and rejected the meeting in the hereafter, those upon whom We granted the riches of this life, said: "This is but a man like our own selves! He eats of what you eat, and he drinks of what you drink!

34. "If you follow a man like your own selves, you will certainly then be the losers.

35. "He promises you that you will be brought back to life even after you die and turn into dust!

36. "Far is what you are promised (from the truth);

37. "It is nothing but life in this world. We die, and we live, and we shall never be raised again.

38. "He is none but a man who has forged a lie about God, and we shall not believe in him."

39. He said: "Lord! Assist me against their charging me of lying."

40. He said: "After a while, they shall soon regret."

41. The (awful) cry overtook them, and We turned them into rubbish; so away with all unjust people!

42. Then We brought forth another generation;

43. No nation shall be brought forth before its fixed time, nor is it capable of postponing it.

44. Then We sent Our messengers, one after the other. Whenever a messenger is sent to a people, they rejected him; so We caused some to follow others, and made others but tales; therefore, away with those who do not believe.

45. Then We sent Moses and his brother Aaron with Our signs and (vested upon them) a manifest authority,

46. (We sent them) to Pharaoh and his chieftains, but they behaved arrogantly, and they were haughty people.

47. So they said: "Shall we believe in two human beings like us whose people are in servitude to us?!"

48. So they rejected them, and they joined those whom We destroyed.

49. We bestowed the Book upon Moses so that they might receive true guidance.

50. We made Mary's son, and his mother, a sign, and We elevated them both to a lofty place, restful, secure, and watered with springs.

51. O messengers! Eat of the good things, and do good deeds, for surely I know what you do.

52. Yet they have certainly rent themselves into sects. Yours is but one nation, and I am your Lord; so, fear (only) Me.

53. Each party among them rejoices in what they possess.

54. So leave them in their overwhelming ignorance till a certain time.

55. They think that the wealth and children with which We provide them.

56. Are (tokens of Our) hastening the good things to them. Nay! They do not perceive.

57. Those who are apprehensive of their Lord's displeasure,

58. While believing in the signs of their Lord,

59. Those who do not associate any with their Lord,

60. Those who spend in charity of what We give them while their hearts are filled with fear of their Lord, they are the ones who shall return to their Lord,

61. They are the ones who hasten to do good deeds and are the foremost to (attain) them.

62. We do not task a soul more than it can bear, and there is a Book with Us that speaks the truth; they shall never be dealt with unjustly.

63. Nay! Their hearts are in overwhelming ignorance about this, and they even commit other deeds too.

64. So when We seize those among them who enjoyed luxuries with Our chastisement, behold! They cry in supplication!

65. Do not groan this day! You shall certainly receive no help;

66. Indeed, My signs were recited unto you, but you used

to turn your heels to them;

67. Puffed up with pride about it, foolishly discoursing by night.

68. Did they ever deliberate upon Our Word, or did they receive something which never came to their forefathers before?

69. Or were they unfamiliar with their (respective) messenger and therefore they rejected him?

70. Or do they (simply) say that he is crazed? Nay! He has brought them nothing but the truth, yet most of them hate the truth.

71. Should the truth be subjected to their own vain desires, then the heavens, the earth, and all that is in them, shall suffer confusion and corruption. Nay! We brought them a reminder, but they turned aside from their own reminder.

72. Or is it that you ask them for a tribute? Your Lord's recompense is the best, and He is the best of sustainers.

73. Verily you call them to the Straight Path;

74. Indeed those who do not believe in the hereafter deviate from the (Straight) Path.

75. Should We have mercy on them and relieve them of their distress, they would obstinately persist in their transgression, blindly wandering on.

76. Indeed, We seized them with a chastisement, but they neither submitted to their Lord, nor did they supplicate.

77. Till We opened upon them a gate of severe torment in which they despaired.

78. He it is Who created for you the hearing, the sight, the hearts; little do you give thanks.

79. He it is Who multiplied you in the earth, and to Him (alone) shall you be gathered.

80. And He it is Who grants life and brings death, and in His control is the alternation of the night and the day; do you not then understand?

81. Nay! But they said just as the ancients had said;

82. They said: "When we die and become dust and bones, shall we still be raised again?

83. "This is something we, and our forefathers before us, were promised; but it is nothing other than fables of the ancients."

84. Say: "To whom does the earth and everything that is in it belong, if you have knowledge?"

85. They will say: "To God;" say: "Will you then reflect?"

86. Say: "Who is the Lord of the seven heavens and the Great Throne?"

87. They will say: "God." Say: "Will you not then fear (Him)?"

88. Say: "In Whose hands is the Kingdom of all things, and Who protects and is never (Himself) protected, if you know?"

89. They will say: "God." Say: "From whence are you beguiled?"

90. Nay! We have brought them the truth, and they are the liars (themselves).

91. God never took to Him a son, and no god has ever been besides Him; otherwise, each god would certainly have taken away what he had created, and one would certainly have overpowered the other(s). Far, indeed, from the glory of God is what they attribute.

92. He knows the unseen; He is above what they associate with Him.

93. Say: "Lord! Would you let me see what (chastisement) they are promised?

94. "Then Lord do not place me among the unjust people!"

95. Verily, We are well able to make you see what We have promised them.

96. So repel evil with that which is the best; We best know what they attribute.

97. And say: "Lord! I seek refuge in You from the temptations of the devils.

98. "I seek refuge in You, Lord, from their access to me."

99. So, when death approaches one of them, he says: "Lord! Send me back again,

100. "So that I may do good deeds which I have never done." Nay! It is but a word he utters. There shall be a barrier behind them till the day they are raised again.

101. When the trumpet is blown, there will be no ties of kinship among them on that day, nor shall they ask one

another.

102. Then those whose scales are heavy shall be the successful ones;

103. While those whose scales are light shall lose their souls and abide (forever) in Hell.

104. The Fire shall scorch their faces, and they shall be groaning therein.

105. "Were My signs not rehearsed to you, and you used to disbelieve in them?"

106. They shall answer: "Lord! Our ill-luck overcame us, and we were people who strayed.

107. "Lord! Take us out of it. If we ever return (to evil), then we shall be the unjust ones."

108. You shall be driven down into it, and do not speak to Me!

109. In truth, there used to be a party among My servants who said: "Lord! We believe, so forgive us and have mercy upon us; You are the best of the merciful ones."

110. Yet you ridiculed them and neglected remembering Me, while you even laughed at them.

111. I have, indeed, rewarded them this day for their patience; they are the victorious.

112. He said: "How many years did you remain on earth?"

113. They said: "We tarried a day or a part of a day; so ask those who keep account."

114. "You tarried but a short while, if you only know."

115. Do you think then that We created you in vain, and that you shall not be returned to Us?

116. Most exalted is God, the True King; there is no god but He, Lord of the Throne of Grace.

117. Whoever invokes any besides God, having no proof thereof, will have his reckoning with his Lord; verily the disbelievers shall never succeed.

118 And say: "Lord! Forgive and have mercy; You are the best of those who offer mercy."

The Light
(an-Nur)

In the name of God, the Beneficent, the Merciful.

1. This is a sura which We have revealed and ordained, and We have revealed therein clear signs so that you may take heed.

2. You shall scourge the fornicatress and fornicator a hundred lashes each, and let no pity for them cause you not to enforce God's judgment, if you believe in God and the Last Day; let their torment be witnessed by a party of the believers.

3. A fornicator marries none but a fornicatress or an idolatress, and a fornicatress marries none but a fornicator or an idolater and the believers are forbidden from that.

4. You shall scourge those who accuse the women who protect their modesty, while failing to bring four eye-witnesses, fourscore lashes, and you shall never accept their testimony, and they are the wicked ones,

5. Save those who repent thereafter and amend themselves, for surely God is oft-Forgiving, all-Merciful.

6. Those who charge their wives, without having witnesses other than their own selves, shall testify by swearing four times by God that they tell the truth,

7. Their fifth oath is invoking God's curse on the liars.

8. If she testifies by swearing four times by God that verily he is a liar, then she shall thus avert the punishment,

9. Her fifth oath is to invoke God's curse on her own self if he (instead) is truthful.

10. Had it not been for God's grace upon you and His mercy, (you would have perished), and God is oft-Returning, all-Wise.

11. Indeed, those who have brought forth slandering are a gang among you. Do not deem it evil to you; nay! It is good for you. To every man among them is the penalty of what sin he committed, and for that who had a greater share of it will be a grievous torment.

12. When the believing men and women heard of it, why did they not think well of their own selves and call it manifest slandering?

13. Why did they not bring four witnesses to testify? Since they did not bring any witnesses, they are in the sight of God liars.

14. Had it not been for God's grace in this life and in the hereafter, a grievous chastisement would have seized you for getting involved in such slandering.

15. For you articulate it and say with your own tongues what you really do not know, surmising it a simple matter to do so, whereas it rests with God as a grievous one.

16. Why did you not say when you heard of it: "It does not befit us that we talk about this (matter); Glory be to You, Lord; this is a serious slander"?

17. God admonishes you not to ever delve in the like of it if you are believers.

18. God makes the signs manifest to you, and God is all-Knowing, all-Wise.

19. Verily those who scandalize the believers shall have a grievous chastisement in this life and the life hereafter, and God knows, while you do not.

20. Had it not been for God's grace and mercy upon you, (you would have been chastised), and God is Compassionate, all-Merciful.

21. O you who believe! Do not follow into Satan's steps, for whoever follows in Satan's steps would enjoin what is shameful and wrong. Had it not been for God's grace and mercy upon you, none of you would have been purified, but God purifies whomsoever He will, and God is all-Hearing, all-Knowing.

22. Let not those among you who are endowed with bounties swear against giving to their kin, to the poor, and to those who migrate for the cause of God, and they should pardon you and overlook. Do not you love that God would forgive you? God is oft-Forgiving, all-Merciful.

23. Verily, those who charge the believing women who safeguard their modesty and are unaware of it, shall be cursed in this life and the life hereafter, and for them shall be a grievous torment.

24. Their tongues and hands and feet will on that day bear witness against them, testifying to what they did.

25. On that day, God will mete out their just dues to them,

and they will know that God is the Truth, the self-Evident.

26. Bad women are for bad men, and bad men are for bad women; good men are for good women, and the good ones are for the good things; these are free from what they allege; for them shall be forgiveness and an honourable sustenance.

27. O you who believe! Do not enter houses other than your own before becoming acquainted and greeting their inhabitants. This is best or you; haply you will remember.

28. But if you find none in them, then do not enter them till you are permitted; if it is said to you to go back, then you should go back, for this is purer for you, and God knows all what you do.

29. You are not to be blamed for entering uninhabited [ware]houses if your goods are inside them, and God knows what you do in the open and in secrecy.

30. Say to the believing men to cast their gaze down and guard their modesty; that is purer for them; verily God is all-Aware of what they do.

31. Tell the believing women to cast their gaze down and guard their modesty, and not to display their adornments save that which is apparent, and to draw their veils over their bosoms, and that they must not display their adornment save to their husbands or fathers, or the fathers of their husbands, or their sons, or the sons of their husbands, or their brothers, or their brothers' sons (nephews), or their sisters' sons, or their women, or those whom their right hands possess, or the male servants who are void of sexual stimulation, or the children who have not yet attained awareness of women's nakedness, and let them not strike their feet to show what adornments they hide, and turn to God all of you, O believers, so that you may be successful.

32. Marry those among you who are single, and those who are righteous among your male and female slaves. If they are needy, then God, out of His benevolence, will free them from want, and God is all-Bounteous, all-Knowing.

33. Let those who find no means to marry be in continence until God, out of His grace, frees them from want. Grant those whom your right hand possesses, who seek to be emancipated, written contracts, should you ascertain their

goodness, and give them of the wealth which God has bestowed upon you. Do not compel your slave girls to prostitution while knowing their desire to remain chaste, if you seek casual fruition in this world. Whoever compels them, then God is oft-Forgiving thereafter, all-Merciful.

34. Indeed We sent down to you manifest signs and (struck for you) the moral of those who passed away before you an admonition to the pious.

35. God is the Light of the heavens and the earth. The similitude of His Light is a niche in which there is a lamp; the lamp is in a glass-ware; the glass-ware is as a shining and bright star, lit from a blessed tree that is neither eastern nor western; its oil almost glows forth even while no fire touches it: light upon light; God guides to His Light whomsoever He pleases, and God sets forth parables for people; God is all-Aware of everything.

36. (The lamps is lit) in houses which God has permitted to be elevated, and His name be mentioned therein; His Glory is praised therein in the mornings and the eves,

37. By men whom neither trade nor sale distracts from remembering God, paying zakat, fearing the Day when hearts and eyes shall writhe in anguish,

38. So that God may reward them with the best of what they earned, and increase it for them out of His Grace. God provides sustenance to whomsoever He pleases without measure.

39. As for those who disbelieve, their deeds are as a mirage in a desert: the thirsty one supposes it to be water until he comes to it and finds it naught, finding God with him; so He recompenses him in full; God is quick in reckoning.

40. Or like utter darkness of the deep sea: a wave above another covers it, and above the wave is the cloud; (layers of) darkness one over the other; when one takes his hand out, he is almost unable to see it; to whomsoever God gives no light, no light he shall ever have.

41. Have you not seen how God is glorified by all those in the heavens and the earth: the birds with their wings stretched out, each knows its own prayer and praise? And God knows all that they do.

42. God's is the kingdom of the heavens and the earth,

and to God is the ultimate return.

43. Do you not see that God gently drives the clouds, then joins them together, then piles them up, then you see rain coming forth from their midst? He sends down from heavens (clouds like) mountains laden with hail whereby He afflicts whom He pleases and He turns it away from whom He pleases; its lightning almost takes sight away.

44. God turns the day and the night over; verily there is a lesson in that for those endowed with insight.

45. God has created every animal of water; some walk upon the belly; some walk upon two feet; some walk upon four; God creates whatever He pleases; verily, God has power over all things.

46. We have, indeed, sent down manifest signs, and God guides whomsoever He pleases to the Right Path.

47. They say: "We believe in God and in the messenger, and we obey;" then a party of them turns back thereafter; these are not believers (at all).

48. When they are invited to God and His messenger to judge between them, lo, a faction of them turns aside.

49. But when right is on their side, they quickly come to him submissively.

50. Has disease afflicted their hearts? Have they some doubt? Or Do they fear that God and His messenger would deal unjustly with them? Nay! They are themselves the unjust ones.

51. The answer of the believers, when invited to God and His messenger to judge between them, is that they say: "We hear and we obey;" these it is that are the victorious.

52. Those who obey God and His messenger, fear God and safeguard (their souls), are certainly the winners.

53. They swear by God with the most solemn of their oaths that if you command them, they would certainly go forth. Say: "Do not swear but rather obey; verily God is well aware of whatever you do."

54. Say: "Obey God and obey the Messenger," and should they turn back, then he carries his burden and you carry yours; if you obey him, you will certainly be rightly guided, and a messenger's duty is but the delivering of a manifest Message.

55. God has promised those of you who believe and do good deeds that He will certainly appoint them successors on earth, just as He appointed those before them, and that He shall certainly establish their religion (Islam) for them, and that He will certainly exchange thereafter their fear for security. They shall worship Me and associate none with Me, and whosoever disbelieves after this are surely the wicked ones.

56. Establish, therefore, prayer, pay zakat, and obey the Messenger, perchance you will be dealt with mercifully.

57. Do not ever suppose that those who disbelieve can frustrate (God's plan) on earth; their abode is the Fire, and certainly it is an evil resort.

58. O you who believe! Let those whom your right hands possess, and those who have not reached puberty yet, ask your permission (to excuse their presence) thrice (a day): before the dawn prayers, when you lay your garments aside in (midday) heat, and after night prayers; these are three periods of privacy for you; thereafter, there is no restriction should you or they attend upon each other. Thus does God explain the signs for you, and God is all-Knowing, all-Wise.

59. When your children reach puberty, let them seek permission just as those (of age) before them did; thus does God clarify His signs; God is all-Knowing, all-Wise.

60. The women who are past child-bearing and do not wish to marry may put on their (fine) garments without displaying their ornaments; but if they restrain (even from this), it is better for them, and God is all-Hearing, all-Knowing.

61. There is no blame on the blind, the lame, the sick, nor is there any on your own selves should you eat at your own homes or those of your fathers', mothers', brothers', sisters', paternal uncles', maternal aunts', or of those whose keys you possess, or at your friends'. It is no sin should you eat together or separately, and when you enter houses, greet your people with a salutation in God's name, blessed and goodly. Thus does God make His signs clear for you so that you may understand.

62. Verily the believers are those who believe in God and His Messenger, and when they are with him on an affair demanding a collective action, they do not disperse before

they seek his permission; verily those who seek your permission are the ones who believe in God and His Messenger; so, when they seek your permission to attend to some affair of theirs, grant permission to whomsoever you please, and seek God's forgiveness for them; verily, God is oft-Forgiving, all-Merciful.

63. Do not call upon the Messenger as you call upon one another; verily God knows those among you who steal away, screening themselves; so let those who go against his order be warned lest a trial should afflict them or a painful chastisement should upon them.

64. Verily God's is whatsoever in the heavens and the earth. He knows your conditions, and on the Day when they are returned to Him, He will inform them of what they did; God is well Aware of everything.

The Criterion
(al-Furqan)

In the name of God, the Beneficent, the Merciful.

1. Blessed is He who revealed the Furqan to His servant (Muhammad) so that he may be a warner to the worlds.

2. His is the kingdom of the heavens and the earth, and He has never taken a son to Himself, nor has there been any partner with Him in his sovereignty. He created every thing, planned according to a fixed measure.

3. Yet they have taken gods besides Him that create nothing, while they themselves are created; they can neither hurt themselves, nor can they profit themselves aught; they have no control over death, life, or resurrection.

4. Those who disbelieve say: "This is nothing but a lie he has forged, and certain other people have aided him thereupon." These have indeed committed iniquity and uttered a slander.

5. They (also) say: "He has written but tales of the ancient recited upon him mornings and eves."

6. Say: "Rather, it is revealed by that Who knows the secrets of the heavens and the earth; indeed He is oft-Forgiving, all-Merciful."

7. They say: "What sort of messenger is he that eats and

walks in the markets? Why has no angel been sent to him to warn with Him?

8. "Or a treasure be hurled to him, or a garden be his of which he eats?" The iniquitous say: "You follow but a bewitched man."

9. See (O Muhammad) how they coin comparisons for you! But they have gone astray, so they shall not be able to find the right way.

10. Blessed is He Who, if He pleases, may grant you what is better than that, gardens beneath which rivers flow, and grant you mansions (too).

11. Nay! They disbelieve in the hour while we have prepared for that who disbelieves in the hour a burning Fire.

12. When it beholds them, even from a distance, it would make its raging and roaring heard.

13. When they, being shackled, are flung into a narrow place therein, they shall announce their own destruction;

14. Nay! Do not announce one destruction but many!

15. Say: "Is this better or the eternal garden reserved for the pious? It shall be their recompense, and a final destination.

16. "They shall have therein whatever they wish, eternally; it is a promise of your Lord worthy of prayers."

17. When He gathers them and all that they served besides God, He shall say: "Did you beguile My servants, these, or did they themselves stray from the Right Path?"

18. They will say: "Glory be to You! It did not behove us to take friends besides You, but You let them and their fathers have enjoyments till they forsook remembering You, becoming people (worthy of) suffering perdition."

19. They have indeed rejected what you say, so you shall not be able to avert the doom or succor, and whosoever commits injustice, We shall let him taste of a great torment.

20. We have sent no messenger before you (O Our Prophet Muhammad), save that they certainly ate food and walked through the markets, and We made some of you a trial for others; will you bear patiently? Your Lord is ever-Seeing.

21. Those who do not wish to meet Us say: "Why has no angel been sent to us, nor have we seen our Lord?" Indeed

they think too highly of their own selves, and they have gone to great excesses.

22. On the day when they do see the angels, there will be no glad tidings on that day for the guilty, and they (angels) shall say: "Forbidden it (enjoyment) is, totally forbidden!"

23. Then We would proceed to what they wrought and We would render them like dust scattered in the air.

24. The dwellers of the Garden on that day shall be in a better abode and a better resting place.

25. On the day when the heavens are burst asunder with cloud, and the angels sent down, descending (in ranks),

26. The kingdom on that day shall in truth belong to the Beneficent Lord, and that day shall be extremely hard for the infidels.

27. On that day, the unjust shall bite their hands saying: "Oh! "Would I had taken a path with the Messenger!

28. "Woe unto me! Would I had not taken such one as a friend!

29. "He then led me astray from remembering (my Lord), and Satan has always been a deserter of man!"

30. The Messenger shall say: "Lord! Indeed my people have forsaken this Qur'an."

31. Thus did We appoint for every messenger an enemy from among the guilty, but your Lord suffices as a Guide and a Helper.

32. Those who disbelieve say: "Why has no Qur'an been revealed to him as a whole?" Thus (did We deem) to strengthen your heart thereby, and We have recited it (unto you) in a well-arranged and gradual stages.

33. They (infidels) shall bring no argument to you, but We shall bring the truth to them and shall provide the best explanation (for it).

34. Those who will be hurled face-ward into the Hell shall have the worst place and the most evil destiny.

35. Indeed, We bestowed the Book upon Moses and We appointed with him his brother Aaron to assist.

36. We said: "Go, both of you, to the people who have rejected Our signs!" So We destroyed them with utter destruction.

37. We drowned the people of Noah when they rejected

the messengers, and made them a sign for mankind, and We have in store a painful chastisement for the unjust.

38. And Ad, Thamud, the inhabitants of the Rass, and generations in-between them in great numbers,

39. To each We gave parables, and each We destroyed with utter extermination.

40. Indeed they have passed by the town that was showered with a fatal rain; did they not then see it? Nay! They do not wish to be resurrected.

41. When they see you, they ridicule you and say: "Is this the one sent by God as a messenger?!

42. "Had we not adhered to them steadfastly, he would almost have led us astray from our gods." When they witness the chastisement, they shall then know who is the one who strayed.

43. Have you seen that who takes his vain inclinations for gods? Would you then be a guardian over him?

44. Do you think that most of them hear or understand? They are but like cattle; nay, they are even farther astray.

45. Do you not perceive (the Might of) your Lord Who extends the shadow? Had He willed, He would certainly have made it stationary, then We would have made the sun to be its guide.

46. Then We draw it to Us by an easy (gradual) contraction.

47. He it is Who has made the night a covering for you, the sleep a rest, and the day to rise up again.

48. He it is Who sends the winds heralding glad tidings before His mercy (rain), and We send water pouring down from heaven,

49. So that We may give life thereby to a dead land, and give it to you, and to the cattle, from among other multitudes We have created, to drink.

50. Indeed We have distributed it among them so that they may (thankfully) be mindful, but do not count most people as thankful.

51. Had We willed, We would certainly have raised up a warner in every town;

52. So do not yield to the infidels, and strive against them strenuously.

53. He it is Who has made both seas to join and flow together: one is palatable and sweet, while the other is salt and bitter; yet He has made a barrier between both of them and an impassable barrage.

54. He it is Who has created man of water, created for him blood relatives and relatives in wedlock, and your Lord is all-Powerful.

55. Yet they worship besides God that which neither profits them nor harms them, and the infidel is a helper against your Lord.

56. We have sent you (O Our Prophet Muhammad) a bearer of glad tidings and a warner.

57. Say: "I ask you no recompense save that you willingly take a path to your Lord."

58. Rely on the ever-Living One Who never dies and celebrate His praise; He suffices as an all-Aware of His servants.

59. It is He, the Beneficent, Who created the heavens and the earth and what is between them in six days, and firmly established Himself on the Throne, so ask about Him the one who knows.

60. When it is said to them: "Prostrate in obeisance to the Merciful," they say: "Who is the Merciful? Shall we prostrate in obeisance to what you bid us?" It only adds to their resentment of the truth.

61. Blessed is He Who made in the heavens constellations, a lamp, and an illuminating moon.

62. He it is Who has made the night and the day to succeed each other (a sign) for him who desires to reflect and offer thanks.

63. The servants of the Beneficent are those who walk on the earth humbly, and when the ignorant ones address them, they say: "Peace!"

64. Those who pass the night prostrating to their Lord and standing,

65. And those who say: "Lord! Turn from us the torment of Hell; verily its torment is a lasting affliction.

66. "Verily it is an evil abode and station."

67. Those who, when they spend, are neither extravagant nor niggardly but in-between the two (extremes).

68. And those who do not call besides God any other gods, nor slay a soul which God has forbidden save in (executing) justice, nor commit adultery. Whosoever does this shall find a requital of the sin;

69. For him there shall be twice the torment on the Day of Resurrection, and he shall abide therein forever in ignominy,

70. Save that who turns repentant and believes and does good deeds; those are they whose evil deeds God shall change into good one, and God is oft-Forgiving, all-Merciful.

71. Whosoever repents and does good deeds, and (sincerely) turns to God,

72. And those who bear no witness to falsehood, and when they pass by vanity, they pass dignified,

73. And those who, when admonished by the signs of their Lord, do not become deaf or blind,

74. And those who say: "Lord! Grant us from our wives and offspring a joy of our eyes, and make us Imams for the pious."

75. These shall be rewarded with a high station for their patience, and they shall be met therein with greetings and salutations,

76. Abiding forever therein, an excellent abode and resting- place.

77. Say: "Had it not been for your prayers, my Lord would not have cared about you, but indeed you rejected (His Message); therefore, you shall be seized."

The Poets
(al-Shu'ara)

In the name of God, the Beneficent, the Merciful.

1. Ta, Sin, Mim.

2. These are the verses of the manifest Book.

3. You may kill yourself grieving for their disbelief,

4. But if We will, We can reveal a sign from heavens to them and keep their necks bent thereto;

5. No reminder comes to them from the Beneficent save they turn aside therefrom.

6. Indeed they rejected it; so soon the tidings of what

they mock shall come to them.

7. Do not they behold the earth and see how many of every noble kind We have planted therein?

8. In that, is a sign, but most of them (still) do not believe.

9. Your Lord is certainly the Almighty, the all-Merciful.

10. When your Lord called upon Moses: "Go to the unjust people,

11. "The people of Pharaoh; will they not fear God?"

12. He (Moses) said: "Lord! I dread their calling me a liar!

13. "And my bosom becomes straitened, and my tongue tied; so, send Aaron (to my aid).

14. "And they have against me a crime, and I fear they may slay me."

15. He (God) said: "No! Go, both of you, with Our signs; verily We are with you listening.

16. "So go to Pharaoh and say: `We are messengers of the Lord of the worlds;

17. "Send, therefore, the children of Israel with us.'"
18. He (Pharaoh) said: "Did we not cherish you as a child, and did you not dwell amongst us for years?

19. "Till you did what you did? You are ungrateful."

20. He (Moses) said: "I did it when I did not yet receive guidance;

21. "So I fled from you when I feared you; then my Lord granted me authority and made me a messenger.

22. "And is it a favour of which you remind me that you enslaved the children of Israel?"

23. Pharaoh said: "What is this `Lord of the world?'"

24. He (Moses) said: "The Lord of the heavens and the earth and what is between them both, if you can rest assured."

25. (Pharaoh) said to those around him: "Do you hear this?"

26. He (Moses) said: "He is your Lord and the Lord of your fathers of old."

27. He said: "Verily, the `messenger' sent to you is insane."

28. He (Moses) said: "He is the Lord of the east and the west and what is between them both, if only you reason."

29. He (Pharaoh) said: "Should you take a god other than myself, I will certainly imprison you."

30. He (Moses) said: "Even if I bring you a manifest (proof)?"

31. He (Pharaoh) said: "Bring it if you are truthful."

32. So he threw his staff down, and lo, it was a manifest serpent,

33. And he drew his hand out, and lo, it seemed white (radiating) to the beholders.

34. He (Pharaoh) said to the chiefs around him: "This is certainly a skilled sorcerer;

35. "He intends to drive you out of your land with his sorcery; what then is your counsel?"

36. They said: "Give him and his brother a respite, and dispatch heralds into the cities,

37. "So that they may bring you all the well-versed sorcerers."

38. So did the sorcerers assemble at the appointed time on an announced day.

39. People were asked: "Will you all assemble?

40. "Haply we may follow the sorcerers should they triumph."

41. When the sorcerers came to Pharaoh, they asked: "Is there a reward for us if we triumph?"

42. He (Pharaoh) said: "Yes, indeed, and you shall be the nearest (to me)."

43. Moses said to them: "Cast whatever you have to cast."

44. They cast down their cords and rods and said: "By Pharaoh's dignity, we shall certainly be triumphant."

45. Then Moses cast down his staff, and lo, it swallowed all that they falsely displayed.

46. The sorcerers flung themselves prostrating.

47. They said: "We believe in the Lord of the worlds;

48. "The Lord of Moses and Aaron."

49. He (Pharaoh) said: "Have you believed in him even before I grant you permission? He is your chief who taught you sorcery; so, soon shall you know. I shall certainly cut your hands and feet from opposite sides, and I will certainly crucify all of you."

50. They said: "(We fear) no harm; verily we shall return

to our Lord.

51. "We certainly wish that our Lord will pardon our wrong- doings, for we are the first to believe."

52. We revealed unto Moses: "Go forth with My servants by night; you will certainly be pursued."

53. Then Pharaoh sent heralds into the cities,

54. Saying: "These (Israelites) are only a small group,

55. "And they have enraged us exceedingly,

56. "And we are a multitude, forewarned."

57. So We turned them out of gardens and fountain-springs,

58. Treasures and goodly dwellings;

59. Thus (did We punish them), and We made the children of Israel their heirs.

60. Then they pursued them at sunrise.

61. When the two parties stood face to face, those with Moses said: "Indeed we are caught!"

62. He (Moses) said: "No; surely my Lord is with me. Soon will He guide me (to safety)."

63. Then We inspired to Moses: "Strike the sea with your staff;" then it cleft asunder, and each part (of the water stood) like a huge mountain.

64. Then We drew near the others,

65. And We saved Moses and all those with him.

66. And We drowned the others.

67. Indeed in this is a sure sign; yet most of them do not believe.

68. Certainly your Lord is the Almighty, the all-Merciful.

69. And recite to them the story of Abraham.

70. He said to his father and people: "What do you worship?"

71. They said: "Idols do we worship, and we shall forever be their devotees."

72. He (Abraham) said: "Do they hear you when you invoke?

73. "Or do they profit or harm you?"

74. They said: "Nay; we found our fathers doing so."

75. "Have you then come to see what you have been worshipping,

76. "You and your fathers of old?

77. "Indeed they are my enemies; the Lord of the worlds is not.

78. "He Who created me shall guide me;

79. "He feeds me and provides me with drink;

80. "When I fall ill, He heals me;

81. "He causes me to die, and then He brings me to life (again).

82. "And I am hopeful that He will forgive my faults on the Day of Judgment.

83. "Lord! Grant me authority, and unite me with the righteous,

84. "And let my tongue utter truth to the posterity,

85. "And make me an heir of the garden of bliss,

86. "And forgive my father; verily he was among those who strayed.

87. "And do not disgrace me on the day when they are raised again,

88. "On the day when no wealth or sons are of avail,

89. "Save him who comes to God with a submitting heart."

90. The garden of bliss was brought to the pious,

91. While Hell shall lay open for those who stray.

92. It shall be said to them: "Where are those whom you used to worship,

93. "Besides God? Can they help you, or can they help their own selves?"

94. So both they and those who stray shall be hurled into the Fire,

95. And Satan's hosts, too, all together.

96. While wrangling therein among themselves, they shall say:

97. "By God! We were in manifest error;

98. "When we equated you with the Lord of the worlds,

99. "None beguiled us save the guilty ones;

100. "Now we have no intercessors,

101. "Nor any loving friend;

102. "If there is a chance for us to return, we would surely believe."

103. Indeed in this is a sign, yet most of them do not believe.

104. Your Lord is truly Almighty, the all-Merciful.

105. Noah's people called the messengers (of God) liars.

106. Their brother Noah said to them: "Will you not guard (yourselves against evil)?

107. "I am truly a trusted messenger;

108. "Therefore, fear God and obey me.

109. "I ask you no recompense for it, for my recompense is only with the Lord of the worlds.

110. "So guard (yourselves against evil), and obey me."

111. They said: "Shall we believe in you while none followed you except those who are the most base (in status) among us?"

112. He (Noah) said: "How should I know what they do?

113. "Their reckoning is with my Lord, if only you know.

114. "I am not here to drive the believers away;

115. "I am but an open warner."

116. They said: "If you, Noah, do not desist, you shall surely be stoned to death."

117. He (Noah) said: "Lord! They have surely rejected me.

118. "So decide between me and them, and deliver me and the believers with me."

119. So We delivered him and those with him in the laden ark.

120. Then We drowned the rest afterwards.

121. Indeed in this is a sign, but most of them do not believe.

122. Your Lord is certainly Almighty, all-Merciful.

123. The (people of) Ad rejected the messengers.

124. Their brother Hud said to them: "Will you not fear God?

125. "Indeed I am to you a trusted messenger,

126. "So guard (yourselves against the wrath of) God, and obey me.

127. "I ask you for no recompense; my recompense is only with the Lord of the worlds.

128. "Do you build on every height a monument for

your vanity?

129. "And you raise strong mansions as if you will abide therein forever?

130. "And when you seize (any) by force, you seize as tyrants.

131. "So guard (yourselves against the Wrath of) God, and obey me,

132. "And fear Him Who has bestowed abundantly on you of what you do not know.

133. "He has provided you with plenty of cattle and children,

134. "And gardens, and springs,

135. "Verily I fear for you against the chastisement of a grievous day."

136. They said: "It is same to us if you admonish us or not;

137. "This (threatening) is but the manner of the ancient;

138. "And we shall never be penalized."

139. So they rejected him; therefore, We destroyed them. In this is a sign, yet most of them do not believe.

140. Your Lord is certainly Almighty, all-Merciful.

141. Thamud rejected the messengers (of God),

142. Their brother Salih said to them: "Will you not guard (yourselves against evil)?

143. "Verily, I am to you a trusted messenger;

144. "So fear God and obey me;

145. "And I ask no recompense for it; my recompense is only with the Lord of the worlds;

146. "Will you be left here forever secure,

147. "In gardens and springs,

148. "And cornfields and palm-trees with fine species?

149. "You exaltingly carve dwellings out of the mountains,

150. "So fear God and obey me,

151. "And do not obey the extravagant,

152. "Those who cause mischief in the earth and do not reform."

153. They said: "Surely you are only bewitched;

154. "You are but a man like us; so, bring a sign if you are truthful."

155. He said: "Behold! This is a she-camel; it shall have her drink and you yours, (each) on an appointed day.

156. "Do not touch her with evil lest the torment of a grievous day touches you."

157. Then they hamstrung her and turned regretful.

158. So the chastisement seized them; verily in this is a sign, yet most of them do not believe.

159. And your Lord is the Almighty, the all-Merciful.

160. The people of Lot rejected the messengers (of God).

161. Their brother Lot said to them: "Will you fear God?

162. "Indeed, I am a trusted messenger sent to you;

163. "Therefore, fear God and obey me;

164. "I seek no reward from you but from the Lord of the worlds.

165. "Do you approach males of the world,

166. "Leaving the wives your Lord has created for you? Nay, you are people who transgress."

167. They said: "If you do not desist, O Lot, you shall surely be expelled."

168. He (Lot) said: "Verily I abhor your deeds.

169. "Lord! Deliver me and my family from what they do."

170. So We delivered him and all his family,

171. Except an old woman who tarried behind.

172. Then We destroyed all others.

173. And We showered down upon them rain, and evil was the rain that showered the warned folks.

174. Indeed in this is a sign, but most of them (still) do not believe.

175. And certainly your Lord is Almighty, all-Merciful.

176. Dwellers of the forest (too) rejected the messengers (of God).

177. Shu'ayb said to them: "Will you fear God?

178. "Verily I am a trusted messenger (sent) to you;

179. "So fear God and obey me.

180. "I seek no recompense from you but from the Lord of the worlds.

181. "Give accurate measure and do not decrease it;

182. "And correctly weigh with accurate balances.

183. "And do not defraud people's goods, and do not fill

the earth with your mischief.

184. "Fear Him Who created you and all the races of old."

185. They said: "Indeed you are among those who are bewitched;

186. "You are but a man like us, and we think you are a liar;

187. "So cause a part of heaven to fall down upon us, if you are truthful."

188. He (Shu'ayb) said: "My Lord knows best what you do."

189. But they rejected him, so the chastisement of a day of cloud seized them; that was a torment of a mighty day.

190. In this there is a sign, but most of them do not believe.

191. And your Lord is surely Almighty, all-Merciful.

192. It (Qur'an) is surely a revelation from the Lord of the worlds.

193. The Trusted Spirit (Gabriel) brought it down,

194. Upon your heart (O Our Prophet Muhammad) so that you warn.

195. Thereby, in plain Arabic;

196. Indeed it is (foretold) in the scriptures of yore.

197. Is it not a sign to them that is recognized by the learned ones among the children of Israel?

198. Had We sent it down to outlanders,

199. Then he would have recited it unto them, and they would have (still) disbelieved it.

200. Thus do We cause it to pass through the hearts of the guilty;

201. They will never believe in it till they behold the grievous torment.

202. It shall come upon them suddenly, before they perceive;

203. Then they shall say: "Shall we have a respite?"

204. Do they truly seek to hasten Our chastisement?!

205. Have you seen how We provided them with means of enjoyment for years,

206. Then that which they were promised came to them,

207. The enjoyment wherewith they were provided

availed them naught.

208. We destroyed no town without first sending warners to it,

209. And something to remember. And We never dealt with them unjustly.

210. The devils did not descend down with it.

211. It does not behove them, nor are they potent to do so.

212. They are furthermost distanced even from hearing it.

213. So do not invoke any god with God lest you should be among the chastised ones.

214. And warn your tribe that is the nearest in kin.

215. And be kind unto that who follows you of the believers.

216. But if they disobey you, then say: "I surely dissociate myself from what you do."

217. And rely on the Almighty, the all-Merciful,

218. Who beholds you when you stand,

219. And witnesses your movements among those who prostrate (in obeisance to God).

220. Indeed He is the all-Hearing, the all-Knowing.

221. Shall I inform you upon whom do the devils descend?

222. They descend upon everyone lying and sinful; .

223. They (eagerly) lend their ears, and most of them are liars.

224. And the poets are followed by the erring ones,

225. Do you not witness how they wander in every valley, bewildered?

226. And that they say what they do not actually do,

227. Save those who believe and do good deeds, quite often remembering God, defending themselves when they are oppressed. Soon shall those who deal with others unjustly come to know what an evil turning their (lot shall) turn.

The Ants
(an-Naml)

In the name of God, the Beneficent, the Merciful.

1. Ta, Sin. These are the verses of the Qur'an, the book that makes truth manifest,

2. A guidance, and glad tidings to the believers,

3. Who establish (regular) prayers and give zakat, and are sure about the hereafter.

4. Verily We have made the deeds of those who do not believe in the hereafter fair-seeming to them, so they wander bewildered.

5. These are those for whom a grievous chastisement is in store, and in the hereafter they shall be the greatest losers of all.

6. Verily you (O Our Prophet Muhammad) receive the Qur'an from the all-Wise, the all-Knowing.

7. Moses said to his family: "Indeed, I behold a fire; soon will I bring you news from there, or a torch, so that you may warm yourselves."

8. So when he came to it, he was called upon: "Blessed are those in the fire and around it, and Glorified is God, Lord of the world.

9. "O Moses! Verily it is I, God, the all-Mighty, the all-Wise;

10. "Cast your staff down." So when he saw it vibrating like a serpent, he turned back fleeing and did not return. "O Moses! Do not fear, for My messengers are not frightened of My presence,

11. "Save he who has committed injustice then succeeded his bad deed with good deeds, for I am the oft-Forgiving, the all-Merciful;

12. "Put your hand into your pocket; when pulled out, it shall brightly glow without a blemish, along with nine signs to Pharaoh and his people; verily they are a transgressing people."

13. So when Our clear signs were brought forth to them, they said: "This is plain sorcery."

14. They unfairly rejected them, though privately they were convinced, out of their own iniquity and arrogance; so

see how the mischief-makers were punished.

15. Indeed, We bestowed knowledge upon David and Solomon. They said: "All praise is God's Who has made us surpass many of His believing servants."

16. Solomon inherited David, and he said: "O people! We have been taught the birds' language, and we have been granted a plentitude of everything; indeed, this is a manifest grace."

17. Solomon's hosts of jinn, men, and birds were gathered together, then they were arrayed in ranks.

18. When they came to the ants' valley, an ant said: "O ants, enter into your dwellings lest Solomon and his hosts should unknowingly crush you."

19. He (Solomon) smiled laughing at her words and said: "Lord! Enable me to thank You enough for the bounty You have bestowed upon me and my parents, and to do good deeds with which You will be pleased, and admit me, by Your mercy, in the company of Your righteous servants."

20. He reviewed the birds then said: "How is it that I do not see the hoopoe, or is he among the absentees?

21. "I shall chastise him with a severe punishment, or I will certainly slaughter him, or he shall bring me a clear evidence."

22. He (hoopoe) tarried not long then said: "I have become acquainted with what you have not, and I have brought you a sure news from Sheba.

23. "Verily I found a woman ruling them. She is plentifully in possession of many things, and she has a magnificent throne.

24. "I found her and her people prostrate to the sun, rather than God; Satan has made their deeds fair-seeming, and thus has he turned them away from the right path, so they are not rightly guided.

25. "Why should they not prostrate in obeisance to God Who brings forth into light that which is hidden in the heaven and the earth, and what you hide and manifest?

26. "God! There is no god but He, Lord of the Mighty Throne."

27. He (Solomon) said: "We shall see if you have uttered the truth or lied;

28. "Take this letter of mine and convey it to them; turn away from them and witness what they come out with."

29. She (the queen of Sheba) said: "Chiefs! Indeed an honourable letter has been delivered to me;

30. "It is in truth from Solomon, and it is: `In the name of God, the Beneficent, the Merciful;

31. "`Do not exalt yourselves against me, and come to me submitting (to God as Muslims).'"

32. She said: "Chiefs! Advise me in this matter; I do not conclude any issue without your counsel."

33. They said: "We are endowed with might and prowess; the command is yours; so, see what your command shall be."

34. Said she: "Verily when kings (victoriously) enter a town, they ruin it and render its most noble people the meanest, and thus will they always do.

35. "I am sending them a present and shall wait to see how the messengers return.

36. When they (messengers) came to Solomon, he said: "Do you provide me with riches? What God has given me is far better than what He has given you. Indeed, you even exult about your present!

37. "Return to them, for surely we will proceed to them with hosts which they shall never be able to meet, and we will certainly expel them out of it abased, contemptible."

38. He (Solomon) said: "Chiefs! Which of you can bring her throne to me before they come to me submitting?"

39. An audacious one among the jinn said: "I will bring it to you before you rise from your place, for verily I am strong and trusted."

40. He who had some knowledge of the Book said: "I will bring it to you before your eye twinkles," and when he (Solomon) saw the throne settled beside him, he said: "This is by the Grace of my Lord that He may test me to witness my gratitude or ingratitude; whoever is grateful (to his Lord) is surely grateful for his own good, and whoever is ungrateful, my Lord is still self-Sufficient, Bounteous."

41. He (Solomon) said: "Transform her throne to her; we will see if she follows the right way or strays."

42. When she (Queen Sheba) came, it was said to her: "Is

this your throne?" She said: "It seems as if it were the same. We were already informed (of your Prophethood), and we were submitting."

43. What she worshipped prevented her from worshipping God; indeed, she belonged to a disbelieving people.

44. It was said to her: "Enter the palace," but when she saw it, she thought it was but a pool of water, and she uncovered her logs; he (Solomon) said: "This is but a place smoothed with (slabs of) glass." She said: "Lord! I have been unjust to my own self, and I submit (along) with Solomon to God, Lord of the worlds."

45. Indeed, We sent to Thamud their brother Salih (who said): "Worship God (alone)." Yet they became two parties wrangling with each other.

46. He (Salih) said: "O people! Why do you seek to hasten to evil deeds before good ones? Should you seek God's pardon, you may receive His mercy."

47. They said: "We augur ill from you and those with you." He said: "(The knowledge of) your ill augury is with God; nay, you are a people being put to test."

48. There were nine men in the town who were making mischief in the land without amending.

49. They said: "Swear by God to one another that, having suddenly attacked him and his family by night, we would say to his heir that we never witnessed the murder of his family, and that verily we are truthful."

50. They plotted, and We, too, plotted, while they could not perceive it.

51. See then what the end of their plot was; We destroyed them and all their people.

52. These houses are their empty ruins, for they were unjust; verily there is a sign in this for people who reason.

53. We delivered those who believed in God and feared Him.

54. And We sent Lot who said to his people: "Do you commit abomination knowingly?

55. "You approach men with lust rather than women; nay, you indeed are ignorant people."

56. His people's answer was nothing but: "Turn Lot's people out of your town, for they are people seeking to

cleanse."

57. So We delivered him and his followers except his wife; We decreed her to stay with those who lagged behind.

58. And We showered rain on them, and evil was the shower that poured upon those who had been warned.

59. Say: "All praise is God's, and peace be with His servants whom He has chosen; is God better, or is it what they associate (with Him)?

60. "Or who is it that created the heavens and the earth, and sent water down from heaven, causing beautiful gardens to grow? It was not within your power to grow trees thereby. Is there any god besides God? Nay; they are but people who equate things with Him.

61. Is not He Who made the earth a resting place, created rivers therein, creating mountains upon it, placing (them as) a barrier between two seas? Is there any god besides God? Nay; yet most of them do not know.

62. Is not He Who answers the distressed one when he invokes Him and removes the distress, and makes you successors in the earth? Is there any god besides God? Little do you reflect.

63. Or who is it that guides you in the darkness of the land and sea, sending the winds as bearers of glad tidings of His mercy? Is there any other god besides God? Exalted is God high above what they associate (with Him).

64. Or who is it that originates the creation then reproduces it, providing sustenance for you from the heaven and the earth? Is there any god besides God? Say: "(If so) bring your proof, if you are truthful."

65. Say: "None knows the unseen in the heavens and the earth save God, and they do not perceive when they shall be resurrected."

66. Nay; their knowledge about the hereafter reached a dead- end; nay, they are unsure about it. Nay! They are blind to it.

67. Those who disbelieve say: "When we become dust, and our fathers, too, shall we still be brought forth again?

68. "Indeed we and our [fore]fathers were promised so; these are nothing but myths of the old."

69. Say: "Roam the earth and see how the guilty were

punished."

70. And do not grieve about them, nor should you feel distressed about what they devise.

71. They ask: "When shall this promise (of chastisement) come to pass, if you tell the truth?"

72. Say: "Perchance a portion of what (chastisement) you are eager to witness will indeed afflict you."

73. Your Lord is verily the Lord of grace to people, but most of them are not grateful.

74. Verily your Lord well knows what enshrouds their breasts and what they declare.

75. Nothing that is hidden in the heavens and the earth but (recorded) in a manifest book.

76. This Qur'an truly relates to the children of Israel that about which most of them dispute.

77. It is sure guidance and mercy to the believers.

78. Indeed, your Lord will judge between them by His decree, and He is the Almighty, the all-Knowing.

79. So rely on God; verily you are on (the path of) manifest truth.

80. Indeed, you cannot make the dead listen, nor can you make the deaf hear the call when they turn away.

81. Nor can you guide the blind out of their straying; you can make none hear save those who believe in Our signs, submitting themselves (to Us).

82. When the word comes to pass regarding them, We shall bring forth to them an earth creature that walks and talks to people, telling them that they did not believe in Our signs.

83. On a day We will collect from every nation a party that rejected Our signs, then they will be formed into groups,

84. When they are brought before God, He shall say: "Did you reject My signs, or did you (simply) fail to comprehend them? Or what were you doing?"

85. The word shall come to pass against them for the injustice they had committed, (so much so that) they shall be unable to speak.

86. Did they not see how We made the night for them to rest therein, and the day a light? Verily in this are signs for people who believe.

87. On the day when the trumpet is blown, those in the heavens and the earth shall be horrified save that whom God wills, and all shall come unto Him abased.

88. You see the mountains and perceive them firmly immovable, while they in fact pass like clouds, God's creation; He has perfected everything He created; He is well-Aware with what you do.

89. Those who do good deeds will be rewarded even with better than their deeds, and they shall be secure on the day of extreme horror.

90. And those who commit bad deeds shall be thrown face-ward into the Fire; should your recompense be anything but according to your deeds?

91. (Say:) "I was enjoined but to worship the Lord of this city which He deemed sacred; His are all things, and I am enjoined to submit to God (in Islam),

92. "And that I should recite the Qur'an; so, whosoever is rightly guided, it is for his own good, and whoever strays, he stays against his own self; I am but a warner."

93. And (also) say: "All praise is God's; He shall make His signs manifest to you, and you shall recognize them; your Lord is not heedless to what you do."

The Narrations
(al-Qasas)

In the name of God, the Beneficent, the Merciful.

1. Ta, Sin, Mim.

2. These are the verses of the manifest Book,

3. We recite unto you of the accounts of Moses and Pharaoh, in truth, for (the benefit of) those who believe.

4. Indeed, Pharaoh exalted himself in the land and divided its people into parties, weakening a group among them, slaughtering their sons and sparing their women; verily he was one of the mischief-makers.

5. And We intend to bestow Our Favour upon those who were considered weak in the land, and to make them THE imams, and the heirs.

6. And to empower them in the world, and to show Pharaoh and Haman and their hosts what they dreaded.

7. We inspired to Moses' mother: "Nurse him, and should you fear for his life, then launch him in the deep (river, Nile), and fear not, nor grieve, for We shall return him to you and make him one of Our messengers."

8. Pharaoh's people picked him, that he might be their enemy and a (cause for their) grief; Pharaoh and Haman and their hosts were surely sinners.

9. Pharaoh's wife said: "Let this be a joy of my eyes and yours; do not slay him; perhaps he will be of use to us, or maybe we will adopt him as a son," and they were not aware (of consequences).

10. The heart of Moses' mother felt relieved, and she almost disclosed it, had We not strengthened her heart so that she might be a believer (in Our promise).

11. She said to his sister: "Follow him," and she watched him from a distance, while they were unaware.

12. We decreed that none could nurse him; so she (his sister) said: "Shall I guide you to a family that might take care of him for you and look after his well-being?"

13. Thus did We restore him to his mother so that her eyes might be delighted, and so that she might not grieve but know that God's promise is true, yet most people do not know.

14. When he reached his prime strength and full growth, We granted him wisdom and knowledge; thus do We reward those who do good deeds.

15. He entered the city while its people were unaware and found therein two men fighting: one of them belonged to his own party, the other to his enemy. The one of his party sought his help against that of his enemy, and Moses struck him with his fist and ended his life; he said: "This is of Satan's doing; he is, indeed, a clear enemy, a misleader."

16. He (Moses) said: "Lord! I have hurt my own self; so, grant me refuge." So He granted him refuge; verily, He is oft-Forgiving, all-Merciful.

17. He (Moses) said: "Lord! Because of the grace You have bestowed upon me, I shall never be a supporter for criminals."

18. He remained in the city frightened, apprehensive when, lo, he whom he had aided the day before was now

again appealing for help. Moses said to him: "You certainly are mischievous."

19. When he was about to assault their (common) enemy, the latter said: "So, Moses! Do you wish to kill me as you yesterday killed another man? Do you intend to be a tyrant in the land, not desiring to be a reformer (instead)?"

20. A man came running from the remotest part of the city and said: "Moses! People are planning to kill you; so, get out; I only wish to give you a sincere advice."

21. So he went out, frightened, apprehensive. He said: "Lord! Rescue me from the unjust people."

22. When he headed towards Midian, he said: "Maybe my Lord will guide me to the right path."

23. Having arrived at Midian's water-place, he found a group of people watering (their flocks), and found besides them two women keeping their flocks away. He asked: "What is the matter with you?" They said: "We cannot water till the (other) shepherds take their herds away, and our father is a very old man."

24. So he watered for them, then he retired to the shade and said: "Lord! Verily, though You have bestowed upon me many bounties, I still am needy."

25. Then one of them came to him walking bashfully. She said: "My father invites you to reward you for watering for us." So when he came to him and narrated the story to him, he (their father) said: "Fear no more. You are secure from the unjust people."

26. One of them said: "Father, employ him. Verily he would be the best to employ, strong and trustworthy."

27. He said: "I desire to wed you to one of these two daughters of mine provided you serve me for eight years, and if you complete ten, then it would be out of your own goodness. I do not intend to place any hardship on you; you will find me, if God wills, righteous."

28. He (Moses) said: "This is an agreement between me and you: should I fulfill either of the two terms, there will be no injustice on my part, and God is a witness to what we say."

29. When Moses had fulfilled the term and was travelling with his family, he perceived on the side of Mount Tur (Sinai)

a fire; he said to his family: I behold a fire; maybe I shall bring you some glad tidings from there, or a torch of fire to warm yourselves."

30. When he came close to it, he was called upon from the right side of the valley, in the blessed area of a tree: "O Moses! Verily it is I, God, Lord of the worlds.

31. "So cast your staff down." Having seen it shake like a serpent, he turned back running in retreat, without looking back. "Come, O Moses, forward, and do not fear, for verily you are secure.

32. "And put your hand in your pocket, it shall come out white, (glowing) without a blemish, and close your sides nearer to you, should you feel any fear; these are proofs from your Lord to Pharaoh and his people; they are people of corruption."

33. He (Moses) said: "Lord! I have surely killed one of them; so, I fear they would slay me;

34. "And my brother Aaron is more articulate then me; so, send him with me as my assistant to testify for me, for I fear they would reject me."

35. He said: "We will strengthen you by your brother, and We will grant you authority so that they cannot approach you both; through Our signs, you and those who support you shall triumph."

36. When Moses brought them Our signs, they said: "This is nothing but a forged sorcery, and we never heard it from our fathers of old."

37. Moses said: "My Lord knows best who brings guidance from Him, and who shall be well rewarded in the hereafter; He never suffers the unjust to succeed."

38. Pharaoh said: "O people! I do not know any god for you besides myself; so, burn for me, O Haman, bricks of clay, and build me a tower so that I may mount it and see Moses' God, and I verily deem him to be a liar."

39. He and his hosts exalted their own selves in the world without a just cause, thinking that they will never be brought back to Us.

40. So We seized him and his hosts, and We cast them into the deep (sea); behold then how the end of the unjust ones was.

41. We made them imams who invite people to the Fire, and on the Day of Resurrection, they shall never be helped.

42. We caused a curse to follow them in this life, and on the Day of Resurrection, they shall be loathed, despised.

43. Indeed, We granted Moses the Book after destroying generations of old: clear arguments for mankind, a guidance and mercy, so that they might reflect.

44. You were not on the western side (of Mount Sinai) when We passed to Moses the commandments, nor were you an eye-witness.

45. But We raised generations, and a long time passed upon them. Nor were you a dweller among the people of Midian, rehearsing Our signs to them, but We sent you (O Our Prophet Muhammad) as one of Our messengers.

46. You were not on the side of Mount Tour (Sinai) when We called (upon Moses), but it is the mercy of your Lord that you warn a people to whom no warner has come before, so that they may reflect.

47. Were it not so, and should a calamity befall them for what their hands commit, then they would say: "O Lord! Why did You not send us a messenger to follow Your signs and believe?"

48. Yet when the truth came to them from Us, they said: "Why is he not given the like of what Moses was given?" Did not they disbelieve in what Moses was given? They said: "Two sorcerers backing each other," and they said: "Verily, we disbelieve in everything."

49. Say: "Then bring a book from God that guides better than both (Torah and Qur'an), so that I may follow it, if you are truthful."

50. If they do not answer you, know then that they only follow their own caprice. Who is more straying than he who follows his own caprice without any (divine) guidance? Verily God does not guide unjust people.

51. Indeed, We caused the Word to come to them continuously, so that they might be admonished.

52. Those whom We gave the Book before are believers therein.

53. When it is recited unto them, they say: "We believe in it; verily, it is the truth from our Lord; verily, we are sub-

mitting (as Muslims) even before."

54. These shall be granted their reward twice for what they have persevered. They repel evil with goodness, and they spend of the sustenance with which We provide them.

55. When they hear vain talk, they turn away from it and say: "For us shall be our deeds, and you shall have yours; peace be with you; we do not desire the (company of the) ignorant."

56. Verily, you cannot guide whomsoever you like; God guides whomsoever He pleases, and He knows best those who follow right guidance.

57. They say: "If we follow the guidance with you, we shall be driven out from our land." Have We not established them in a sacred and safe precinct to which all kinds of fruit are brought, a sustenance with which We have provided them? But most of them do not know.

58. How many a town, in which means of subsistence exulted, did We destroy? These are their dwellings: they have never been inhabited after them save a little, and We are their heirs.

59. Your Lord destroys no town until He raises in its metropolis a messenger rehearsing Our signs to them, and we destroyed no town except when its inhabitants were unjust people.

60. Whatever things you have been given are but a provision of this life and its adornment, and whatever is (in store) with God is better and more lasting. Do you not then understand?

61. Is he, then, whom We have promised a goodly promise which he shall meet is equal to him whom We have provided the provision of this life, then on the Day of Resurrection he shall be arraigned?

62. On that Day, God will call unto them and say: "Where are the partner whom you ascribed to Me?"

63. Those against whom the sentence has been confirmed will say: "O Lord! These are they whom we led astray: we led them astray even as we had ourselves been led astray: we declare to You to be free of them; they were not worshipping us."

64. It will be said: "Call upon your associate (gods);" so

they called, but they gave them no answer, and they shall witness the chastisement and wish that they had been rightly guided.

65. On that day, He shall call upon them and say: "How did you answer My messengers?"

66. The tidings shall that Day be so confusing that they shall not even ask each other.

67. Yet, as regarding that who turned repentant to God, believed (in Him), and did good deeds, he may be among the successful ones.

68. Your Lord creates whatever He pleases, and chooses, too. It is not they that choose; Praised is God, and Highly Exalted is He above what they associate with Him.

69. Your Lord knows what their hearts conceal and what they declare.

70. He is God; there is no god but He. His is all the praise, in the beginning and the end; His is the authority, and to Him (only) you shall be returned.

71. Say: "Have you seen how God has made the night to continue on you until the Day of Resurrection? Who is the god other than God that could bring light to you? Do you then hear?"

72. Say: "Have you seen how God has made the day to continue on you until the Day of Resurrection? Who is the god other than God that could bring night to you to rest therein? Do you not then see?"

73. Of His mercy is making the night for you and the day, so that you may rest therein, and that you may seek His Grace, and that you may be grateful (to Him).

74. On that Day, He shall call unto them and say: "Where are My partners whom you used to claim?"

75. We will draw forth a witness from each nation, and We will say: "Bring forth your proof." They shall know then that the truth is God's, and whatever they used to forge shall depart from them.

76. Indeed, Korah (Qarun) belonged to the people of Moses, but rebelled against them. We had given him treasures, so much so that their keys would have been a burden even for a group of many strong. When his people said to him: "Do not exult, for God does not love those who exult.

77. "And seek by means of what God has given you the abode of the hereafter, and do not forget your share in this world; be good unto others even as God has been good unto you, and do not seek mischief in the world; verily, God does not love mischief-makers."

78. He (Korah) said: "It has been granted to me only on account of the knowledge I possess." Did he not know that God has surely destroyed generations before him who were mightier in prowess than him and greater in hoarding? The criminals shall not be questioned about their crimes.

79. So he went forth to his people, pompous, and those who coveted (the pleasures of) this world said: "Would that we had the like of what Korah has been given! Verily he owns a great fortune."

80. Those who were endowed with knowledge said: "Woe unto you! God's reward is better for him who believes and does good deeds, but none shall attain it save the steadfast ones."

81. Then We caused the earth to swallow him and his abode; there was no group that could help him against God, nor was he able to defend his own self.

82. Those who coveted his position only the day before began saying: "Oh! As if God amplifies or straitens the sustenance of whomsoever He pleases of His servants! Had God not been gracious to us, He would certainly have let the earth swallow us, too. Oh! As if He never let the ungrateful ones succeed."

83. We assign the abode of the hereafter for those who do not intend to exult themselves in this life nor make mischief, and the end is best for the pious.

84. Whosoever does good deeds, there shall be better than it for him, and whosoever commits evil, those who commit evil shall not be recompensed save with what they had been doing.

85. Indeed, He it is Who has ordained the Qur'an to you is certainly the One that brings you back home. Say: "My Lord best knows whoever brings guidance, and whoever is in manifest error."

86. You (O Our Prophet Muhammad) did not expect the Book to be revealed unto you, but it is a mercy from your

Lord; therefore, do not side with the disbelievers.

87. Let them not turn you aside from God's signs after having been revealed to you, and call unto your Lord and do not be a polytheist.

88. And do not call with God any other god; there is no god but He. All things are perishable save He. His is the authority, and to Him shall you all return.

The Spider
(al-Ankabut)

In the name of God, the Beneficent, the Merciful.

1. Alif, Lam, Mim.

2. Do people imagine that they will be left alone on saying: "We believe," without being tried?

3. We did, indeed, try those before them, so that God may distinguish those who are truthful from those who are liars.

4. Or do they imagine that they will escape (Our judgment)? Ill is their judgment.

5. Whoever hopes to meet God, then meeting Him is forthcoming, and He is all-Hearing, all-Knowing.

6. Whoever strives hard does so only for his own good; verily God is independent of all creation.

7. We shall blot out the sins of those who believe and do good deeds, and We shall reward them with the best of what they were doing.

8. We have enjoined man to be good unto his parents. Should both of them strive to make you associate (other gods) with Me, without having any knowledge thereof, then do not obey them. To Me is your return, and I shall inform you of what you were doing.

9. We shall lodge those who believe and do good deeds among the righteous.

10. Among people are there those who say: "We believe in God." When they are persecuted in the Way of God, they think that people's persecution is a sign of God's chastisement; yet if your Lord's aid comes unto them, they would certainly say: "Verily, we were with you." Does not God know best what is in the bosoms of all the people of the

worlds?

11. God shall certainly distinguish those who believe and those who are hypocrites.

12. Those who disbelieve say to those who believe: "Follow our path, and we will certainly bear your sins." They shall not bear any of their sins; indeed they are liars.

13. They shall certainly bear their own burdens and (other) burdens with theirs, too, and they shall certainly be questioned on the Day of Judgment about what they were forging.

14. We did, indeed, send Noah (as messenger) to his people, and he stayed among them for a thousand years and fifty, and the deluge seized them while they were unjust.

15. So We rescued him and those who accompanied him in the ark and made them a sign to the nations of the world.

16. And (also) Abraham who said to his people: "Worship God (alone) and fear Him; this is best for you, if only you know.

17. "What you worship besides God is nothing but idols; you forge a lie; verily those whom you worship besides God have no sustenance for you; so, seek God's sustenance, and worship Him. Give thanks to Him, for to Him shall you all be returned.

18. "If you reject (the truth), then indeed nations before you rejected it, and nothing is incumbent upon the messenger except the delivery of a clear message."

19. Have they not seen how God originates the creation then causes it to return again? Verily this is easy for God.

20. Say: "Travel in the world and see how He originates the creation; He shall likewise bring the later development; verily God has power over all things.

21. "He tortures whomsoever He pleases and grant His mercy to whomsoever He wills, and to Him will you all be returned.

22. "You shall not frustrate His Might on earth, nor in the heaven, and there is none for you other than Him to protect or aid."

23. Those who disbelieved in God's signs and in meeting Him despaired of My Mercy, and these it is who shall have a painful torment.

24. The answer of his people was nothing except that they said: "Slay him, or burn him." Then God delivered him from the fire; verily in this are signs for people who believe.

25. He (Abraham) said: "You have only taken for yourselves idols besides God in friendship between you in the life of this world, then on the Day of Judgment, some of you shall deny others and some of you shall curse the others; your abode shall be the Fire, and you shall have no helper."

26. Lot believed in Him and said: "I am leaving (others) for my Lord, for verily He is the Almighty, the all-Wise."

27. We bestowed upon him Isaac and Jacob and ordained prophethood and the Book to his progeny; We granted him a recompense in this life, and in the hereafter he shall be among the righteous.

28. Lot said to his people: "Verily you commit lewdness to which none among the nations of the world has ever preceded you.

29. "Do you approach men (in lust) and cut the highways, and you commit evil deeds in your assemblies?" The answer of his people was nothing other than they said: "Bring us the chastisement of God if you are truthful."

30. He (Lot) said: "Lord! Help me against the mischief-makers!"

31. When Our messengers came to Abraham with glad tidings, they said: "Verily we are destroying the people of this town for they are unjust people."

32. He (Abraham) said: "Lot is surely therein." They said: "We know best who is in it; we shall certainly rescue him and his family save his wife; she shall lag behind."

33. When Our messengers came to Lot, he grieved on their account and felt powerless (to protect them). They said: "Do not fear or grieve. We shall deliver you and your family save your wife; she shall stay behind.

34. "Verily, we are bringing down a punishment upon the people of this town from heaven for what they were transgressing."

35. We have, indeed, left a clear sign of it for people who understand.

36. And to Midian (We sent) their brother Shu'ayb. He

said: "O my people! Worship God (alone), and fear the Last Day, and do not indulge in evil on earth, making mischief."

37. But they rejected him; so, an earthquake seized them, and they lay (dead) in their abodes, motionless.

38. And We (destroyed) Ad and Thamud, and indeed it had been made manifest to you from their dwellings (now in ruins). Satan rendered their deeds fair-seeming to them; so, he kept them away from the (right) Path, though they were endowed with sight.

39. And (We destroyed) Korah, Pharaoh, and Haman. Moses brought them clear proofs, but they behaved arrogantly in the world, and they were not the first.

40. So, each We seized for his sin. Of them was he on whom We sent a stone-laden violent gale. Of them was he whom the blast seized. Of them was he whom We caused to be swallowed up in the earth, and of them was he whom We drowned. It was not God Who did them injustice; they were themselves committing injustice.

41. The similitude of those who take others for guardians besides God is like the spider that makes for itself a house; verily the frailest of all houses is the spider's, if they only know.

42. Verily, God knows whatever they invoke besides Him, and He is the Almighty, the all-Wise.

43. We set forth such similitudes to people, yet none comprehend them except the learned ones.

44. God created the heavens and the earth in truth; verily in this there is a sign for those who believe.

45. Recite what has been revealed unto you of the Book, and establish prayers; verily prayer restrains from filth and evilness. Verily, remembering God is the greatest (duty), and God knows what you do.

46. Do not argue with the people of the Book but in the best manner, except those among them who act unjustly, and say: "We have believed in what has been sent down to us and to you; our God and yours is One, and we submit to Him."

47. Thus have We revealed the Book (Qur'an) unto you. Those whom We have given the Book believe therein, and among these are those who also believe in it, and none dis-

pute about Our signs except the disbelievers.

48. You never recited any book before it (Qur'an), nor did you ever transcribe one with your hand; then those who utter falsehood would have doubted it.

49. Nay! It (Qur'an) is but a clear sign in the hearts of those who have been endowed with knowledge, and none disputes Our signs except the unjust ones.

50. They say: "Why has no sign been sent down unto him from his Lord?" Say (O Our Prophet Muhammad): "The signs are with God (alone), and I am only a clear warner."

51. Is it not enough for them that We have sent down unto you the Book which is recited to them? Verily in this there is mercy and a reminder for people who believe.

52. Say: "God suffices for a witness between me and you; He knows what is in the heavens and the earth; those who believe in falsehood and disbelieve in God shall certainly be the losers."

53. They challenge you to hasten the chastisement upon them. Had not the term been decreed, chastisement would certainly have come to them suddenly while they do not perceive it.

54. They challenge you to hasten the chastisement on them and verily Hell will encompass the disbelievers.

55. On the Day when the chastisement covers them, from above them and from beneath their feet, He shall say: "Taste what you were doing."

56. O My servants who believe! Verily My earth is vast; therefore, you should worship Me alone.

57. Every soul shall taste death; then to Us will you all be returned.

58. We shall certainly lodge those who believe and do good deeds in exalted places, gardens beneath which rivers flow; they shall abide therein forever; how excellent is the reward of those who act rightly!

59. Those who are steadfast and on their Lord they rely.

60. How many moving creatures that do not carry their sustenance does God sustain? God sustains them and your own selves; He is the all-Hearing, the all-Knowing.

61. If you ask them: "Who created the heavens and the earth and made the sun and the moon subservient?" They

will certainly say: "God." So, whence are they turned away?

62. God makes sustenance abundant for whomsoever He wills of His servants. He (similarly) causes it to be straitened from others; verily God is well-Cognizant of all things.

63. If you ask them: "Who sends water down from heaven and thereby gives life to a land that had died?" They will certainly say: "God." Say: "All praise is His." Nay! Most of them do not understand.

64. This life is but a vain sport and play, and verily the abode of the hereafter is the true life if you only know.

65. When they embark upon a ship, they sincerely invoke God, vowing to worship Him, and when He brings them safely to land, behold, they associate (others with Him).

66. Let them not offer thanks for what We have granted them, and let them enjoy it; but soon shall they come to know.

67. Have they not seen how We have established a sacred precinct that is secure, while people are ravaged all around them? Will they yet believe in falsehood, disbelieving in God's bounty?

68. Who is more unjust than he who forges a lie against God or belies the truth when it comes to him? Is not in Hell an abode for the disbelievers?

69. We shall certainly guide those who strive hard for Us to Our ways, and verily God is with those who do good deeds.

The (east) Romans
(ar-Rum)

In the name of God, the Beneficent, the Merciful.

1. Alif, Lam, Mim.

2. The [East] Romans have been defeated,

3. In the nearer land, yet after their defeat, they will soon triumph,

4. Within a few years; God's is the Sovereignty before and after, and day shall come when the believers rejoice,

5. Due to God's victory (upon them); He renders whomsoever victorious as He pleases; He is the Almighty, the all-Merciful.

6. It is God's promise; God never fails His promise, but most people do not know.

7. They (only) know what is apparent in life, heedless to the hereafter.

8. Have they not reflected upon their own themselves? God never created the heavens and the earth, and what is in-between, except in truth, and for an appointed term; most people, indeed, disbelieve in the meeting of their own Lord.

9. Have they not travelled throughout the world and seen how the outcome of those before them had been? They were mightier than them, and they left stronger marks, dug the earth and built more than what these people have built; Our messengers brought them manifest proofs; so, God did not have to do them injustice, but they were unjust to their own selves.

10. Then evil was the end of those who committed evil by rejecting God's manifest signs and mocking them.

11. God originates the creation, then He causes it to recur, then to Him shall you all be returned.

12. On the Day when the Hour comes, the guilty ones shall surely despair.

13. They shall have no intercessors from among their partner gods, and they shall (even) deny their partners.

14. On the Day when the Hour arrives-it is then that they shall separate.

15. As to those who believed and did good deeds, they shall be in the Garden, well-pleased.

16. As to those who disbelieved and rejected Our signs and the meeting in the hereafter, these shall be brought to the chastisement.

17. So glory be to God when you approach the eve or the morn.

18. And His (alone) is the Praise in the heavens and the earth, and at dusk, and when you approach noon.

19. He brings forth a living out of the dead, and brings forth the dead out of the living, and He brings life to the earth after its death-thus shall you, too, be resurrected.

20. Among His signs is that He created you of dust, then you became human beings scattering (in the world).

21. And among His signs is that He created for you, from

your own selves, mates so that you dwell (in tranquility) with them, creating love and compassion between you; indeed, there are signs in this for people who reflect.

22. And among His signs is the creation of the heavens and the earth, and the variety of your languages and complexions; verily in this are signs for those endowed with knowledge.

23. And among His signs is your slumber at night and day, and your seeking of His grace; verily in this there are signs for people who listen.

24. And among His signs is that He shows you lightning, causing awe and hope, sending water down from the heavens and giving life with it to the earth after it had died; verily there are signs in this for people who understand.

25. And among His signs is that the heavens and the earth carry out His command, then if He summons you to come out of the earth (your tombs), you shall come forth.

26. His are whosoever in the heavens and the earth: all are subservient to Him.

27. He it is Who originates the creation, then He causes it to recur again, and the latter (case) is even easier to Him; His are the most exalted similitudes in the heavens and the earth, and He is the Almighty, the all-Wise.

28. He sets forth parables for you from your own creation. Have you had partners from those your right hands possess in what We have provided you for sustenance, so that you are alike in its regard, fearing them as you fear each other? Thus do We make Our signs clear for those who understand.

29. Nay! Those who are unjust followed their own desires without any knowledge, so who can guide those whom God has permitted to stray? They shall have no helpers.

30. So set your face uprightly for religion, in natural devotion to the truth, the nature caused by God in which He has made people; there can be no change in God's creation; this is the established religion, but most people do not know.

31. Turn to Him; fear (only) Him, and establish prayer, and do not be polytheists,

32. Each party of those who split up their religion and became sects rejoices in what is therewith.

33. When people are afflicted with harm, they call upon their Lord, turning to Him; then when He causes them to taste of His mercy, lo, some of them even associate partners with their Lord.

34. Let them be ungrateful for what We have granted them; enjoy for a while, for soon you shall come to know.

35. Or have We sent down upon them an authority that speaks of what they associate with Him?

36. And when We cause people to taste of Our Mercy, they rejoice therein, and if an evil befalls them for what they wrought with their own hands, lo, they are in utter despair.

37. Have not they seen that God amplifies the provision for whomsoever He pleases and straitens? Verily in this are signs for people who believe.

38. Then give the near of kin his dues, and to the needy and the wayfarer; this is best for those who desire to please God, and these it is who are the successful ones.

39. And what you give out at interest so that it may increase people's wealth, it does not increase with God, and whatever you give as zakat, desiring to attain the Pleasure of God, it is these that shall get manifold (rewards).

40. God is He Who created you then provided you with sustenance, then He causes you to die, then He brings you to life again; is there any of your associate gods that does aught of these things? Glory be to Him, and Exalted is He far above what they ascribe (to Him).

41. Mischief has appeared in the land and the sea on account of what the hands of men have wrought, that He may make them taste a part of what they have done, so that they may return (to Him).

42. Say: "Travel in the earth, then see how the end of those who were before you was; most of them were polytheists."

43. Then set your face upright to the established Religion before a Day comes from God when, on that Day, which can never be averted, they shall surely be separated.

44. Whoever disbelieves shall bear the burden of his disbelief, and whoever does good deeds, it is for his own self what he prepares.

45. So that He may recompense those who believe and do good deeds with His Grace; verily He does not love the disbelievers.

46. Among His Signs is that He sends forth the wind bearing glad tidings, and that He may make you taste of His Mercy, and that ships may sail by His Command, and that you should seek of His Grace, and that you may show gratitude.

47. Indeed, We sent messengers before you to their (respective) people, and they came to them with clear proofs, then We took vengeance upon those who were guilty; the succor of the believers was indeed incumbent upon Us.

48. God it is Who sends forth the winds so that they raise clouds, then He spreads it forth in the skies as He wills and causes it to break up so that you see the rays coming forth from inside it. When He causes it to fall upon whomsoever He pleases from among His servants, lo, they rejoice therein-

49. Though before it was sent down upon them they were in mute despair.

50. Behold the traces of God's Mercy: how He gives life to the earth after it had died; verily He is the giver of life to the dead; He has power over all things.

51. If We send the wind, and they see (their tilth) yellow, they become disbelievers thereafter;

52. For you cannot make the dead hear, nor can you make the deaf hear the call when they withdraw, turning upon their heels.

53. Nor can you lead the blind away from straying; you cannot make anyone hear except those who believe in Our Signs, for they are resigned to Our Will as Muslims.

54. God it is Who created you out of weakness and then turned your weakness into strength, then your strength into weakness and grey hairs; He creates whatsoever He wills; He is the all-Knowing, the omni-Potent.

55. When the Hour (of Judgment) arrives, on that Day the guilty will swear that they tarried but an hour; thus did they use to utter lies.

56. Those who have been endowed with knowledge and faith shall say: "Indeed, you tarried according to the decree of God till the Day of Resurrection, but you did not know."

57. On that Day, the plea shall not avail those who were unjust, nor will they be able to please God.

58. Indeed, We have set forth for people every kind of parable in this Qur'an; yet if you bring a Sign to them, those who disbelieve will certainly say: "You are but a false claimant."

59. Thus does God set a seal on the hearts of those who do not know.

60. Be patient, therefore; verily the promise of God is true, and let not those who have no belief in God make you despair of His promise.

Luqman

In the name of God, the Beneficent, the Merciful.

1. Alif, Lam, Mim.

2. These are the verses of the Book of Wisdom,

3. A guidance and a mercy for the righteous,

4. Who establish prayer and pay zakat, having no doubt about the hereafter;

5. These are the ones who are on the right guidance of their Lord, and they are the ones that shall succeed.

6. Among the people there is one who buys vain talk to lead others astray from the path of God without knowledge, mocking thereat; awaiting these is a disgracing chastisement.

7. When Our signs are recited unto them, they turn back puffed up as if they had not heard them, as if heaviness is in their ears; so, convey the tidings of the painful chastisement.

8. Verily, for those who believe and do good deeds shall be the gardens of bliss,

9. Dwelling therein eternally, a true promise from God; He is the Almighty, the all-Wise.

10. He created the heavens without pillars as you behold them, and He cast mountains upon the earth lest it should shake with you, and He spread in it of every kind of animals; We sent down water from the skies, then We caused vegetation to grow therein of every noble kind.

11. Such is the creation of God; show me what those besides Him have created. Nay! The unjust are in manifest stray-

ing.

12. Indeed, We granted Luqman wisdom saying: "Be grateful to God, for whoever is grateful is indeed grateful for his own self, and whoever is ungrateful, God is surely self-Sufficient, Most Praised."

13. Luqman, exhorting his son, said: "O son! Do not associate aught with God, for verily associating aught with God is the greatest iniquity."

14. And We enjoined man concerning his parents; his mother bore him in weakness upon weakness, and his weaning in two years, saying: "Be grateful unto Me and unto your parents; to Me is the ultimate return.

15. "Should they pressure you to associate (any) with Me of which you have no knowledge, then do not obey them but consort them kindly in this world, and follow the path of that who turns to Me (penitent); to Me is your return, and I will then inform you of what you were doing."

16. "O son! Verily even if a mustard seed is (enclosed) in a rock, in the heavens, or in the earth, God shall bring it forth to light; verily, God is all-Subtle, all-Aware.

17. "O son! Establish prayer, enjoin goodness, and forbid evil; be patient against what befalls you; verily this is the task of steadfastness.

18. "Do not turn your face to people (in scorn), nor should you walk exultingly; verily, God does not love a self-conceited braggart.

19. "Be moderate in your gait, and lower your voice; indeed the most unpleasing of voices is the braying of donkeys."

20. Have you not seen how God has made all that is in the heavens and the earth subservient, and completed upon you His bounties both apparent and hidden? Yet among people is that who disputes about God even without knowledge or guidance or an illuminating book.

21. When it is said to them: "Follow what God has sent down," they say: "Nay! We rather follow that which we found our fathers doing." Even if Satan beckons them to a chastisement of the blazing Fire?

22. Whosoever sets his face in submission to God, doing good deeds, indeed he has then laid hold on a most firm

handhold, and to God is the end of all affairs.

23. Let not the disbelief of a disbeliever grieve you; to Us is their (ultimate) return, and We will then inform them of what they used to do; verily God well-knows what is in their hearts.

24. We provide them to enjoy a little, then We shall drive them to a severe chastisement.

25. If you ask them: "Who created the heavens and the earth?" they would certainly say: "God." Say: "(All) praise be to God!" Nay! Most of them do not know.

26. God's is whatever in the heavens and the earth; verily God is self-Sufficient, Most Praised.

27. Had all the trees on earth been turned pens, and the sea multiplied seven seas of ink, yet they will not exhaust the Words of God; verily God is Almighty, all-Wise.

28. Neither your creation, nor your resurrection, is any but as a single soul; verily God is all-Hearing, all-Seeing.

29. Do you not see that God causes the night to pass into the day, and the day to pass into the night, and He has made the sun and the moon subservient, each passing an appointed term? God is all-Aware of all what you do.

30. It is so because God is the Truth, and what they call upon besides Him is falsehood; God is He, the most Sublime, the most Great.

31. Do you not see how the ships sail onto the sea by the favour of God, that He may show you (some) of His signs? Verily in this are signs for everyone steadfast, grateful.

32. When a wave like mountains covers them, they call unto God in sincere devotion; but when He brings them safe to land, some of them halt between right and wrong; none dispute about Our signs except the perfidious, the ungrateful.

33. O people! Guard yourselves against (the Wrath of) your Lord, and dread the Day when (even) a father cannot avail his son, nor a child avails its father; verily the promise of God is true; so, let not the life in this world beguile you, nor let the deceiver deceive you concerning God.

34. Verily, God is He Who has the knowledge of the Hour; He sends rain down and knows what is in the wombs; no soul knows what it shall earn in the morrow, and no soul

knows in what land it shall die; verily God is all-Knowing, all-Aware.

Prostration
(Sajdah)

In the Name of God, the Beneficent, the Merciful.

1. Alif, Lam, Mim.

2. A revelation of a Book (Qur'an) with no doubt therein from the Lord of the worlds.

3. Or do they say: "He has forged it"? Nay! It is the truth from your Lord that you may warn thereby a people to whom no warner before you came, haply they may be guided aright.

4. God it is Who created the heavens and the earth and what is between them in six days, and firmly established on His Throne (Authority); for you there is none besides Him as the guardian, nor any intercessor; will you not then reflect?

5. He regulates the affairs from the heaven to the earth, then it shall ascend to Him on a day whose measure is (like) a thousand years of what you reckon.

6. Such is the Knower of the hidden and the manifest, the all-Mighty, the all-Merciful.

7. It is He Who created and began the creation of man from clay.

8. Then He made his progeny out of an extract of despised liquid water.

9. Then He shaped him and breathed into him of His Spirit and made ears for you, and eyes, and hearts; little do you give thanks.

10. They said: "When we become lost in the earth, shall we, even then, still return in a new creation?" Nay! They even disbelieve in meeting their Lord.

11. Say: "The angel of death, put in charge of you, shall take your life away, then to your Lord you shall be brought back.

12. Could you but see how the guilty ones droop their heads before their Lord: "Lord! We have seen and heard; so send us back to do good deeds; verily we now truly be-

lieve."

13. Had it pleased Us, We would certainly have granted every soul its guidance, but true is the word which went forth from Me: "I shall certainly fill Hell with the jinn and man together;

14. "So taste (the recompense), for you had forsaken the meeting of this day of yours; verily We too forsake you today, and taste the perpetual chastisement for what you were doing."

15. Verily, only those who, when reminded of Our signs, fall down prostrating in obeisance and celebrate the praise of their Lord, are the ones who believe therein, and they do not exalt themselves with pride.

16. Their sides forsake their beds, praying to their Lord in fear and in hope, and they spend benevolently of what We provide them with.

17. No (righteous) soul knows what is hidden for it of the joy of the eyes, as recompense for what it was doing.

18. Is he then who is a believer like unto him that who is a transgressor? They shall never be held akin.

19. As for those who believe and do good deeds, for them are the gardens of bliss, their heavenly abode, an entertainment for what they were doing.

20. As for those who transgress, their abode shall be Hell- fire; whenever they desire to get out of it, they shall be brought back into it, and it shall be said to them: "Taste the chastisement of the fire in which you used to disbelieve."

21. We shall certainly make them taste of the minimum chastisement instead of the maximum one, so that they may haply return (penitent).

22. Who is more unjust than he who, when reminded of the signs of his Lord, turns away therefrom? Verily, We shall exact retribution from the guilty ones.

23. Indeed We bestowed the Book upon Moses; so, do not be in doubt of receiving this from Him, and We made it (Torah) a guidance to the children of Israel.

24. And We made some of them leaders (Imams) guiding by Our command, steadfast, and they were quite certain of Our signs.

25. Verily your Lord will Himself decide between them

on the Day of Judgment concerning what they were disputing therein.

26. Does it not guide them rightly to see how many generations We destroyed? They walk (now) in (the ruins of) their abodes; verily in this are signs; will they not then listen?

27. Do they not see how We drive water to a parched earth and bring forth therewith crops of which the cattle and they themselves eat? Will they not then behold?

28. They say: "When will this judgment take place, if you are truthful?"

29. Say: "On the Day of Judgment, the belief then of those who used to disbelieve will not avail them, nor will they be respited."

30. So turn away from them and wait, verily they too are waiting.

The Confederates
(al-Ahzab)

In the Name of God, the Beneficent, the Merciful.

1. O Our Prophet (Muhammad)! Fear God (alone) and do not obey the disbelievers and hypocrites; verily God is all-Knowing, all-Wise.

2. And follow what is revealed unto you from your Lord; verily God is all-Aware of what you do.

3. And rely on God (alone), for God is sufficient Protector.

4. God has never made two hearts in the breast of any man, nor has He made your wives, whom you declare to be your mothers, as your mothers, nor has He made those whom you call your sons as your sons; these are mere words of your mouths, and God speaks the truth and He guides to the (Right) Path.

5. Call them after their fathers, this is more just with God, but if you do not know their fathers, then they are your brethren in Faith and friends. It shall not be a crime upon you concerning that in which you commit error, but that which you do with the intent of your heart, and God is oft-Forgiving, Most Merciful.

6. The Prophet (Muhammad) has a greater claim unto

the believers than they have on their own selves, and his wives are (as) their mothers, and blood-relations have a better claim regarding one to the other according to the Book of God than the believers and emigrants, save that you do some good to your friends. Thus is the decree (of God) written.

7. Behold! We took a Covenant from the Prophets and from you, from Noah and Abraham, Moses and Jesus son of Mary, and We took from them a firm Covenant,

8. That He may question the truthful of their truth, and He has prepared for the disbelievers a painful chastisement.

9. O you who believe! Remember the bounty of God unto you when the hosts came upon you, then We sent upon them a strong wind and hosts that you did not see, and God sees all what you do.

10. They came upon you from above you and from below, and the eyes were turned dull, and the throats reached the hearts, and you even imagined about God diverse thoughts.

11. There, the believers were tried and shaken tremendously.

12. The hypocrites, and those in whose hearts was a disease, began to say: "God and His Messenger did not promise us but a deception."

13. A party among them said: "O people of Yathrib! There is no place for you to stand; so, return," and a party of them asked permission of the Prophet saying: "Verily our houses are exposed (to deterioration)," they were not indeed exposed (to deterioration); they only intended to flee away.

14. Had the entry been made upon them from all sides, and had they been incited to treachery, they would certainly have brought it to pass only if they stayed a while longer.

15. Indeed they had made a Covenant with God before, that they would not turn their backs, and their Covenant with God shall be questioned. Say: "Never shall your flight benefit you if you flee away from death or slaughter, and even then, you will not be allowed to enjoy yourselves but only for a short while."

16. Say: "Who is he that can screen you from God if He intends to harm you, or to be merciful unto you?" And they

will find for themselves no other guardian or helper besides God.

17. Say: "Who is he that can screen you from God if He intends to punish you, or be merciful unto you?" They will then find neither guardian nor helper besides God.

18. Indeed, God knows those who hinder others among you and those who say to their brethren: "Come hither to us," and they do not go to fight but for a short while.

19. Being niggardly to you, but when fear approaches them, you find them looking to you; their eyes rolling like one on whom death has cast its shadow, and when fear passes away, they smite you with sharp tongues, being niggardly of the good things; these have not believed at all; so, God has made their deeds vain, and this is easy for God.

20. They think the allies have not gone. Should the clans come (again), they would fain be dwelling with the wandering Arabs in the desert, seeking news about you. Had they been amidst you, they would have fought you save for a short while.

21. Indeed, there is for you in the Messenger of God (Muhammad) an excellent pattern of conduct for him who places his hope in God and the latter day and remembers God much.

22. And when the believers saw the allies, they said: "This is what God and His Messenger promised us; God and His Messenger had spoken the truth," and it increased their faith and supplication.

23. Among the believes are men who are true to their covenant with God; of them is he who has fulfilled his vow, and of them is he who awaits it, and they have not changed in the least,

24. That God may recompense the truthful for their truthfulness and chastise the hypocrites if He wills, or turn to them (Mercifully); verily God is oft- Forgiving, Most Merciful.

25. God turned back those who disbelieve in their rage; they reaped no benefit, and God suffices the believers in their fighting, for God is Almighty, omni-Potent.

26. He drove down those of the people of the Book who backed them from their fortresses, and He cast an awe into

their hearts; some you killed and others you took captive.

27. He made you inherit their land, dwellings and possessions, and a land where you have never set your foot in, and God has power over all things.

28. O Our Prophet (Muhammad)! Say to your wives: "If you desire (to enjoy) the life of this world, and its adornment, come then so I provide for you and allow you to depart on good terms.

29. "And if you desire God and His Messenger and the abode in the hereafter, then verily God has prepared for the righteous among you a great reward."

30. O wives of the Prophet! Whosoever among you commits an open indecency, her chastisement shall be doubled, and this is easy for God.

31. And whoever of you is obedient to God and His Messenger, and does good deeds, We will grant her twice her recompense, and We have prepared for her an honourable sustenance.

32. O wives of the Prophet! You are not like any other women if you guard yourselves against evil, and be not soft in (your) speech lest that in whose heart is a disease should feel lust for you, and speak plainly.

33. Stay in your abodes, and do not display your finery like the display of the days of ignorance of yore; establish prayer; pay zakat, and obey God and His Messenger; verily God intends but to keep off from you (every kind of) abomination, O you People of the (Prophet's) Household (Ahl al-Bayt) and purify you with a perfect purification.

34. And remember what is recited in your abodes of the signs of God and the wisdom; verily God is Benignant, all-Aware.

35. Indeed, God prepared forgiveness and a great recompense for Muslim men and women, believing men and women, obedient men and women, truthful men and women, patient men and women, humble men and women, alm-giving men and women, fasting men and women, men and women who safeguard their chastity, men who remember God much and women who remember God much.

36. It is not for a believing man or woman to have any choice in their affair when God and His Messenger have (al-

ready) decided a matter; whoever disobeys God and His Messenger indeed has strayed off a manifest straying.

37. When you said to the one upon whom God has bestowed His bounty, and to whom you have shown favour: "Retain your wife, and fear God," you did, indeed, hide in yourself that which God would (eventually) bring to light, and you feared people while God has a greater right that you should fear Him. But when Zayd concluded his concern with her, We joined her (in wedlock) as your wife, so that there should be no difficulty for the believers concerning the wives of their adopted sons, when they have concluded their concerns with them, and the command of God shall be carried out.

38. On the Prophet there is no blame in doing what was ordained by God unto him, and such has been the Way of God with those who have passed before, and the behest of God is a decree irrevocable.

39. Those who convey the Message of God and fear Him, and fear none but Him, God suffices to take their account.

40. Muhammad is never the father of any of your men, but a Messenger of God and the Seal of the Prophets, and God ever knows all things.

41. O you who believe! Remember God most frequently,

42. And glorify Him in the morn and the eve;

43. He it is Who confers upon you His blessings and the angels, that He may bring you forth from the darkness into the light, and He is to the believers all-Merciful.

44. Their greetings on the Day when they meet Him shall be: "Peace!" and He has prepared for them an honourable reward.

45. O Our Prophet (Muhammad)! Verily We have sent you as a Witness, a bearer of glad tidings, and a warner,

46. And the one who invites to God by His command, and an illuminating lamp.

47. Convey the glad tidings to the believers that there shall be a great grace for them from God.

48. Do not comply with the infidels and hypocrites; do not heed their annoying talk, and rely on God; God is sufficient as (your) Protector.

49. O you who believe! When you wed the believing

women, then you divorce them before touching them, there is no iddat (term) on them which you should reckon; so, make some provisions for them and send them away in a gracious manner.

50. O Our Prophet (Muhammad)! Verily We have made lawful to you your wives whom you have given their dowries, and those whom your right hand possesses out of those whom God returns to you (without war), and the daughters of your paternal uncles, the daughters of your paternal aunts, the daughters of your maternal uncles and the daughters of your maternal aunts who fled with you, a believing woman if she gives herself to the Prophet, if the Prophet desires to wed her, especially for you other than the (rest of) believers; indeed We know what We have ordained for them about their wives and those whom their right hands possess in order that no blame may be attached to you, and God is oft-Forgiving, Most Merciful.

51. You may defer whom you please of them, and you may take to yourself whom you please, and whom you desire of those whom you have set aside, no blame shall be on you; this is nearer to giving them the joy of their eyes, that they may not grieve, and that they all be pleased with what you give them; God knows what is in your heart; God is all-Knowing, most Patient.

52. It is not allowed to take women afterwards, nor should you change them for other wives, though their beauty may charm you, save what your right hand possesses, and God is watchful over all things.

53. O you who believe! Do not enter the houses of the Prophet unless it is permitted to you for a meal, without waiting till the meal is served, but when you are invited, enter, and when you have taken the food, disperse without seeking any familiar talk; verily this annoys the Prophet. Indeed he is too shy to dismiss you, but God is never too shy of the truth, and if you ask them for any goods, ask them from behind the curtain; thus is purer for your hearts and theirs. It is not right for you to annoy the Messenger of God, nor should you ever wed his wives after him; verily this is grievous in the sight of God.

54. If you manifest anything or hide it, verily God is

well-Aware of all things.

55. There is no blame on them regarding their fathers, nor their sons, nor their brothers, nor their brothers' sons, nor their sisters' sons, nor their own women, nor of what their right hands possess; fear God! Verily God is a witness on all things.

56. Verily God and His angels bless the Prophet! O you who believe, send blessings unto him and greet him with a salutation worthy of respect.

57. Verily those who annoy God and His Messenger (Muhammad), God has cursed them in this world and the hereafter, and He has prepared for them a disgraceful torment.

58. And those who annoy believing men and women without having committed anything wrong, indeed they bear the guilt of slander and a manifest sin.

59. O (Our) Prophet (Muhammad)! Tell your wives and daughters, and believing women, to let their garments down to cover them, lest they should be known and troubled; God is oft- Forgiving, Most Merciful.

60. If the hypocrites, and those in whose hearts there is a diseases, and the agitators in the city, do not desist, We shall certainly stir you against them; they shall not be allowed to be your neighbours therein except for a short time.

61. They are cursed wherever they are found; they shall be seized and slain horribly.

62. Such is the way of God concerning those who have passed away before, and never shall you find in the way of God any change.

63. When people ask you (Muhammad) about the Hour; say: "The knowledge of it is only with God, and what will make you know? Haply the Hour may be nigh."

64. Verily God has cursed the disbelievers and prepared a flaming fire for them.

65. They shall abide therein forever; they shall not find a protector or a helper.

66. On that Day, when their faces are turned into the Fire, they shall say: "Oh! Would that we had obeyed God and the Messenger!"

67. And they shall say: "Lord! Verily we obeyed our

chiefs and elders, and they led us astray from the Path.

68. "Lord! Give them double the torment, and curse them with a great curse."

69. O you who believe! Do not be like those who afflicted Moses (with slander), but God cleared him of what they said, and he was held by God in high esteem.

70. O you who believe! Guard yourselves and utter what is right.

71. He will set your deeds right and forgive your faults; whoever obeys God and His Messenger has indeed achieved a great success.

72. Verily We offered the trust to the heavens and the earth and the mountains, but they refused to bear it, and were afraid thereof, and man undertook it; verily he was (proved) unjust, ignorant.

73. So will God chastise the hypocrites, men and women, and the polytheists, men and women, and God will turn (merciful) to the believing men and women; God is oft-Forgiving, Most Merciful.

Saba

In the name of God, the Beneficent, the Merciful.

1. All praise is due to God to Whom (the domain) of the heavens and in the earth belongs, and His is all praise in the hereafter; He is the all-Wise, the all-Aware.

2. He knows whatever passes into the earth and whatever comes out of it, and whatever comes down from the heavens and whatever goes upto it; He is the Most Merciful, the oft-Forgiving.

3. Those who disbelieve say: "The Hour shall not come upon us." Say: "Yea; by my Lord, the Knower of the unseen, it shall certainly come upon you, from Him nothing is hidden (not even) the weight of an atom in the heavens nor in the earth, nor is there aught less than this, nor aught greater, but is in the manifesting Book,

4. "That He may recompense those who believe and do good deeds; these it is for whom there is forgiveness and an honourable sustenance.

5. For those who strive hard to invalidate Our Signs

there is a chastisement of a painful torment.

6. Will those to whom knowledge has been given see that which has been revealed to you from your Lord is the truth, and it guides to the Path of the Almighty, the Most Praised?

7. Those who disbelieve say (in ridicule): "Shall we point out to you a man who informs you that when you are wholly scattered, totally disintegrated, (even then) you are certainly returned into a new creation?

8. "Has he forged a lie against God, or is he possessed?" Nay! Those who do not believe in the hereafter are in a torment and are straying far from the truth.

9. Do not they see then what is before them and what is behind them of the heavens and the earth? If We please, We will make them sink into the earth, or We bring down upon them a piece from the heavens; verily in this there is a sign for every servant turning (to his Lord).

10. And indeed We gave a boon to David from Us saying: "O mountains! Sing the praise of God along with him, and the birds, too," and We softened the iron for him.

11. "Make coats of mail, and measure its links and do good deeds; verily I see all what you do."

12. And for Solomon (We subjected) the wind which travelled in the morning a month's journey and a month's journey in the eve, and We caused for him a fountain of molten brass to flow, and among the jinn were those who worked for him by the Command of his Lord, and whoever among them turned away from Our command, We shall make him taste of the chastisement of the flaming fire.

13. They made for him whatever he wills of fortresses and statues, basins as reservoirs and huge cooking cauldrons immovable from their place; "Act gratefully, O family of David! And very few of My servants are grateful!"

14. And when We decreed his death, nothing showed them his death except the worm of the earth that gnawed away his staff; when it fell down, the jinn plainly saw that had they come to know the unseen, they would not have tarried in their humiliating torment.

15. Indeed, for (the children of) Saba in their abode was a sign: two gardens on the right and the left; "Eat of the

sustenance of your Lord and offer thanks to Him," and a good land, and an oft-Forgiving Lord!

16. But they turned away, so We sent upon them a torrent irresistible, and in place of their two gardens We gave them two gardens yielding bitter fruits and tamarisks and a few lotetrees.

17. This We recompensed them for what they disbelieved; but do We (thus) recompense any save the ungrateful?

18. And We caused between them and the towns which We had blessed (other) towns to be seen, and We have made easy the journey therein; travel through them nights and days, secure.

19. Then they said: "Lord! Make the spaces to be longer between our journey" and they were unjust to their own selves. We made them tales and scattered them with a total scattering; verily in this are signs for every one patient, grateful.

20. And indeed Iblis found his conjecture concerning them true, so they followed him except a party of the believers.

21. And there is no authority for him save that We would distinguish him that believes in the hereafter from him that is in doubt concerning it, and your Lord is a Guardian over all things.

22. Say: "Call upon those whom you deemed (as gods) besides God; they do not own the weight of an atom in the heavens nor the earth, nor is there for them any partnership in either, nor for Him is there from among them anyone to help."

23. No intercession with Him will avail them save of him whom He has permitted, until terror is removed from their hearts, they shall say: "What is it that your Lord said?" They (angels) shall say: "The truth, and He is the Most High, the Greatest!"

24. Say: "Who provides you with sustenance from the heavens and the earth?" Say: "(It is none but) God, and verily (either) we or you are guided aright, or in manifest error?"

25. Say: "You will not be questioned about what we are guilty of, nor shall we be questioned about what you do."

26. Say: "Our Lord will gather us together, then He will

judge between us with justice; He is the Greatest Judge, the all-Knowing."

27. Say: "Show me those whom you associate with Him: By no means! Nay! He is God the Almighty, the all-Wise."

28. And We sent you (Muhammad) but to the whole world as a bearer of glad tidings and a Warner, yet most people do not know.

29. And they say: "When will this promise be, if you are truthful?"

30. Say: "For you there is an appointed day which you cannot hold back even a while, nor can you hasten it on."

31. And those who disbelieve say: "We shall never believe in this Qur'an, nor in that which is before it," but could you see when the unjust are made to stand before their Lord, returning reproaches from one to another? Those who were despised as weak will say to those who had prided: "Had it not been for you, we would certainly have been believers."

32. Those who had prided shall say to those who were despised as weak: "Did we turn you away from the guidance after it had come to you? Nay! You were yourselves the guilty ones."

33. Those who had been despised as weak shall say to those who had prided: "Nay! (It was your) planning by night and day, when you bade us disbelieve in God and set up equals with Him." And they shall feel regretful when they see the torment; We will put shackles on the necks of those who disbelieved; they are recompensed with aught save that which they did.

34. We sent no warner to a town except that the opulent ones of it said: "Verily we are disbelievers in what you are sent with."

35. And they said: "We are more (than you) in wealth and descendants, and we shall not be chastised."

36. Say: "Verily my Lord amplifies the sustenance for whomsoever He wills and straitens it for whomsoever He pleases, but most people do not know."

37. Neither your wealth, nor your children, can bring you nigh to Us, but whosoever believes and does good deeds, they are the ones for whom there is a double recompense for what they did, and they are in exalted places, secure.

38. And those who strive hard to invalidate Our Signs, they shall be brought to chastisement.

39. Say: "Verily my Lord increases or restricts the sustenance for whomsoever He wills of His servants, and whatever you spend, He returns it (with rewards); He is the best of sustainers."

40. On the Day when He gathers them all together, He will then say unto the angels: "Did these worship you?"

41. They shall say: "Glory be to You! You are our Guardian, not they. Nay! They worshipped the jinn; most of them were believers in them."

42. So on that Day, none of you will own any profit or harm, and We will say unto those who did injustice: "Taste the torment of the Fire in which you disbelieved."

43. And when Our clear Signs are recited to them, they say: "This is but a man; he desires to turn you away from what your fathers used to worship," and they say: "This (Qur'an) is naught but a falsehood forged." Those who disbelieve say of them: "This is nothing but a clear sorcery."

44. We have not given them any book to read nor did We send them before you any warner.

45. Those before them rejected, and these have not attained (even) the tithe of what We gave them, yet they rejected My messengers, so how (intense) was My abhorrence (of them)?

46. Say: "I exhort you only to one thing: that you rise up for God's sake in pairs and singly, then ponder: your companion (Muhammad) is not possessed; he is but a warner to you, before a severe chastisement."

47. Say: Whatever recompense I have asked of you is only for your own souls; my recompense is from God (alone), and He is witness over all things."

48. Say: "Verily my Lord does hurl out the Truth, the Greatest Knower of the unseen."

49. Say: "Truth has come and falsehood does not bring forth anything, nor does it reproduce."

50. Say: "If I stray, I stray only against my own self, and if I am guided rightly, it is (the guidance) of what my Lord has been revealed to me; verily He is all-Hearing, Most Nigh."

51. If only you could see when they get terrified, no

escape there shall be, and they shall be seized from a near place!

52. They shall say: "We (now) believe in it." And when shall the approach (to faith) be for them from such a distant place?

53. Indeed they disbelieved in it before, and aimed their conjecture about the unseen from a distant place.

54. A gap shall be set between them and that which they desire, as was done to their likes of yore; verily they have been in a disquieting doubt.

The Originator
(Fatir)

In the name of God, the Beneficent, the Merciful.

1. (All) praise is God's, Originator of the heavens and earth, Creator of the angels as messengers flying on wings in two, three, and four (pairs); He adds to His creation whatever He wills; verily God has power over all things.

2. Whatever God bestows of His Mercy upon people, none can withhold it, and whatever He holds back, none besides Him can send it forth; He is the Almighty, the all-Wise.

3. O people! Remember God's bounty on you; is there any creator other than God who provides you with your sustenance from the heaven and the earth? There is no god but He; whence then are you turned away?

4. If you reject you (Muhammad), indeed people have rejected messengers before you, and to God (alone) are all affairs returned.

5. O people! Verily the Promise of God is true; so, let not the life of this world beguile you, and let not the arch-beguiler (Satan) beguile you about God.

6. Verily Satan is your enemy; so, you (too) take him as your enemy; he only invites his party to follow the path of the flaming Fire.

7. For those who disbelieve shall be a severe chastisement, and as for those who believe and do good deeds, for them shall be forgiveness and a great recompense.

8. Is he then whose evil deed is made so alluring to him that he sees it good (equal to the rightly guided? Nay!

Verily God leaves whomsoever He pleases to stray, and He guides whomsoever He wills; so, let not yourself go in (vain) grief for them; verily God knows all that they do.

9. God is He Who sends the winds, and they raise clouds, then We drive them on to a country that is dead, and We give life therewith to the earth after its death; even so is the (rising of the dead in) resurrection.

10. Whosoever desires dignity, God's (alone) is all dignity; to Him (only) ascend all the good words; as for those who plot evil deeds, for them shall be a severe chastisement; their plot shall be in vain.

11. God created you of dust, then of a life- germ, then He made you pairs (of male and female); the knowledge of whatever a female bears is with Him, and none ages nor any diminishes from one's life except what is in a Book; verily this is easy for God.

12. Nor are the two seas alike: this one is sweet; its sweetness quenches your thirst and it is pleasant to drink, while the other is salty and bitter; yet from both of them do you eat fresh (fish) meat and take forth ornaments to wear; you see the ships cleave through it that you may seek of His Grace, and that you may be grateful.

13. He causes the night to enter into the day and the day to enter into the night, and He has made the sun and the moon subservient: each turns in its orbit till an appointed term: this is God your Lord! His is the kingdom; those whom you call upon besides Him do not own (even) a straw.

14. Should you call upon them, they shall not hear your call, and even if they hear it, they shall not answer it, and on the Day of Judgment they will denounce your associating them (with God)! None can inform you (of this) save the all-Aware.

15. O people! You are the needy to God, and God is self-Sufficient, Most Praised.

16. If He wills, He can take you off and bring about a new creation.

17. Nor is this difficult for God.

18. No bearer shall bear the burden of another. Should the heavily laden one cry for (another bearer to carry) his burden, none of it shall be carried, even if he be his near of

kin. You can warn only those who fear their Lord in the unseen and keep up regular prayer; whosoever purifies himself, he only purifies it for his own good; to God (alone) is the destination (of all).

19. The blind and the seeing are never alike unto each other.

20. Nor are the darkness and the light.

21. Nor are the shade and the heat;

22. Nor are the living and the dead alike; verily God hears whomsoever He wills, and you cannot make those in the graves hear you.

23. You are but a warner.

24. Verily We sent you with the truth as a bearer of glad tidings and a warner. No people have ever been left without a warner among them.

25. If they call you a liar, then so indeed did those before them do: their messengers had come to them with clear proofs, with scriptures, and with an enlightening book.

26. Then I seized those who disbelieved; so, how (intense) was My abhorrence?

27. Do you not see that God sends down water from the heaven, then We bring forth with it fruits of various colours, and in the mountains are streaks of white and red hues, while others are intensely black?

28. And of the people, beasts and cattle, are likewise various complexions; verily God is feared only by those of His servants who are endowed with knowledge; indeed God is the Almighty, the oft-Forgiving.

29. Those who recite the Book of God, establish (regular) prayer and spend out of what We have provided them with secretly and openly are the ones who put their trust in a bargain that will never perish.

30. That He may give them back their full recompense and increase His Grace unto them; verily He is the oft-Forgiving, the Greatest to appreciate.

31. That which We have revealed unto you of the Book is but the truth testifying to that which has already come before it; indeed, God is all-Aware, fully-Observant of His servants.

32. Then We made the inheritors of the Book (Qur'an)

those whom We chose from among Our servants. Among them is he who causes himself to suffer a loss, and among them is he who follows a middle course, and among them is he who is the foremost in doing good deeds by God's permission; this is the greatest of God's favours.

33. They shall enter the gardens of eternity, wherein they shall wear bracelets of gold and pearls, and their raiment therein shall be silk.

34. They shall say: "All Praise is God's Who has taken away from us all grief; verily our Lord is oft- Forgiving, the greatest to appreciate (good deeds).

35. "He Who has settled us, through His Grace, in an eternal abode; no toil shall touch us therein, nor any fatigue shall affect us."

36. For those who disbelieve shall be the fire of Hell; it shall not be decreed that they should ever die, nor shall aught of its torment be decreased from them. Thus do We retribute everyone who is ungrateful.

37. They shall cry aloud therein for help: "Lord! Take us out; we will do good deeds different from what we used to do." - "Did We not keep you alive long enough, for (the good of that) who reflected to reflect therein? A warner came to you (too); so now taste (the fruits of your deeds); no helper shall ever be for the unjust."

38. Verily God knows the unseen in the heavens and the earth; He knows all that is concealed in the heart.

39. He is the One Who made you successors in the earth; so, whosoever disbelieves, his disbelief shall be (weighed) against him. The disbelief of the infidels shall increase nothing with their Lord but Wrath, and disbelief shall increase the infidels nothing but loss.

40. Say: "Do you not see your partners whom you call upon other than God? Show me what part of the earth they have created, or have they any share in the heavens, or have We given them any scripture so that they may produce proof therefrom (of their claim)?" Nay! The unjust promise one another nothing but delusion.

41. Verily God holds the heavens and the earth lest they should come to naught. If they came to naught, none besides Him can hold them back; verily He is the Most For-

bearing, the oft-Forgiving.

42. They swore by God with the strongest of their oaths that if a warner came to them, they would surely be guided aright better than (all) other people; but when warner did come to them, they increased in naught but aversion.

43. Priding in the world, and plotting evil. Their evil plans shall beset none but the devisers themselves; then they shall wait for aught save the course of the people who went before them. You shall never find any change in the Course of God, and never shall you find in the Course of God any alteration.

44. Have they not travelled throughout the world and seen how the end of those before them was, though they were stronger than them in might? God is not such that anything can frustrate Him in the heavens nor in the earth; verily He is the all-Knowing, the all-Powerful.

45. Were God to seize (punish) man for what they wrought, He would not leave on the face of earth any moving being, but He gives them a respite till an appointed term, and when their doom comes, then verily God is all-Observant of His servants.

Ya-Sin

In the name of God, the Beneficent, the Merciful.

1. Ya-Sin.

2. By the Qur'an, the Word of (God's) Wisdom,

3. Verily you (Muhammad) are the Messenger,

4. On the Straight Path,

5. Sent by the Almighty, the all-Merciful,

6. So that you may warn a people whose [fore]fathers were not warned and who therefore are heedless

7. Indeed the word has been proven true about most of them, and wherefore they do not believe.

8. Verily We have put chains around their necks, reaching up to their chins; their heads are forced up, stiff.

9. We have set a barrier before them, and behind them a barrier, and We covered them over, so that they cannot see.

10. It is the same if you warn them or do not; they will

never believe.

11. Verily you can warn only him that abides by the Reminder (Qur'an) and fears the Beneficent (God), the Unseen; so convey to him the glad tidings of forgiveness and an honourable reward.

12. Verily We, and We (alone) give life to the dead, and We write down what they have sent before them, and the footprints they leave behind; We have confined everything into a Manifesting Imam.

13. Set forth to them the instance of the people of a town when Our messengers came to them;

14. We sent them two (messengers); they rejected them both then We strengthened them with a third. They said: "Verily we are messengers sent to you."

15. They said: "You are but human beings like us; the Beneficent has not sent anything; you only utter a lie."

16. They said: "Our Lord knows that we truly are messengers sent to you.

17. "On us is naught but the clear delivering (of the message)."

18. They said: "Verily we augur ill from you; if you do not desist, we will certainly stone you, and a painful torment shall afflict you from us."

19. They said: "Your augury of ill is with your own selves; is it so even when you are admonished?! Nay! You are people transgressing."

20. A man came to them from the furthermost part of the city saying: "O people! Follow (these) messengers;

21. "Follow these who do not ask you any reward, and they are rightly guided.

22. "Why should I not worship Him who brought me into being and to Whom you shall all be returned?

23. "Shall I take besides Him any gods? If the Beneficent wills to afflict harm upon me, their intercession shall not avail me, nor can they save me.

24. "Verily I shall then be in manifest error;

25. "Verily I believe in your Lord; so, listen to me."

26. It was said (to him): "Enter the garden (of bliss)." He said: "Oh! Would that my people had known-

27. "Of my Lord's forgiveness unto me, including me

among the honoured ones!"

28. We sent no hosts upon his people after him, nor were We to send any.

29. It was nothing but a terrifying cry and, lo, they were all extinct.

30. Alas for the servants: whenever a messenger comes to them, they mock at him.

31. Do not they see how many generations We destroyed before them? They will never return to them.

32. All shall surely be gathered together before Us.

33. A sign for them is the dead earth; We give it life and bring forth grain therefrom, of which they eat.

34. We make therein gardens of date-palms and grape-vines, and We cause springs to flow therein.

35. That they may eat of its fruits and of what they make with their own hands; should they not be grateful?

36. Hallowed is He Who created pairs of all things, of what grows on earth, of their own selves, and of what they do not know.

37. And (another) sign to them is the night: We draw forth the day from it and lo, they are in the dark!

38. And (another is) the sun travels to a resting-place fixed for it; that is the decree of the Almighty, the all-Knowing.

39. As for the moon, We have fixed for it stages till it returns bent like an old palm branch.

40. It is not (expedient) for the sun that it should over-take the moon, nor can the night outstrip the day; each rotates on its sphere.

41. And (another) sign to them is that We carry their offspring in the laden ark.

42. And We have created for them like it a conveyance on which they ride.

43. If We only will, We can drown them (all), then there shall be none to help them nor shall they be ever rescued,

44. Save by a mercy from Us, and an enjoyment for yet awhile.

45. When it is said to them: "Guard (yourselves) against what is before you and what is behind you, that you may be treated with mercy,"

46. (Yet) no sign comes to them from their Lord but they turn away from it.

47. And when it is said to them: "Spend of what God has provided you with of sustenance," those who disbelieve say to those who believe: "Shall we feed those who, if God wills, He could have fed them? You are but in manifest error."

48. And they say: "When will this promise come to pass if you are truthful?"

49. They wait but for a single (terrifying) cry to seize them even while they wrangle with one another.

50. Then they shall not be able to make a bequest, nor shall they be able to return to their families.

51. When the trumpet is blown, lo, they shall all hasten to their Lord from their graves.

52. They shall say: "Oh! Woe unto us! Who has raised us up from our place of repose?" - "This is what the Beneficent promised and the messengers spoke only the truth."

53. There will be but a single cry when, lo, they are all brought to Us.

54. So this day no soul shall be dealt with unjustly in the least, nor will you be recompensed but with that which you were doing.

55. Verily the inmates of the garden shall on that day be busy enjoying themselves.

56. They and their mates shall be in shades, reclining on raised couches.

57. They shall have fruits therein, and for them shall be whatever they would call for.

58. "Peace!" shall be the word from the Most Merciful Lord.

59. - "And get you aside this day, O you guilty ones!

60. "Did not I enjoin on you, O children of Adam, that you should not worship Satan, for he is your open enemy?

61. "And that you should worship (only) Me: this is the Right Way?

62. "And yet he led a great multitude of you astray; did you not then reason?

63. "This is Hell which you were promised;

64. "Enter into it for what you used to disbelieve."

65. On that Day, We will set a seal upon their mouths, and their hands shall speak to Us, and their feet shall bear witness regarding what they used to earn.

66. If We will, We could certainly put out their sight, then they would struggle (groping) to get first to the way, but how could they see?

67. And if We will, We would certainly transform them in their own places, then they would not be able to go on, nor will they ever return.

68. Whomsoever We increase in life-span, We reverse him to an abject state in life. Do they not understand?

69. We have taught him no poetry, nor would it befit him (to compose); it is (not poetry) but a reminder and a manifesting Qur'an,

70. To warn any who is alive, and the word be proven against the disbelievers.

71. Do they not see that We created the cattle for them, among what Our hands have created, and over them they are the masters?

72. And We subjected them (cattle): you ride upon some of them, and of some you eat.

73. And for them therein are benefits and drinks; will they not then be grateful?

74. And yet they have taken gods besides God so that they may be helped.

75. They shall not be able to help them, yet they are their host to be brought to account.

76. So let not their speech grieve you (Muhammad), for verily We know what they hide and what they reveal.

77. Does man not see that We created him from (a drop of) sperm? Yet, lo, he is an open disputant!

78. He sets to Us an argument, forgetting his own creation; he says: "Who will bring the bones that are decayed back to life?"

79. Say: "The One Who created them the first time shall bring them back to life, and He is fully cognizant of all creation,

80. "He Who made a fire for you from the green tree and, lo, you kindle (a fire) therefrom!

81. "Is not He Who created the heavens and the earth

capable of creating the like of them? Yea! And He is the Creator, the all-Knowing."

82. His Command, when He wishes anything, is only that He says: "Be!" and it is.

83. Hallowed, therefore, is He in Whose hand is the kingdom of all things, and to Him you shall all be returned.

The Ranks

(as-Saffat)

In the name of God, the Beneficent, the Merciful.

1. By those who range themselves in ranks,

2. And by those who drive away the evil with reproof,

3. And by the reciters of the Qur'an:

4. Verily your Lord is One;

5. Lord of the heavens and the earth and what is between them, Lord of the places of the rising (of the sun).

6. Verily We have adorned the heaven nearest to this world (earth) with an adornment, the stars.

7. And (also) a guard against every rebellious Satan;

8. So they may not hear the assembly on high, and they are darted from every side.

9. Driven off, and for them is a perpetual chastisement,

10. Except he who steals (a word) by stealth, then a glistening flame pursues him.

11. Ask them then: "Are they stronger in creation or those whom We have created?" Verily We created them of a sticky clay.

12. Nay! You wonder while they mock.

13. And when they are warned, they are heedless.

14. And when they see a sign, they incite its ridicule.

15. And they say: "This is but open sorcery.

16. "When we are dead and (turned into) dust and bones, shall we still be raised again?

17. "And so shall our [fore]fathers of yore?"

18. Say: "Yes, indeed; you shall be disgraced."

19. Then it will only be a single roar when, lo, they shall gaze (around).

20. And they shall say: "Woe unto us! This is the Day of Reckoning!"

21. - "This is the Day of Judgment in which you used to disbelieve."

22. - "Gather (now) together those who were unjust, and their mates, too, and that which they used to worship-

23. "Besides God and lead them all to Hell.

24. "And stop them, for verily they have to be questioned:

25. "How now that you cannot help one another?"

26. Nay! On that Day, they shall (all) be submitting themselves;

27. Some of them shall advance to the others, questioning each other.

28. They shall say: "Verily you did come to us from the right side beguiling."

29. They shall say: "Nay! You yourselves were not believers.

30. "We had no authority over you. Nay! You were rebellious people.

31. "So now the sentence of our Lord has been proven true that we shall surely taste (the doom).

32. "We led you astray, for verily we ourselves strayed."

33. Indeed, they shall on that Day share in the punishment.

34. Thus do We deal with the guilty ones.

35. When it was said to them that there was no god but God, they used to behave arrogantly.

36. They used to say: "Are we to give up our gods for a crazed poet?"

37. Nay! He has come with the truth and testified to the (preceding) messengers.

38. Verily you will taste the painful chastisement.

39. And you shall be recompensed only with what you were doing.

40. Save the sincere servants of God.

41. For these there is a known sustenance.

42. Fruits, and they shall be highly honoured,

43. In the gardens of bounties,

44. Upon couches facing each other,

45. Round will go to them a cup from a clear spring,

46. Limpid white, delicious to those who drink it.

47. Nothing therein to oppress the senses, nor shall they be exhausted therewith.

48. With them shall be chaste women with modest gaze, with large (lustrous) lovely eyes,

49. As if they were eggs securely hidden!

50. Some of them shall advance to others, questioning each other.

51. A speaker among them shall speak: "In truth, there was an intimate friend of mine,

52. "Who used to say: `Are you, too, a believer (in the resurrection?

53. "`When we are dead and are turned into dust and bones, shall we even then be brought to account?'"

54. He shall say: "Will you look?"

55. Then he would look down and see him in the midst of Hell- fire.

56. He shall say: "By God! You have almost caused me to perish!

57. "Had it not been for the bounty of my Lord, I would have certainly been brought with you into the Fire.

58. "Is it then that we do not die?

59. "Save our first death, and we shall not be chastised?

60. "Verily this is the great achievement."

61. For the like of this should every active one act.

62. Is this better entertainment, or is it the tree of zaqqum?

63. Verily We have made it a trial for the unjust.

64. Verily it is a tree that grows in the pit of Hell.

65. Its produce is as (ugly as) the heads of the devils.

66. And verily they shall eat from it and fill their bellies therewith.

67. Then verily for them shall be to drink over it a mixture in a boiling water.

68. Then their return shall surely be to Hell.

69. Indeed they found their fathers going astray,

70. So they hastened in their footsteps.

71. And indeed most of the ancient ones before them went astray.

72. And indeed We did send warners to them from among themselves.

73. See then how the end of those who were warned had

been,

74. Save the servants of God, the sincere ones.

75. And indeed Noah called upon Us and We were the Most Excellent in answering him.

76. We delivered him and his followers from the great distress.

77. We made his progeny the survivors.

78. We perpetuated for him (his praise) in the later generations.

79. "Peace be unto Noah in all the worlds!"

80. Thus do We recompense those who do good deeds.

81. Verily he was one of Our faithful servants.

82. Then We drowned all others.

83. Indeed of his party was Abraham;

84. He came unto his Lord with a submissive heart;

85. He said to his father and people: "What is that you worship?

86. "Do you desire but false gods other than the (True) God?

87. "What do you then think about the Lord of the worlds?"

88. Then he cast a glance at the stars,

89. Then he said: "Verily I am sick (of your worship)."

90. So they turned back from him.

91. Then he turned to their gods secretly and said: "Do you not eat?

92. "What ails you that you do not speak?"

93. Then he attacked them in secrecy, striking them with his right hand.

94. Then they came hastening to him.

95. He said: "Do you worship that which you yourselves carve out?

96. "While God has created you and all what you make?"

97. They said: "Erect for him a structure and fling him (from it) into the flaming Fire."

98. So they desired to plot against him, but We made them lowly.

99. He said: "Verily I am going to my Lord; He will guide me.

100. "Lord! Grant me a righteous son."

101. So We conveyed to him the glad tidings of a son extremely forbearing.

102. When he reached (the age of) working with him, he said: "O son! I truly saw in my vision that I sacrificed you; now what is your view?" He said: "O father! Do as you are bidden; you will find me by the Will of God steadfast."

103. When they both surrendered to the Will of God, and he threw him upon his forehead,

104. We called out unto him: "O Abraham!

105. "Indeed you have fulfilled the dream; verily thus do We recompense the doers of good deeds!

106. "Verily this is a manifest trial."

107. And We ransomed him with a momentous sacrifice.

108. And We shifted (this blessing) on him (who is from) among the generations (to come).

109. Peace be upon Abraham:

110. Thus do We reward those who do good deeds.

111. Verily he was one of Our faithful servants.

112. We gave him the glad tidings of Isaac, a prophet from among the righteous ones.

113. And We bestowed Our blessings upon him and upon Isaac: from their progeny are those who did good deeds, and those who were openly unjust to their own selves.

114. Indeed We conferred Our favour upon Moses and Aaron.

115. We delivered them both, and their people, from the great distress.

116. And We succored them, so they were triumphant.

117. We gave them both the Book that made things clear.

118. We guided them both on the Right Way.

119. We perpetuated their praise in the later generations;

120. Peace be upon Moses and Aaron.

121. Indeed thus do We reward the doers of good deeds.

122. They both were, indeed, among Our faithful servants.

123. And verily Elias was one of the messengers.

124. He said to his people: "Would you not fear God?

125. "You call upon Ba'l (idol) and forsake the best of

creators-

126. "God, your Lord and the Lord of your [fore]fathers of yore?"

127. But they called him a liar, so they will certainly be brought to account,

128. Save the sincere servants of God.

129. We perpetuated his praise in the later generations;

130. Peace be upon the family of Ya-Sin;

131. Verily thus do We reward the doers of good deeds.

132. He was one of Our faithful servants.

133. And verily Lot was one of the messengers.

134. We delivered him and all his followers,

135. Save an aged woman among those who tarried,

136. Then We destroyed the rest.

137. Verily you pass by (their ruins) at morn,

138. And at eve; do you still not understand?!

139. Jonah was truly one of the messengers.

140. He fled to a ship fully laden,

141. They drew lots, and he was among those who were to be cast off.

142. And the whale swallowed him while he was blamed.

143. So, had it not been for his glorification of Us,

144. He would certainly have remained in its belly till the Day (of Resurrection) when they all are raised;

145. So We cast him forth on the naked shore, and he was (surly) sick.

146. And We caused a gourd plant to grow (and shade) over him.

147. And We sent him to a hundred thousand or more,

148. And they all believed, so We gave them provision till a time.

149. So ask them: "Is it that your Lord has daughters, while they have sons?

150. "Or have We created the angels females? Did they witness their creation?"

151. Beware! Verily it is of their own falsehood that they say-

152. That God has begotten; verily they utter a lie.

153. Has He preferred daughters to sons?

154. What has happened to you? How do you judge?

155. Will you then not reflect?

156. Or have you any clear authority?

157. (If so) then bring your book if you are truthful.

158. They assign between him and the jinn a kinship, and indeed the jinn know that they shall surely be brought to account.

159. Hallowed is God far above what they ascribe,

160. But (contrariwise are) the sincere servants of God.

161. Indeed you and what you worship,

162. Do not tempt any against Him,

163. Except him that goes to Hell.

164. And there is no place for him from Us except an assigned place.

165. We are the ones who shall arrange them in ranks.

166. And we are the ones who celebrate His praise.

167. And they certainly used to say:

168. "Had we had a reminder from those of yore,

169. "We would certainly have been true servants of God, devoted."

170. Then they disbelieved therein; so, they will soon come to know.

171. Our word has already gone forth about Our servant- messengers.

172. Verily they shall be the succored ones.

173. And verily only Our hosts shall be victorious.

174. So turn away from them till a time,

175. And show them the light, for they shall come to see (their doom).

176. Do they hasten Our chastisement on?

177. When it descends in their court, evil shall then be the morning of the warned ones.

178. And turn away from them for a while,

179. Then behold, for they too shall soon behold (their doom).

180. Hallowed is your Lord, the Lord of Majesty, far above what they ascribe (to Him).

181. And peace be upon the messengers;

182. And all praise is God's, Lord of the worlds.

Saad

In the name of God, the Beneficent, the Merciful.

1. Saad; by the Qur'an which is full of admonition;

2. Nay! Those who disbelieve are steeped in self-exaltation and opposition.

3. How many did We destroy of generations before them? They cried when there was no time to escape.

4. And they wondered that a warner from among themselves came to them and the disbelievers said: "This is a sorcerer, a great liar.

5. "Does he make (all) the gods into one single God? Verily this is a strange thing."

6. The chiefs among them get away saying: "Walk away (from him), and be steadfast to your gods; verily this is but something planned.

7. "We heard none of this in the former creed; this is nothing but an imposture.

8. "Has the Reminder been revealed only to him from among us?" Nay! They are in doubt about My Reminder. Nay! They have not yet tasted My torment.

9. Or do they have the treasures of the mercy of your Lord, the Almighty, the Greatest Bestower?

10. Or is it that to them belongs the kingdom of the heavens and the earth and what is between them? Then let them ascend (to it) with means.

11. The mighty host of clans shall surely be routed.

12. Before them, the people of Noah rejected, and so was Ad and Pharaoh, lord of stakes,

13. And Thamud, and the people of Lot, and the dwellers of the wood: these were the clans.

14. All of them rejected the messengers, so (My) retribution was just.

15. And these (infidels) do not wait but for a single (trumpet) blast; there shall be no delay in it.

16. And yet they say: "O Lord! Hasten our lot on to us before the Day of Reckoning."

17. Bear with patience with what they say, and remember Our servant David was (blessed) with the strength of his

hand; verily he oft-turned to Us.

18. We subjected the mountains to join him in declaring Our Praises, in unison, at the nightfall, and at the break of the day.

19. And the birds assembled together (to sing the hymns) and they were all obedient to him.

20. And We made his kingdom strong, and We bestowed upon him wisdom, and the clear power of judgment.

21. Has the story of the litigants come to you? When they climbed the wall into the prayer-room?

22. When they entered upon David, he was frightened of them. They said: "Fear not; (we are but) two litigants. One of us has exceeded against the other; so, you decide between us with justice, and do not be unfair, and guide us to the right way.

23. "This brother of mine has ninety-nine ewes, while a single ewe is mine, yet he said: `Let me be the owner of that, too,' and he has prevailed over me in arguing."

24. He (David) said: "Indeed he has been unjust to you in demanding your ewe to add to his own; verily many associates act wrongfully towards each other, save those who believe and do good deeds, and they are a few." David perceived that We had tried him; so he asked forgiveness of his Lord and he fell down prostrating, oft-turning (to Us).

25. So We forgave him that (lapse), and verily for him is a near approach with Us and an excellent resort.

26. O David! Verily We have appointed you as a vicegerent in the earth; so, judge between people with justice, and do not follow vain desires lest they should lead you astray from the Way of God; for them shall be a severe chastisement because of forgetting the Day of Reckoning.

27. And We did not create the heavens and the earth in vain; that is the imagination of those who disbelieve; then woe unto those who disbelieve because of the Fire.

28. Shall We treat those who believe and do good deeds as we treat the mischief-makers in the world? Or shall We treat the pious as we treat the wicked?

29. We have revealed the Book unto you abounding in blessings, that they may ponder over its verses, and bear in mind those (who are) endowed with understanding.

30. And to David We bestowed Solomon: an excellent servant (of God); verily he was oft-turning (to Us).

31. Remember when light-footed coursers of the highest breeding were shown to him at eventide;

32. He said: "Verily I have loved the good things besides the remembrance of my Lord, until they got hidden in the veil (of the dark).

33. "Bring it back to me!" And he began to rub the legs and the necks.

34. And indeed We did try Solomon, and a (mere) body (corpse) was cast on his throne, then he turned (to God).

35. He said: "Lord! Forgive me and grant me a dominion such as none shall befit after me; verily You alone are the Bounteous Bestower!"

36. Then We made the wind subservient to Him: it flew gently at his command wherever he desired.

37. And the satans, every builder and diver,

38. And the others bound in chains;

39. This is Our Gift; now give freely or withhold it, without rendering any account.

40. Verily he enjoyed a near approach to Us and an excellent resort.

41. Remember Our servant Job when he cried unto his Lord: "Verily Satan has touched me with affliction and pain."

42. - "Stamp this spring with your foot (O Job); it is a cool one to wash therewith and drink therefrom."

43. And We endowed upon him his family and the like of them, a mercy from Us and a reminder for those endowed with understanding.

44. "Take in your hand a bundle of thin (fiber) sticks and strike (your wife) with it, and do not break your oath." Verily We found him steadfast, an excellent servant; he was oft-turning (to Us).

45. And remember Our servants Abraham, Isaac and Jacob, men of strength and insight.

46. Verily We freed them (from sinning) with a distinction of remembrance of the (eternal) abode.

47. Verily, they are with Us among the chosen and the good ones.

48. And remember Ishmael, Elisha, and Zulkifl; they

were among the elect and the good.

49. This is a Reminder, and verily for the pious there is an excellent resort,

50. Gardens of eternal bliss, opened for them are the doors thereof,

51. Reclining therein, calling for many a fruit and drink.

52. And with them shall be mates equal in age, modest in gaze.

53. This is what you are promised on the Day of Reckoning.

54. Verily this is Our sustenance; it shall never fail.

55. As for the wicked ones, there shall be a wretched resort,

56. Hell-fire, they shall enter it, an evil place it is.

57. Even so, let them then taste it: boiling water and gore,

58. And other (torment) similar to it, of various sort.

59. "This army (of your follows) shall be thrown headlong with you! No welcome for them! Verily they shall enter the Fire!"

60. They shall say: "Nay! You too! There shall be no welcome for you; indeed you prepared this for us, and wretched is the abode."

61. They shall say: "Lord! Whoever brought this unto us, double the torment of the Fire for him."

62. They shall say: "What has happened to us that we do not see the men whom we counted as the wicked ones?

63. Was it that we treated them with scorn, or have our eyes failed to perceive them?"

64. Verily this is the truth-the wrangling of the inmates of the Fire, one with another.

65. Say (O Muhammad): "I am only a warner, and there is no god but the One God, the Almighty,

66. "Lord of the heavens and the earth and what is between them twain, the Almighty, the Most Forgiving."

67. Say: "It is a message of great import,

68. "And you are still turning away from it.

69. "I had no knowledge of the exalted chiefs when they disputed!

70. "It is revealed to me that I am an open warner."

71. Remember when your Lord said to the angels: "Verily I am about to create a man from clay,

72. "And when I complete his creation and breathe into him of My own Spirit, then you fall prostrating in obeisance to him."

73. All the angels fell prostrating in obeisance,

74. Save Iblis; he was proud, and he disbelieved.

75. (God) said: "O Iblis! What prevented you that you did not prostrate in obeisance to what I have created with My own hands? Are you proud or are you of the exalted ones?"

76. He said: "I am better than him; You have created me of fire and created him of clay."

77. (God) said: "Get then out of it, for surely you are an outcast.

78. "And verily My curse shall be upon you till the Day of Judgment."

79. He said: "Lord! Then grant me a respite till the day when they are raised."

80. (God) said: "Verily then you are respited,

81. "Till the Day of the time made known."

82. He said: "Then by Your Might, I will certainly beguile them all,

83. "Save Your servants from among them who are sincere."

84. He said: "Then it is in truth, and the truth do I speak,

85. "I will certainly fill Hell with you and with those who follow you all together."

86. Say (O Our Messenger Muhammad): "I ask you for no reward, nor am I an impostor.

87. "It is but a reminder to the world,

88. "And you will certainly come to know about it after a time."

The Hordes
(az-Zumur)

In the name of God, the Beneficent, the Merciful.

1. The revelation of the Book (Qur'an) is from God, the Almighty, the all-Wise.

2. We have surely revealed to you the Book (Qur'an) with the truth so that you may worship God (alone) and be sincere to Him in faith.

3. Beware! To God alone is all obedience due, and those who take others as guardians besides Him say: "We worship them only so that they may bring us closer to God;" God will surely judge between them about what they differ; surely God does not guide a liar, an ingrate.

4. Had God intended to take a son unto Himself, He would have certainly selected those whom He pleases of His creation; hallowed is He; He alone is God, the One, the Almighty.

5. He has created the heavens and the earth with the truth; He causes the night to enter the day and the day to enter the night, and He subjected the sun and the moon, each speeds on to an assigned term. Beware! He is the Almighty, the oft-Forgiving.

6. He created you from a single being, then He created from him, of like nature, his mate, and sent down for you eight in pairs of the cattle; He creates you in the wombs of your mothers one creation after another, in triple darkness; that is God your Lord; His is the Kingdom; there is no god but He; how then are you turned away?

7. If you are ungrateful, verily God is Independent of you; He does not like ingratitude in His servants. If you are grateful, He likes it in you. No bearer of a burden shall bear the burden of another; then to your Lord is your return; He will then inform you of what you were doing; verily, He knows all what is hidden in the hearts.

8. When distress touches man, he cries unto his Lord, oft- turning to Him, and when He bestows upon him a favour from Him, he forgets that for which he cried unto Him before, and he even sets up rivals with God that he may beguile men to stray away from His Path! Say: "Enjoy yourself in your ingratitude for a little while; verily you are of the inmates of Hell-fire."

9. (Unlike) the one who offers prayers during the hours of the night, prostrating in obeisance and standing, taking heed of the hereafter, and hoping for the mercy of his Lord; say: "Can those who know be equal to those who do not?

Verily only men of understanding heed the warning."

10. Say to My believing servants: "Fear your Lord; for those who do good deeds in this world there shall be good, and God's earth is spacious; verily, only the patient ones receive their reward without any account."

11. Say: "I have been bidden to worship God (alone) and be sincere to Him in faith,

12. "And I am bidden to be the foremost in belief (Muslim)."

13. Say: "Verily I fear lest I should disobey my Lord the chastisement of a great Day."

14. Say: "God (alone) do I worship, being devoted to Him in my religion,

15. "Worship then whatsoever you like besides Him." Say: "Verily the losers are those who have lost their own souls and their own families on the Day of Judgment. Beware! That is the manifest loss."

16. For them shall be the coverings of fire from above them and from beneath them, with that, God causes His servants to fear; so fear Me, O My servants.

17. And for those who shun the worship of the idols and turn to God shall be the glad tidings; so, convey the glad tidings to My servants,

18. Those who hearken to the word and follow the best of it; those are they whom Go has guided, and those are the men of understanding.

19. Is he upon whom the sentence of chastisement has been justly passed, could you rescue any from the Fire?

20. As for those who fear their Lord, they are in lofty pavilions built (for them); beneath them do rivers flow, a promise from God; God never fails His promise.

21. Have you not seen how God sends water down from heaven, then He causes it to go into the earth in springs, then He brings forth herbage therewith of various colours, then it withers till you see it yellow, then He makes it chaff? Verily in this is a reminder for men of understanding.

22. Is he whose heart God has opened for Islam and follows the Light from God (like the hard-hearted one)? Nay! Woe unto those whose hearts are hard against the remembrance of God; those are in clear error.

23. God has revealed the best recital, a Book consistent with criterion at which the skins of those who fear their Lord shudder, and so do their hearts when remembering God; this is God's guidance; He guides with it whomsoever He pleases, and allows whomsoever He pleases to stray; there is no guide (for the latter).

24. Is he then who shuns his face against the torment of the chastisement on the Day of Judgment (like unto him who is secure therefrom)? It will be said to the unjust ones: "Taste what you were earning."

25. Those before them rejected too, so there came to them a chastisement from whence they could not perceive.

26. Then God made them taste the disgrace of this life and certainly the chastisement of the hereafter is even greater if they only knew.

27. Indeed We have set forth examples in this Qur'an of every sort that haply they may reflect.

28. An Arabic Qur'an without any crookedness so that haply they may be pious.

29. God sets forth an example of a man (in the service of) associates quarrelling with each other, and of a man wholly devoted to a single man: can they both be alike in condition?! All praise is God's. Nay! Most of them do not even know.

30. Verily you shall come to die, and so shall they too.

31. Then verily you, on the Day of Judgment, will wrangle with one another before your Lord.

32. Who is then more unjust than he who lies about God and falsifies the truth when it comes to him? Is there no place in Hell for the disbelievers?

33. He who brings forth the truth and he who testifies to it are indeed the pious ones.

34. For them is whatever they please with their Lord; that is the reward of those who do good deeds;

35. That God may take away from them the worst of what they did and reward them with the best of rewards for what they used to do.

36. Is not God sufficient for His servant? And they frighten you with those besides Him! Whomsoever God allows to stray, for him there shall be none to guide.

37. And whomsoever God guides, none shall beguile him. Is not God the Almighty Lord of retribution?

38. And if you ask them who created the heavens and the earth, they would certainly say "God;" say: "Consider then what you call upon besides God. If God wishes me any harm, could they remove His harm, or if He wishes me His mercy, could they withhold His mercy from me?" Say: "God suffices me. On Him do the reliants rely."

39. Say: "O people! Act (as you please); verily I too do act; soon will you come to know-

40. "To whom a disgracing chastisement will come, and upon whom will the everlasting doom fall."

41. Verily we revealed the Book (Qur'an) unto you for the good of people with the truth; whosoever is guided aright, it is for his own good, and whosoever goes astray, he strays only to his own harm; you are not a custodian over them.

42. God takes the souls away at death. Those that do not die (He takes) during their sleep; God withholds (the life of) those on whom He has passed the decree of death; but He sends the others (to their bodies) till a fixed time. Verily in this are signs for people who reflect.

43. Or have they taken as intercessors others besides God? Say: "Even if they have no power over anything, nor do they understand?"

44. Say: "God's is intercession altogether; His is the kingdom of the heavens and the earth, then to Him you shall all be returned."

45. When God alone is mentioned, the hearts of those who do not believe in the hereafter shrink, and when those besides Him are mentioned, lo, they rejoice.

46. Say: "God is the Originator of the heavens and the earth, Knower of the unseen and the manifest. You (alone) shall judge between Your servants in the matter wherein they were differing."

47. Had it been for those who committed injustice, whatever is in the earth and the like of it added thereto, they will surely seek to ransom themselves with it from the pain of the chastisement on the Day of Judgment, and there shall appear to them from God that which they had not been

expecting.

48. The evils of what they wrought shall appear to them, and they shall be surrounded by that which they used to ridicule.

49. When harm touches man, he cries unto Us; then when We grant him a favour from Us, he says: "I have been granted it only on account of my own knowledge." Nay! It is only a trial, but most of them do not know.

50. Indeed, the same was said by those before them; what they had been earning did not avail them in the least.

51. So the evils of what they earned afflicted them; for those who committed injustice, the evil of what they earned shall soon befall upon them, and they shall not frustrate Us in the least.

52. Have they not come to know that God alone amplifies the sustenance to whomsoever He pleases and straitens it (from whomsoever He pleases); verily in this are signs for people who believe.

53. Tell My servants who have been extravagant unto their own selves: "Do not despair of God's mercy; verily God forgives all your sins; He is the oft- Forgiving, the Most Merciful;

54. "And return to your Lord and resign yourselves to Him before the chastisement comes to you, for you shall not be helped then;

55. "And follow the most excellent thing of what has been revealed to you from your Lord before the chastisement suddenly comes to you even before you perceive it."

56. (It is so) lest a soul should say: "Oh! Alas! Woe unto me for what I failed (in my duty) to God! Certainly I was of those who mocked."

57. Or it should say: "Had God guided me, I would certainly have been among the pious."

58. Or it should say, when it sees the chastisement, "Had there been a return for me, I would have been among the righteous."

59. Nay! Indeed My signs did come to you, but you rejected them; you acted proudly, and you were among the disbelievers."

60. On the Day of Resurrection, you shall see those who

uttered lies against God with their faces blackened; is there no place in Hell as the abode of the arrogant?

61. God shall deliver those who shunned evil and were successful; no harm shall touch them, nor shall they grieve.

62. God (alone) is the Creator of everything, and He (alone) is guardian over all things.

63. His are the keys of the heavens and the earth; those who disbelieve in the Signs of God are truly the losers.

64. Say: "Do you bid me worship others besides God, O you ignorant folks?!"

65. Indeed, it has been revealed to you and to those before you: "Verily if you associate (others with God), your deeds would come to naught, and you would certainly be among the losers.

66. "Nay! God alone do I worship and be among the grateful ones."

67. They did not esteem God justly, as is His due, while the whole earth is within His grip on the Day of Judgment, and the heavens rolled up in His right hand; hallowed is He, the Exalted, the Most High, above what they associate (with Him).

68. The trumpet is blown, and whoever is in the heavens and the earth are stunned save those whom God has wished; then it shall be blown again and lo! They shall stand up waiting.

69. The earth shall get radiant with the light of its Lord, and the Book (of deeds) shall be set; the prophet shall be brought and the witnesses too; it shall be judged between them, and they shall not be dealt with unjustly.

70. Every soul shall be paid in full for what it wrought, and He best knows what they did.

71. Those who disbelieved shall be driven to Hell in flocks until, when they come to it, its gates shall be opened, and its keepers shall say to them: "Did any messengers from among you not come to you to recite for you the signs of your Lord and warn you of the meeting of this Day of yours?" They shall answer: "Yes, indeed," yet the sentence of punishment is justice for the disbelievers.

72. It shall be said to them: "Enter the gates of Hell to abide therein forever; wretched is the abode of the arro-

gant."

73. Those who feared (their Lord) shall be conveyed in groups to the Garden; when they come to it, its gates shall be opened, and its keepers shall say to them: "Peace be upon you! You shall be happy here; enter it to abide therein forever."

74. And they shall say: "All praise belongs to God Who had made His promise good to us, and He has permitted us to inherit the earth and dwell in the gardens wherever we please; goodly is the reward of those who do good deeds."

75. You shall see the angels surrounding the Throne, celebrating the Praise of their Lord, and it shall be judged between them with justice, and it shall be said: "All praise is to God, Lord of the Worlds."

The Believer
(al-Mu'min)

In the name of God, the Benéficent, the Merciful.

1. Ha', Meem.

2. The revelation of the Book (Qur'an) is from God, the Almighty, the all-Knowing,

3. Who forgives sins and accepts repentance; He is severe in chastising, Lord of bounties; there is no god but He; to Him is the ultimate end of the journey.

4. None dispute about the signs of God save those who disbelieve; so, let not their going to and from the cities deceive you.

5. The people of Noah before them disbelieved, and so did the parties after them; every nation schemed against their own messenger to seize him, and they disputed in falsehood that they might thereby render the truth null; so, I seized them; how (terrifying) was then My retribution?

6. Thus did your Lord's sentence prove true regarding those who disbelieved that they were the inmates of the Fire.

7. Those who bear the Throne, and those around it, celebrate the praise of their Lord and believe in Him; they seek forgiveness for those who believe in Him: "O Lord! You comprehend all things in (Your) mercy and knowl-

edge; therefore, forgive those who turn (to You) and follow Your way, and save them from the torment of Hell-fire;

8. "Lord! Admit them into the ever-blissful gardens which You have promised them, their wives and descendants; You are the all-Mighty, the all-Wise;

9. "Keep them away from evil; whomsoever you keep from evil, You have on this Day bestowed mercy upon him; that is the mighty achievement."

10. Verily, to those who disbelieve shall be a voice crying: "God's hatred (of you) is greater than your hatred of your own selves when you were called upon to believe and you (instead) disbelieved."

11. They shall say: "O Lord! Twice did You cause us to die, and twice did You grant us life; (now) we do confess our sins; is there then a way to get out (of this)?"

12. (It is so because) when God alone was called upon, you disbelieved, and when associates were attributed to Him, you believed (in them); all authority is God's, the Most Sublime, the Most Great.

13. He it is Who shows you His signs and sends down your sustenance for you from the heaven; none heeds this but he who turns (to Him).

14. So call upon God, devoting religion exclusively to Him, though averse the disbelievers are.

15. Exalter of the ranks, Lord of the Throne; He causes forth the spirit at His own behest on whomsoever He wills of His servants that He may warn man of the Day of the Meeting.

16. A Day when they come forth (from their graves), when naught about them shall be hidden from God: "Whose is the Kingdom this day? God's, the One, the Subduer."

17. This Day shall every soul be recompensed for what it earned; no injustice shall ever be done; verily God is quick in reckoning.

18. And warn them of the approaching Day when hearts rise up to the throats choking; there shall be no sincere friends for the unjust, nor any intercessor to prevail.

19. He knows the deceit of the eye and what the hearts conceal.

20. God judges in truth; those whom they call upon be-

sides Him cannot judge anything; verily God is the all-Hearing, the all-Seeing.

21. Have not they travelled through the world and seen how (destructive) has the end of those who were before them been? They were mightier in strength than these ones and more in relics on earth, but God seized them for their sinning, and no shelter was there for them to protect them against God's Wrath.

22. This is so because there came to them their messengers with clear proofs, but they disbelieved; so, God seized them; verily He is Almighty, Vehement in retribution.

23. Indeed We sent Moses with Our signs and a clear authority,

24. To Pharaoh and Haman and Korah, but they said: "A sorcerer and a great liar!"

25. He brought them the truth from Us, yet they said: "Slay the sons of those who believe with him, and let their women live;" yet the plot of the disbelievers is nothing but utter failure.

26. Pharaoh said: "Let me slay Moses myself, and let him call upon his Lord; verily I fear lest he might change your religion, or he might cause mischief in the land."

27. Moses said: "Indeed I take refuge with my Lord and yours from every arrogant one who does not believe in the Day of Reckoning."

28. A man who was a believer from among the house of Pharaoh, concealing his faith, said: "Do you slay a man for saying that his Lord is God? And indeed he has brought you clear proofs (of his mission) from your Lord. If he is a liar, his lie will weigh against him, and if he is truthful, then some of what he warns you with will surely afflict you; verily God does not guide any extravagant liar.

29. "O people! Yours is the kingdom today, prevailing in the land, but who will help us against the Wrath of God when it comes upon us?" Pharaoh said: "I show you naught but what I myself see, and I guide you but to a right way."

30. He who believed said: "O people! Verily I fear for you the like of what befell the parties;

31. "The like of what befell the people of Noah, Ad and Thamud, and those who succeeded them; God does not in-

tend injustice to His servants.

32. "And O people! I fear for you the Day of Calling (each other) out;

33. "The day when you are turned back; there shall be no saviour for you then from God; whomsoever God allows to stray, no guide shall ever be for him."

34. Indeed, Joseph came to you before with clear proofs, but you doubted what he had brought; when he died, you said: "God will not raise any messenger after him." Thus does God allow him who is an extravagant doubtful to stray.

35. Those who dispute about the signs of God with no authority coming to them are greatly despised by God and by those who believe in Him; thus does God set a seal over every heart which is arrogant and haughty.

36. Pharaoh said: "O Haman! Build me a tower so that I may reach the means of access,

37. "To heavens, so that I may mount up to reach the God of Moses, and I surely think he is a liar." Thus was Pharaoh's evil deed made seemingly fair to him, and he was turned away from the (right) way; and Pharaoh's plot was only to his own ruin.

38. The one who believed said: "O people! Follow me so that I show you the way to the right guidance;

39. "O people! The life of this world is only (a transient) enjoyment; verily the hereafter is the lasting abode.

40. "Whosoever commits an evil deed, he shall only be recompensed with the like of it, and whosoever male or female does good deeds, while being a believer, they shall enter the garden wherein they shall be provided with sustenance without measure.

41. "O people! How is it that I invite you to salvation and you invite me to the Fire?

42. "Do you invite me to disbelieve in God and associate with Him that for which I have no knowledge, and I invite you to the Almighty, the oft-Forgiving Lord?

43. "No doubt that what you invite me to has no right to be invoked in this world nor in the hereafter, and our return is to God; the extravagant ones shall be the inmates of the Fire.

44. "And you shall remember what I say to you, and I

entrust my affair to God; verily God is ever watchful for His servants."

45. God protected him from the evils of what they planned; the awful chastisement surrounded the people of Pharaoh.

46. They are exposed to the Fire every morn and eve, and on the Day when the Hour (of reckoning) is established, "Admit the people of Pharaoh into the most severe of the torment."

47. When they wrangle with each other in the Fire; the weak shall say to those who were arrogant: "Verily, we were your followers; will you then relieve us from some of the (torture of the) Fire?"

48. Those who were arrogant shall say: "Verily God has judged between His servants."

49. Those in the Fire shall say to the guards of Hell: "Call upon your Lord to decrease the torture (at least) a day."

50. They shall say: "Did not your messengers come to you with clear proofs?" They shall say: "Yes." They (guards) shall say: "Call (upon Him) yourselves; the call of the disbeliever shall be in utter vain."

51. Verily We help Our messengers and those who believe in the life of this world and on the Day when the witnesses stand forth,

52. The Day when excuses shall not benefit the unjust ones, and for them there shall be a curse; for them shall be an evil abode.

53. Indeed, We bestowed guidance upon Moses, and we permitted the children of Israel to inherit the Book,

54. A guidance and a reminder to those endowed with understanding.

55. So (Muhammad) be patient; verily the promise of God is true; seek protection for your (followers') shortcomings, and celebrate the praise of your Lord in the evening and in the morning.

56. Verily those who dispute about the signs of God without any authority coming to them, there is nothing in their hearts but (the desire) to become great which they shall never attain; therefore, seek refuge with God; verily He is the all-Hearing, the all-Seeing.

57. Surely the creation of the heavens and the earth is greater than the creation of people, yet most people do not know.

58. Not equal are the blind and the seeing, nor those who believe and do good deeds are equal to the doers of evil; little do you reflect.

59. Verily the Hour (of reckoning) is to approach; there is no doubt therein, yet most people do not believe.

60. Your Lord says: "Call unto Me; I will answer you." Verily those who are too arrogant to serve Me shall soon enter Hell in disgrace.

61. God is He Who has made the night for you a rest, and the day a light; verily God is gracious to people, but most people are not thankful.

62. That is God, your Lord, Creator of everything; there is no god but He; why then are you (still) turned away?

63. Thus did those who denied the signs of God turn away.

64. God is He Who made the earth for you a resting place, and the heavens a canopy; He shaped your form, making it (look) good, and provided you the sustenance of goodly things; that is God your Lord; hallowed is God, Lord of the worlds.

65. He is the ever-Living; there is no god but He; so, call upon Him devoting to Him the religion; all praise is God's, Lord of the worlds.

66. Say: "Verily I am forbidden to worship those whom you call upon besides God when clear proofs have (already) come to me from my Lord, and I have been commanded to submit myself to the Lord of the worlds.

67. He it is Who created you from dust, then from a lifegerm, then from a clot, then He brings you forth as a babe, then you may reach your full strength, or you may age; of you are those who are caused to die early, and that you may reach the appointed term, haply you may understand.

68. He it is Who gives life and causes death, and when He decrees an affair, He only says: "Be," and it is.

69. Do you not see how those who dispute about the signs of God are turned away?

70. Those who falsify the Book and what We revealed to Our messengers shall soon come to know,

71. Fetters and chains shall surround their necks, and they shall be dragged-

72. Into the boiling water, then in the Fire to be burned;

73. Then it shall be said to them: "Where are those whom you used to associate (as gods)-

74. "Besides God?" They shall say: "They have gone away from us; nay, we used not to call upon anything before." Thus does God leave the disbelievers stray.

75. - "This is so because you exulted in the land without any right, and you were insolent;

76. "Enter the gate of Hell to abide therein." Wretched shall then be the arrogant ones."

77. So be patient; verily the promise of God is true; whether We let you see what We threaten them with, or whether We cause you to die (before then), to Us they shall all be returned.

78. And verily We sent messengers before you (O Our Messenger Muhammad). Of them there are those whom We have mentioned to you, and of them are those whom We have not; it was not given to any messenger to bring a sign (miracle) save with God's leave, but when the behest of God came, it was executed in truth, and those who stood on falsehood were then the losers.

79. God is He Who created the cattle for you to ride on some and eat of some others.

80. For you in them are other benefits, and that you may achieve thereby the need you cherish in your hearts, and upon them, and on board the ships, are you borne.

81. He shows you His signs; which of the signs of God will you then deny?

82. Have they not travelled in the earth and seen how the end of those before them was? They were more (numerous) than these and mightier in strength, and (also) greater in relics in the world, but what they were earning did not avail them aught.

83. When their messengers came to them with clear proofs, they exulted in what measure they had with them of knowledge, but that which they were wont to scoff encom-

passed them.

84. But when they witnessed Our punishment, they said: "We believe in God alone, and we deny what we used to associate with Him."

85. Yet their faith then did not avail them upon witnessing Our punishment; (such is) the procedure of God which has indeed been employed concerning His servants; it is then that the disbelievers lost their all.

Ha Mim

In the name of God, the Beneficent, the Merciful.

1. Ha-Meem:

2. A revelation from the Beneficent, the Most Merciful;

3. A book fully expounded in its verses, an Arabic Qur'an for people who know,

4. Bearer of glad tidings, and a warner, yet most of them turn away, so they do not hearken.

5. They say: "Our hearts are under coverings from that to which you invite us, and in our ears is heaviness, and between us and you hangs a veil; so, do what you please, for so are we doing."

6. They say: "I am only a man like you; it is revealed to me that your God is One, so seek a straight path unto Him, and seek His forgiveness; woe unto those who associate others with God,

7. "Who do not pay zakat, even denying the hereafter."

8. Verily for those who believe and do good deeds there is a ceaseless recompense.

9. Say: "Do you indeed disbelieve in Him Who created the earth in two days (periods) and you (still) set up equals with Him? That is the Lord of the worlds."

10. He has made therein lofty mountains, and He has bestowed His blessings thereupon; He measured its nourishment in four equal days (periods) for the seekers.

11. Then He applied Himself to the firmament which was yet only a smoke; so He said to it and to the earth: "Come you twain willingly or reluctantly." The twain said: "We come willingly."

12. And He made them seven heavens in two days (periods), and assigned His Will unto every heaven; We adorned the lower heavens with lamps (stars) and provided them with (angel) guards; that is the decree of the Almighty, the all-Knowing.

13. If they turn away from you (Muhammad), then say: "I warn you of thunderbolt like the one that afflicted the people of Ad and Thamud."

14. When Our messengers came to them from before and from behind them saying: "Worship none save God," they said: "Had our Lord willed, He would certainly have sent angels; so, verily we in what you have been sent with disbelieve."

15. As to the people of Ad, they prided in the land without right, and they said: "Who is mightier than us in power?" Behold! Is not God Who created them mightier than them in power? And they used to deny Our signs, too.

16. So We sent upon them a violent wind in inauspicious days that We may make them taste the chastisement of disgrace in the life of this world, and certainly the torment of the hereafter is more disgracing, and they shall not be helped.

17. As to (the people of) Thamud, We guided them aright, but they favoured misguidance to guidance; so a thunderbolt of a disgracing chastisement seized them for what they used to earn.

18. And We rescued those who believed and feared God.

19. On the Day when the enemies of God are gathered together for the Fire, they shall be ranked in groups.

20. When they come to it (Hell), their ears, eyes, and skins shall bear witness against them as to what they used to do.

21. And they shall say to their skins: "Why do you bear witness against us?" They shall say: "God Who makes everything speak has caused us to speak; He it is Who created you the first time, and to Him you shall all be returned."

22. And you could not seek to hide yourselves lest your ears, eyes, and skins should bear witness against you, but you thought that God does not know most of what you used to do.

23. That was but your (evil) conjecture which you conjec-

tured about your Lord, (now) it has tumbled you into ruin, so you have become the losers.

24. If they bear patiently, the Fire shall still be their abode, and if they seek favours, then they shall not be among the favoured ones.

25. We have appointed for them intimate companions, so for them fair-seeming have been made what is before them and what is behind them, and the sentence proved just against them, as it did with the peoples of the jinn and the human beings who passed away before them; verily they were the losers.

26. Those who disbelieve say: "Do not listen to this Qur'an but make noise (while it is recited), perhaps you may have the upper hand."

27. We will certainly make those who disbelieve taste a severe chastisement, and We will certainly reward them with the worst of what they used to do.

28. The Fire shall be the recompense of the enemies of God to abide therein for denying Our sign.

29. Those who disbelieve will say: "Lord! Show us those who led us astray of both the jinn and the humans; we will trample upon them with our feet so that they may be the lowest."

30. Verily those who say: "Our Lord is God" and remain on the Right Path, the angels descend upon them: "Do not fear nor grieve, and receive the glad tidings of the garden which you were promised.

31. "We are your guardians in the life of this world and in the hereafter, and for you shall be whatever you desire,

32. "A hospitable welcome from the oft-Forgiving, the Most Merciful."

33. And who is better in speech than he who calls unto God and does good deeds saying: "Verily I am a Muslim."

34. The good and the evil cannot be equal; repel evil with what is best when, lo, he between whom and you was enmity shall turn as if he were a warm friend.

35. None receive it save those who are steadfast, and none receive it save those who are most fortunate.

36. If an enticement from Satan entices you, seek refuge then with God; verily He is the all-Hearing, the all-Seeing.

37. Among His signs are: the night and the day, the sun and the moon. Do not prostrate in obeisance to the sun nor to the moon, but prostrate in obeisance to God (alone) Who created them both, if you worship Him.

38. But if the are too arrogant (to do so), then those (angels) with your Lord glorify Him night and day, and they are never tired. (COMPULSORY PROSTRATION HERE)

39. Among His signs is that you see the earth barren, but when We send water down on it, it stirs and swells; verily He Who gives it life will certainly give life to the dead; verily He has power over all things.

40. Verily those who distort Our signs are not hidden from Us. Is then he who is cast in the Fire better, or he who comes safe on the Day of Judgment? Do as you please; verily He sees all what you do.

41. Those are disbelievers who disbelieve in the reminder (Qur'an) when it is brought to them, though it is a book that is unassailable.

42. Falsehood cannot approach it from front or from behind, a revelation from the all-Wise, the Most Praised.

43. Nothing is said to you save what was said to the messengers before you; surely your Lord is the Lord of forgiveness and the Lord of grievous retribution.

44. Had We made it a colloquial Qur'an, they would certainly have said: "Why are not its verses made plain? In a slang (tongue)?! While the Prophet is Arabian?!" Say: "It is for those who believe, a guidance and a cure. As to those who do not believe, there is heaviness in their ears, and they are blind thereto. These are like those who are called upon from a far off place."

45. Indeed We bestowed the Book upon Moses, but disputes arose therein. Had no word already gone forth from your Lord, there would certainly have been judgment passed between them, and they are certainly about it in a disquieting doubt.

46. Whosoever does good deeds, it is for his own self, and whosoever commits evil, it is against his own self; your Lord is not unjust to the servants.

47. To Him is referred the knowledge of the Hour (of reckoning); no fruits come out of its covering, and no fe-

males are big with child nor deliver except with His knowledge. On the Day when He calls them: "Where are My partners?" they shall say: "We declare to You that there is no witness from us thereto."

48. What they used to call upon before shall pass away from them, and they shall know that for them there is no escape.

49. Man never tires praying for good (things), yet when a harm touches him, he is despaired, hopeless.

50. If We make him taste mercy from Us after distress had touched him, he will certainly say: "This is my due, and I deem the Hour (of reckoning) would never be established, and if I am returned to my Lord, verily there will be the best for me with Him." We will certainly inform those who disbelieve of what they used to do, and We will surely make them taste of a stiff torment.

51. When We bestow bounties on man, he turns away, and when any distress touches him, he abounds in long prayers.

52. Say: "Do you behold that it (Qur'an) is from God, yet you still disbelieve in it? Who is farther astray than he who is in opposition far away (from the truth)?"

53. Soon will We show them Our signs in the horizons, and in their own selves, until it becomes manifest to them that He is the truth. Does it not suffice you that He is witness over all things?

54. They doubt the meeting with their Lord! Verily He encompasses everything.

Consultation
(ash-Shura)

In the name of God, the Beneficent, the Merciful.

1. Ha, Meem.

2. Ain, Sin, Qaf.

3. Thus does God, the Almighty, the all-Wise, reveal to you as He did to those before you.

4. His is whatever in the earth, and He is the Highest, the Greatest.

5. Nigh it is that the heaven may cleave asunder from

above (in awe), while angels are celebrating the praise of their Lord, seeking forgiveness for the inhabitants of the earth. Be it known that God alone is the oft-Forgiving, the Most Merciful.

6. God watches over those who take aught besides God as their guardians, and you are not a guardian over them.

7. Thus have We revealed to you (Muhammad) an Arabic Qur'an so that you may warn the mother-city (Mecca) and those around it, and that you may warn of the day of gathering together, the day wherein there should be no doubt. A party shall (then) be in the garden, and a party in the burning Fire.

8. Had God so pleased, He would certainly have made them a single nation, but He admits whomsoever He wills into His mercy. There is no guardian nor helper for the unjust.

9. Or have they taken besides Him other guardians? Yet God is the Guardian, and He grants life to the dead and He is omni-Potent over all things.

10. In whatever you differ, its decision is to God; that is your God, my Lord; on Him do I rely, and unto Him (alone) do I return,

11. Originator of the heavens and the earth; He created mates for you, of your own selves, and of the cattle pairs (male and female) thereby He may multiply you. Nothing whatsoever is like unto Him, and He is the all-Hearing, the all-Seeing.

12. His are the treasures of the heavens and the earth. He amplifies the sustenance to whomsoever He wills and straitens; verily He knows all things.

13. He has prescribed for you the religion of what He ordained to Noah and that which We revealed to you and what We ordained to Abraham, Moses and Jesus; that is: "Establish the religion and do not be divided therein." Hard is it to the disbelievers that which you call them to. God chooses to Himself whomsoever He wills, and He guides to Himself whosoever turns to Him.

14. Nor were they divided until the knowledge had come to them out of rivalry among themselves. Had no word gone forth from your Lord (respiting them) to a fixed time,

the affairs would have certainly been decided between them. Verily those who were made the heirs to the Book after them are certainly in disquieting doubt about it.

15. For this then you invite on, and be steadfast as you are commanded. Do not follow their vain desires, and say: "I believe in what God as sent down of the Book, and I have been commanded to do justice among you; God is our Lord and yours; upon us (is the responsibility of) our deeds, and upon you yours. No contention (need be) between us and you; God will gather us together, and to Him is the ultimate return."

16. Those who dispute about God after response was made unto Him, their argument is vain to their Lord, and upon them is the Wrath, and for them is a severe chastisement.

17. God is He Who sent down the Book with truth and the balance, and what do you know? Haply the Hour (of reckoning) is nigh.

18. Those who do not believe in it hasten it on, and those who believe are dreadful thereof. Do not they know that it is the truth? Beware! Verily those who dispute about the Hour are far astray.

19. God is Benign to His servants; He provides sustenance to whomsoever He wills, and He is the Almighty, the omni-Potent.

20. Whosoever desires the tilth of the hereafter, We increase for him in his tilth; whosoever desires the tilth of this world, We give him thereof, and for him shall be no share in the hereafter.

21. Or do they have partners (unto God) who have prescribed for them any religion which God does not sanction? Had it not been for the word of decision, the decision would have certainly been made between them, and verily for the unjust there shall be a painful chastisement.

22. (On that day) you will see the unjust alarmed for what they earned and (the chastisement) shall be in the meadows of the garden; for them shall be whatever they please with their Lord; that is the greatest grace.

23. That is (one) of the glad tidings of which God gives to those who do good deeds. Say: "I do not ask you for any

reward for it save the love of my relatives, and whosoever earns good, We increase for him the good therein; verily God is oft- Forgiving, Appreciator (of good deeds)."

24. Or do they say "He has forged a lie against God"? Had God willed, He would have sealed your heart, and yet He would blot out the falsehood and prove the truth with His words; verily He knows best whatever is in the hearts.

25. He it is Who accepts repentance from His servants and forgives sins, and He knows whatever you do.

26. He responds to those who believe and do good deeds and increases to them of His grace. For the disbelievers shall be a severe torment.

27. Should God amplify the sustenance to His servants, they would certainly rebel in the world, but He sends it down by measure as He pleases; verily He is all-Aware, all-Seeing of His servants.

28. He it is Who sends down the rain after they have despaired and spreads His mercy. He is the Guardian, the Praised.

29. Among His signs is the creation of the heavens and the earth and (the creation of) what He has spread out in both of them of the animate beings and for their gathering together when He wills; He is the omni-Potent.

30. Whatever befalls you of a misfortune, it is (due to) what your own hands have wrought, and He pardons most of your sins.

31. You cannot frustrate God's Will in the earth, and there is no guardian or helper for you other than God.

32. And among His signs are the ships sailing in the sea like mountains.

33. If He wills, He lulls the wind that they lie motionless on the surface; verily in this are signs for every one steadfast, grateful.

34. Or He may cause them to perish for what they have wrought, and (yet) He (still) pardons most.

35. That haply those who dispute Our signs may know; for them there is no refuge.

36. And whatever you are given is but a provision for the life of this world, and what is with God is better and more lasting for those who believe and on their Lord rely.

37. Those who shun the great sins and filthiness, and when angry they forgive;

38. Those who respond to their Lord and establish prayer, and conduct their affairs with counsel among themselves, and they spend of what We have provided them with,

39. And those who, when afflicted with great wrong, become (eventually) victorious.

40. The recompense for an evil shall be an ill-return like it, but if one pardons and amends, his reward is incumbent on God; verily He does not love unjust people.

41. Whosoever defends himself after being oppressed, then there is no way against these to be blamed.

42. The way (to blame) is against those who do injustice to people and transgress in the world unjustly; for these shall be a painful chastisement.

43. Indeed, whosoever remains patient and forgives, verily it is an act of great resolution.

44. Whomsoever God permits to stray, there shall be no guardian after it for him, and you shall behold the unjust when they see the chastisement, saying: "Is there any way to return?"

45. And you shall see them brought to it humiliated, disgraced, looking with a stealthy glance. Those who believe shall say: "Verily the losers are those who lost their people on the day of reckoning." Beware! The unjust shall surely be in a lasting torment.

46. There shall be no guardian for them to help besides God. Whomsoever God allows to stray, there shall be no other way for him to be guided to the right path.

47. Respond to your Lord before a day comes to you from God for which there is no averting; you shall not have any refuge on that day, nor will your denial be of any avail.

48. If they turn away (from you, O Muhammad), then We have not sent you as a watcher over them. On you is naught but only to convey (Our Message). Verily when We make man taste mercy from Us, He rejoices thereby, and if any harm afflicts them for what they did with their own hands, man will surely then turns ingrate.

49. God's is the kingdom of the heavens and the earth. He creates whatever He wills. He blesses whomsoever He

pleases with females, and He blesses whomsoever He wishes with males.

50. Or He mingles them, males and females, and makes whomsoever He wills barren; verily He is the all-Knowing, the all-Powerful.

51. It is not for any man that God should speak to him save by revelation or from behind a veil, or by sending a messenger (angel) and to reveal by His permission what He pleases; verily He is the Most High, the all-Wise.

52. Thus did We reveal to you Our guidance by Our command; you did not know what the Book (Qur'an) was, nor the faith, but We made it a light, guiding thereby whomsoever We please of Our servants, and verily a guide to the Right Path,

53. The path of God Whose is whatsoever in the heavens and the earth. Be it known that to God (alone) shall all affairs be referred.

The Ornaments
(az-Zukhruf)

In the name of God, the Beneficent, the Merciful.

1. Ha, Meem.

2. By the Book manifesting,

3. Verily We have made it an Arabic Qur'an that you may gain understanding.

4. And verily it is in the mother-book with Us, Most Exalted, full of Wisdom.

5. Shall We then turn the Reminder away from you wholly since you are extravagant people?

6. How many of Our prophets did We send to those who have gone by?

7. Whenever a prophet came to them, they mocked him.

8. Then We destroyed those who were mightier than these in strength, and such has gone examples among those gone before.

9. Should you ask them "Who created the heavens and the earth?" they would certainly say: "The Almighty, the all-Knowing, created them."

10. He Who made the earth for you a cradle, and made

paths therein for you that you may be rightly guided.

11. He sends down [rain]water from the heavens in a measure; then We raise with it a town that is dead (dried); even so shall you be brought forth (to life again).

12. He created pairs of all things and made ships for you, and the cattle to ride on,

13. That you may mount their backs, then haply remember the bounty of your Lord, and when you mount it you say: "Hallowed is He Who subjected this to us, and we (on our own) were not able to attain this.

14. "Verily we, to our Lord, shall all return."

15. Yet they (still) assign to some of His servants partnership with Him! Verily man is openly ungrateful.

16. Has He taken daughters (unto Himself) of what He has Himself created, and chosen you to have the sons?!

17. When the news is given to anyone of them of what similitude the Beneficent sets, his face becomes darkened and he is choked with rage.

18. Can then one brought up amidst ornaments and in disputes, unable to give a clear account (be associated with God)?

19. They (even) make the angels, who are servants of the Beneficent, females; did they witness their creation? Their witness shall be written down, and they shall be questioned.

20. They say: "Had the Beneficent willed, we should not have worshipped them." They have no knowledge of this; they only surmise.

21. Or have We given them a Book before it which they fast uphold?

22. Nay! They say: "Verily we found our [fore]fathers on a creed and verily in their footsteps are we guided."

23. Thus, We sent no warner before you to a town except that the luxurious in it said: "Verily, we found our [fore]fathers on a creed, and verily in their footsteps are we following."

24. (The warner) said: "Even if I bring you a guidance that is better than that on which you found your [fore]fathers?" They said: "Verily we are disbelievers in whatever you are sent with."

25. So We inflicted retribution upon them, and behold

how the end of those who falsified (Our messengers) was.

26. And (remember) when Abraham said to his father and people: "Verily I am free of what you worship.

27. "I worship but Him Who created me, for surely He will guide me."

28. He made it a word to continue in his progeny that they might return (to God).

29. Nay! I provided these and their fathers to enjoy until the truth (Qur'an) came to them and the Messenger (Muhammad) manifesting it.

30. When the truth came to them, they said: "This is sorcery. We are disbelievers in it."

31. And they said: "Why was no Qur'an sent to a leading man in both cities?"

32. Do they distribute your Lord's mercy? It is We Who distribute their own livelihood in the life of this world, and We raised some of them above the others in ranks, so that some of them may take others in subjection; and the mercy of your Lord is better than all that they hoard.

33. Were it not that all people might follow one (evil) way of life, We would certainly have provided those who disbelieve in the Beneficent God silver roofs and stairs on which they ascend.

34. And the doors of their houses, and the couches on which they recline,

35. And ornaments of gold; but all these are only provisions of this life, and the hereafter with your Lord is for the pious.

36. Whosoever is blinded against the remembrance of the Beneficent, for him shall We appoint a Satan, and he shall be his close companion.

37. Verily (Satan) turned them away from the Right Path, and they (still) deem it that they are rightly guided.

38. Until, when he comes to Us, he would say: "Would that between me and you (Satan) there were a distance of two Easts!" Indeed, an evil companion Satan is.

39. Never shall it profit you on this day since you committed injustice that you be partners in the chastisement.

40. Can you then make the deaf hear you, or can you guide the blind and him who is manifestly astray?

41. Even if We take you away, then verily We shall exact retribution from them,

42. Or We shall show you that which We have promised them, for verily We are over them (fully) Powerful.

43. Hold fast, therefore, to what has been revealed to you; verily you (Muhammad) are on the Right Path.

44. And verily it is a Reminder for you and your people, and you shall soon be questioned about it.

45. Ask those of Our Messengers whom We sent before you if We appointed besides the Beneficent God any gods to be worshipped.

46. And indeed We sent Moses with Our signs to Pharaoh and his chiefs, and he said: "I am truly the messenger of the Lord of the worlds."

47. When he came to them with Our signs, lo, they held them in ridicule.

48. We showed them no sign but was greater than the other, and We seized them with chastisement so that they might return.

49. They said: "O sorcerer! Call on us to your Lord to do as He has promised you; verily we will (then) be rightly guided."

50. But when We relieved them from the chastisement, lo, they did not honour the pledge.

51. Pharaoh proclaimed to his people: "O people! Is not the kingdom of Egypt mine? And these rivers flow beneath me? Do you not behold?

52. "Nay! Am I not better than this fellow (Moses) who is contemptible, scarcely capable of speaking distinctly?

53. "Why have no bracelets of gold been put upon him? Why no angel came with him as his companion?"

54. Thus did he persuade his people to levity, and they obeyed him; verily they were a transgressing people.

55. When they angered Us, We inflicted them with Our retribution. So did We drown them altogether.

56. We made them a precedent and an example for later generations.

57. When (Jesus) the son of Mary set forth an instance (of Our Power), lo, your people laughed in ridicule.

58. They say: "Are our gods better or is He?" They do

not set it forth to you but a way of disputation. Nay! They are a contentious people.

59. None was he but a servant (of Ours). We bestowed upon him Our Favour, and We made him an example (of Our Power) to the children of Israel.

60. Had We pleased, We could certainly have let the angels be the successors on earth.

61. Verily he shall be a sign of the Hour. Do not doubt then about it, and follow Me: this is the Right Path.

62. Let no Satan prevent you; verily he is your open enemy.

63. When Jesus came with clear proofs (miracles), he said: "Indeed I have come to you with wisdom, that I may clarify some (issues) in which you differed; so Fear God and obey me.

64. "God (alone) is my Lord and yours, so serve (only) Him; this is the Right Path."

65. But parties among them differed; so, woe of the chastisement of a painful day unto those who were unjust.

66. Do they wait for aught but the Hour (of reckoning) to come to them suddenly while they do not perceive?

67. Friends that day shall be enemies of one another save the pious.

68. O My servants! No fear shall be on you this day, nor shall you grieve.

69. Those who believed in Our signs and were Muslims,

70. Enter the garden, you and your mates; you shall be delighted.

71. Dishes of gold and cups (of drinks) shall be passed around to them, and they shall have whatever their souls desire therein, and whatever would delight their eyes, to abide therein eternally.

72. This is the garden (Paradise) you are made to receive as a heritage for what you have been doing.

73. For you therein are fruits in abundance, of which you eat.

74. Verily the guilty ones shall abide in the torment of Hell forever.

75. It shall not be abated from them, and they shall be despairing therein.

76. We were not unjust to them, but it was they who were unjust to their own selves.

77. They shall cry out: "O Malik! Would that your Lord puts an end to us!" He shall say: "Verily you shall remain (here forever)."

78. Indeed We have brought you the truth, but most of you were hateful of the truth.

79. Or have they settled any device (among themselves)? Then verily We too shall settle Ours.

80. Or do they think that We do not hear their secret and concealed discourses? Aye! And Our messengers write down everything.

81. Say: "Had the Beneficent God had any son, I would have been the first to worship."

82. Hallowed is the Lord of the heavens and the earth, Lord of the Throne, far above what they attribute.

83. So leave them to plunge on and sport until they meet the day they have been (ominously) promised.

84. He it is Who is God in the heavens and the earth, the all-Wise, the all-Knowing.

85. Holiest is He Whose is the Kingdom of the heavens and the earth and whatsoever is between them twain, and with Him is the knowledge of the Hour, and to Him shall you all return.

86. Those whom they call besides Him do not own any power or intercession save he who bears witness to the truth and they know it.

87. If you ask them who created them, they would certainly say: "God." Whence are they then deluded away (from the truth)?

88. And his (Prophet's) cry: "Lord! Verily these are people who do not believe!"

89. So turn away from them (O Muhammad) and say: "Peace," for they shall soon come to know.

The Smoke
(ad-Dukhan)

In the name of God, the Beneficent, the Merciful.

1. Ha, Meem.

2. By the manifesting Book (Qur'an),

3. Verily We revealed it on a blessed night-indeed, We have ever been warning-

4. Therein, all wise affairs are made distinct,

5. (Becoming) a command from Us; surely We send (revelations),

6. As a mercy from your Lord; He is the all-Hearing, the all-Knowing.

7. Lord of the heavens and the earth and whatever is between them twain, if you are sure of faith.

8. There is no god but He; He gives life and causes death; your Lord and the Lord of your fathers of yore.

9. Yet they are sporting in doubt.

10. So await the day when the heaven gives out a smoke clearly visible,

11. Enveloping the people; this will be a painful chastisement.

12. - "O Lord! Remove from us the torment; we are (now) truly believers."

13. How shall they be admonished when a messenger came to them making the truth manifest?

14. (Yet) they turned their backs to him and said: "He is tutored (by others), mad."

15. Verily We will remove the torment a little; you will surely return (to evil).

16. That day We shall seize them with a great seizure; We shall certainly afflict retribution upon them.

17. And indeed We tried the people of Pharaoh before them. A noble messenger came to them-

18. Saying: "Deliver to me the servants of God, verily I am a trusted messenger to you,

19. "And do not exalt yourselves against God; I come to you with a manifest authority.

20. "And I take refuge with my Lord and yours lest you

should stone me;

21. "And if you do not believe in me, then leave me alone."

22. (But they tormented him); then he cried unto his Lord: "These are a guilty people."

23. - "Then march forth with My servants by night; you will surely be pursued,

24. "And leave the sea calm; they are certainly a host that shall be drowned."

25. How many have they left of gardens and fountains!

26. Cornfields and dwellings noble!

27. And pleasant things in which they delighted!

28. So was it: and We gave them all as a heritage to another people;

29. So neither the heavens nor the earth wept over them, nor were they respited.

30. And indeed We delivered the children of Israel from the degrading affliction,

31. From Pharaoh; he surely was haughty, extravagant.

32. And indeed We chose them, with prescience, above all other creation;

33. And We gave them the signs wherein was a clear trial.

34. These do say:

35. "There is naught save our first death, and we shall not be raised again.

36. "Then bring our fathers back, if you are truthful."

37. Are they better or the people of Tubba', and those before them? We destroyed them, for verily they were guilty.

38. And We did not create the heavens nor the earth and what is between them both in sport.

39. We created them but with the truth, yet most of them do not know.

40. The day of sporting is the appointed term for all of them,

41. The day when a friend shall not avail his friend aught, nor shall they be helped,

42. Save those on whom God shall have mercy; verily He is the Almighty, the all-Merciful.

43. Verily the tree of Zaqqum,

44. Shall be the food of the sinful,

45. Like molten brass; it shall boil in their bellies.

46. Like the boiling of scalding water.

47. - "Seize him, then drag him down into the midst of Hell,

48. "Then pour on his head of the torment of the boiling water."

49. "Taste it! You were forsooth the Mighty, the Honourable;

50. "Verily, this is what you used to dispute."

51. The pious will be in a place secure,

52. In gardens and springs,

53. Attired in fine silk and rich brocade, facing each other;

54. So shall it be, and We will unite them with fair ones, large, lustrous, lovely eyes.

55. They shall call therein for every kind of fruit, being in peace and security;

56. They shall taste no death therein save the first death, and He will save them from the chastisement of Hell.

57. A grace from your Lord; this is the great achievement.

58. So We have made it (Qur'an) easy in your own tongue so that they may be admonished.

59. So wait, therefore, verily they, too, are waiting.

The Kneeling
(al-Jathiya)

In the name of God, the Beneficent, the Merciful.

1. Ha, Meem.

2. This Book (Qur'an) is revealed from God, the all-Mighty, the all-Wise.

3. Verily in the heavens and the earth are signs for the believers.

4. And in your own creation, and in what He scatters in the earth of animals are signs for people sure in faith,

5. And in the alternation of the night and the day, and what God sends down from heaven of sustenance, (in His) giving life thereby to the earth after its death, and in the changing of the winds., are signs for people who understand.

6. These are the signs of God We recite them unto you

with truth; then in what (other) argument after (rejecting) God and His signs would they believe?

7. Woe unto every sinning liar,

8. Who hears the signs of God recited to him, yet he persists arrogantly, as if he never heard them; so announce to them a painful torment.

9. When he comes to know of any of Our signs, he takes it jestingly. These shall have a disgracing chastisement.

10. Behind them is Hell, and naught of what they earned shall avail them, nor those whom they took as guardians besides God, and for them shall be a grievous chastisement.

11. This (Qur'an) is guidance, and for those who disbelieve in the signs of their Lord shall be a most painful torment.

12. God is He Who made the sea subservient to you that you may traverse the ships therein by His command, and that you may seek of His grace, and that you may be thankful.

13. And He made subservient to you whatever is in the heavens and the earth, all on His behalf. Verily in this are signs for people who reflect.

14. Say to those who believe that they may forgive those who do not hope for the Days of God, that He may reward people for what they earned.

15. Whoever does good deeds, it is for his own self, and whoever does evil deeds, it is against his own self; then to your Lord you shall all be returned.

16. Indeed, We bestowed upon the children of Israel a Book, and wisdom and prophethood, and We provided them with sustenance from the goodly things, and We favoured them over all other peoples.

17. And We gave them clear arguments of the affairs, but they differed only after knowledge had come to them through rivalry among themselves. Your Lord will surely judge between them on the Day of Reckoning about that wherein they differed.

18. Then We have set you (O Muhammad) on a definite course of Law, so follow it, and do not follow the vain desires of those who do not know.

19. They shall not avail you aught against God. The unjust are friends of one another, and God is the Guardian of the pious.

20. These are proofs for the people, a guidance and a mercy to people who are sure in faith.

21. Do those who have wrought evil deeds deem that We will treat them as We treat those who believed and did good deeds, in life and in death? Ill is their judgment.

22. God created the heavens and the earth in truth, and every soul shall be rewarded for what it earned, and they shall not be dealt with unjustly.

23. Have you seen him who takes as god his own vain desires, while God has allowed him to stray, knowing it, and set a seal upon his ear and heart and put upon his eyes a veil? Who can guide him besides God? Will you not then reflect?

24. They say: "It is naught save our life in this world; we die and we live, and nothing annihilates us save time." There is no knowledge for them of that; they only surmise.

25. And when Our clear signs are recited unto them, their argument is only that they say: "Bring our fathers back if you are truthful."

26. Say: "God grants you life, then He causes you to die, then He will gather you to the Day of Reckoning; there is no doubt about this, yet most people do not know."

27. God's is the kingdom of the heavens and the earth; on the Day when the Hour is established, on that Day the believers in falsehood shall be the losers.

28. And you (O Our Messenger Muhammad!) shall see every nation kneeling down, every people called upon to their own book; today you shall be recompensed for all that you used to do.

29. This is Our Book (Qur'an) that speaks against you with justice; verily We used to record whatever you used to do.

30. And those who believed and did good deeds, their Lord admits them into His mercy; that is the manifest achievement.

31. And those who disbelieved (it shall be said to them): "Were not My signs recited to you? Yet you acted arrogantly, and you were a guilty people."

32. It was said to them: "Verily the promise of God is true, and there is no doubt in the Hour;" you said: "We know not what the Hour is. We deem it naught but a mere guess, and we are not sure."

33. The evils of what they wrought shall (appear) manifest to them and that which they used to mock shall surround them.

34. And it shall be said to them: "Today, We neglect you even as you neglected the meeting of this Day of yours, and your abode shall be the Fire, and for you there will be no helpers."

35. "You took the signs of God for a jest and the life of this world deceived you;" so on that day, they shall not be taken out thence, nor shall they be granted any grace.

36. Therefore, God's (alone) is the praise, Lord of the heavens and the earth, Lord of the worlds.

37. His (only) is greatness in the heavens and the earth, and He is the Almighty, the all-Wise.

The Winding Sand-tracts
(al-Ahqaf)

In the name of God, the Beneficent, the Merciful.

1. Ha, Meem.

2. The revelation of this Book (Qur'an) is from God, the Almighty, the all-Wise.

3. We did not create the heavens and the earth and what is between them save with truth, and for a determined term; yet those who disbelieve turn away from what they are warned.

4. Say: "Have you seen what you called upon besides God? Show me what part of the earth they created, or if there is any share for them in the heavens. Bring me a book before this, or traces of knowledge, if you are truthful."

5. Who is more astray than he who calls upon others besides God, such that will not respond to him till the Day of Judgment, and they are not even aware of being invoked?

6. When people are gathered together, they shall be hostile to them, and there shall be those who would deny their worship.

7. When Our clear signs are recited to them, those who disbelieve in the truth when it comes to them say: "This is but open sorcery."

8. Or do they say that he has forged it? Say: "If I have forged it, then you have naught for me against (the Wrath of) God. He knows best what you utter about it; He suffices for witness between me and you, and He is the oft-Forgiving, Most Merciful."

9. Say: "I am not the first of the messengers. I do not know what will happen to me or to you; I only follow what is revealed to me, and I am but an open warner."

10. Say: "Do you see if (this Qur'an) is from God and you still disbelieve in it (although) a witness from among the children of Israel has testified to its similarity (with its pre-decessors), and has believed therein? Yet you even pride in exalting yourselves! Verily God does not guide the unjust people."

11. Those who disbelieve say about those who believe: "Had it been good, they would not have gone ahead of us to it." Since they do not seek to be guided by it, they say: "This is only a lie of old."

12. Before it, the Book of Moses was a guide and mercy, and this (Qur'an) is a Book confirming it in the Arabic language that it may warn those who are unjust, and contains glad tidings for the doers of good.

13. Verily those who say "Our Lord is God" and are firm on the Right Path, there shall be no fear for them, nor shall they grieve.

14. They shall be the inmates of the garden, abiding therein (forever), a recompense for what they did.

15. We have enjoined man to be good to his parents. His mother bore him in pain, and delivered him in pain, and his weaning is thirty months, until, when he attains his maturity and reaches forty years, he says: "Lord! Bestow upon me and my parents that I may do good deeds to please You, and do good to me in respect to my offspring; verily I turn to You (repentant), and I am one of the Muslims."

16. These are they from whom We accept the best of what they have done and pass by their evil, (they shall be) among the dwellers of the garden, a promise of truth which

they were promised.

17. But (there is one) who says to his parents: "Fie upon you both! You promise me that I shall be brought forth (from the grave alive) when many generations have passed away before me?" and they both implore God's aid saying: "Woe unto you! Believe, for verily the promise of God is true;" then he will say: "This is naught but stories of the ancient."

18. These are they against whom the sentence has been proven among the people of the jinn and the men that have passed away before them; verily they were the losers.

19. And for all are ranks according to what they used to do, and that He may (fully) reward their deeds, and they shall not be dealt with unjustly.

20. On the Day when those who disbelieved shall be exposed to the Fire: "You did away with your good things in the life of the world, and you took your fill of pleasure in them; this Day, therefore, you shall be recompensed with shameful chastisement for what you used to act in arrogance on earth without any right, and for what you used to transgress."

21. Remember the brother of Ad when he warned his people of al-Ahqaf, and (while) indeed warners have been sent before him and after him: "Worship none but God! Verily I fear for you the chastisement of a grievous Day."

22. They said: "Do you come to us to turn us away from our gods? Then bring upon us what you threaten us with if you are truthful."

23. He said: "The knowledge of it is only with God. I only convey to you the message with which I am sent, but I see you a people who are ignorant."

24. So when they saw (the punishment in the form of) a cloud advancing to their valleys, they said: "This is a cloud which will give us rain." Nay! It is what you sought to hasten on, a blast of a violent wind in which there is a painful chastisement.

25. Destroying everything by the command of its Lord; so they became unseen, even thus do We reward the guilty people.

26. And certainly We had firmly established them (in a

way that) We never established for you. We bestowed upon them ears, eyes and hearts, but neither their hearing, nor sight, nor hearts availed them aught, since they rejected the signs of God, and they were encircled by that which they used to mock.

27. And indeed We destroyed (many) of the towns which are around you, and We displayed Our signs that they might turn (to Us).

28. Why then did not those whom they took for gods besides God, hoping that they would bring them closer to God, assist them? Nay! They failed them, and this was but their lie and what they used to forge.

29. When We turned to you, the party of jinn, who came unto you, listened to the Qur'an; they said: "Be silent!" Then when the recital was finished, they returned to their people to warn;

30. They said: "O people! Verily we have heard a Book revealed after the time of Moses testifying to what was before it, guiding to the truth and to a Straight Path.

31. "O people! Respond to the Summoner of God and believe in Him. He will forgive your sins and guard you against a painful torment."

32. Whosoever does not respond to the Summoner of God, he cannot frustrate God's will in the world, and for him there shall be no guardian other than Him; these are in manifest error.

33. Have they not seen that God, Who created the heavens and the earth, and their creation did not wary Him, has power to give life to the dead? Aye! Verily He is powerful over all things.

34. On the Day when those who disbelieved shall be exposed to the Fire: "Is this not justice?" They shall say: "Aye! By our Lord!" Then He will say: "Taste (now) the chastisement for what you used to disbelieve."

35. Bear with patience, therefore, as the messengers endowed with uncompromising determination did, and do not seek to hasten (their doom) for them; on the Day when they see what they were promised, it shall be as though they did not tarry but an hour of the day; (a clear) deliverance Who shall then be destroyed other than transgressing people?

Muhammad

In the name of God, the Beneficent, the Merciful.

1. God shall render vain the deeds of those who disbelieve and hinder others from His Path.

2. As to those who believe and do good, believing in what has been sent down to Muhammad, which is the truth from their Lord, He shall forgive their sins, remove their evils from them, and improve their conditions.

3. That is so because those who disbelieve follow falsehood, whereas those who believe follow the truth from their Lord; thus does God set forth examples to the people.

4. So when you encounter those who disbelieve (on battlegrounds), smite their necks until you have wounded them heavily and routed them, then take them captives in fetters, or set them free as an obligation, or they may be ransomed, till they lay their weapons down; thus are you commanded. If God pleases, He would certainly exact retribution from them, but He would rather try some of you through the others. He will never permit the deeds of those who are slain in His way to go in vain.

5. Soon will He guide them rightly and please their conscience,

6. And admit them to the garden with which He has acquainted them.

7. O you who believe! If you support (the Cause of) God, He will also support you and set your feet firm.

8. As to those who disbelieve, stumbling with destruction shall be their fate, and He shall render their deeds vain.

9. That is so because they hated what God revealed, so He shall render their deeds null.

10. Have they not travelled in the earth and seen how the end of those before them was? God brought destruction to them, and there shall be the like of it for the disbelievers.

11. That is so because God is the Guardian of those who believe, and there shall be no guardian for the infidels.

12. Verily God will admit those who believe and do good deeds into gardens beneath which rivers flow. As to those who disbelieve, they shall enjoy themselves and eat

as beasts eat, then the Fire shall be their final abode.

13. How many a town, mightier in power than your own, from which you (Muhammad) have been driven out, did We destroy? There was none to help them.

14. Is he who is on clear proofs from his Lord like unto him whose evil work is made fair-seeming to him, following his own vain desires?

15. A similitude of the garden which has been promised to the pious ones. Rivers of water therein that are incorruptible, and rivers of milk whose taste suffers no change, and rivers of wine, delicious to those who drink it, and rivers of honey, pure and clear. For them therein are (also) all kinds of fruits, and a complete forgiveness from their Lord. Are they similar to those who shall dwell in the Fire and who shall be made to drink boiling water so that it will render their bowels asunder?

16. Among them are those who seek to listen to you until, when they go forth from you, they say to those who have been given the knowledge: "What was it that he said just now?" These are they on whose hearts God has set a seal, and they only follow their own vain desires.

17. Those who avail of the guidance. He increases their guidance and grants them the rewards of their piety.

18. Do they wait then save for the Hour that it comes suddenly to them? Indeed the signs of it have already come; of what avail can the reminder be to them when it has already come unto them?

19. So know that there is no god but God, and seek (His) protection for your sins and for the believing men and women; God well knows the place of your movements, and the place of your final rest.

20. Those who believe say: "Why has no chapter been sent?" but when a chapter is revealed in which war is mentioned, you see those in whose hearts there is a disease look at you with a look of one on whom the shadow of death has fallen; woe unto them!

21. Obedience and a fair word; but when the affair is determined, then if they are true to God, it would certainly be better for them;

22. Then belike you are if you hold authority that you

make mischief in the earth and sever the ties of kinship?

23. Those are they whom God has cursed, and so has He made them deaf, and their sights blind.

24. Do not they (ever) reflect upon the Qur'an? Nay! Locks are set on their hearts.

25. Verily those who return on the backs after manifest guidance has become, Satan has beguiled them, and has given them a respite.

26. That is so for those who hate what God has revealed say: "We will obey you in a part of this matter," but God knows well their secret reservations.

27. How if the angels cause them to die, smiting their faces and backs?

28. It is so for they follow that which displeases God and hate what pleases Him; so, He has made their deeds null.

29. Or do those in whose hearts there is a disease deem it that God will never bring their spite forth?

30. Had We willed, We would certainly have acquainted you with them, and you would certainly have known them by their features; you can certainly recognize them by the tone of their speech, and God well knows whatever you do.

31. Certainly We shall try you until We know who among you strives and who perseveres, and shall make your affairs known.

32. Verily those who disbelieve and hinder others from the Path of God, and oppose the Messenger after guidance has been made manifest to them, can never harm God in any way, and He will make their deeds null.

33. O you who believe! Obey God, obey the Messenger, and do not render your deeds null.

34. Verily those who disbelieve and hinder others from the Way of God shall die disbelievers, then God will never forgive them.

35. So do not be faint-hearted, and call (the infidels) to peace, while you have the upper hand, and God is with you; He will never depreciate your deeds.

36. The life in this world is but idle sport and play, and if you believe and fear God, He will grant you your recompense and will not ask you (to give up) your possessions.

37. Should He ask them of you, you will be niggardly,

and He will bring your spite forth.

38. Lo! You, who are called upon to spend in the way of God, are niggardly, and whosoever is niggardly harms his own soul, and God is self-Sufficient, and you are in need (of Him). If you turn back, He will bring in your place people other than you, then they surely will not be like you.

The Victory
(al-Fath)

In the name of God, the Beneficent, the Merciful.

1. Verily, We have granted you a manifest victory.

2. (So) that God may forgive the past faults of your followers and the faults to come, and thus does He perfect His bounty unto you and guide you on the straight path.

3. And that God might help you with a prevailing triumph.

4. He it is Who sent down tranquility into the hearts of the faithful that they might add further faith to their faith, and God's are the hosts of the heavens and the earth; God is all-Knowing, all-Wise.

5. That He may admit the faithful men and women to gardens beneath which rivers flow to abide therein, and remove their ills; that is in the sight of God a great achievement,

6. And that He may chastise the hypocrites, men and women, and the polytheist men and women, those who think evil thoughts about God; upon them is God's wrath, and His curse; He has prepared Hell for them; what an evil journey's end!

7. God's are the hosts of the heavens and the earth; God is the ever-Prevalent, the all-Wise.

8. Verily We have sent you (Muhammad) a witness, a bearer of glad tidings, and a warner,

9. That you may believe in God and His messengers, and aid and revere him, and that you may celebrate His glory morning and eve.

10. Verily those who swear fealty to you do but swear it to God; the hand of God is above their hands; so, whosoever violates his oath does so only to harm his own soul, and

whosoever fulfills what he has covenanted with God, soon will God grant him a great reward.

11. Those of the desert Arabs who stayed behind will say to you: "Our wealth and families distracted us; so, ask pardon for us." They say with their tongues what is not in their hearts; so, say (O Muhammad): "Who then can control anything for you from God if He intends to do you any harm, or if He intends to profit you? Nay! God is well-Aware of whatever you do.

12. "Nay! You thought that the Messenger would never return, nor would the believers return to their families, and that was made fair-seeming in your minds, and you even entertain an evil thought, and you were a people lost (in wickedness)."

13. And whosoever does not believe in God and His messenger, verily We have prepared for the disbelievers a flaming Fire.

14. And God's is the kingdom of the heavens and the earth; He forgives whom He pleases and chastises whom He wills; God is oft-Forgiving, Most Merciful.

15. Soon will those who stayed behind you, when you went forth, say when you march to take the spoils of war: "Let us follow you." They desire to change the Word of God. Say: "You shall never follow us; thus has God already said before." But they will say: "Nay! You are jealous of us." Nay! They understand but only a little.

16. Say to those desert Arabs who stayed behind: "You shall be called against a people of mighty prowess; you shall fight against them until they submit; then if you obey, God will grant you a goodly recompense, and if you turn back as you did before, He will chastise you with a painful chastisement."

17. No blame shall there be on the blind, the lame, nor the sick; whosoever obeys God and His messenger, He will admit him into gardens beneath which rivers flow, and whosoever turns back, He will chastise him with a painful chastisement.

18. Indeed God was well pleased with the believers when they pledged their fealty to you under the tree, as He did know what was in their hearts; so did He send down tran-

quility on them and rewarded them with a victory soon to come,

19. And gains great many which they will take, and God is ever-Prevalent, all-Wise.

20. God promised you great many spoils; He sped this (promise) to you, and withheld people from harming you, that it may be a sign to the believers, and that He may guide you on the Straight Path.

21. And other (gains) not within your reach yet; indeed God has encompassed them, and God has power over all things.

22. If those who disbelieve fight you, they would certainly turn back, then they would find neither protector nor a helper.

23. (Such has been) the course of God that came to pass before; you shall never find any change to the course of God.

24. And He it is Who withheld their hands from you and your hands from them in the valley of Mecca, after having granted you victory over them; God sees whatever you do.

25. They are the ones who disbelieved and obstructed you from reaching the Sacred Mosque and the offering (which was) prevented to reach its destination. Were it not for the believing men and women, not having known them, you might have trodden down, a crime would have afflicted you on their behalf without knowledge, that He may admit into His mercy whomsoever He pleases; had they been separated, We would certainly have chastised the disbelievers among them with a painful chastisement.

26. When those who disbelieved fostered zealotry in the hearts, the zealotry of (pagan) ignorance, God sent down tranquility upon His messenger and the believers, and made them bound to the word of piety, and well were they entitled to it, worthy of it; God well knows all things.

27. Indeed God has fulfilled for His messenger the vision with the truth that: "Certainly you shall enter the sacred Mosque, if God pleases, in security, heads shaved, (some) with their hair shortened, and without fear; He knew what you did not know, and He has ordained besides this a speedy victory.

28. He it is Who sent His messenger with the guidance and the true religion that He may make it prevail over all religions, and God suffices for a witness.

29. Muhammad is the messenger of God, and those are with him are vehement against the infidels, compassionate among themselves. You see them bowing down, prostrating in obeisance (to God), seeking grace from God and (His) pleasure. Their marks are in their faces showing the effect of their (frequent) prostrations; their similitude in the Torah, and in the Evangel, is like a seed which sends forth its stalk then strengthens it, then it becomes stout, and rises firmly upon its stem, delighting the sowers-that He may cause the disbelievers to be enraged at them; God has promised those who believe and do good deeds forgiveness and a great recompense.

The Private Chambers
(al-Hujurat)

In the name of God, the Beneficent, the Merciful.

1. O you who believe! Be not forward in the presence of God and His messenger and fear God; verily God is all-Hearing, all-Knowing.

2. O you who believe! Do not raise your voice above the Prophet's voice, do not speak loudly to him as you speak to one another lest your deeds should become null while you do not perceive.

3. Verily those who lower their voices in the presence of the messenger of God are the ones whose hearts God has tested for piety; theirs shall be forgiveness and a great reward.

4. Verily most of those who call out to you (O Muhammad) from outside the private chambers do not understand.

5. If they wait patiently till you come out to them, it would certainly be better for them, and verily God is oft-Forgiving, Most Merciful.

6. O you who believe! If a wicked man comes to you with some news, ascertain it carefully lest you harm some people in ignorance and then you repent for what you have

done.

7. And know that the messenger of God is in your midst; should he obey you in many matters, you would certainly be in distress, but God has endeared faith to you and made it attractive in your hearts and made disbelief and transgression abhorrent to you; these are they who are on the Right Guidance,

8. By grace from God and as a bounty; God is all-Knowing, all-Wise.

9. If two parties of the believers fall into an armed dispute, restore peace between them both; but if one of the two parties transgresses against the other, then you shall fight the one that transgresses till it complies with the Command of God; if it complies, then restore peace between the two parties with justice, and act justly; verily God loves the just ones.

10. The believers are brethren; so, make peace among the brethren and fear God that you may be blessed with mercy.

11. O you who believe! Let not some people laugh at other people who may be better than them, nor let women laugh at other women who haply may be better than the latter; find no fault with your own selves nor call one another by (bad) nicknames; evil is a bad name after his accepting the faith; whoso does not repent such conduct are surely the unjust ones.

12. O you who believe! Avoid much suspicion, for verily suspicion in some cases is a sin, and do not spy. Do not let some of you backbite others; does any of you like the eating of the flesh of his dead brother? You would surely abhor it, and fear God; verily God is oft-Returning, Most Merciful.

13. O people! Verily We have created you of a male and a female, and made you nations and tribes so that you may recognize each other; verily the most honoured among you in the sight of God is the most pious; verily God is all-Knowing, all-Aware.

14. The desert Arabs say: "We believe;" say: "You did not believe," but say: "We submit," for faith has not yet entered your hearts; and if you obey God and His messen-

ger, He will not belittle any of your deeds; verily God is oft-Forgiving, Most Merciful."

15. The believers are those who believe in God and His messenger; they do not doubt thereafter, and they strive with their wealth and lives in the way of God; they are the truthful ones.

16. Say: "Do you instruct God about your religion? While God knows everything in the heavens and the earth, and God knows all things?"

17. They impress on you as a favour that they have submitted (to God in Islam); say: "Lay no obligation upon me by your submission; rather, God lays an obligation upon you that He guided you to faith, if you are truthful.

18. "Verily God knows the unseen in the heavens and the earth, and God sees all that you do."

Qaf

In the name of God, the Beneficent, the Merciful.

1. Qaf; by the Glorious Qur'an,

2. Nay! They wonder that a warner from among their own selves has come to them; so, the disbelievers say: "This is an amazing thing!

3. "What! When we die and become dust (shall we still return?) This is a return far (from the truth)."

4. Indeed We know how much of them the earth reduces, and with Us is a written record that is secure.

5. Nay! They falsified the truth when it came to them, so they are in a confused condition.

6. Have they not looked up to the heavens and seen it adorned? No gaps are therein.

7. And the earth We have spread out, and We have cast therein mountains and caused therein the growth of all beautiful kinds (of vegetation),

8. To serve insight and as a reminder to every servant who turns (to his Lord).

9. We sent down water from the heavens with blessings, and We caused the growth thereby of gardens and grain which is harvested,

10. And the tall palm-trees with fruit-stalks, closely set

one above the other,

11. A sustenance for the servants, and We give life thereby to a dead town; thus will be the resurrection.

12. Before them, the people of Noah rejected, and so did the dwellers of ar-Rass, and the people of Thamud.

13. And so did Ad and Pharaoh, and the brethren of Lot,

14. And the dwellers of the wood, and the people of Tubba; all rejected the messengers; so, My promise (of the doom) proved true.

15. Were We then wearied out with the first creation? Yet they still are in doubt about a new creation.

16. Indeed We created man, and We know whatever thoughts whisper to him within himself, and We are nearer to him than his jugular vein.

17. Two (guardian angels) are appointed to scribe, seated, one on his right and one on his left.

18. Man shall not utter a word but what is already written by a trusted watcher.

19. And the stupor of death comes in truth: - "This is what you wished to shun."

20. The trumpet shall be blown; it is the promised Day.

21. Every soul shall come along with its (angel to) drive, and (an angel to) witness;

22. - "You were heedless of this; (since) now We have removed your veil from you, your sight today is sharp."

23. And his companion shall say: "This is (his record) ready with me."

24. - "Cast into Hell every ingrate rebel,

25. "Forbidder of good, transgressor, doubter,

26. "Who set up other gods with God; then cast him, you two, into the severe torment."

27. His companion will say: "O Lord! I did not lead him to rebellion, but he himself had gone far astray."

28. He shall say: "Do not wrangle in My presence; indeed I had sent beforehand warnings to you;

29. "The word with Me cannot be changed, nor am I unjust to the servants."

30. We will ask Hell on that day: "Are you filled up?" and it will answer: "Are there any more?"

31. And the garden (Paradise) shall be set aside, not far,

for the pious:

32. - "This is what you have been promised, for every one who turns to God and guards (his limits),

33. "Who fears the Beneficent God in secret and comes (to Him) with a devoted heart;

34. "Enter it in peace; this is the Day of eternity."

35. For them therein shall be whatever they desire, and with Us is yet even more.

36. How many a generation did We destroy before them who were mightier than them in power? They wandered throughout the land; was there any place of refuge for them?

37. Verily in this is a reminder for him who has a heart or listens with a mindful presence.

38. Indeed We created the heavens and the earth and what is between them twain in six periods and no fatigue ever touched Us.

39. So be patient (O Muhammad) about what they say, and celebrate the praise of your Lord before sunrise and before sunset.

40. And during the night, glorify Him, and after the prostrations.

41. And listen for the day whereon the crier shall cry from a near place,

42. The Day when they hear the cry in truth is the Day of coming forth (from the graves).

43. Verily We give life and cause death, and all shall return to Us.

44. On the Day when the earth is cleft asunder under them, they will hasten; their gathering together is easy for Us.

45. We best know what they say, and you are not to compel them; therefore, remind through the (medium of the) Qur'an whoever fears My threat.

The Scatterers
(al-Dariyat)

In the name of God, the Beneficent, the Merciful.

1. By the scatterers that scatter,

2. Then by those that bear their load,

32. Or is it that their deliberations bid them do this, or are they an inordinate people?

33. Or do they say: "He has forged it (Qur'an)"? Nay! They do not believe.

34. Let them then bring a discourse like it, if they are truthful.

35. Or were they created by nothing? Or are they themselves the creators?

36. Or did they create the heavens and the earth? Nay! They have no certainty.

37. Or are the treasures of your Lord with them, or do they hold absolute authority?

38. Or is there for them a ladder whereby they can listen (to the angels)?

39. Or are daughters His and sons yours?!

40. Or do you ask them for any recompense (so much so) that they are burdened with the weight of debt?

41. Or is the unseen with them and they write it down?

42. Or do they intend to lay snares for you? But those who disbelieve are themselves the snared ones.

43. Or is there a god for them other than God? Hallowed is God from what they associate with Him.

44. And if they see a portion of the heavens coming down, they say: "Clouds piled up."

45. Leave them then until they encounter the day of theirs wherein they shall be smitten (with terror) to swoon,

46. A day wherein their stratagem shall not avail them aught, nor shall they be helped.

47. And verily there shall be a chastisement for those who did injustice besides that, yet most of them do not know it.

48. And wait patiently for the Command of your Lord, for verily you are before Our Eyes; and celebrate the praise of your Lord when you rise.

49. And in the night, too, celebrate His glory, and at the setting of the stars.

The Star
(an-Najm)

In the name of God, the Beneficent, the Merciful.

1. By the star when it goes down,

2. Your companion (Muhammad) does not err, nor is he led astray;

3. Nor does he speak of his own inclination;

4. It is naught but a revealed revelation.

5. The one mighty in power taught him.

6. The one endued with wisdom; hence he (stately) appeared,

7. While he was in the highest horizon,

8. Then he drew nigh and became so close to him,

9. As close as the distance between two bows or nigher still,

10. Then He revealed to His servant what He revealed.

11. His heart did not reject what he saw.

12. Do you then dispute with him as to what he saw?

13. And indeed he saw him at another descent,

14. At the sidra (lote-tree) of the all-Comprehensive Terminus,

15. Nigh to it is the garden-abode.

16. When the sidra is covered by that which covers it;

17. Neither did his eye dazzle, nor did it rebel.

18. Indeed he saw of the greatest signs of his Lord.

19. Do you then see the Lat and the Uzza?

20. And Manat, the third one, too?

21. Are the males yours and the females His?

22. This indeed is an unjust division;

23. They are nothing but (mere) names which you and your fathers have named. God sent no authority for them. They follow but a conjecture and what their own selves are inclined to; indeed, right guidance has now come to them from their Lord.

24. Shall man have whatever he wishes?

25. Nay! God's is the life hereafter, and the former one.

26. How many an angel in heaven are those whose intercession is of no avail at all save that whom God permits and with whom He is pleased?

27. Verily those who do not believe in the hereafter give the angels female names.

28. They have no knowledge of it at all; they follow nothing but a conjecture; verily conjecture avails the truth nothing at all.

29. Turn aside, therefore, from him who turns his back against Our reminder and desires nothing but the life of this world,

30. That is the last reach of their knowledge; verily your Lord knows best who is astray from His Path and He knows best who is guided aright.

31. And God's is everything in the heavens and in the earth that He may reward those who do evil for what they did, and that He may reward those who do good with what is best.

32. Those who do avoid the great ones of the sins and shameful deeds save accidentally; verily your Lord is (the Lord of) vast forgiveness; He knows best about you when He raised you from the earth and when you are embryos in the wombs of your mothers; so assert no purity of your own selves; He knows best he who guards (himself against evil).

33. Have you then seen the one who has turned his back?

34. He gives a little and withholds (more).

35. Is the knowledge of the unseen with him?

36. Or has he not been told of what is in the scriptures of Moses?

37. And of Abraham who fully discharged his mission?

38. That no bearer of a burden shall bear the burden of another,

39. And that there is none for man save what he strives for,

40. And that his striving shall soon be scrutinized.

41. Then he shall be rewarded to the fullest measure,

42. And that to your Lord is the end of all,

43. And verily He it is Who causes one to laugh or to weep,

44. And that He it is Who causes death and grants life,

45. And He it is Who creates pairs, male and female,

46. From the sperm when it is discharged;

47. And that on Him (alone) is the raising for a second

time,

48. And that He it is Who enriches and bestows contentment,

49. And that He it is Who is the Lord of Sirius,

50. And that He destroyed (the mighty) Ad of ancient times,

51. And He did not spare Thamud,

52. Nor the people of Noah before them; verily they were the most unjust, the most transgressing.

53. And the One Who overthrew the overthrown cities is but He;

54. So, they were covered with whatever covered them,

55. About which of the bounties of your Lord do you then dispute?

56. This (Muhammad) is a warner (like those) of the old times.

57. The Hour (of reckoning) ever draws nigh;

58. None is there to lay it bare other than God.

59. Do you wonder even at this statement?

60. And you laugh and do not weep?

61. And you still sport (indifferently)?

62. Prostrate, therefore, in obeisance to God and worship Him alone.

The Moon
(al-Qamar)

In the name of God, the Beneficent, the Merciful.

1. Nigh has come the Hour (of reckoning) and the moon has been rent asunder,

2. And if they see a sign, they turn away and call it transient sorcery.

3. They reject and follow their vain inclinations, and every affair is unalterably fixed.

4. Indeed some of the tidings have come to them wherein there is restraint (from evil),

5. Consummate wisdom, yet the warnings did not avail them aught.

6. So withdraw yourself (O Muhammad) from them on the day when the caller calls them to the hard task (of reck-

oning),

7. With their eyes cast down, they shall go forth from their graves as if they were locusts scattered,

8. Hastening to the caller. The disbelievers shall say: "This is a hard day!"

9. Before them did the people of Noah reject Our Servant (Noah) and called him mad, and he was (even) driven out.

10. So he called upon his Lord: "Verily I am overcome (by these people); so, give help."

11. We therefore opened the gates of heaven with water pouring down;

12. And We caused the earth to gush forth with springs, and the water met together for a destined purpose.

13. And We bore him on (an ark) made of planks and nails.

14. It floated under (the supervision of) Our eyes, a recompense for those who had been rejected.

15. And indeed We have left it (ark) as a sign, but is there any who remembers?

16. How (great) was then My chastisement and warning?

17. Indeed We have made the Qur'an easy (to memorize), but is there any who remembers?

18. The people of Ad rejected the truth, then how (great) was My chastisement and warning?

19. Verily We sent on them a violent wind on a day of constant ill-luck,

20. Flinging the people away as if they were uprooted palm- trunks.

21. How (great) was then My chastisement and warning?

22. And indeed We have made the Qur'an easy (to memorize), but is there any who remembers?

23. (The people of) Thamud called the warners liars,

24. They said: "A single man from among our own selves? And we are to follow him? Verily then we shall go astray and be in distress;

25. "Is it that reminding has been bestowed upon him (alone), of all people among us? Nay! He is a great liar, an

insolent one!"

26. Soon shall they come to know, tomorrow, who is the liar, the insolent.

27. Verily We are going to send the she-camel as a trial for them; so watch them (O Our Messenger Salih) and be patient.

28. And make them aware beforehand that the water is to be divided between them; every drinking share shall be witnessed.

29. But they called upon their companion, and pursued (the she- camel) and hamstrung her.

30. How (great) was then My chastisement and warning?

31. Verily We sent upon them a single blast, and they became like dry stubble used by a fencer in a fence.

32. Indeed We have made the Qur'an easy (to memorize), but is there any who remembers?

33. The people of Lot rejected the warners.

34. Verily We sent upon them a stone-storm, save the followers of Lot; We saved them by early dawn,

35. A bounty from Us; thus do We recompense him who gives thanks.

36. And indeed he warned them of Our severe seizure, but they disputed about the warner.

37. Indeed they demanded him of his own guests (to satisfy their own sinful desires), so We blinded their eye (saying): "Taste then My chastisement and warning!"

38. And indeed a lasting chastisement dawned upon them in the morning;

39. - "Now taste My chastisement and warning!"

40. And indeed We have made the Qur'an easy (to memorize), but is there any who remembers?

41. The warners came to the people of Pharaoh.

42. They rejected all Our signs, so We seized them after the manner of the One, the ever-Prevalent, the Almighty.

43. Are your disbelievers (O Meccans) better people than these? Or is there an exemption for you in the sacred scriptures?

44. Or do they say: "We are a host joined together to help each other"?

45. Soon shall the host be routed, and they shall turn their backs fleeing.

46. Nay! The Hour (of reckoning) is their promised time, and the Hour shall be most grievous and bitter.

47. Verily the guilty ones are straying and are in distress.

48. On that day, they shall be dragged upon their faces into the Fire: "Taste the touch of Hell!"

49. Verily We have created everything according to a determined measure.

50. And Our command is but one word: "Be!" and it becomes, like the twinkling of the eye.

51. Indeed We have destroyed the like of you, but is there any to receive the warning?

52. Everything they have done is in the books (of deeds);

53. Every matter, small and big, is recorded in writing.

54. Verily the pious shall be in gardens and rivers.

55. In the seat of truth, with the Sovereign, the omni-Potent.

The Beneficient
(ar-Rahman)

In the name of God, the Beneficent, the Merciful.

1. (God is) the Beneficent,

2. He taught the Qur'an;

3. He created man;

4. He taught him (the power of) expression;

5. The sun and the moon follow the (prescribed) timings,

6. And the herbs and trees prostrate in obeisance,

7. And the heavens He raised high, and placed the scales,

8. So that you may not transgress the scales,

9. And you may maintain the measure with justice and do not cut the scale short.

10. And the earth He has made for (His living) creatures.

11. Therein is fruit and palms having sheathed clusters.

12. And corn with leaves and stalks, and with

sweet-smelling herbs;

13. Which, then, of the bounties of your Lord will you twain (man and jinn) reject?

14. He created man from dry clay like that of earthen vessels,

15. And He created the jinn of a flame of fire.

16. Which, then, of the bounties of your Lord will you twain (man and jinn) reject?

17. Lord of the two easts and the two wests;

18. Which, then, of the bounties of your Lord will you twain (man and jinn) reject?

19. He has let loose the two seas that they may flow together, meeting each other.

20. Between them He has caused a barrier, that they may not encroach one upon the other;

21. Which, then, of the bounties of your Lord will you twain (man and jinn) reject?

22. Pearls and corals come forth out of the twain;

23. Which, then, of the bounties of your Lord will you twain (man and jinn) reject?

24. And His are the ships towering up at the sea like mountains,

25. Which, then, of the bounties of your Lord will you twain (man and jinn) reject?

26. Everyone upon its (earth's) face shall perish,

27. But forever will the Face of your Lord, the Glorious, the Gracious, remain.

28. Which, then, of the bounties of your Lord will you twain (man and jinn) reject?

29. All those in the heavens and the earth beseech Him; every day He is in a (new) splendorous manifestation.

30. Which, then, of the bounties of your Lord will you twain (man and jinn) reject?

31. Soon will We attend to you, O you two groups (man and jinn).

32. Which, then, of the bounties of your Lord will you twain (man and jinn) reject?

33. O people of the jinn and humans! If you can penetrate the bounds of the heavens and the earth, then do penetrate through them, but you cannot do so except with (Our)

authority.

34. Which, then, of the bounties of your Lord will you twain (man and jinn) reject?

35. On you both shall the flames of fire and molten brass be sent, then you shall not be able to protect yourselves.

36. Which, then, of the bounties of your Lord will you twain (man and jinn) reject?

37. And when the firmament is rent asunder, becoming red like tanned hide.

38. Which, then, of the bounties of your Lord will you twain (man and jinn) reject?

39. And on that Day, no man or jinn shall be asked of his sin;

40. Which, then, of the bounties of your Lord will you twain (man and jinn) reject?

41. The guilty ones shall be recognized by their marks, and they shall be seized by their forelocks and feet.

42. Which, then, of the bounties of your Lord will you twain (man and jinn) reject?

43. This is Hell in which the guilty ones used to disbelieve.

44. They shall run between it and boiling water;

45. Which, then, of the bounties of your Lord will you twain (man and jinn) reject?

46. And for him who fears the time of standing before his Lord are two gardens.

47. Which, then, of the bounties of your Lord will you twain (man and jinn) reject?

48. With over-branching trees.

49. Which, then, of the bounties of your Lord will you twain (man and jinn) reject?

50. In both of them are two fountains flowing.

51. Which, then, of the bounties of your Lord will you twain (man and jinn) reject?

52. In each of them are two kinds of every fruit.

53. Which, then, of the bounties of your Lord will you twain (man and jinn) reject?

54. Reclining on beds, the inner coverings of which are silk brocades; the fruit of the gardens shall be nigh.

55. Which, then, of the bounties of your Lord will you

twain (man and jinn) reject?

56. Therein shall be damsels with retiring glances whom no human nor jinn had ever touched before.

57. Which, then, of the bounties of your Lord will you twain (man and jinn) reject?

58. As though they were rubies and pearls.

59. Which, then, of the bounties of your Lord will you twain (man and jinn) reject 60. Is the recompense for good any but good?

61. Which, then, of the bounties of your Lord will you twain (man and jinn) reject?

62. And besides these (two) are two other gardens.

63. Which, then, of the bounties of your Lord will you twain (man and jinn) reject?

64. Dark green in colour.

65. Which, then, of the bounties of your Lord will you twain (man and jinn) reject?

66. In them both are two springs gushing forth.

67. Which, then, of the bounties of your Lord will you twain (man and jinn) reject?

68. In both are fruits, palms, and pomegranates.

69. Which, then, of the bounties of your Lord will you twain (man and jinn) reject?

70. In them are virtuous women, beautiful ones.

71. Which, then, of the bounties of your Lord will you twain (man and jinn) reject?

72. Fair ones, restrained, in pavilions.

73. Which, then, of the bounties of your Lord will you twain (man and jinn) reject?

74. No human being nor jinn had ever touched them before.

75. Which, then, of the bounties of your Lord will you twain (man and jinn) reject?

76. Reclining on green cushions and beautiful carpets.

77. Which, then, of the bounties of your Lord will you twain (man and jinn) reject?

78. Hallowed is the name of your Lord, Lord of Glory and Grace!

The Inevitable Event
(al-Waqi'ah)

In the name of God, the Beneficent, the Merciful.

1. When the (momentous) Event takes place,
2. No belying there shall be for its happening.
3. Abasing, Exalting.
4. When the earth is shaken with a (tremendous) shaking,
5. And the mountains crumbled a terrible crumbling,
6. And they shall become scattered dust,
7. And you shall be three kinds:
8. Then the people of the right - O What (happiness awaits) the people of the right!
9. And the people of the left-Ah! Wretched are the people of the left!
10. And (thirdly) the foremost (in faith and virtue) shall be the first (to receive their reward),
11. These are they who shall be brought closer (to God),
12. In the gardens of bliss:
13. Many from the first (group),
14. And a few of the latter (third) one;
15. On couches encrusted, bedecked,
16. Reclining face to face,
17. Around shall go about (serving them) youths of unchanging bloom,
18. With goblets and ewers, and a cup of pure drink,
19. Their brows ache not from it, nor their sense fails,
20. And fruits of any that they choose,
21. And the meat of fowls of what they like,
22. And the houris (maidens pure) with large, lustrous (lovely) eyes,
23. Like pearls hidden (in their shells):
24. (Such is) the recompense for what they used to do.
25. They shall hear no frivolity therein, nor any taint of sin,
26. (None) save: "Peace!" and ever "Peace!" talked of.
27. And the people of the right, Oh what (happiness awaits) the people of the right!
28. Amid thornless lote-trees,

29. And banana-trees (with fruits) piled one above the other,

30. And shade spreading out,

31. And water flowing,

32. And abundant fruit,

33. Neither failing (by season) nor forbidden.

34. And on thrones exalted.

35. Verily We have created them (maidens) a special creation.

36. And made them pure virgins,

37. Lovable (by nature), of equal age,

38. For the people of the right.

39. Many of the first group,

40. And many of the latter one.

41. As for the people of the left, - Ah! What (wretches) are the people of the left!

42. In scorching wind and scalding water,

43. In the shadow of a black smoke,

44. Neither cool nor graceful.

45. Verily they were before that extravagant (spend-thrift).

46. They used to persist in heinous sins,

47. They used to say: "When we die and become dust and bones, shall we even then be raised up again?

48. "And our fathers of yore, too?"

49. Say (O Muhammad): "Verily the ancient, and the later ones,

50. "Shall all be gathered together, to the tryst of the known Day."

51. Then verily you who went astray and falsified,

52. Shall certainly eat of the tree of Zaqqum,

53. And fill your bellies therewith,

54. And drink over it of boiling water,

55. Then you shall drink of it as thirsty camels drink.

56. This shall be their repast on the Day of reckoning.

57. It is We Who created you; why then do you not admit the truth?

58. Have you seen what (sperms) you emit?

59. Is it you who create it, or are We the Creators?

60. It is We Who have decreed death among you, and

We are not to be frustrated.

61. To Us is the changing of your forms, and raising you in forms that you do not know.

62. And indeed you know the first growth; why then do not you reflect?

63. Have you seen what you sow?

64. Is it you who grow it or are We the growers?

65. Had We willed, We could have crumbled it to dry bits, and you would be left only to lament.

66. (Saying): "Verily we have been burdened with loss!

67. "Nay! We are deprived (of benefits)."

68. Have you seen the water which you drink?

69. Is it you who send it down from the heavens or are We its senders?

70. Had We willed, We would have made it salty; why then do not you offer thanks?

71. Have you seen the Fire which you kindle?

72. Is it you who produce its tree, or are We the producers?

73. It is We Who have made it a reminder and a provision for the needy ones.

74. So hallow is the name of your Lord, the Great.

75. Nay! I swear by the setting of the stars,

76. And it is a great oath, only if you knew,

77. That is an honourable Qur'an,

78. Embedded in a Book,

79. None touch it save the purified ones.

80. Revealed by the Lord of the worlds.

81. Do you then hold even this statement with scorn?

82. And have you made your sustenance that you should declare it false?

83. Why then do you not help when (the soul of the dying man) comes up to the throat?

84. And you then (remain) only gazing.

85. And We are nearer to him than you, yet you do not perceive Us.

86. Why, then, if you are not in bondage (to Us),

87. Do you not send the soul back, if you are truthful?

88. Then if he is of those drawn nigh (to God),

89. (For him is then) rest and happiness, and a delightful

garden,

90. And if he is of the people of the right,

91. Then peace be unto you from the (other) people of the right.

92. And if he is of those who have falsified, staying,

93. Then he shall have an entertainment of boiling water,

94. And the burning of Hell-fire,

95. Verily this is the certain truth.

96. Hallow therefore the name of your Lord, the Great.

Iron

(al-Hadid)

In the name of God, the Beneficent, the Merciful.

1. Everything in the heavens and the earth celebrates the praise of God; He is the ever-Prevalent, the all-Wise.

2. His is the Kingdom of the heavens and the earth; He grants life and causes death, and He has power over all things.

3. He is the first and the last, the manifest and the hidden; He is the Knower of all things.

4. He it is Who created the heavens and the earth in six days (periods), then He firmly established Himself over the Throne; He knows whatever enters the earth and whatever goes forth from it, and whatever descends from the heavens and whatever goes up into it; He is with you wherever you may be; God is the Seer of whatever you do.

5. His is the Kingdom of the heavens and the earth, and to God (alone) are all affairs returned.

6. He causes the night to enter upon the day, and causes the day to enter upon the night, and He is the Knower of whatever in the hearts.

7. So believe in God and His Messenger (Muhammad) and spend (in charity) of what He has made you successors thereof; for whosoever among you believes and spends (charitably), for them is a great recompense.

8. What reason do you have that you do not believe in God, while the Messenger invites you to believe in your Lord and has indeed taken a covenant from you if you are

believers?

9. He it is Who sends His servant manifest signs so that He may bring you out of the darkness (of infidelity) into the light (of faith); verily God is the Most Kind and Merciful unto you.

10. And what reasons do you have that you do not spend in the Way of God, while God's is the heritage of the heavens and the earth? Alike are not among you those who spend before the victory and fought, and those who are more exalted in rank than those who spent and fought afterwards; to all has God promised goodness; verily God is all-Aware of whatever you do.

11. Who is he who would loan God a goodly loan? So that He may double it for him, and for him shall be a noble recompense.

12. The Day you see the faithful men and women with their light running before them, and on their right hand (shall be given) glad tidings for you of that Day: gardens beneath which rivers flow to abide therein; that is the great achievement.

13. On that Day, the hypocritical men and women will say to those who believe: "Tarry for us so that we may borrow some of your own light." It shall be said to them: "Turn back and seek light!" So there will be a wall set between them with a door therein; there shall be mercy therein, and the outside shall have the chastisement.

14. They will cry out to them: "Were we not with you?" They shall answer: "Yea! But you cast yourselves into temptation, and you waited (for us to be beguiled) and you doubted (God's warning), and your own vain desires deceived you about God's decree, and the Deceiver deceived you about God."

15. So, this Day no ransom shall be accepted from those who disbelieved. Your abode shall be the Fire; it is your guardian, and what a wretched resort it shall be!

16. Has not time come yet for those who believe that their hearts become humble for the remembrance of God and for what has been revealed of the truth? They should not be like those who were given the book before, but when ages passed over them, it only hardened their hearts, and

many of them are transgressors.

17. Know that God enlivens the earth after its death; indeed We have made the signs clear to you that you may understand.

18. Verily charitable men and women, and those who offer a goodly loan to God, it shall be doubled for them, and a noble reward shall be theirs.

19. Those who believe in God and His Messenger are the truthful, and the witnesses with their Lord; for them shall be their recompense and their light; those who disbelieve and falsify Our signs are the inmates of Hell.

20. Know that the life of this world is only sport, play, and boasting, and the lustful are vying in the multiplying of wealth and children, like rain therewith vegetation springs up, pleasing the tillers; then it withers away, and you see it becoming yellow; then it becomes stubble, crumbling down, and in the hereafter is a severe chastisement and (also) forgiveness from God and (His) pleasure; the life of this world is but means of illusion.

21. Vie in hastening to forgiveness from your Lord and to a garden whose extent is like that of the heavens and the earth (combined) prepared for those who believe in God and His messengers; that is the grace of God; He bestows it upon whomsoever He pleases; God is the Lord of Mighty Grace.

22. No disaster befalls the earth save it is in a Book before We cause it to be; verily that is easy for God,

23. Lest you should distress yourselves for what escapes you, and be over-joyous for what He has granted you; God does not love any arrogant boaster,

24. Those who are niggardly and enjoin upon people niggardliness; and whosoever turns away (from charity), then verily God is He Who is self-Sufficient, Most Praise-worthy.

25. Indeed We sent Our messengers with clear proofs, and We sent down with them the Book and the Scale that people might establish themselves in justice; We sent down iron wherein is latent mighty power and also benefits for mankind, and that God may test who it is that will help Him and His messengers in secret; verily God is the Almighty, the ever- Prevalent.

26. Indeed We sent Noah and Abraham, and We endowed upon their seed the prophethood and the Book, so among them are some who are rightly guided, and most of them are transgressors.

27. Then We made Our messengers follow in their footsteps, and We sent after them Jesus son of Mary, and We gave him the Evangel and put into the hearts of those who followed him kindness and compassion; but (as to) the monastic life, they invented it themselves. We never prescribed it upon them save seeking the pleasure of God, and this they did not observe as they should have been, and We gave those of them who believed their due recompense; but many of them are transgressors.

28. O you who believe! Fear God and believe in His Messenger; He will give you two-fold of His mercy. He will appoint you a light wherein you shall walk, and He will forgive you; God is oft-Forgiving, Most Merciful.

29. So that the people of the Book may know that they control naught of the grace of God, and that God's grace is in His Hand; He bestows it upon whomsoever He pleases; God is the Lord of Mighty Grace.

The Pleading Woman
(al-Mujadilah)

In the name of God, the Beneficent, the Merciful.

1. God has indeed heard the statement of the woman pleading about her husband and petitions God; verily God hears the contention of both of you; God is all-Hearing, all-Seeing.

2. Those of you who abandon any of their wives through zihar, their wives are certainly not their mothers. Their mothers are only those who gave birth to them, and they certainly utter a word that is hateful and false; verily God is pardoning, oft-Forgiving.

3. Those who abandon any of their wives through zihar and then recall what they have uttered may free a captive before touching each other, that you may be admonished; verily God is well-Aware of whatever you do.

4. But whosoever finds no means (to do so), then he

may fast for two consecutive months before touching each other. Whosoever is not able to do so shall feed sixty needy ones; that is so in order that you may believe in God and His Messenger; these are the bounds set by God; as for the disbelievers, there shall be a painful chastisement.

5. Verily those who oppose God and His Messenger shall be humiliated as those before them were, and indeed We have sent down clear signs, and for the disbelievers there shall be a humiliating torment.

6. On the Day when God raises them all to life and informs them of what they did, God has encompassed (everything) in His record; while they might have forgotten it, and God is a Witness over all things.

7. Do not they see that God knows whatever is in the heavens and the earth? Nowhere does any secret counsel between three persons take place except that He is their fourth, nor between five except that He is their sixth, nor between less than that nor more except that He is with them wherever they may be. Then He will inform them of whatever they did on the Day of Judgment; verily God well knows all things.

8. Do you not see those who have been forbidden secret counsels, yet they return to what has been forbidden and they (still) hold secret counsels to sin and revolt and in disobedience of the Messenger. When they come to you, they do not greet you as God greets you, and they ask themselves: "Why does God not chastise us for what we say?" Hell suffices them; they shall enter it-what a wretched destination it is!

9. O you who believe! When you counsel each other, do not counsel in secrecy, nor should you counsel to sinning and revolting and disobeying the Messenger, but counsel among yourselves for goodness, and restrain yourselves; fear God to Whom you shall all be gathered.

10. Secret counsels are only Satan's, that he may cause mischief to those who believe, but he shall not harm them in the least except with the permission of God; upon God alone depend those who believe.

11. O you who believe! When it is said to you "Make room in your assemblies," then do make room. God will

make room for you. And when it is said to you to rise up, then do rise up, God will exalt in ranks those who believe among you, and those who have been granted knowledge, and God is all-Aware of whatever you do.

12. O you who believe! When you (wish to) consult in private with the Messenger, then offer something in charity before your consultation; that is better for you and purer. But if you find no means to do so, then verily God is oft-Forgiving, Most Merciful.

13. Do you restrain against giving alms before your consultation? Since you did not do it, and God turned to you (with mercy), then keep up (regular) prayer, and pay zakat and obey God and His Messenger; God is all-Aware of what you do.

14. Have you not seen those who befriend the ones on whom the Wrath of God has fallen? They are neither of your party nor are they of theirs; they swear for falsehood while they know (what you do).

15. For them God has prepared a severe penalty; verily evil is what they do.

16. They make their oaths a shield, and they obstruct (others) from the Way of God; so, for them shall be a humiliating torment.

17. Never shall they avail aught against God, nor their wealth nor children. They are fellows of the Fire; they shall forever abide therein.

18. On the Day when God raises them all, they will then swear to Him as they (now) swear to you, and they deem that it will avail them. Nay! Verily they are liars.

19. Satan has gained hold of them, so he made them forget the remembrance of God. They are Satan's party. Beware! Verily the party of Satan are the losers.

20. Those who are opposed to God and His Messenger will surely be most humiliated.

21. God has decreed: "I shall prevail; I and My Messenger." Verily God is the Almighty, the ever- Prevalent.

22. You shall find no people who believe in God and the hereafter to befriend those who oppose God and His Messenger, be they even their own fathers, sons, brothers, or kinsmen; they are those upon whose hearts God has in-

scribed faith, and He has strengthened them with a spirit
from Him; He will admit them into gardens beneath which
rivers flow. They shall abide therein with God well-pleased
with them, and they will be well-pleased with Him. They are
the party of God. Be it known that surely the party of God
alone shall be the successful ones.

The Gathering
(al-Hashr)

In the name of God, the Beneficent, the Merciful.

1. Everything in the heavens and the earth praises the
glory of God; He is the ever-Prevalent, the all-Wise.

2. He it is Who caused those who disbelieved from
among the people of the Book to go out from their homes to
the first banishment. You deemed not that they would go
out, while they thought that their fortresses would protect
them against God, but (the Wrath of) God came upon them
from whence they did not look for Him and caused (such)
terror into their hearts that they demolished their homes
with their own hands and the hands of the believers; therefore, get warned O you who have eyes!

3. Were it not that God had decreed against them the
exile, certainly He would have chastised them in this world;
and for them in the hereafter shall be the chastisement of the
Fire.

4. That is so because they opposed God and His Messenger, and whosoever opposes God, then verily God is
severe in retribution.

5. Whatever you cut down of palm-trees or spare it
standing upon its roots is only by God's permission, and
that He may put the transgressors to shame.

6. And whatever God bestows upon His Messenger
from them, while you make no expedition with cavalry or
camelry, God grants authority to His messengers over
whomsoever He pleases, and God has power over all things.

7. Whatever God has bestowed upon His Messenger
(taken) from the people of the towns belongs to God, to the
Messenger, to his (Prophet's) kindred, the orphans, the needy
and the wayfarer, so that it may not circulate among the rich

among you, and whatever the Messenger gives you, accept it, and from whatever he prevents you, stay away (therefrom), and fear God; verily God is severe in retribution.

8. (And also) for the poor immigrants, those who were expelled from their homes and possessions seeking God's Grace and Pleasure, and aiding God and His Messenger; these are the truthful ones.

9. And those (who believed) before them and had made (their) homes (in Medina) and are (firm) in faith, love those who have fled to them and find in their hearts no need for what has been given to them, and they even prefer them over their own selves, though their own lot is poverty. Whosoever is saved from the niggardliness of his own self is surely the successful one.

10. And they who come after them say: "O Lord! Forgive us and our brethren who have preceded us in (accepting) faith, and create not in our hearts any ill-will to those who believe. Lord! Verily You are the ever-Kind, the all-Merciful."

11. Have you not seen those who are hypocrites? They say to those of their brethren who disbelieve from among the people of the Book: "If you are driven out, we shall certainly go with you, and we will not obey anyone at all in as much as you are concerned, and if you are fought, we will certainly help you." God bears witness that they are liars.

12. Nay! If they were driven out, they will not go out with them, and if they are fought, they would not help them. Even if they help them, they will certainly turn their backs (fleeing), then they shall not themselves be helped.

13. Of surety you are more vehement in being feared in their hearts than God, for they are people who do not understand.

14. They will not fight you together except in fortified towns or from behind walls. Their fighting among themselves is severe; you may deem them united, but their hearts are divided. That is so because they are people who do not understand.

15. They are like those who preceded lately, (who also) tasted the evil result of their own deeds, and for them is a painful chastisement.

16. Like Satan who says to man: "Disbelieve!" and when he disbelieves, he says: "Verily I dissociate myself from you. Verily I fear God, Lord of the worlds."

17. So the end of both of those two (Satan and disbelievers) is that the two shall be in the Fire to abide therein forever, and that shall be the recompense of the unjust.

18. O you who believe! Fear God! Let every soul (carefully) look well to what (provision) it has sent forth for the morrow, and fear God; verily God is all-Aware of whatever you do.

19. Do not be like those who forsook God. So He made them forsake their own selves; those are the transgressors.

20. Equal are not the fellows of the Fire and the dwellers of the Garden. The dwellers of the Garden are they who are the successful.

21. Had We revealed this Qur'an on a mountain, you would have certainly seen it (mountain) humbling itself, and being rent asunder for fear of God. And We set forth these similitudes to mankind that they may reflect.

22. He is God; there is no god but He, Knower of the unseen and the seen; He is the Beneficent, the Most Merciful.

23. He is God; there is no God but He, the King, the Holy, the Peace-loving, the Guardian, the ever-Prevalent, the Supreme, the Great Absolute! Hallowed is God above what they associate with Him.

24. He is God, the Creator, Maker, Fashioner; His are all the excellent names; hallows Him everything in the heavens and the earth; He is the ever-Prevalent, the all-Wise.

The Woman Put To Test
(al-Mumtahenah)

In the name of God, the Beneficent, the Merciful.

1. O you who believe! Take not My foes and yours for friends: offering them your love while they deny what has come unto you of the truth, driving the Messenger and your own selves out for believing in God, your Lord. If you go forth striving in My Path and seeking My Pleasure (do not take them for friends by) manifesting to them your love in secret, and I know best what you conceal and what you

reveal. Whosoever of you does so, he has indeed strayed from the Straight Path.

2. If they find any opportunity against you, they will antagonize you and will stretch forth their hands and tongues with evil to you, and they anxiously desire that you too should disbelieve.

3. Neither your relations nor your children shall avail you aught on the day of reckoning; He (alone) will decide between you, and God sees all that you do.

4. Indeed, there is for you a good pattern of Abraham and those with him. They said to their people: "Verily We dissociate ourselves from you and what you worship other than God. We renounce you, and enmity and hatred have prevailed between us forever until you believe in God alone." But not what Abraham said to his father: "I shall certainly seek forgiveness for you, and I own nothing for you from God. Lord! On you (alone) do we rely, and to You (only) do we return! And to You (alone) is our final return.

5. "Lord! Do not expose us to a trial for those who disbelieve, and forgive us, O Lord! Verily You are the ever-Prevalent, the all-Wise."

6. Indeed there is for you in them a good pattern (of conduct), for him who hopes in God and the Last day, and whosoever turns away, then verily God is self-Sufficient, Most Praised.

7. Maybe that God will cause friendship between you and those whom you take to be enemies among them; God is all-Powerful, and God is oft-Forgiving, Most Merciful.

8. God does not forbid you regarding those who have not fought you due to your religion, nor drove you out of your homes, if you show them kindness, and be just to them; verily God loves the just ones.

9. God only forbids you regarding those who waged war against you in the matter of your religion and drove you out of your own homes and aided in your expulsion, that you make friends with them. Whosoever makes friends with them are surely the unjust ones.

10. O you who believe! When believing women-refugees come to you, then ascertain them; God best knows their faith, and if you find them to be believing women, then do

not return them to the disbelievers. These women are neither lawful for them nor are those men lawful for them. And give them what they have spent, and no blame shall be on you should you marry them having paid them their dowries. Hold no ties of marriage to the disbelieving women, and demand what (dowries) you have spent, and let them demand for what (dowries) they have spent. This is the Decree of God; He enforces it among you, and God is all-Knowing, all-Wise.

11. If any of your wives deserts you and join the disbelievers, and thereafter you have your turn (of triumph), then give those whose wives have deserted the equivalent of what (dowries) they have spent, and fear God in Whom you believe.

12. O (Our) Prophet (Muhammad)! When believing women come to you pledging that they will associate none with God, and that they will not steal, nor commit adultery, nor kill their own children, nor utter slander nor falsehood which they had forged themselves between their hands and feet and will not disobey you in what is fair, then accept their pledge and ask God's forgiveness for them; verily God is oft-Forgiving, Most Merciful.

13. O you who believe! Do not befriend a people with whom God is angry; indeed they despair of their hereafter as the disbelievers despair of those in the graves.

The Rank
(as-Saff)

In the name of God, the Beneficent, the Merciful.

1. Whatever is in the heavens and the earth hallows God, and He is the ever-Prevalent, the all-Wise.

2. O you who believe! Why do you say what you yourselves do not do?

3. Most hateful it is to God that you say what you do not do.

4. Verily God loves those who fight in His Way in ranks as if they were an unbreakable metalloid wall.

5. Behold! Moses said to his people: "O my people! Why do you harm me? While indeed you know that I am a mes-

senger of God to you?" But when (yet) they went astray, God too allowed their hearts to stray, and God does not guide the people who transgress.

6. When Jesus the son of Mary said: "O children of Israel! Verily I am a messenger of God to you confirming what is before you of the Torah and bearing the glad tidings of a Messenger who shall come after me whose name is Ahmed (i.e. Muhammad)," but when he (Ahmed) came to them, they said: "This is a manifest sorcery!"

7. Who is more unjust than he who forges a lie against God while he is invited to Islam? God does not guide the unjust people.

8. They intend to put out the Light of God with their own mouths, but God insists on perfecting His Light, though averse the disbelievers may be.

9. He it is Who has sent His Messenger (Muhammad) with the guidance (Qur'an) and the religion of truth (Islam) that He may bring about its triumph over all other religions, though averse the polytheists may be.

10. O you who believe! Shall I lead you to a merchandise that will deliver you from a painful chastisement?

11. That you believe in God and His Messenger, and strive in the way of God with your possessions and your lives; that is better for you, if you only know.

12. He will forgive you your sins and admit you into gardens beneath which rivers flow, and an excellent abode there is in the gardens of eternity? That is the supreme achievement.

13. And another (blessing) which you love: victory from God at hand; so give the glad tidings to the believers.

14. O you who believe! Be the helpers (in the cause) of God as Jesus the son of Mary said to his disciples: "Who will be my helpers to (the work of) God?" The disciples said: "We are the helpers (in the cause) of God." Then a party of the children of Israel believed, while another party disbelieved; then We aided those who believed against their enemy; so, they became the victorious.

Friday Congregation
(al-Jumu'ah)

In the name of God, the Beneficent, the Merciful.

1. Whatsoever is in the heavens and the earth hallows the glory of God, the King, the Most Holy, the ever-Prevalent, the all-Wise.

2. He it is Who raised among the unlettered a Messenger from among their own selves, reciting to them His Signs, purifying them and teaching them the Book (Qur'an) and the wisdom, although they were before that in manifest straying.

3. And to the others from among them who have not yet joined with them, and He is the ever-Prevalent, the all-Wise.

4. That is the grace of God; He grants it to whomsoever He pleases, and God is the Lord of Great Bounty.

5. The similitude of those who were entrusted with the Torah, and they did not honour the trust, is like a donkey bearing books; wretched is the similitude of the people who falsify the signs of God, and God does not guide the unjust people.

6. Say: "O you who profess Judaism! If you claim that you (alone) are the favourites of God, excluding every other nation, then desire death if you are truthful."

7. But they will never desire it for what their own hands had sent before, and God well knows all about those who commit injustice.

8. Say: "The death from which you flee will surely meet you, then you shall be returned to the Knower of the unseen and the seen, then He will inform you of whatever you used to do."

9. O you who believe! When the call is made for prayer on Friday, then hasten, all of you, to remembering God, and abandon all trading; that is better for you, if you only know.

10. And when the prayer commences, disperse in the land and seek of the grace of God, and remember God much so that you may be successful.

11. And when they see a bargain or amusement, they break away to it, leaving you (O Muhammad) standing.

Say: "What is with God is better than sport and merchandise, and God is the best of sustainers."

The Hypocrites
(al-Munafiqun)

In the name of God, the Beneficent, the Merciful.

1. When the hypocrites came to you, they said: "We bear witness that you are the Messenger of God," and surely God knows that you (Muhammad) are His Messenger, and surely God bears witness that the hypocrites are liars.

2. They make their oaths a shield, thus obstructing others from the way of God; verily evil are their deeds.

3. That is because they believed, then they disbelieved; therefore, a seal was set upon their hearts, so they do not understand.

4. When you see them, their bodies please you, and when they speak, you listen to their speech, as if they were blocks of wood propped up in garments. They deem that every cry is against them. They are your enemy; so beware of them; God annihilate them whence they deviate.

5. When it is said to them: "Come; the Messenger of God will seek God's forgiveness for you," they turn their heads back, and you see them turning away in arrogance.

6. It is the same for them whether you seek forgiveness for them or not; God will never forgive them; verily God does not guide the transgressing people.

7. They are the ones who say (to those who help the believing refugees): "Do not spend anything on those who are with the Messenger of God until they break up." God's are the treasures of the heavens and the earth, but the hypocrites do not understand.

8. They say: "If we return to Medina, the honourable ones shall drive the meaner ones out;" but to God all honour belongs, and to His Messenger, and to the believers, but the hypocrites do not know.

9. O you who believe! Let not your wealth nor children distract you from remembering God; whosoever does so is a losers.

10. And spend of what We have provided you with (in

the way of God) before death approaches any of you, then he would say: "O Lord! Why do not You grant me a respite till a near term so that I may give alms and do good deeds?"

11. God does not grant a respite to any soul when its fixed time approaches, and God is all-Aware of whatever you do.

Cheating Exposed
(at-Taghabun)

In the name of God, the Beneficent, the Merciful.

1. Whatever is in the heavens and the earth hallows the glory of God; His is the Kingdom, and to Him is all praise due, and He (alone) has power over all things.

2. He it is Who created you, then (some) of you are disbelievers, while others believe, and God sees all what you do.

3. He created the heavens and the earth with truth and fashioned you and made your forms good, and unto Him is the ultimate return.

4. He knows everything in the heavens and the earth, and He knows whatever you conceal and reveal; God knows all what the hearts contain.

5. Has not the story of those who disbelieved before come to you? They tasted the evil consequences of their own deeds, and for them there is a painful torment in store.

6. It is so because their messengers came to them with clear proofs, but they said: "Shall (mortal) men guide us?" So they disbelieved, turning away. God can do without them; He is self- Sufficient, Most Praised.

7. Those who disbelieve think that they shall never be resurrected. Say: "Aye! By my Lord, you shall certainly be raised, then you shall certainly be informed of what you did; that, for God, is surely easy."

8. So believe in God and His Messenger and the Light which We have sent, and God is well-Aware of all what you do.

9. The Day when He gathers you for the Day of Gathering is surely a day of mutual loss. Whosoever believes in God and does good deeds, He will wipe out his sins and

admit him into gardens beneath which rivers flow to abide therein forever; that is the great achievement.

10. As for those who disbelieved and falsified Our signs, they are the fellows of the Fire to abide therein, and wretched is the destination.

11. No affliction afflicts any save by the leave of God; whosoever believes in God, He shall guide his heart, and God well-knows all things.

12. Obey God and obey the Messenger. If you turn away, then only the clear delivery (of Our message) is incumbent upon Our Messenger.

13. God! There is no god but He; upon God (alone) should the believers rely.

14. O you who believe! Verily of your wives and children (are some who are) an enemy to you; wherefore beware of them, and if you forgive, overlook and cover up (their faults), then verily God is oft-Forgiving, Most Merciful.

15. Your possessions and offspring are surely a trial, and verily with God is a great recompense.

16. So fear God as much as you can; listen (to His Word) and obey, and spend (in His Way); that is better for your own souls. Whosoever is saved from the greed of his own self is the successful one.

17. If you lend God a goodly loan, He will double it to you and forgive you, and God is Most Appreciative, Most Forbearing,

18. Knower of the unseen and the seen, the ever-Prevalent, the all-Wise.

Divorce
(at-Talaq)

In the name of God, the Beneficent, the Merciful.

1. O Our Prophet! (Tell the believers): When you divorce your women, divorce them at their prescribed period, and reckon their iddat, and fear God, your Lord. Do not turn them out of their homes, nor shall they (themselves) go out, unless they commit an open indecency. These are the limits of God; whosoever transgresses the limits of

God indeed commits injustice against his own soul. You do not know that perchance God may bring about some new situation thereafter.

2. When they reach their iddat, either retain them with fairness or part with them with kindness, and call to witness two men (endowed) with justice, and establish the witness (as though it were) before God. Thus admonished is he who believes in God and the last day. Whosoever fears God, He will make for him a way (out of trouble).

3. And provide him with sustenance from whence he reckons not. Whosoever relies on God, then He is sufficient for him; verily God accomplishes His purpose; indeed God has prescribed for everything its due measure.

4. And (such of) those of your women who despair of menstruation, should you doubt, their prescribed term shall be three months, and (the same is the case) of those who have not yet had the course; (as for) those pregnant women, their prescribed iddat shall be till they deliver their burden. Whosoever fears God, He will ease his affair for him.

5. This is the Command of God which He has revealed to you, and whosoever fears God, He will wipe out from him his sins and will increase for him the recompense.

6. Lodge them wherever you lodge according to your means, and do not harm them so as to restrict them. If they are pregnant, spend on them until they lay their burden down; if they suckle (your offspring) for you, give them their recompense, and deal with one another fairly. If you find yourselves in (physical and/or psychological) difficulties, then some other woman shall suckle for him.

7. Let him with abundance spend of his abundance, and let him whose resources are restricted spend of what God has given him; God lays no burden on any soul save to the extent to which He has enabled it; God will soon bring about ease after difficulty.

8. How many a town which rebelled against the Command of its Lord and His Messenger did We call to a severe account? We chastised it with a stern chastisement.

9. So it tasted the evil consequences of its deeds, and the end of its conduct was perdition.

10. God has prepared for them a severe chastisement, so

fear God, O believers endowed with understanding! Indeed God has sent down to you a reminder,

11. A Messenger who recites to you the clear signs of God, that he may bring out those who believe and do good deeds out of the darkness into the light. He shall admit whoever believes in God and does good deeds into gardens beneath which rivers flow to abide therein forever. God has bestowed upon him a goodly sustenance.

12. God is He Who created the seven heavens and the earth, a similar number, and commands are sent down amidst them, that you may know that God has power over all things, and that God's knowledge encompasses all things.

Prohibition

(at-Tahrim)

In the name of God, the Beneficent, the Merciful.

1. O Our Prophet! Why do you forbid that which God has made permissible to you? Do you seek to please your wives? (Yet) God is oft- Forgiving, Most Merciful.

2. Indeed God has made lawful for you the dissolution of your oaths, and God (alone) is your Lord; He is the all-Knowing, the all-Wise.

3. When the Prophet confided to one of his wives regarding a matter, she divulged it (to others) and God apprised him thereof. He made known a part of it and repudiated another; so when he informed her of it, she asked: "Who has informed you of this?" He said: "The all-Knowing, the all-Aware has informed me."

4. If you both turn (in repentance) to Him, then indeed your hearts are inclined (to this), but if you two support each other against him, then verily God is his Protector, and so is Gabriel, and (most) virtuous ones among the believers, and the angels thereafter will support him.

5. Haply his Lord, if he divorces you, will give him in your place better wives than you, Muslims, mu'mins, devout, repentant, worshippers of God, travellers (for faith), observers of fast, widows and virgins.

6. O you who believe! Save yourselves and your families from the Fire whose fuel shall be men and stones, over

which angels shall be stern and strong; they do not disobey God in what He commands them, and only act as they are bidden.

7. (The angels will say): "O you who disbelieve! Make no excuses this Day; you shall be recompensed just as you used to do."

8. O you who believe! Turn (in repentance) to God with a turning of sincere penitence, haply your Lord will wipe out your sins from you and admit you into gardens beneath which rivers flow. On the Day, God will not abase the Prophet nor those who believe with him. Their light will run before them, and on their right hand they shall say (in prayers): "Lord! Perfect our light for us, and grant us forgiveness. Verily You have power over all things."

9. O Our Prophet! Strive against the disbelievers and hypocrites, and be firm with them. Their abode is Hell, and what an evil destination!

10. God sets forth, as a similitude to those who disbelieve, the wife of Noah, and the wife of Lot. Both were under two of Our righteous servants, but they were unfaithful (to their husbands), and they (husbands) availed them naught against God. It was said (to them): "Enter, both of you, into the Fire along with those who enter."

11. God sets forth the similitude to those who believe the wife of Pharaoh. She said: "Lord! Build me a house in Paradise and deliver me from Pharaoh and his deeds, and deliver me from the unjust people."

12. And Mary the daughter of Imran (Amram) who guarded her chastity. We breathed into it (her body) of Our spirit, and she testified to the truth of the words of her Lord and His scriptures, and she was among the obedient ones.

The Kingdom
(al-Mulk)

In the name of God, the Beneficent, the Merciful.

1. Hallowed is He in Whose hand is the kingdom (of the heavens and the earth), and He has power over all things.

2. He created death and life that He may try you (to ascertain) which of you is best in deeds; He is the

ever-Prevalent, the oft- Forgiving.

3. Who created the seven heavens layer above layer (spheres); you cannot find any defect or incongruity in the creation of the Beneficent. Then look again; do you see any gap?

4. Then repeat your gaze again and again; your gaze shall return to you dulled, wearied.

5. Indeed We have adorned the lower heavens with lamps (stars) and made them (like) missiles to repulse the satans, and We have prepared for them the chastisement of the flaming Fire.

6. As for those who disbelieve in their Lord, there is the chastisement of Hell, and evil is the destination.

7. When they are flung into it, they hear its roaring as it boils up,

8. As though it is bursting with rage. Whenever a group is flung into it, its keepers shall ask them: "Did any warner come to you?"

9. They shall say: "Yes, indeed, a warner did come to us, but we rejected and said ` God has sent naught; you are but in vast delusion.'"

10. And they shall say: "Had we but listened or pondered, we would not have become among the fellows of the flaming Fire."

11. So they shall confess their sins, but far will be (from mercy) the inmates of the blazing Fire.

12. Verily, for those who fear their Lord in secret shall be forgiveness and a great reward.

13. You conceal your word or declare it; verily He knows the secrets of the hearts.

14. Would He Who created not know? He is the Subtle, the all-Aware.

15. He it is Who made the earth subservient to you; so traverse its broad sides, and eat of His provision. To Him (alone) is the ultimate return.

16. Do you deem yourselves secure of Him Who rules the heavens, that He may not cause the earth to swallow you up? Then lo! It shall quake,

17. Or do you deem yourselves secure of Him Who rules the heavens, that He will not send down upon you a tor-

nado with showers of stone, then you shall know how (terrible) My warning is?

18. And indeed those before them rejected (My signs): how (terrible) then was My wrath?

19. Do they not behold the birds above them outstretching (their wings), and contracting them? None upholds them save the Beneficent. Verily He well sees everything.

20. Or who is it that can be a host for you to succor besides the Beneficent? The disbelievers are but in mere delusion.

21. Or who is it that can provide you with sustenance should He withhold His sustenance? Yet they persist in disdain and aversion (against the truth).

22. Is he who goes along grovelling on his face better guided than he who walks upright upon the Straight Path?

23. Say: "It is He Who brought you (into existence) and made for you ears, eyes, and hearts; yet how little is it that you thank?"

24. Say: "He it is Who has multiplied you throughout the world, and to Him (alone) shall you all be gathered."

25. They say: "When shall this appointment come to pass, if you are truthful?"

26. Say: "Verily the knowledge of it is only with God, and verily I am but an open warner."

27. Yet when they see it nigh, grieved shall be the faces of those who disbelieve, and it shall be said to them: "This is what you have been calling for."

28. Say: "Do you see if God were to destroy me and those with me, or if He were to bestow mercy upon us, who would protect the disbelievers against the painful chastisement?"

29. Say: "He is the Beneficent. We believe in Him and on Him (alone) do we rely; so you shall come to know who is in manifest straying."

30. Say: "Do you see should your water go down (into the ground), who then (other than God) can bring you flowing water?"

The Pen
(al-Qalam)

In the name of God, the Beneficent, the Merciful.

1. Nun; by the pen, and by what they write,

2. You (Muhammad), by the grace of your Lord, are not insane.

3. Verily there is for you a reward without an end.

4. And most certainly you stand on a sublime standard of morality.

5. So you will see, and so will they too,

6. Which of you is demented.

7. Verily your Lord best knows who strays from His Way, and He knows best those who are rightly guided.

8. So do not yield to the falsifiers;

9. They wish that you too should be pliant so that they would be pliant.

10. And do not yield to any despicable swearer,

11. Defamer, slanderer,

12. Vehement hinderer of good, uncontrolled transgressor, deeply sunk in sin,

13. Cruelly violent, besides all that, baseborn.

14. Just because he has wealth and sons,

15. When Our signs are recited to him, he says: "Stories of yore."

16. We will brand him on the snout.

17. Verily We will try them as We tried the owners of the garden. They vowed that they would certainly gather the fruits at morn,

18. They made no room for exception (for the will of God),

19. So it was encircled with destruction from your Lord, even while they were asleep,

20. And it became like a black barren soil,

21. And they cried out one to another at morn:

22. "Be early at your tilth if you would gather (the fruits)."

23. And they went whispering to each other,

24. Saying: "No poor man shall ever enter it today."

25. At morn, they went strong in their resolve (to pre-

vent the poor).

26. But when they beheld it, they said: "Verily we have strayed.

27. "Nay! We are deprived (of its fruits)."

28. The most just among them said: "Did I not tell you that you should glorify (God)?"

29. They said: "Hallowed is our Lord! Verily we have been unjust."

30. Then some of them proceeded against the others, reproaching each other.

31. They said: "Woe unto us! Verily we have been arrogant;

32. "Haply our Lord will give us in its place a better one; verily to our Lord do we turn (repenting)."

33. Such has been Our chastisement, and certainly the chastisement of the hereafter is still greater, if they but know it.

34. Verily the pious are with their Lord in the gardens of bliss.

35. Shall We make the Muslims like the guilty ones?

36. What is the matter with you? How do you judge?

37. Or have you a scripture to read-

38. Wherein there is for you what you choose?

39. Or have you a sworn covenant from Us reaching to the Day of Judgment that you shall surely have whatever you judge?

40. Ask them which one of them will guarantee that.

41. Or have they any partners (unto Us), if they are truthful?

42. On the Day when the shin is laid bare, and they shall be called upon to prostrate in obeisance, but they shall not be able (to do so).

43. Casting their looks down, abasement covering them, and indeed they had been called upon to prostrate in obeisance, while they were still healthy.

44. So leave Me and him who belies this announcement. We will lead them on (to ruin) by steps from whence they do not know.

45. And yet respite them for My stratagem is firm.

46. Or do you ask them for a recompense, that they are

burdened with a load of debt?

47. Or is the knowledge of the unseen with them, (so much so) that they write it down?

48. So wait patiently for the judgment of your Lord. Do not be like the fellow of the whale. He cried when he was confined.

49. Had no bounty from his Lord reached him, he would certainly have been cast forth on the naked shore in disgrace.

50. But his Lord chose him and made him one of the righteous.

51. And those who disbelieve would almost smite you with their eyes when they hear the reminder, and they say: "Verily he is mad."

52. It is naught but a reminder to the worlds...

The Reality
(al-Haqqah)

In the name of God, the Beneficent, the Merciful.

1. The reality:

2. What is the reality?

3. And what makes you comprehend the reality?

4. Thamud and Ad belied the striking calamity,

5. So as to Thamud, they were destroyed by an exceedingly terrible thunder;

6. And as to Ad, they were destroyed by a roaring violent blast.

7. He made it rage against them for seven nights and eight days uprooting, that you might see the people therein prostrate as if they were trunks of hollow palms.

8. Then do you see if any of them survived?

9. Pharaoh and those before him, and the ones who were overthrown, committed evil sins;

10. They disobeyed the messenger of their Lord; so, He seized them with an increasing seizure.

11. Verily We, when the water (of Noah's flood) rose beyond the limits, transported you in the ark made to float,

12. That We might make it a reminder for you, and that retaining ears might retain it.

13. And when the trumpet is blown a single blast,

14. The earth and mountains shall be borne away and crushed with a single crush.

15. On that day, the great event shall come to pass,

16. And the heavens shall cleave asunder; on that day, it shall be (mere) frail.

17. And the angels shall be on its sides, and above them shall bear the Throne of your Lord that day eight strong.

18. On that day, you shall be exposed, and no secret of yours shall remain hidden.

19. Then he who is given the book (of deeds) in his right hand will say: "Lo! Read my book!

20. "Verily I felt that I would meet my account,"

21. So shall he be in a life (of bliss), pleased,

22. In the exalted garden,

23. Its fruits being low and near at hand.

24. - "Eat and drink in health and pleasure for what goodness you sent before in the days that passed!"

25. But he who is given the book in his left hand will say: "O would that the book had never been given to me;

26. "And that I had not known what my account was;

27. "O would that it had put an end to me.

28. "My wealth availed me naught;

29. "And all my power has gone from me."

30. Seize him, and fetter him!

31. Then into the glazing Fire burn him!

32. Then into a chain, seventy cubits long, tie him!

33. Verily he used to disbelieve in God, the Great;

34. And he did not urge the feeding of the poor;

35. So there is no friend for him today;

36. No food for him save the puss from the washing of wounds;

37. Eaten by none other than the sinners.

38. So I swear by what you see,

39. And what you do not see,

40. Verily it is the word of the most honoured Messenger,

41. And it is not the word of a poet; little do you believe.

42. Nor is it the word of a soothsayer; little do you reflect.

43. It is a dispatch from the Lord of the worlds.

44. And if (Our Messenger Muhammad) had fabricated against Us any of the sayings,

45. We would certainly have seized him by the right hand,

46. Then We would certainly have cut off his aorta,

47. And of you none could have withheld (Us) against him,

48. And verily it (Qur'an) is a reminder to the pious,

49. And verily We know that some of you are falsifiers,

50. And verily it is a great grief to the disbelievers,

51. And it is the very truth, fully assured;

52. So, hallow the name of your Lord, the Most High.

The Ways Of Ascent
(al-Ma'arij)

In the name of God, the Beneficent, the Merciful.

1. A demander demanded an inevitable chastisement,

2. Unavoidable for the disbelievers,

3. From God, Lord of the Ways of Ascent;

4. To Him do the angels and the spirit ascend in a day whose measure is fifty thousand years,

5. So be patient (O Muhammad) with excellent patience,

6. Verily they regard it distant,

7. While We see it nigh;

8. On that Day, the heavens shall be like molten brass,

9. And the mountains shall be like (flakes of) wool,

10. And no friend will inquire about his friend,

11. (Though) they will be given the sight of each other; the guilty one would fain redeem himself from the punishment of that Day at the price of his own children,

12. And his wife and brother,

13. And his kindred that gave him shelter,

14. And all that are in the earth combined together, to deliver him;

15. By no means! Verily it is the flaming of Hell-fire,

16. Dragging the scalp,

17. Claiming him that turned his back and went away (from the truth),

18. And amassed wealth, and hid it.

19. Verily man is created avaricious,

20. When any evil afflicts him, he is fretful;

21. When any good reaches him, he is niggardly (ungrateful).

22. Save those who offer (regular) prayer,

23. Those who are ever constant at their prayer,

24. And those in whose wealth is a right declared (by Us),

25. For him that asks, and him that is deprived;

26. And those who testify to the truth about the Day of Judgment,

27. And those who are afraid of the chastisement of their Lord;

28. Verily none should feel secure against the chastisement of their Lord.

29. Those who guard their modesty,

30. Save to their wives or those whom their right hands possess—for then they are not to be blamed:

31. Whoso seeks beyond this transgresses.

32. And those who are faithful to their pledge and covenant,

33. And those who are firm in their testimonies,

34. And those who are careful about their (regular) prayers,

35. (All) those shall be in the gardens (duly) honoured.

36. But what has happened to the disbelievers that they hasten on around you?

37. On your right and on your left, in groups?

38. Does everyone of them covet to enter the garden of bliss?

39. By no means! For We have created them of what they (already) know!

40. But nay! I swear by the Lord of the Easts and the Wests, We are certainly able—

41. To substitute them for better ones, and We shall not be overtaken.

42. So leave them (to themselves) to remain in discoursing and (vain) sporting, until they come face to face unto the Day which has been promised (to them),

43. On that Day, they shall come forth from their graves in haste, as if they were rushing to a signpost in haste.

44. With their eyes cast down, covered with disgrace; that is the day they were promised.

Noah
(Nuh)

In the name of God, the Beneficent, the Merciful.

1. Verily We sent Noah to his people saying: "Warn your people before a painful chastisement approaches them."

2. He said: "O my people! Verily I am an open warner to you,

3. "That you worship God (alone), fear Him, and obey me;

4. "He will forgive you your sins and respite you to an appointed term; verily when the term of God comes, it cannot be put off, if you but only know."

5. He said: "Lord! I surely called upon my people by night and day,

6. "But my call increased them in naught but fleeing (from the Right Way).

7. "Whenever I called them that You may forgive them, they thrust their fingers in their garments and persisted (in their error), and became puffed up with pride.

8. "Then verily I called upon them aloud,

9. "Then I spoke openly to them, and I confided in them in secrecy;

10. "Then I said: `Seek forgiveness of your Lord! Verily He is the Most Forgiving,

11. "`He will send down clouds to rain upon you in torrents,

12. "`And bestow upon you wealth and offspring, and make gardens for you, and make rivers, too;

13. "`What has befallen you that you do not take God as Great?

14. "`While He created you through regular stages?

15. "`Do you not see how God has created the seven heavens one above the other?

16. "`And made the moon a light and the sun a lamp?

17. "`And God made you grow of the earth vegetation,

18. "`Then He returns you therein, and again He will bring you forth a new creation;

19. "`And verily God has made for you the earth spacious,

20. "`That you may walk therein along wide paths?'"

21. Noah said: "Lord! They have disobeyed me and followed him whose riches and offspring only increase his loss,

22. "And they have plotted a great plot,

23. "And they said (to each other): `Do not forsake your gods; do not forsake Wudd, Suwa', Yaghuth or Nasr.'

24. "And indeed they have led many astray, then they would increase the unjust naught but error."

25. Because of their own sins they were drowned and were made to enter the Fire, and even then, they found no helper for them besides God.

26. Noah said: "Lord! Leave none of the unjust ones, not a single dweller, alive on earth;

27. "Verily if You leave them, they would lead Your servants astray, and they will not beget but immoral ingrates;

28. "Lord! Forgive me and my parents and the believer who enters my abode, and believing men and women, and increase the unjust in naught save perdition."

The Spirits
(al-Jinn)

In the name of God, the Beneficent, the Merciful.

1. Say: "It has been revealed unto me that a party of the jinn has heard (the Qur'an) and said: `We have surely heard a recitation of the Qur'an that is wonderful,

2. "`It guides to the Right (Path) wherein we believe, and we will never associate any with our Lord;

3. "`And that He, our Lord, Exalted in Majesty, has taken no wife nor son,

4. "`And that the fools among us want to speak against God atrocious things,

5. "`And that we thought that the humans and the jinn

would never utter falsehood against God,

6. "`And that individuals from among the humans used to seek protection of individuals from among the jinn, so they increased them (only) in rebelling (against God),

7. "`And that they (too) thought as you thought, that God would never raise anyone (to life);

8. "`And that we sought the heavens and found it filled with strong guards and flaming darts;

9. "`And that we sat on some of the seats (there) to steal a hearing, but any who would (try to) listen would find a flaming dart awaiting him,

10. "`And that we do not understand whether he has meant evil for those on earth, or whether their Lord wishes to guide them aright,

11. "`And that some among us are good ones, and others are contrariwise; we are sects following different ways,

12. "`And that we knew that we can never defeat (the will of) God on earth, and we can never defeat Him by fleeing,

13. "`And that when we heard the guidance, we believed in it; whosoever believes in his Lord shall fear neither loss nor oppression,

14. "`And that some of us are Muslims while others are deviators (from the Right Path), and whoever submits pursues the right guidance,

15. "`As for the deviators, they shall be the fuel of Hell,

16. "`And if they are steadfast on the Right Path, We would certainly give them water in abundance,

17. "`That We may try them thereby. Whosoever turns away from remembering his Lord, He will make him undergo a severe torment,

18. "`And that the places for prostration are for remembering God; so, do not call therein any besides God!

19. "`And that when the servant of God (Muhammad) stands praying to Him, they surround him, almost stifling...'"

20. Say: "I only pray to my Lord, and I do not associate any with Him."

21. Say: "I do not possess any power to harm or profit you."

22. Say: "None of you can ever protect me against God,

and I can find no place as refuge besides Him,

23. "Save a delivery (of the message) from God, and His Messenger; whosoever disobeys God and His Messenger shall surely have the Fire of Hell to abide therein forever."

24. Till when they see that which they are promised, they shall come to know who is weaker in help and fewer in number.

25. Say: "I do not know whether what you are promised is near, or if my Lord has appointed a distant term for you."

26. Knower of the unseen; He does not reveal His secrets to anyone-

27. Save to the messengers whom He chooses, for surely He causes a guard to march before and after him.

28. That He may know that indeed they have delivered the Message of their Lord, and He encompasses (the knowledge of) all that is with them, and takes account of everything.

The Mantled One
(Al-Muzzammil)

In the name of God, the Beneficent, the Merciful.

1. O you who is wrapped up in the mantle!

2. Rise by night to pray but a little.

3. Half of it or curtail a little.

4. Or add to it, and recite the Qur'an in a regulated tone.

5. Verily We will soon send down upon you weighty words.

6. Verily the rising at night when impression is intense and straightest in word.

7. Verily, for you is the day-long occupation with duties,

8. And remember the name of your Lord, and devote yourselves to Him exclusively.

9. Lord of the East and the West; there is no god but He; take Him then as the Protector.

10. And be patient against whatever they say, and avoid them a decorous avoidance.

11. And leave Me (to deal with the) the falsifiers, pos-

sessors of bounties, and respite them for a while.

12. Verily with Us are strong fetters and a flaming Fire.

13. The food that chokes, and torment that is dire.

14. On the Day when the earth and mountains are shaken and the mountains become heaps of sand, rendered loose;

15. Verily We have sent you a Messenger to witness against you, as We sent Pharaoh a messenger,

16. But Pharaoh disobeyed the messenger, whereupon We seized him with a severe seizure.

17. How then will you guard yourselves, if you disbelieve, against the Day which shall turn children grey-headed?

18. The heavens shall be rent asunder by it; His promise is always be fulfilled.

19. Verily this is a reminder; so let him, whoever wills, adopt the (Right) Way to his Lord.

20. Verily, your Lord knows that you stand up (in the night prayer) nigh two-thirds of the night, and (sometimes) half of it, and (sometimes) a third thereof, with a group of those with you; and God well measures the night and the day; He knows that you can never take (correct) account of it; so, He turns to you (with mercy); therefore recite whatever is easy (in prayers) to be recited of the Qur'an. He knows that there may be some sick among you, and others travelling in the world seeking the grace of God, and others fighting in the way of God, so recite as much as it can easily be recited thereof, establish regular prayers, pay zakat and offer God a goodly loan. Whatever good you send beforehand for your own selves, you will surely find it with God. That is the best and the greatest recompense; and seek God's forgiveness; verily God is oft-Forgiving, Most Merciful.

The Cloaked One
(Al-Muddathir)

In the name of God, the Beneficent, the Merciful.

1. O you (i.e. Muhammad) who is covered under the mantle (i.e. Muhammad)!

2. Arise and warn!

3. And glorify your Lord!

4. And purify your raiment!

5. And shun every kind of abomination!

6. And bestow no favours (expecting) that you may receive them back increased;

7. And for (the sake of) your Lord (endure) in patience;

8. For when the trumpet is sounded.

9. That shall be the Day of distress,

10. To the disbelievers nothing easy.

11. Leave Me (to deal with) him whom I created alone;

12. And to whom I granted wealth in abundance,

13. And offspring abiding in his presence,

14. And to whom I made (life) adjustably smooth,

15. And yet he desires that I should further add!

16. Never! For he was a foe to Our signs,

17. Soon will I afflict him with a severe punishment.

18. Surely he thought and estimated,

19. But may he be ruined how he estimated,

20. May he again be ruined how he estimated!

21. Then he looked around,

22. Then he frowned and scowled,

23. Then he turned his back and swelled in pride!

24. Then he said: "This is naught but the sorcery of old!

25. "This is naught but the word of a human being!"

26. Soon will I cast him into Hell;

27. And what will make you realize what Hell is?

28. It leaves out none, nor does it spare;

29. It shrivels the human body;

30. Above it are nineteen (guardians);

31. We have made no guardians for the Fire other than angels, and We have made their number but a trial for those who disbelieve, that certainly those who have been given the Book may be certain, and it may increase those who believe in faith, so that those who have been given the Book, and the believers, may not doubt therein, and that those in whose hearts there is distress, and the disbelievers, may say: "What does God mean by this similitude?" Thus does God allow whomsoever He pleases to stray, and He guides whom He pleases. None knows the hosts of God save He Himself. This is naught but a reminder to man.

32. Nay! By the moon!

33. And by the night when it retreats!

34. And by the morn when it brightens!

35. Surely it (Hell) is one of the grievous woes!

36. A warning to mankind,

37. To him among you who desires to go forward (in goodness) or to remain behind:

38. Every soul is pawned to what it earned,

39. Save the people of the right,

40. In gardens shall they all be asking each other-

41. About the guilty ones:

42. - "What has brought you into Hell?"

43. They shall say: "We were not among those who offered regular prayers,

44. "And we used not to feed the poor,

45. "And we used to talk vanities with vain talkers,

46. "And we used to falsify the Day of Judgment;

47. "Till the certain (death) came upon us."

48. So the intercession of intercessors shall not (now) avail them.

49. What has happened to them that they turn aside from the warning?

50. As if they were frightened donkeys,

51. Fleeing before a lion,

52. Nay! Everyone of them wishes that he may be given (the heavenly Book) in open pages spread out;

53. Nay! They do not fear the hereafter!

54. Nay! Surely it is a reminder;

55. So, whosoever pleases may heed it;

56. They will not heed it unless God pleases! He is worthy to be feared, and He is worthy to be sought as the refuge.

The Resurrection
(Al-Qiyamah)

In the name of God, the Beneficent, the Merciful.

1. Nay! I swear by the day of Resurrection!

2. Nay! I swear by the self-accusing spirit!

3. Does man think that We will never reassemble his bones?

4. Yea! We can put his very finger tips together in per-

fect order!

5. Nay! Man wills but to do evil before him.

6. He asks: "When is the day of resurrection to come)?"

7. So when the eye is confounded,

8. And the moon is darkened,

9. And the sun and the moon brought together,

10. Man shall cry that day: "Is there anywhere to flee?"

11. By no means! No refuge there shall ever be!

12. To your Lord (alone) shall be the place of final abode!

13. Man shall be informed on that day of whatsoever he put behind.

14. Nay! Man shall bear witness even against his own self!

15. And even if he puts forth excuses!

16. Do not move your tongue with it in haste!

17. Surely on Us is its collection and recitation!

18. So when We have recited it, then follow the recitation.

19. Again it is on Us to explain it,

20. Nay! You love but the fleeing life,

21. And neglect the life hereafter,

22. On that day, (some) faces shall be splendid,

23. To their Lord attentive,

24. And (other) faces shall be despondent,

25. Thinking that some great calamity shall befall them.

26. Nay! When it reaches the throat,

27. And it will be said: "Who is the charmer?"

28. Man shall think that it is the parting;

29. And when one leg (twists) with the other (in agony),

30. To your Lord on that day shall be the drive;

31. For he did not believe in the truth, nor did he offer regular prayers,

32. Instead he falsified the truth and turned away,

33. Then he went to his people in haughtiness;

34. Nearer to you (O man) is the destruction, and still nearer!

35. Yet again nearer to you (O man) is the destruction, and even still nearer!

36. Does man think that he will be left uncontrolled?

37. Was he not a (mere) drop of emitted sperm?

38. Then he was a clot of blood, then He created (him) and made him proportioned,

39. Then He made him of two sexes: male and female.

40. Is not He then potent enough to give life (again) to the dead?

Time Or Man
(ad-Dahr)

In the name of God, the Beneficent, the Merciful.

1. Has there been any period to pass when man was nothing, unmentioned?

2. Surely We created man of a life-drop of intermingled life germ, so that We might put him to trial, and We endowed him with hearing and sight.

3. Surely We have shown him the (right) Way, be he grateful or ungrateful.

4. Surely We have prepared chains for the disbelievers and shackles, and a flaming fire.

5. Surely the righteous shall drink of a cup tempered at the fountain of Camphor [Kawthar].

6. The fountain whereof the servants of God shall drink; they shall cause it to flow to a desirable measure.

7. Those who fulfill their vows and fear the day the woe of which stretches far and wide.

8. And they give away food out of love for Him to the poor man, the orphan, and the captive,

9. (Saying): "We feed you only for God's sake; we seek no recompense nor thanks from you.

10. "Surely we dread from our Lord a stern day of distress."

11. So did God protect them against the evil of that day and caused them to meet beauty and (blissful) pleasure;

12. And He rewarded them, for what they patiently persevered, with a garden and silk-wear,

13. Reclining therein on elevated couches. They shall find no sun[heat] therein, nor any chill.

14. And close low over them (shall be) its shades, and the clustered fruits thereof (shall be) bowing down;

15. And shall pass round among them vessels of silver

and goblets of crystal (glass),

16. Bright as glass, made of silver, measure they to a well- measure.

17. They shall be supplied with the drink therein of a cup, tempered with Zanjabil (ginger).

18. A spring therein is named Salsabil,

19. And around them in their service shall be boys (graced) with eternal youth; when you see them, you will deem them scattered pearls.

20. And when you behold there, you shall behold bounties (abundant), and a kingdom magnificent.

21. Upon them shall be robes of fine green silk and rich brocade, and they shall be adorned with bracelets of silver, and their Lord gives them to drink a pure and holy drink.

22. - "Surely this is to you a reward, and your endeavour is accepted (with appreciation).

23. Verily We ourselves have sent down to you (Muhammad) the Qur'an in a proper revelation;

24. Await, then, with patience, for the Command of your Lord, and do not obey any sinner or an ungrateful one among them.

25. And remember the name of your Lord at morn and at eve,

26. And during a part of the night, prostrate in obeisance to Him, and celebrate His Praise a long night through.

27. Surely these people love the present fleeting life, putting away behind them the day which shall be hard.

28. We have Ourselves created them, and made their parts strong, and if We will, We can replace them with the like of them.

29. Surely this is a reminder; so whomsoever pleases, let him take the (right) Way to his Lord.

30. And you do not wish save only if God wishes; verily God is all-Knowing, all-Wise.

31. He admits whomsoever He wills into His mercy, and (as for) the unjust ones, He has prepared for them a painful torment.

The Dispatched Angels
(al-Mursalat)

In the name of God, the Beneficent, the Merciful.

1. By those (winds) dispatched (to man's profit), one after another,

2. Which then rage in violent rage,

3. And by those that spread (goodness) far and wide,

4. Then by those that separate them from one another,

5. Then by those that give forth the reminder,

6. Either to justify (the punishment), or to warn,

7. Surely what has been promised to you shall come to pass.

8. So when the stars are caused to cease radiating,

9. And when the heavens are rent asunder,

10. And when the mountains are carried away like dust,

11. And when the messengers are made to reach their appointed time,

12. To what day is the appointment (fixed)?

13. To the Day of Decision!

14. And what will make you know what the day of Decision is?

15. Woe on that day unto the falsifiers;

16. Did We not destroy the former people?

17. Then did We not make the later people follow them?

18. Thus do We deal with the guilty ones.

19. Woe on that day unto the falsifiers.

20. Did We not create you of a despicable fluid?

21. Then We placed it in a safe place,

22. Till the appointed term?

23. So We planned, then how excellent are the Planners?

24. Woe on that day unto the falsifiers.

25. Have We not made the earth a receptacle?

26. For the living, and for the dead?

27. And We made therein mountains high and given you sweet water to drink?

28. Woe on that day unto the falsifiers.

29. Begone to that which you falsify!

30. Begone to the shadow with three columns!

31. (Which yields) no shade (for coolness) nor availing

against the flames.

32. Surely it sends up sparks (huge) like palaces,

33. As if they were (a string of) tawny camels,

34. Woe on that day unto the falsifiers.

35. This is the day when they shall not speak,

36. And it shall not be permitted to them so that they may offer excuses,

37. Woe on that day unto the falsifiers.

38. This is the day of Decision. We will gather you and all those of yore,

39. If you have any stratagem, try your stratagem (now)!

40. Woe on that day unto the falsifiers.

41. Surely the pious shall be amidst shades and springs,

42. And fruits of whatever they desire:

43. - "Eat and drink in health and delight, a reward for what you used to do."

44. Surely thus do We reward the doers of good deeds.

45. Woe on that day unto the falsifiers.

46. Eat and enjoy yourselves for a short while, for surely you are the guilty ones.

47. Woe on that day unto the falsifiers.

48. And when it is said to them: "Bow down," they do not bow;

49. Woe on that day unto the falsifiers.

50. In what other word after this will they (ever) believe?

The News
(an-Naba')

In the name of God, the Beneficent, the Merciful.

1. About what are they all disputing with one another?

2. About the great news,

3. That which they differ therein,

4. Verily they shall soon come to know,

5. Then verily they shall soon come to know,

6. Did We not make the earth a wide expanse?

7. And the mountains belts?

8. And created you in pairs?

9. And caused your sleep a rest?

10. And caused the night a covering?

11. And caused the day for seeking livelihood?

12. And We have erected above you seven strong firmaments,

13. And We made therein a lamp burning,

14. And We send down from the clouds water in torrents,

15. That We may bring forth thereby corn and herbs,

16. And gardens of thick foliage.

17. Verily the Day of Decision is a time appointed,

18. The Day when the trumpet is blown, and you shall come forth in huge groups,

19. And (they will find) the heavens opened, full of portals,

20. And (they will find) the mountains set in motion like mere vapour;

21. Verily (they will find) Hell waiting-

22. For the transgressors: their destination,

23. To abide therein for ages.

24. They shall taste no coolness therein nor any drink,

25. Save boiling water and running puss,

26. A recompense fitting (their evils).

27. Verily they did not look forward to their reckoning,

28. And they falsified Our signs with a persistent falsification.

29. And everything We have recorded is in a Book:

30. Taste then! And We will increase you nothing but torment!

31. Verily for the pious ones is a great fulfillment (of their desire):

32. Gardens enclosed, and vineyards,

33. And mates and beautiful maidens,

34. And a brimful cup,

35. They shall hear no vain talk therein, nor any falsehood,

36. A recompense from your Lord, a reward according to the reckoning,

37. The Lord of the heavens and the earth and whatever is between them twain, the Beneficent God; they shall have no right to address Him,

38. On that Day, whereupon the spirit shall stand, and the angels arrayed; they shall speak not save he whom the Beneficent God permits, and he shall speak the truth.

39. That is the certain Day. Whoso then desires, let him take refuge with his Lord.

40. Verily We have warned you of a chastisement nigh at hand, on the day when man sees what his hands sent forth, and when the disbelievers say: "Oh! Would that I were dust!"

The Snatchers
(an-Nazi'aat)

In the name of God, the Beneficent, the Merciful.

1. Those who drag forth violently,

2. And those who untie (the knot) briskly,

3. And those who glide on swiftly,

4. Then those who go ahead with a foremost speed,

5. Then those who manage the affairs (as commanded),

6. On the day when the quake shall be quaking,

7. The (second) trumpet shall follow the quake,

8. Hearts on that day shall palpitate;

9. Their eyes shall be cast down.

10. They shall say: "Are we indeed to be restored to our first (state)?

11. "Even when we are rotten bones?"

12. They said: "That will then be a return in vain."

13. Verily it shall be but a single (violent) blast,

14. When lo! They shall all be in the awakened state.

15. Has not the story of Moses come to you?

16. Behold! His Lord called him in the holy valley of Tuwa:

17. - "Go to Pharaoh! Verily he has transgressed the bounds,

18. "And say (to him): `Have you (any desire) to cleanse yourself?

19. "`And I will guide you to your Lord, so that you may fear Him."`

20. And he showed him the greatest sign,

21. But he falsified and disobeyed,

22. Then he turned his back in haste,

23. And gathered people and proclaimed,

24. And said: "I am your lord, the most high!"

25. So God seized him with the chastisement of the hereafter and of the life before.

26. Verily in this there is a lesson to him who fears (God).

27. Are you the harder to create or the heavens He built?

28. He raised its heights and established it,

29. And He darkened its night, and brought its moonlight forth,

30. And afterwards He stretched forth the earth,

31. He brought forth from it its water and pasturage,

32. And set the mountains firm,

33. A provision for you and your cattle.

34. When the great calamity comes,

35. It is then that man shall recollect all that he strove for,

36. And Hell shall be displayed to him who sees,

37. As for him who has transgressed the bounds,

38. And preferred the life of this world,

39. Then verily Hell shall be his abode,

40. As for him who fears the standing of his Lord, and forbids himself from following his inclination,

41. The garden shall then be his abode.

42. They ask you of the Hour, "Whereto its anchorage?"

43. Wherein are you of its motion?

44. To your Lord (alone) is its termination!

45. You (Muhammad) are only a warner to him who fears it.

46. It shall seem to them on the day when they see it as though they tarried not in (their graves) but an evening, or till the following morning.

He Frowned
(Abasa)

In the name of God, the Beneficent, the Merciful.

1. He frowned and turned away,

2. Because the blind man came to him;

3. And what makes you know that he might cleanse himself?

4. Or he is warned and avails himself of the warning?

5. As for him who thinks himself independent (on account of being wealthy),

6. To him do you attend,

7. It shall be no blame on you if he did not cleanse himself,

8. But as to him who comes to you striving in earnest,

9. And he fears (at heart),

10. To him should you be indifferent,

11. Nay! But it (Qur'an) shall be a reminder;

12. So let those who please keep it in mind.

13. Written in the books greatly honoured,

14. Exalted with elevation, purified,

15. In the hands of the emissary angels,

16. Noble, virtuous.

17. Cursed be man; how ungrateful he is!

18. Of what did He create him?

19. Of a seminal drop; He created him, then He fixed his measure,

20. Then He made the way (for him) easy,

21. Then He causes him to die, and gets him buried,

22. Then when He wills, He will again raise him (to life).

23. Nay! He has not fulfilled what He bade him.

24. Then let man look at his food:

25. It was We Who poured down [rain]water in abundant pouring,

26. Then We cleft the earth with a (necessary) cleaving,

27. Then We caused grain to grow therein,

28. And grapes and vegetables,

29. Olives and palms,

30. And gardens enclosed, thick with trees,

31. And fruits and herbage,

32. A provision for you and your cattle.

33. But when the deafening trumpet blast comes,

34. That Day man will flee from his own brother,

35. From his mother and his father,

36. And from his wife and offspring,

37. For every man of them on that Day will have a concern enough to make him heedless (of all others).

38. (Some) faces on that Day shall be radiant,

39. Joyously laughing,
40. And (other) faces on that Day shall (look like) dust,
41. Darkness shall cover them,
42. These are they who are the disbelievers, the wicked.

The Cessation
(at-Takwir)

In the name of God, the Beneficent, the Merciful.

1. When the sun is folded,
2. And the stars darkened,
3. And the mountains removed (like scattered dust),
4. And the she-camels, ten months with young, are abandoned,
5. And the wild beasts herded together,
6. And the oceans are caused to boil and burn,
7. And the souls are reunited (with their bodies),
8. And the female babe that was buried alive is asked-
9. For what sin she was put to death,
10. And when the books (of deeds) are unfolded,
11. And the heaven is removed,
12. And Hell is set to blaze,
13. And the garden (Paradise) is brought nigh,
14. Every soul shall then know what it has presented.
15. And I swear by the receding planets,
16. That run and glide,
17. And by the night when it ends,
18. And the dawn when it brightens,
19. Verily it (Qur'an) is the word of a most honoured messenger,
20. Endowed with mighty power, honoured in the presence of the Lord of the Universe.
21. The obeyed One, the Trustworthy above all.
22. O people! Your companion (Muhammad) is not insane,
23. And indeed he saw him (Gabriel) on the clear horizon,
24. And he is not avid about the unseen,
25. Nor is it the word of the cursed Satan;
26. Whither then shall you go?

27. It (Qur'an) is naught but a reminder to all the worlds,

28. To him among you who wishes to remain upright;

29. And you shall not wish save if God, Lord of the worlds, pleases.

The Violent Upheaval
(al-Infitar)

In the name of God, the Beneficent, the Merciful.

1. When the sky cleaves asunder,

2. And the stars disperse,

3. And the seas burst forth,

4. And the graves are overturned;

5. Every soul shall know then what it has sent forth and left behind.

6. O man! What has beguiled you from your Lord, the Most Gracious?

7. Who created you and fashioned you and justly proportioned you?

8. In whatever form He pleases, He casts you.

9. Nay! But you reject the reckoning,

10. While verily watchers are posted over you,

11. Recorders honourable,

12. They comprehend whatever you do,

13. Verily the righteous shall be amidst blissful bounties,

14. And verily the wicked shall be in the flaming Fire,

15. They shall be committed to it on the Day of Judgment.

16. Nor will they themselves be absent therefrom,

17. And what will make you know what the Day of Judgment shall be?

18. Then what makes you know what the Day of Judgment is?

19. It is the Day on which each soul shall own nothing (helpful) for another, and the Supreme Command shall that Day be God's (alone).

The Frauds
(at-Tatfif)

In the name of God, the Beneficent, the Merciful.

1. Woe unto the defrauders in measuring,

2. Who, when they measure from people, demand it full,

3. But when they themselves measure to them, or weigh to them, they deceive.

4. Do not they think that they shall be raised-

5. For a mighty Day?

6. On the Day when mankind stands before the Lord of the worlds?

7. Nay! The record of the wicked has been preserved in Sijjin,

8. And what will make you know what Sijjin is?

9. It is a written Book;

10. Woe unto the falsifiers on that Day,

11. Who rejected the Day of Judgment,

12. And none belies it save a transgressing sinner,

13. When Our signs are recited unto him, he says: "These are only stories of yore."

14. Nay! What they used to do has rusted their hearts.

15. Nay! Verily on that Day, they shall be shut out, away from the mercy of their Lord.

16. Verily they shall be committed to the flaming Fire,

17. Then it shall be said (to them): "This is that which you rejected!"

18. Nay! The record of the righteous shall be in Illiyin,

19. And what will make you know what Illiyin is?

20. (It is) a Book written,

21. Those who are the near ones to God see it.

22. Verily the righteous shall be in the bounties of bliss,

23. On exalted couches, viewing (the delightful sights),

24. You (Muhammad) will recognize in their faces the (delightful) radiance of the bliss!

25. They shall be provided to quaff of pure sealed drink.

26. The seal thereof is musk; for that, let those with aspiration (for bliss) aspire.

27. Mixed therewith shall be the water of Tasnim,

28. (Which is) a spring wherefrom the near ones drink,

29. And verily the guilty ones used to laugh at those who believed.

30. And when they pass by them, they wink at each other (mocking),

31. And when they return to their people, they return jesting.

32. And when they see them, they say: "Verily these are truly astray."

33. While they themselves are not sent to be watchers over them.

34. So today those who believe shall laugh at the disbelievers;

35. On couches (exalted, they shall be) seeing (delights).

36. Shall not the disbelievers be (also) recompensed for what they used to do?

The Rending Asunder
(al-Inshiqaq)

In the name of God, the Beneficent, the Merciful.

1. When the firmament is rent asunder,

2. And it shall hearken to its Lord-as it ought to,

3. And when the earth is flattened,

4. And everything in it is cast forth, and it becomes empty,

5. And it shall hearken to its Lord, as it ought to,

6. O mankind! Verily you strive and are surely to meet Him!

7. He who is given his book in his right hand-

8. Shall soon be reckoned an easy reckoning,

9. And he shall return to his people delighted;

10. While he, who is given his book from behind his back,

11. Shall invoke destruction,

12. And he shall be committed to the flaming Fire.

13. Verily he was joyous among his people,

14. He thought that he will never return (to God).

15. Yea! Verily his Lord was always vigilant about him,

16. And I swear by the glow of sunset,

17. And by the night and what it enshrouds,

18. And by the moon when it is full,

19. That you shall certainly march from state to state,

20. But what then has happened to them that they do not believe?

21. And when the Qur'an is recited unto them, they do not prostrate in obeisance?

22. Nay! Those who believe falsify (the truth).

23. And verily God best knows what they hide (in their hearts),

24. So announce to them the tidings of a painful chastisement,

25. Save those who believe and do good deeds, for theirs shall be a recompense that will never fail.

The Constellations
(al-Buruj)

In the name of God, the Beneficent, the Merciful.

1. By the heavens full of constellations,

2. By the promised Day,

3. By the witness and the witnessed,

4. The fellows of the ditch self-destructed,

5. Of the Fire with fuel.

6. They sat facing it,

7. Witnessing what they did to the believers,

8. They tormented them for naught except that they believed in God, the ever-Prevalent, the Most Praised,

9. He to Whom the kingdom of the heavens and the earth belongs, and God witnesses all things.

10. Verily those who persecute the believing men and women, and do not repent it, for them shall be the chastisement of Hell, and for them is the torture of burning.

11. Verily, for those who believe and do good deeds shall be gardens beneath which rivers flow; that is the great achievement.

12. Verily the grip of your Lord is mighty.

13. Verily He originates (everything) and causes it to return,

14. He is the oft-Forgiving, the Most Compassionate,

15. Lord of the Glorious Throne,
16. The Mighty Doer of whatever He pleases.
17. Has not the story of the hosts come to you—
18. (The story) of Pharaoh and Thamud?
19. Nay! Those who disbelieve are used to falsify.
20. While God is encompassing over them.
21. Nay! It is a Glorious Qur'an,
22. (Inscribed) in the guarded tablet.

The Night Visitant
(at-Tariq)

In the name of God, the Beneficent, the Merciful.

1. By the heavens and the nightly visitant,
2. -What will let you know what the nightly visitant is?
3. (It is) the star of piercing radiance—
4. There is no soul without a watcher!
5. Let man then reflect about what he is created of;
6. He is created of ejected water,
7. Coming forth from between the backbone and the ribs,
8. Verily He is well-Able to resurrect him,
9. On the Day when all hidden things shall be tried,
10. Then for him there shall be neither power nor any to help.
11. By the heavens endued with rotation,
12. And by the earth endued with splitting (and sprouting),
13. Verily it (Qur'an) is a decisive word,
14. And it is not a jest.
15. Verily they scheme quite a scheming,
16. And I, too, do scheme such a scheme,
17. So respite the disbelievers; let them alone for a while.

The Most Sublime
(al-A'la)

In the name of God, the Beneficent, the Merciful.

1. Hallow the name of your Lord, the Most Sublime,
2. Who creates and fashions (all things),
3. And plans and guides them,
4. And brings the herbage forth,
5. Then He reduces it to dusty stubble,
6. We shall read unto you, and you shall not forget,
7. Save what God pleases; verily He knows the declared and the hidden.
8. We shall ease (your way) to an ease (for you).
9. So keep reminding them, when reminding avails.
10. He who fears (God) will heed the warning,
11. And the most reprobate will avoid it.
12. Who shall be committed to the great Fire,
13. Then he shall not die therein, nor shall he live.
14. Indeed he who purifies himself shall succeed,
15. And remembers the name of his Lord, and (regularly) prays.
16. Nay! You prefer the life of this world,
17. Although the hereafter is better and more lasting.
18. Verily this is (recorded) in the earlier scriptures,
19. The scriptures of Abraham and Moses.

The Overwhelming Event
(al-Ghashiyah)

In the name of God, the Beneficent, the Merciful.

1. Have you come to know of the tidings of the overwhelming event?
2. (Some) faces on that day shall be downcast,
3. Toiling, weary,
4. Entering into the blazing Fire,
5. Made to drink from a spring (fiercely) boiling;
6. For them there shall be no food except bitter thorny fruit,
7. Which will neither fatten nor satisfy;
8. (Other) faces on that Day shall be happy,

9. With their past efforts well-pleased,

10. In a grand garden.

11. They shall hear no vain talk therein.

12. Therein is a flowing spring,

13. Therein are exalted couches,

14. And goblets readily placed,

15. And cushions set in rows,

16. And carpets spread forth.

17. Can they not see how the camels are created?

18. And how the sky is raised?

19. And the mountains are set up?

20. And the earth is spread out?

21. So keep reminding them; you are only a reminder.

22. You are not compeller over them.

23. Except whosoever turns back and disbelieves,

24. Then God will chastise him with the greatest chastisement.

25. Verily to Us is their return.

26. Then verily We shall reckon with them.

The Dawn

(al-Fajr)

In the name of God, the Beneficent, the Merciful.

1. By the dawn,

2. And by the Ten Nights,

3. And by the even and the odd,

4. And by the night as it passes away,

5. Verily there is in this an oath for those who have understanding.

6. Have you (O Our Prophet Muhammad!) not seen how your Lord dealt with the people of 'Ad -

7. Of (the city of) Iram with lofty pillars,

8. The like of which were not created in any other city (of the world)?

9. And of Thamud who hewed out the rocks in the valley,

10. And of Pharaoh, lord of the stakes,

11. Who (all) transgressed in the cities,

12. And multiplied wickedness therein,

13. So (much so that) your Lord let fall on them the whip of chastisement;

14. Verily your Lord is ever Watchful.

15. As for man, when his Lord tries him and honours him and is bounteous unto him, he then says, "My Lord has honoured me!"

16. But when He tries him then straitens to him his sustenance, he then says, "My Lord has disgraced me!"

17. Nay! You rather do not honour the orphan,

18. Nor do you urge one another to feed the poor!

19. And you devour inheritance in greed,

20. And you love wealth exceedingly.

21. Nay! When the earth is pounded to powder,

22. And the Command of your Lord comes, and the angels are in ranks arrayed,

23. And Hell is made to appear that Day, man shall that Day get awakened, but of what avail to him shall be the awakening?

24. He shall say, "Oh! Would that I had sent forth (good deeds) for (this future) life!"

25. On that Day, none shall chastise the way He shall,

26. Nor shall any bind the way He binds,

27. - "O tranquilled soul at (complete) rest!

28. "Return to your Lord well-pleased (with Him), and He with you!

29. "Enter thus among My servants,

30. "And enter into My garden!"

The City
(al-Balad)

In the name of God, the Beneficent, the Merciful.

1. Nay! I swear by the city (Mecca)!

2. While you (Muhammad) are settled in this city!

3. And (by) the begetter (Adam), and by whom he begot (mankind),

4. That indeed We have created man (to dwell) amidst hardship.

5. Did he think that none has power over him?

6. He says: "I have wasted an enormous wealth!"

7. Does he think that none sees him?

8. Did We not make for him his two eyes?

9. A tongue, and two lips?

10. And We showed him the two paths (of goodness and evil).

11. But he did not strive to (cross over the) steep ascent;

12. (But) what would make you know what the steep ascent is?

13. (It is) the freeing of a slave or a captive,

14. Or the feeding on a hungry day-

15. Of an orphaned kin,

16. Or the poor man who lies in the dust,

17. Besides this, to be of those who believe and enjoin steadfastness on each other, and enjoin mercy.

18. These are the people of the right hand,

19. And those who disbelieve in Our signs are the people of the left hand,

20. On whom the Fire shall close in.

The Sun
(ash-Shams)

In the name of God, the Beneficent, the Merciful.

1. By the sun and his radiation,

2. By the moon when she follows after him,

3. By daytime when it unfolds its light;

4. By night-time when it enshrouds it;

5. By the sky and of which it is built;

6. By the earth and what expands it;

7. By the soul as it is perfected.,

8. He inspired to it (against) its vices and about its virtues;

9. Indeed he who purifies it shall succeed,

10. And indeed he who corrupts it shall fail!

11. Thamud rejected (the truth) due to their rebellious impiety,

12. When the worst wretch among them rose up (with mischief),

13. Then the messenger of God (Salih) said to them: "It is the she-camel of God, (so leave her) and its drink!"

14. But they rejected him and hamstrung her, so their Lord crushed them for their sins and levelled them (with the ground);

15. He fears no consequence.

The Night
(al-Layl)

In the name of God, the Beneficent, the Merciful.

1. By the night when it spreads its veil,

2. By the day when it shines,

3. By Him Who created the male and the female;

4. Verily your striving is to diverse (ends)!

5. Then as for him who gives (alms) and fears God,

6. And believes in the best (of religions),

7. We will then smoothen the path to bliss for him.

8. And as for him who acts niggardly and deems himself free from need,

9. And he belies the best,

10. We will then smoothen for him the path to affliction,

11. And his wealth will not avail him when he perishes.

12. Verily on Us (depends) the guidance,

13. And verily Ours is the hereafter and the beginning;

14. So I warn you of the Fire that flames,

15. None shall be cast into it save the most wretched,

16. (He) who falsifies (the truth) and turns back (to it),

17. And he who fears God shall be far removed therefrom,

18. Who gives his wealth away and purifies himself.

19. None has (done) to Him any favour, that he should be recompensed,

20. Save the seeking of the pleasure of his Lord, the Most High,

21. And soon shall he be fully content.

Daylight
(ad-Duha)

In the name of God, the Beneficent, the Merciful.

1. By the bright morning light,
2. By the night when it darkens:
3. Your Lord (O Muhammad) has not forsaken you, nor has He been displeased (with you)!
4. Verily the end is better for you than the beginning,
5. And soon your Lord will grant you till you are well-pleased.
6. Did He not find you an orphan and sheltered you?
7. And He found you in loss and guided you?
8. And He found you in need and made you independent?
9. So do not oppress the orphan,
10. And as to the beggar, do not chide him;
11. And as to the bounties of your Lord, announce (them to others).

The Expansion
(al-Inshiraah)

In the name of God, the Beneficent, the Merciful.

1. Have We not expanded your breast (O Muhammad)?
2. And We removed your burden from you?
3. Which weighed your back down?
4. And exalted your name for you?
5. Verily with every difficulty there is ease,
6. (Again) verily with every difficulty there is ease.
7. And when you have commenced (your mission), then establish it!
8. And return unto your Lord with fervour.

The Fig
(at-Tin)

In the name of God, the Beneficent, the Merciful.

1. By the fig and the olive,
2. By the Mountain of Sinai,
3. And by this city declared inviolable,
4. Indeed We created man in the best form,
5. Then We reverted him to the lowest of the low,
6. Save those who believe and do good deeds, for them shall be an incessant recompense.
7. What then causes you to reject the final judgment (to come)?
8. Is not God the judge of judges?

The Blood Clot
(al-Alaq)

In the name of God, the Beneficent, the Merciful.

1. Read (recite)! In the name of your Lord Who created (everything),
2. He created man from a clot!
3. Recite (O Muhammad!) And your Lord is the Most Honourable!
4. Who taught the use of the pen,
5. Taught man what he never knew,
6. Nay! Verily man is a wont rebel!
7. He deems himself needless!
8. Verily to your Lord (alone) is the return!
9. Have you seen the man who forbids-
10. A servant from praying?
11. Have you seen if he were on right guidance?
12. Or enjoined piety?
13. Have you seen if he belies the truth and turns back?
14. Does he not know that God sees?
15. Nay! If he does not desist, We shall surely drag him by the forelock!
16. A forelock that is lying, sinful!
17. Then let him summon his fellows in council,
18. We too will summon the angels of Hell.

19. Nay! Do not heed him, and prostrate in obeisance, and draw yourself nearer (to Him).

The Destiny
(al-Qadr)

In the name of God, the Beneficent, the Merciful.

1. Verily We revealed it (Qur'an) in the Night of Qadr (Power).
2. What can make you know what the Night of Qadr is?
3. The Night of Qadr is better than a thousand months,
4. The angels and the spirit descend therein by permission of their Lord with (decrees) of all affairs.
5. Peace is the whole (Night) till dawn-break.

The Testimony
(al-Bayyinah)

In the name of God, the Beneficent, the Merciful.

1. Those who disbelieved from among the people of the Book and the polytheists could not have separated themselves (from falsehood) till the clear evidence came to them,
2. A Messenger from God reciting to them the Purified Scripture (Qur'an),
3. Wherein are decrees correct and forceful,
4. Nor were those people of the Book divided except after the clear evidence came to them.
5. Yet nothing was enjoined on them except that they should worship only God in perfect sincerity, truth in faith, and that they should pay zakat: that is the correct (and straight) religion.
6. Verily those who disbelieve from among the people of the Book and the polytheists shall be in the fire of Hell to abide therein forever. It is they who are the worst of creation.
7. Verily those who believe and do good deeds are the ones who are the best of creation.
8. Their recompense with their Lord shall be everlasting gardens beneath which rivers flow to abide therein for-

ever. God is well-pleased with them and they with Him; that is for him who fears his Lord.

The Earthquake
(al-Zilzal)

In the name of God, the Beneficent, the Merciful.
1. When the earth is quaked with a (terrible) quaking,
2. And the earth brings forth her burdens,
3. And man says: "What has befallen her?"
4. On that Day, she shall relate her news-
5. That your Lord has revealed to her.
6. On that Day, people shall come out (from their graves) in scattered groups, to be shown their deeds.
7. Then he who has done an atom's weight of a good deed shall see it,
8. And he who has done an atom's weight of evil shall (also) see it.

The Chargers
(al-Adiyat)

In the name of God, the Beneficent, the Merciful.
1. By the snorting chargers,
2. And those that dash off (their hoofs) striking fire,
3. And those that scour to the morn attack,
4. And stir thereby dust aloft,
5. And all penetrate through (the foe),
6. Verily man is ungrateful to his Lord.
7. And verily He is a witness thereto.
8. And verily he is violent in his love for wealth.
9. Does he not know that all those in the graves shall be raised (to life)?
10. And all things in the hearts shall be made manifest?
11. Verily their Lord, on that Day, will be fully aware concerning them.

The Clamour
(al-Qari'ah)

In the name of God, the Beneficent, the Merciful.
1. The striking calamity:
2. What is the striking calamity?!
3. What makes you know what the striking calamity is?
4. The Day when people shall be like moths scattered about,
5. And the mountains like wool carded,
6. Then as for him whose scales (of good deeds) are heavy,
7. He shall be in a life with which he is well-pleased,
8. And as for him whose scales (of good deeds) are light,
9. His home shall be a burning abyss.
10. And what explains to you what this is?
11. It is a Fire fiercely blazing!

The Piling Up
(at-Takathur)

In the name of God, the Beneficent, the Merciful.
1. Your vying engages you in exuberance,
2. Until you come to the graves.
3. Nay! Soon shall you come to know,
4. Nay! Soon shall you come to know!
5. Nay! Would that you know it with the knowledge of certainty,
6. That you shall surely see Hell!
7. Then you shall surely see it with the vision of certitude,
8. Then you shall be questioned on that Day about the bounties (you used to enjoy).

Time
(al-Asr)

In the name of God, the Beneficent, the Merciful.

1. By the Time!
2. Verily man is in loss!
3. Save those who believe and do good deeds and exhort each other to truth, and to endurance.

The Slanderer
(al-Humazah)

In the name of God, the Beneficent, the Merciful.

1. Woe unto every slanderer, defamer,
2. Who amasses wealth and hoards it.
3. He deems that his wealth will make him live forever.
4. Nay! Verily he will be flung into the Hutama!
5. And what makes you know what the Hutama is?
6. It is the Fire God has kindled,
7. It shall mount above the hearts;
8. It shall be upon them, closed over,
9. In columns outstretched.

The Elephant
(al-Fil)

In the name of God, the Beneficent, the Merciful.

1. Have you not seen how your Lord dealt with the fellows of the elephant?
2. Did He not cause their treacherous scheme to err?
3. And He sent down upon them birds in flocks,
4. Pelting them with stones of baked clay,
5. Thus did He render them like straw, eaten up (by cattle).

Custodians of the Ka'ba
(Quraysh)

In the name of God, the Beneficent, the Merciful.

1. For the covenant of Quraysh,
2. The covenant of their winter and summer journeys,
3. So let them worship the Lord of this House,
4. Who fed them against hunger, and secured them against fear.

The Neighbourly Needs
(al-Ma'un)

In the name of God, the Beneficent, the Merciful.

1. Have you seen him who belies the final judgment?
2. He it is who repulses the orphan,
3. And he does not urge others to feed the poor,
4. So woe unto those who pray-
5. While being heedless to (the commandments of) their prayers,
6. Who do (a good deed only) to be seen.
7. And (also) they withhold alms.

The Abundance
(al-Kawthar)

In the name of God, the Beneficent, the Merciful.

1. Verily We have given you (O Muhammad) the abundance,
2. So pray to your Lord and offer sacrifice.
3. Verily your enemy shall be the one who is cut off (in his progeny).

The Disbelievers
(al-Kafirun)

In the name of God, the Beneficent, the Merciful.

1. Say (O Muhammad): "O you who disbelieve!
2. "I do not worship what you worship,
3. "Nor do you worship Whom I worship,

4. "Nor shall I ever worship what you worship,
5. "Nor will you ever worship Whom I worship.
6. "To you is your religion, and to me is mine."

Victory
(an-Nasr)

In the name of God, the Beneficent, the Merciful.

1. When the help of God and His victory come,
2. And you see people entering the religion of God in multitudes,
3. Then celebrate the praise of your Lord and seek His protection; verily He is oft-Turning (with mercy).

The Flame
(Lahab)

In the name of God, the Beneficent, the Merciful.

1. May both the hands of Abu-Lahab perish, and may he too;
2. Neither his wealth nor what he earns shall avail him.
3. Soon shall he burn in the flaming Fire,
4. And his wife, the bearer of the firewood,
5. Upon her neck shall be a halter of twisted rope.

The Purity Of Belief
(al-Ikhlas)

In the name of God, the Beneficent, the Merciful.

1. Say: "He is God, the One and only God,
2. "The Needless (independent) God;
3. "He begets not, nor is He begotten,
4. "And there is none like unto Him."

The Dawn
(al-Falaq)

In the name of God, the Beneficent, the Merciful.

1. Say: "I seek refuge with the Lord of the Dawn,

2. "From the evil of what He has created,
3. "From the evil of the dark night when it overtakes,
4. "And from the evil of malignant witchcraft,
5. "And from the evil of the envious one when he envies."

Mankind
(an-Nas)

In the name of God, the Beneficent, the Merciful.
1. Say: "I seek refuge with the Lord of people!
2. "The King of people!
3. "The God of people!
4. "From the evil of the slinking whisperer,
5. "Who whispers into the hearts of man!
6   "(Be he) from among the jinn or man."

INDEX

INDEX

INDEX

INDEX

INDEX

INDEX

INDEX

INDEX

INDEX

INDEX

INDEX

INDEX

INDEX

INDEX

INDEX

INDEX

INDEX

INDEX

INDEX

INDEX

INDEX

INDEX

INDEX

INDEX

INDEX

INDEX

INDEX

INDEX

INDEX

INDEX

INDEX

INDEX

INDEX

INDEX

INDEX

INDEX

INDEX

INDEX

INDEX

INDEX

INDEX

LIST OF BOOKS:

Holy Qur'an by Abdullah Yusufali:

The Qur'an, English,	Paperbound	$ 6.95
The Qur'an, Arabic Translation,	Hardbound	$30.00
The Qur'an, Arabic Translation,	Paperbound	$25.00
The Holy Qur'an, Arabic-	Hardbound	$25.00
Translation-Transliteration	Paperbound	$20.00

Holy Qur'an by M.H. Shakir

The Qur'an, English	Paperbound	$6.95
The Qur'an, Arabic-Translation	Paperbound	$8.00
The Qur'an, Arabic-Translation		
(features 41 translations of the	Hardbound	$24.00
First Chapter-Sura Fateha)	Paperbound	$19.00
Wedding Edition	Hardbound	$24.00

Holy Qur'an by Muhammad Pickthall

The Glorious Qur'an, English	Paperbound	$ 6.95
The Glorious Qur'an, Arabic Transl	Paperbound	$ 8.95
The Meaning of the Glorious Qur'an,	Hardbound	$25.00
Arabic-Translation-Transliteration	Paperbound	$20.00
	Hardbound	$39.95

Holy Qur'an by S.V. Mir Ahmed Ali

The Qur'an, English	Paperbound	$ 6.95
Holy Qur'an, Arabic-Translation	Hardbound	$59.95
& Commentary	Paperbound	$39.95

Holy Qur'an by S. V. Ahamed

The Glorious Qur'an;	Paperbound	$7.95
A simplified translation for young people		

Spanish Qur'an by Julio Cortes

El-Coran , Spanish	Paperbound	$12.00
El-Coran, Arabic-Spanish	Hardbound	$24.00

Tahrike Tarsile Qur'an, Inc.

Publishers and Distributors of Holy Qur'an

80-08 51st Avenue, Elmhurst, New York 11373, USA

http://www.koranusa.org, E-mail: read@koranusa.org

NOTES

NOTES